T0318159

Complex Social Networks

The book provides a systematic and self-contained account of the fast-developing theory of complex social networks. Social networks are central to the understanding of most socio-economic phenomena in the modern world. The classical approach to studying them, however, relies on a methodology that abstracts from their size and complexity and is thus hardly suitable for the task. In contrast, the approach taken here keeps complexity at the core but aims at integrating it fruitfully with the incentive considerations that are preeminent in traditional economic analysis. The treatment starts with a detailed discussion of the basic models that act as "benchmarks" for the complex-network literature: random networks, small worlds, and scale-free networks. Then, it separately studies the three different forces that underlie, with varying intensities, almost all interesting network phenomena in social contexts: diffusion, search, and play. Finally, these forces are combined into a unified framework that is brought to bear on the important issue of network formation and the coevolution of agents' behavior and their pattern of interaction.

Fernando Vega-Redondo is Professor of Economics at the University of Alicante, Spain, and the University of Essex, UK. He also taught at the Autonomous University of Barcelona and has held visiting positions at Harvard University, Hebrew University of Jerusalem, University of California–San Diego, Boston University, and Cornell University. Professor Vega-Redondo is the author of *Economics and the Theory of Games* (Cambridge University Press, 2003) and *Evolution, Games, and Economic Behavior* (1996). He has written more than 70 articles in professional journals, including the *Journal of Economic Theory*, *Econometrica*, *International Economic Review*, and *Games and Economic Behavior*. Professor Vega-Redondo received his Ph.D. from the University of Minnesota in 1984.

Econometric Society Monographs

Editors:

Andrew Chesher, University College London
Matthew Jackson, Stanford University

The Econometric Society is an international society for the advancement of economic theory in relation to statistics and mathematics. The Econometric Society Monograph Series is designed to promote the publication of original research contributions of high quality in mathematical economics and theoretical and applied econometrics.

Other titles in the series:

Continued on page following the Index

Complex Social Networks

Fernando Vega-Redondo

University of Alicante
and University of Essex

CAMBRIDGE UNIVERSITY PRESS
Cambridge, New York, Melbourne, Madrid, Cape Town, Singapore,
São Paulo, Delhi, Dubai, Tokyo, Mexico City

Cambridge University Press
The Edinburgh Building, Cambridge CB2 8RU, UK

Published in the United States of America by Cambridge University Press, New York

www.cambridge.org
Information on this title: www.cambridge.org/9780521674096

© Fernando Vega-Redondo 2007

First published 2007

A catalogue record for this publication is available from the British Library

Library of Congress Cataloging in Publication Data

Vega-Redondo, Fernando.
Complex social networks / Fernando Vega-Redondo.
  p.   cm. - (Econometric Society monographs ; 44)
Includes bibliographical references and index.
ISBN-13: 978-0-521-85740-6 (hardback)
ISBN-10: 0-521-85740-6 (hardback)
ISBN-13: 978-0-521-67409-6 (pbk.)
ISBN-10: 0-521-67409-3 (pbk.)
1. Social networks. 2. Sociometry. I. Title.
HM741.V44   2007
302.3'5-dc22   2006030242

ISBN 978-0-521-85740-6 Hardback
ISBN 978-0-521-67409-6 Paperback

A Mireia

Contents

Preface

The aim of this book is to provide a systematic account of a recent body of theoretical research that lies at the intersection of two fertile strands of literature. One of these strands, the study of complex networks, is a new field that has been developing at a fast pace during the last decade. The other one, social network analysis, has been an active area of research in sociology and economics for quite some time now – only lately, however, has it started to be seriously concerned with the implications of complexity. There is, I believe, much potential in bringing these two approaches together to shed light on network-based phenomena in complex social environments. This monograph is written with the intention of helping both the social scientist and other network researchers in this fascinating endeavor.

For the social scientist, the monograph may be used, *inter alia*, as a self-contained introduction to some of the main issues and techniques that mark the modern literature on complex networks. Since this literature has largely developed as an outgrowth of statistical physics, some of the powerful methodology being used is often alien to researchers from other disciplines. On the other hand, for the network theorist who lacks an economic background, the present monograph can fulfill a reciprocal role. Specifically, it may serve as an illustration of the questions and concerns that inform the economists' approach to the study of socioeconomic networks. I hope that this twin, admittedly ambitious, objective is at least partly achieved in the following pages.

Writing this book has truly been a team effort. This concerns, in particular, the help provided by some of my (ex-)students, who have read through all the material and made a large number of useful suggestions. I want to highlight, specifically, the role played by José Antonio García-Martínez, Dunia López-Pintado, Miguel Ángel Meléndez-Jiménez, and Arnold Polanski. But a special mention must go to Constanza Fosco, whose thorough review of every detail has been most important. Some of my colleagues and coauthors, such as V. Bhaskar, Coralio Ballester, Antonio Cabrales, Andrea Galeotti, Sanjeev Goyal, and Juana Santamaría-García, have also contributed specific comments or general points on different parts of the manuscript.

My original interest in the field of complex networks has been substantially bolstered through numerous collaborations with statistical physicists over the last few years. Alex Arenas, Albert Díaz-Guilera, George Ehrhardt, Roger Guimerà, Enrique Louis, Conrad Pérez, Frantisek Slanina, and, in a particularly intense and sustained way, Matteo Marsili have been providing both valuable stimuli and expert help all along. Despite our quite different backgrounds, it has generally been surprisingly easy to "talk science" with them, since we share a similar view and excitement of what is interesting in research. Finally, I also want to express my sincere thanks to Matthew Jackson, for his advice and support as coeditor of the *Econometric Society Monograph Series,* to which I am privileged to contribute this work.

The completion of the book has imposed quite a toll on some people, and I am very grateful to all of them for their indulgent understanding. These certainly include my coauthors, who have seen how some of the ongoing projects advanced more slowly than desired. My students and colleagues, at both Alicante and Essex, have also experienced some occasional blackouts, as I concentrated on the task of finishing different parts of the manuscript. But those who have probably been most affected, and certainly deserve my highest gratitude, are my family. In my view, inevitably subjective, they represent a vivid example that a "complex" and coevolving network of immensely rich relationships can also arise on the small scale!

Other titles in the series *(continued from page iii)*

CHAPTER 1

Introduction

1.1 THE NEW FIELD OF COMPLEX NETWORKS

In the last decade, the study of complex networks has become a booming field of research with a marked interdisciplinary character. Many different phenomena in the physical, biological, and social worlds can be understood as network based. They build upon some complex (as well as evolving) pattern of bilateral connections among individual entities *and* the overall performance of the system is largely shaped by the intricate architecture of those connections.

A brief review of alternative domains of application should serve to illustrate the rich diversity of phenomena that are distinctly governed by complex networks. This is the task carried out in Subsection 1.1.1, where the primary aim is to illustrate such diversity with empirical illustrations gathered from a large number of different areas. Next, in Subsection 1.1.2 we elaborate on the idea that, given the nature of the endeavour, a genuinely interdisciplinary approach is well in order in the field of complex networks.

1.1.1 Realms of Application and Empirical Evidence

We may start, as the most tangible, with *transportation networks*. These include the connections through which modern economies channel the physical movement of all sorts of commodities and signals. Pertaining, for example, to the conveyance of signals, a paradigmatic instance is of course the internet network, the huge mesh of bilateral connections through which bit-codifying electronic impulses across computers are transferred all around the world. This network has been recently studied by a number of authors, e.g. Govindan and Reddy (1997) [129], Faloutsos *et al.* (1999) [107], Magoni and Pansiot (2001) [194] and Siganos *et al.* (2003) [256].

The exploration of the internet topology can be done at two different levels of detail: at a finer level, focusing on the connections among all routers or, at a coarser one, where only the connections among so-called autonomous systems (or domains) are considered.[1] In either case, the aforementioned studies find a complex network architecture with a broadly skewed distribution of connectivities, i.e. while many nodes (routers or domains) have a few links, some others have many more connections. Or, to be more precise, the empirical observation is that node connectivity is distributed according to a power (or Pareto-like) law. This implies that the degree distribution is *scale-free,* in the sense that the proportional rate ("elasticity") at which the frequency decays with higher degrees is the *same at all scales*. Such an absence of a well-defined scale is often regarded as one of the key factors explaining the intricate complexity of the internet network. In a sense, it is an indication that all scales of the phenomenon are relevant and thus cannot be ignored.

In addition to studying the "physical" internet network, there have also been substantial efforts devoted to understanding the essential features of the "virtual" network defined by the World Wide Web (WWW). In this case, nodes represent the different webpages and a (directed) link joining a webpage to some other is taken to exist if a hyperlink to the latter is found in the former – see e.g. Albert *et al.* (1999) [5] and Kleinberg *et al.* (1999) [176]. The WWW is what might be called an *informational network* since the links present at any given webpage have informational content rather than represent a physical connection.

Another phenomenon whose informational flows can be usefully represented through networks is that of citation, either in patents (cf. Jaffe and Trajtenberg (1996) [163]) or scientific papers (cf. Otte and Rousseau (2002) [229]). In the latter case, for example, the nodes represent scientific papers and a link (again directed) is taken to exist from some paper A to another paper B if A cites B. An early precursor in the study of such citation networks was Price (1965) [239], while a more recent study has been undertaken by Redner (1998) [247].

Interestingly enough, the distribution of connectivities displayed by informational networks so disparate as those of scientific citation and the WWW also happen to be scale-free (at least if we focus on the number of in-connections *received* by each paper or webpage). Moreover, the frequency decay for higher-connectivity nodes (as reflected by the exponent of the power distribution) is so slow that the entailed dispersion of node connectivities is very high – so high, in fact, that second-order moments diverge. This means that the average connectivity cannot be conceived as "typical" and, therefore, there is not even a meaningful way of speaking of a characteristic scale for the connectivity of the network.[2]

---

[1] While routers are specialized computers directing the flow of internet traffic, the so-called autonomous systems are subnetworks composed of routers that are all under the same administrative control. Two such autonomous systems are understood to be linked if there is at least a pair of routers, one in each system, that are connected.

[2] To make sure, notice the distinction between the notion that a distribution is *scale-free* (which means that is defined by a power law) and the statement that the induced node connectivity *lacks a characteristic scale* (usually identified with infinite, or very high, second-order moments). Even though they are sometimes equated (in part, due to the similar terminology used in both cases),

An additional striking feature that has been documented about the WWW concerns the distance between its nodes, as measured by how many (hyper-) links separate them. Despite the many millions of nodes forming part of the WWW, their average distance turns out to be exceedingly low. For instance, Broder *et al.* (2000) [43] sample (through "crawling strategies") a huge subset of the WWW including more than 200 million nodes and find that their average distance is around 16. This means that, on average, an arbitrary pair of web-pages in the sample are only 16 "clicks" away, following a chain of hyperlinks connecting them.

The networks such as the WWW that enjoy short average distances between their nodes are often said to satisfy the *small-world property* (see Watts (1999) [284] and Buchanan (2002) [44]). This important property has been found to hold in a wide array of large real-world networks, even if these networks display substantial differences pertaining to many other topological features (see Amaral *et al.* (2000) [10]). In this respect, it is worth stressing that the small-world property does *not* require (or implicitly presume) either a broad dispersion in connectivities or that these be distributed in a scale-free fashion.

Indeed, neither broad nor scale-free distributions can be expected to arise in a number of interesting cases where, nevertheless, the average distance between nodes is known to be quite short. This applies, for instance, to contexts where the nature of the phenomenon at hand is such that establishing new links is rather difficult; or it is prohibitively costly to maintain them beyond a certain number; or they tend to age and then vanish at a relatively fast rate. To illustrate the point, we may return to the realm of transportation networks and refer to the data gathered on airline networks by Guimerà *et al.* (2003*b*) [146], or the evidence on networks of electric power distribution reported by Watts and Strogatz (1998) [288]. These networks satisfy the small-world property. And in both of them, the aforementioned circumstances on linking costs apply as well quite naturally.[3] This seems to explain why neither of them is found to display a scale-free distribution of connectivities, in contrast with the evidence outlined above for other transportation and informational networks. But, clearly, analogous considerations may apply as starkly to other kind of networks, such as those arising in biological and social contexts. Next, we review some interesting examples in both of these domains.

Biology has been a fertile area of network applications in recent years. One first (and vast) subarea of research has been molecular biology, the aim being to understand various molecular processes such as metabolic reactions (Jeong *et al.* (2000) [166] and Fell and Wagner (2000) [110]), gene regulation (Kauffman (1993) [170] and Jeong *et al.* (2001) [165]), or the folding of proteins and other polymers (Scala *et al.* (2001) [254] and Amaral *et al.* (2000) [10]).

---

the former notion implies the latter only if the decay displayed by the degree distribution is not too steep. See Sections 2.1 and 2.5 for an elaboration on these matters.

[3] For example, congestion alone makes adding a new connection to an already busy airport very costly.

In the latter case, for example, each feasible conformation of the polymer chain is identified with a node in the network and a link is defined between two nodes if there is a conformational change of a local character (i.e. one that affects few monomers) that permits switching from one to the other. In a simple two-dimensional representation of the problem, Scala *et al.* (2001) [254] show that the resulting network not only displays the small-world property and a characteristic connectivity but also exhibits significant clustering – i.e. there is a high probability that any two nodes that are neighbors of a third node be neighbors themselves (see Section 2.1 for a formal definition).

High clustering is an indication of a marked local structure (or, analogously, low local dimensionality). It will be seen to have multifarious and important implications for the analysis of networks – in particular for social networks, as explained below. In much of the network literature, it is common to label simply as a *small world* any network that satisfies the twin requirements of short distances (i.e. what has been called the small-world property) *and* high clustering. We shall also abide by this terminology throughout.[4]

Other far-reaching applications of networks in the field of biology have centered on the study of neural networks (Koch and Laurent (1999) [179]) and food webs (Williams and Martinez (2000) [291]). Let us take up each of them in turn. In a sense, we may regard neural networks as a kind of "transportation networks," fulfilling for living beings a role analogous to the internet network in a modern society – i.e. the conveyance of signals (now of an electrochemical nature) across neurons. The best known research that has succeeded in mapping *completely* the neural network of a living being was undertaken by White *et al.* (1986) [290] for the nematode worm *C. elegans*. Abstracting from neurological detail, Watts and Strogatz (1998) [288] translated that mapping into a corresponding (undirected) network of neurons. Interestingly, they found that they are small worlds, i.e. display short distances and a significant degree of clustering.

Food webs, on the other hand, can also be conceived as networks, the nodes standing for the different species in a certain ecological environment and the links embodying predator–prey relationships. Pursuing this approach, specific food webs have been constructed for many disparate ecological systems. To focus on just one example, consider the evidence reported by Montoya and Solé (2002) [205] for three different large ecosystems, two aquatic and one terrestrial. In all three cases, these authors encounter a complex small-world topology with short distances and high clustering.[5] It is remarkable, however, that unlike what occurs in many other small-world networks, the distributions

---

[4] The expression "small world" was used in the seminal paper of Watts and Strogatz (1998) [288] that introduced a very stylized formalization of the notion. Their model is discussed at some length in Section 2.4.

[5] Naturally, a food web is inherently directed in view of the asymmetry of the predator–prey relationship. This asymmetry notwithstanding, empirical studies in this area (including Montoya and Solé (2002) [205] itself) often abstract from this feature and work with an undirected network representation.

of connectivities is scale-free with a slow decay. This points to environmental conditions that are rich enough to allow at least some species to enjoy substantial trophic versatility.

To conclude our review, let us now turn to the context that is the primary object of this monograph: *social networks*. In the social sciences, the earliest efforts to understand the pattern of inter-agent relationships through "sociograms" – a set of points representing agents and edges joining some of them – goes back to the early work of Moreno (1934) [206], a European socio-psychologist who emigrated in the 1920's to the USA, where he founded the journal *Sociometry*. A mathematical formalization of his ideas, which relies on the concepts and tools of Graph Theory, was later undertaken by Cartwright and Harary (1956) [57]. They explored, in particular, the implications of the innovative "equilibrium-like" notion of structural balance, originally proposed by Heider (1946, 1958) [151, 152]. Heuristically, a network structure is said to be balanced if it equilibrates the overall "tensions" induced by agents' behavior and attitudes toward others (positive and negative).

With such a novel network perspective, lively groups of scholars (psychologists, anthropologists, and sociologists) arose at both sides of the Atlantic, undertaking both theoretical and empirical research. In Europe, the leading group was based at Manchester University – cf. Barnes (1954) [25], Bott (1957) [41], and Mitchell (1969) [201]. In the United States, it was centered at Harvard University around Harrison White (cf. White *et al.* (1976) [290]), followed by Nancy Lee (1969) [188] and Mark Granovetter (1973) [136]. A very useful account of these early developments in social network analysis can be found in Scott (2000, Ch. 2) [255]. This handbook also contains a review of the modern tools and applications in the field of social networks, for which a more complete account can be found in the encyclopedic monograph of Wasserman and Faust (1994) [280].

Unfortunately, the real-world networks that have been studied in detail by the sociological literature mostly focus on small setups, which cannot possibly display the overall complexity that is our main concern here. By way of illustration, we may refer to the empirical cases discussed by Wasserman and Faust (1994, Ch. 2) [280]. They range from the 21 managers of a small firm (Krackhardt (1987) [181]), the 16 leading families of 15th century Florence (Padgett and Ansell (1993) [230]), the 50 researchers of a scientific conference (Freeman (1984) [114]), or the 26 CEO of large firms headquartered in the Minneapolis/St. Paul metropolitan area (Galaskiewicz (1985) [117]). Even the empirical studies that were largely motivated as applications of Rapoport's (1957) [244] *theory of random and biased nets* (an early precursor of the modern theory of complex networks – see Chapter 2) have considered only relatively small contexts. A paradigmatic example is the study conducted by Fararo and Sunshine (1964) [109] – see also Rapoport and Horvath (1961) [245] – who used the individual responses obtained from 417 students of a high school at Madison (Wisconsin) to construct the "sociogram" (network) representing their pattern of friendship.

Only recently, with the wealth of information (and the ability to process it) afforded by modern information technologies, has it become possible to gather data on real-world social networks in a truly large scale.[6] The range of empirical evidence available is still quite limited, but two particular contexts have received special attention: research collaboration and email communication.

Research collaboration is a widespread phenomenon, both among academic scientists and industry researchers. In the academic realm, recent empirical work on collaboration networks has covered a wide variety of disciplines. For example, Newman (2001) [212] has studied the fields of physics, biomedical research, and computer science; Grossman (2002) [143] has focused on mathematics; and Goyal *et al.* (2003) [132] have considered academic economists. The number of authors involved in each case is quite large. It ranges from 11 994 in computer sciences to 52 909 in physics, 81 217 in economics, 337 454 in mathematics, and 1 388 989 in biomedical research, all pertaining to the publication window 1995–99. Qualitatively, the main regularities observed can be summarized as follows.

- Firstly, all of the aforementioned studies report short average distances, which never exceed 10 in any of them.
- A second important observation is that clustering is high. Specifically, the probability that two coauthors of any given researcher be coauthors themselves is above 0.4 in physics and computer science, although significantly lower in the other disciplines (the lowest, 0.072, occurs in biomedical research). Clustering, therefore, must be regarded as quite high in every case, since the populations involved are very large.
- Thirdly, concerning the distribution of connectivities (i.e. of the number of coauthors), one common observation is that, among those academics lying in the lower and middle range, it is scale-free. In contrast, when we move to the higher range, a truncation appears with the frequency of researchers that display a larger number of coauthors decaying much more steeply. Naturally, the latter feature is to be expected in the present context, given the sharp limitations in time and effort faced by authors in writing scientific papers.

Overall, we may confidently conclude that research collaboration networks, at least in the above considered scientific disciplines, are small worlds. Incidentally, it is interesting to note that similar conclusions have also been

---

[6] In fact, this same ability to handle large data sets effectively has been used by the recent empirical literature in sociology to obtain extensive (and therefore statistically significant) data on *small-* or *mid-size* networks through a large number of *independent materializations* observed in separate groups. Consider, for example, the work of Lubbers (2003) [193] who integrates data on 20,000 students divided in 800 classes to estimate the key considerations affecting class network structure. She relies on the exponential random graph model (also known as the $p*$ model) originally proposed by Frank and Strauss (1986) [113] – see also Wasserman and Pattison (1996) [281]. Another interesting recent example of such a *multilevel* approach is the study by Snijders and Baerveldt (2003) [258] on the spread of delinquent behavior, again integrating behavior (at a "macro" level) of a number of different school classes (at the "micro" level).

obtained concerning collaboration in *industrial* research in a number of different contexts. A good case in point is the network of Italian inventors studied by Balconi *et al.* (2002) [22], where two inventors are taken to be connected if they have collaborated in a joint patent. These networks also happen to display a small-world topology, across a wide range of different industries (chemicals, electronics, consumer goods, etc.).

As mentioned, another social context where large-scale empirical evidence has become recently available is electronic (email) communication.[7] Specifically, Ebel *et al.* (2002) [93] and Guimerà *et al.* (2003a) [144] study two different networks representing email communication in university environments. Both of them find small-world features (i.e. low distances and high clustering) in the corresponding network. But whereas Ebel *et al.* (2002) [93] report a broad distribution of connectivities (more specifically, scale-free with a large exponential cut-off), Guimerà *et al.* (2003a) [144] identify an exponential distribution with fast decay (and thus a well-defined characteristic scale). This disparity seems to be grounded on the fact that the latter paper chooses to discard bulk email, under the belief that it does not reflect genuine communication. A quite related piece of empirical evidence has been studied by Newman *et al.* (2002) [219], who focus on address books of a large university system. Here, the idea is that individuals keep the email addresses of only those with whom they are in frequent email contact. As by-now expected, they obtain a network with small-world topology. It is also interesting to observe that its connectivity distribution is exponential. This is in line with the conclusion obtained by Guimerà *et al.* (2003a) [144], suggesting that when effective communication is involved, individuals face a binding limit on their possible connectivity. From a general viewpoint, this can be viewed as a further illustration of a formerly advanced tenet: a network (be it social or biological) should display a well-defined characteristic connectivity whenever the establishment or maintenance of links is a costly affair.

Lastly, an additional important observation that vertebrates heuristically much of the empirical evidence available on large social networks is that individuals typically do not find it difficult to reach each other. This was the original meaning of the term "small world," coined by Stanley Milgram (1967) [200] to describe a situation where, despite facing a very large population, an individual can typically succeed in *contacting* any other in the population through a short path of intermediaries.[8] Specifically, one of the experiments reported in that seminal article involved delivering a letter from randomly selected individuals

---

[7] See also the empirical evidence on long-distance phone calls collected by Aiello *et al.* (2000) [3].

[8] As explained in a subsequent article of Stanley Milgram with his student Jeffrey Travers (cf. Travers and Milgram (1969) [270]), the problem was motivated in part as a test of whether some of the related insights obtained by Rapoport and coworkers (cf. in particular the aforementioned Rapoport and Horvath (1961) [245]) extend to a genuinely large and heterogenous population. In fact, the problem was first posed in an even earlier unpublished paper by Ithiel de Sola Pool and Manfred Kochen, which was later published as the inaugural paper of the journal Social Networks, de Sola Pool and Kochen (1978) [260].

living in Nebraska to a stockbroker working in Massachusetts. There was a single simple rule to be respected by the participants: the letter should be sent to someone whom the sender knew on a first-name basis. In the end, a significant fraction of letters arrived to their destination, requiring a median number of steps around six. This, of course, is a direct confirmation that a short path joining them indeed existed in the social network. But, as stressed by some of the latest papers reconsidering the issue (see e.g. Kleinberg (2000 *a,b*) [173, 174]), the truly remarkable feature about the world being "small" is not so much that short paths exist between heterogenous individuals but that these paths can indeed be found! The intriguing aspect of the problem, therefore, concerns the *searchability* – rather than the mere existence – of short paths.

The empirical side of this phenomenon has been recently revisited by Dodds *et al.* (2003) [83], who set up a large-scale, internet-based search experiment similar to that of Milgram's. Eighteen heterogenous targets were selected around the world and more than 24 000 individuals were involved in initiating the search chain. Unfortunately, only a scant 384 chains were completed by reaching the destination, which casts some doubts on the interpretation of the exercise. In particular, as the authors themselves suggest, it underscores the importance of individual incentives (besides searchability) as a primary factor in chain completion. However, when suitably accounting for a reasonable rate of attrition (that is assumed random), they find that Milgram's original conclusions are somewhat reconfirmed: the median number of steps can be estimated to range between 5 and 7.

1.1.2   An Interdisciplinary Approach

The profusion of examples just reviewed suggests the idea that a truly interdisciplinary approach to the study of complex networks may be quite fruitful. A common area of research thus arises where physics, biology, and the social sciences share not only objectives and insights, but also organizing concepts and analytical tools. More specifically, we can single out the following three levels of convergence among these different disciplines.

First, we find that complex networks not only emerge in quite different contexts (from molecular biology to economics, or from ecological systems to the World Wide Web) but also tend to display some analogous topological features. For example, we have seen that large networks with short distances and high clustering (what has been labelled a "small world") appear to prevail in many such contexts. It is conceivable, therefore, that it could respond to similar mechanisms of network formation.

Clustering, specifically, might often be the result of intense *local* search (appropriately defined in the context at hand) in the creation of new links. This introduces a force toward transitivity into link formation that, overall, must tend to enhance clustering. Concerning short typical distances, on the other hand, they could simply follow from the operation of some *global* mechanism that establishes just a few *long-range* links acting as effective shortcuts. Finally, another dimension where general principles might also be at work pertains to the distribution of node connectivities. As hinted before, it may well be that whether or not node connectivity displays a characteristic scale simply depends on the magnitude of linking costs, whether these are biological, ecological, or economic in nature. In general, therefore, we find that striving to unveil common mechanisms and principles that may apply to a wide range of different setups should be one of the distinctive marks of the modern field of complex networks.

A second related basis of interdisciplinary convergence involves the nature of the questions being asked. Thus, for example, some common questions that naturally arise in complex networks, be they biological, technological, or social concern the following phenomena.

- *Robustness*, i.e. the resilience of certain network features (e.g. its overall connectivity, which may crucially affect performance) to the operation of occasional perturbations.

  In this respect, a natural question to ask is how such robustness is affected by the topological characteristics of the network. Relatedly, a further interesting question to pose is when and why may it matter that the perturbations be random ("errors") or guided ("attack"). See e.g. Albert *et al.* (2000) [6], Solé and Montoya (2001) [261], and Carlson and Doyle (2002) [54] for a discussion of these matters in different contexts and with a different perspective.

- *Search*, i.e. the procedure by which individual nodes may look for, and then access, disperse information.

  Here, some natural questions are the following. Is the effectiveness of search influenced by network topology? Are different search algorithms better suited to alternative topologies? Can one design the network architecture so that search is optimized? See e.g. Adamic *et al.* (2001, 2003) [2, 1] and Kleinberg (2000 *a,b*) [173, 174].

- *Diffusion*, i.e. the multifaceted phenomenon that governs the gradual spread over time of any kind of signals (physical or chemical), knowledge, opinions and fads, or behavior.

  In any of these cases, of course, the key issue is to understand how the network architecture bears on the reach of the process. This has been studied in different disciplines, ranging from sociology and economics to molecular biology and neurology. By way of illustration of the breadth of setups considered, see e.g. Granovetter (1973) [136], Bikhchandani *et al.* (1998) [31], Chwe (2000) [63], Kauffman (1993) [170], Sporns (2002) [263], and Amaral *et al.* (2004) [9].

Finally, a third element that makes the field of complex networks distinctively interdisciplinary is of a methodological sort. Complex networks do not lend themselves easily to the tools of analysis that have been traditionally used in the social and biological sciences. Their intricate detail makes it virtually hopeless to attempt a microscopic description of their structure. Besides, even if such minute descriptions were at all feasible, it could hardly be expected that most of the interesting properties of the network would depend on them. For example, the robustness of any large-scale communication network, if it is truly complex, cannot hinge upon very small-scale details on its pattern of connections. Or, in a complex (and thus large) social context, the access to relevant information by the agents (say, on job openings or retail prices) should generally depend on "global" features of the social network. Of course, the same would apply if the problem pertained instead to, say, technological diffusion and the objective were to predict the extent to which the population will eventually come to adopt some innovation.

But, what are the global features of the network that should play a significant role in the analysis? The modern theory of complex networks suggests focusing on those network properties that can be suitably described statistically (e.g. average distances between nodes, their distribution of connectivity, etc.). Correspondingly, the tools used in the analysis must also be of a statistical nature and thus only applicable to very large systems. Statistical physics has a long and fruitful tradition in this type of analysis. It should therefore come to no surprise that much of the methodology used in the analysis of complex networks bears the trace, if not the evident imprint, of this origin. This, of course, reinforces the interdisciplinary character of the field. But it also has an unfortunate side effect: it raises the "entry cost" for outsiders, rendering it more difficult that research becomes a truly interdisciplinary endeavor.

Such a methodological convergence notwithstanding, the different areas of application in the field of complex networks naturally maintain many specificities of their own. This applies, in particular, to the economic and other social networks that will concern us here, for which the distinctive characteristics of socioeconomic environments cannot be ignored. Most importantly, it must be recognized that individual agents (the "nodes" of the social network) have their behavior shaped by what are their prevailing objectives and expectations. The latter, in turn, are sharply affected by the social network, which implies that agents' behavior must be conceived and modeled as embedded in the social network. This leads us to the so-called *issue of network embeddedness*, whose importance was forcefully stressed in a very influential paper by the sociologist Mark Granovetter (1985) [139]. We elaborate on this issue and illustrate its implications in the following subsection.

1.2 SOCIOECONOMIC NETWORKS AND THE ISSUE OF EMBEDDEDNESS

In his appraisal of mainstream economic analysis, Granovetter (1985) [139] sharply criticized it for having traditionally circumscribed to two polar paradigms: *markets* and *hierarchies*. He argued that markets, on one hand, are modeled as an extremely under-socialized setup where social relations play virtually no role. Concerning hierarchies, on the other hand, he suggested that there is an analogous de-socialization, but now resulting, ironically, from an extreme oversocialization. A case in point is the monolithic view of the firm where all its members (worker, managers, and owners) operate in perfect coordination, either voluntarily or by the influence of authority. Both perspectives, Granovetter contended, embody similarly desocialized views of economic behavior that markedly contrast with how economic agents actually behave in the real world.

Even though one might well quarrel with the above simplified view of economic analysis, the gist of Granovetter's criticism merits some justification concerning what has been the conventional paradigm of economics until recent times. Matters, however, are rapidly changing in economics, both concerning theoretical and empirical work. There is a recent surge of economic research that is keenly striving to understand economic phenomena as *embedded in the underlying social structure*, i.e. integrated in the network of connections that define how agents interact and communicate. It is not our objective here to provide a systematic or comprehensive survey of this by-now extensive body of work. Rather, what will be done is simply to illustrate its richness and importance by listing some of the fundamental economic problems that have been approached in this vein.

The discussion will be somewhat more detailed concerning two prominent economic applications: the functioning of labor markets and processes of technological diffusion. We will also review, but more succinctly, a number of other socioeconomic examples: the dynamics of social movements (such as revolutions or mass protests), mechanisms of informal insurance (most important in less-developed countries), peer effects in promoting (anti)social behavior, buyer–seller networks that facilitate trust and trade, interfirm agreements for conducting joint R&D, and a network view of organizations that stresses the importance of information flows and adaptability. All this should effectively convey the rich diversity of network-based phenomena that naturally arise in many social contexts. It will also serve to illustrate the main shortcomings of the received theoretical literature, in turn motivating the complex-network approach pursued in this monograph.

1.2.1 Labor Markets

At least since the early work of Rees (1966) [248] there has been a clear understanding of the importance of (informal) social networks in labor markets. In his study of the Chicago area, Rees reports that around a half of the hiring of white-collar workers was done through informal channels, while the proportion rose to 80% in the case of blue-collar workers. The importance of social networks was later confirmed in the thorough and systematic study of the labor market in the Boston area conducted by Granovetter (1974, 1995) [137]. He again found that over 50% of the jobs were found through personal contacts, in contrast with any other mechanism such as formal means or direct application. A richer perspective on the issue is provided by the recent work of Topa (2001) [268]. Using Census Tract data on Chicago, he obtains empirical support for a model with local exchange of information on employment opportunities. He also discovers that these information spillovers are strongest among low-education workers and minorities. Further interesting evidence on the importance of social networks in labor markets is provided by Munshi (2003) [208] with his analysis of Mexican migrants in the United States.

Probably the first *theoretical* analysis of the problem can be found in Boorman (1975) [40], who proposed a simple "combinatorial" model where agents have to decide how to allocate their time and effort among strong and weak links. The difference between each type of link simply reflects considerations of priority: stronger links always receive information on job openings first. Boorman's analysis focuses on symmetric equilibria where every agent is choosing an optimal allocation, given the *same* allocation selected by all others. He concludes, for example, that under certain conditions (i.e. if the risk of losing one's job is high), the equilibrium networks are inefficient because they are overconnected. This brings in a theme (the inefficiency caused by equilibrium overconnectedness) that reappears in different forms through much of modern network theory – see e.g. Jackson and Wolinsky (1996) [161]. A recent paper that revisits Boorman's combinatorial approach and casts it in a full-fledged network setup is Calvó-Armengol (2004) [50]. Its characterization of equilibrium networks, however, also eschews complexity by restricting to symmetric situations.

Two key additional papers that must be singled out are Montgomery (1991) [204] and Calvó-Armengol and Jackson (2004) [52]. The first paper studies the implications of employee referral in labor markets. It explores a setup where younger workers may be referred by older employed workers, the quality of the latter being partially informative of that of the former for hiring firms. The implicit social network under consideration is again simple. It is characterized by only two parameters: the probability that a young worker has a tie to (and thus can be referred by) an employed referee; the correlation between the qualities of connected individuals. Montgomery finds that, in equilibrium, referrals are indeed used by firms in spanning a certain range of wage differentiation.

Finally, I summarize the paper by Calvó-Armengol and Jackson (2004) [52], which represents an important advance over previous literature in at least two respects. First, it is explicitly dynamic in modeling how information flows along the social network. Second, it does not restrict to simple network architectures but in principle allows for any (possibly complex) pattern of connections. One of its main results is that, as indeed confirmed by empirical evidence, the employment situation of individuals that are connected (directly or indirectly) is correlated. Another interesting conclusion is that, for an unemployed individual, the expected future duration of its unemployment spells (in part a consequence of the network conditions faced by this individual) is increasing in the length of time she has been unemployed (an indication of what are those network conditions). Neither of these *qualitative* conclusions depends on network *structure*. However, as illustrated in the paper by means of simple examples, the architecture of the networks will generally affect the *magnitude* of those effects, determining the strength of the implied spatial and temporal correlations of unemployment.

1.2.2   Technological Diffusion

In economics, technological diffusion has long been a topic of central interest, with multiple ramifications in areas such as development and growth, industrial organization, or law and economics. An early and very well-known contribution was made by Griliches (1957) [142], who studied the determinants of the different rates of diffusion of hybrid corn across different US states. Since then, there has been an enormous body of empirical research, which we will not even attempt to summarize here. However, even though diffusion usually presumes some interpersonal "contact," only a relatively small part of this literature has approached the problem from a network viewpoint. A celebrated precursor of this approach is the investigation conducted by the sociologist James Coleman and coauthors (see Coleman *et al.* (1966) [72]) on the spread of a new drug, tretracycline, as prescribed by the doctors of four communities in Illinois. In their survey, doctors were asked not only about their prescription of this drug, but also about the name of another doctor whom they most relied upon for discussion, friendship, and advice (at most three in total). The main conclusion of their study was that the diffusion of the drug spread faster among those doctors who were better "integrated" in the community – i.e. among those who were listed more frequently by their colleagues in at least one of the aforementioned categories.

Many similar studies have been subsequently pursued by the sociological literature, as summarized for example in the excellent monograph by Everett Rogers (1962, 1995) [249]. In economics, but only quite recently, there has also been an analogous flurry of empirical research highlighting the importance of social networks in processes of technological diffusion – see e.g. Foster and Rosenzweig (1995) [112], Conley and Udry (2001) [73], and Munshi (2004) [209]. In contrast with the sociological literature, its emphasis has been on understanding the informational considerations and interagent asymmetries that underlie technological adoption. And, as expected, a robust conclusion is that the wider the heterogeneity of agents and the more uncertain and idiosyncratic the induced performance, the slower the pace of diffusion.

Turning now to theoretical studies of technological diffusion, the older literature, in line with its empirical counterpart, eschewed the implications of networks. Its approach to the problem fell into two main categories: epidemic models and probit models, both of them contemplating population-wide scenarios displaying global interaction (see Geroski (2000) [123] for a good survey). Later work introduced network considerations, giving rise to what have been called "network threshold models" – see e.g. Valente (1996) [273]. These represent an adaptation to a network context of population-based threshold models of the sort proposed by Granovetter (1978) [138]. The characteristic feature of threshold models is the assumption that there is a nondegenerate distribution of *acceptance thresholds* in the population, each individual adopting some new behavior or technology exactly when the fraction of adopters in the relevant (sub-)population exceeds her particular threshold. When these models are applied to a network context, the "relevant subpopulation" is simply identified with the neighbors of the agent in question. The approach, however, is purely local, in that there is no attempt to bring these idiosyncratic thresholds together into a global understanding of how overall network structure impinges on the process of diffusion.

In contrast, there is a body of recent literature in economics that has adopted a full-fledged network analysis of diffusion. In line with the empirical papers discussed above, its main emphasis is on the *differential* information and beliefs held by the agents and on how those evolve over time. Two prominent examples are the papers by Bala and Goyal (1998) [20] and DeMarzo *et al.* (2003) [78].

In the first one, the model has agents located in an arbitrary network and experimenting with a so-called multiarmed bandit – i.e. several actions are available, their corresponding realized (and observed) payoffs having a (nonobserved) stochastic component. The diffusion dimension of the model derives from the fact that an agent is taken to observe not only the outcome of her own experimentation but also that of her neighbors in the network.[9] Over time, agents always choose the action that they perceive maximizes immediate expected payoff given their current beliefs. Their beliefs, on the other hand, are updated in a statistically consistent manner (i.e. through Bayes Rule) in view of the results of her own and her neighbors' experimentation.

The model studied by DeMarzo *et al.* (2003) [78] may also be interpreted as one of belief evolution. Beliefs on the part of each agent are one-dimensional and identified with a real number statistic. Over time, these beliefs change as determined by a matrix of interagent influences – i.e. "persuasion weights" that reflect the impact of an agent's beliefs on those of others. In essence, this matrix embodies a weighted social network, specifying not only who is connected to whom but the strength (persuasion bias) embodied by each of these connections.

Despite the significant differences between the models studied by Bala and Goyal (1998) [20] and DeMarzo *et al.* (2003) [78], both deliver a similar qualitative implication: in the long run, the process converges to a homogenous configuration (identical actions in the first case and identical beliefs in the second), irrespectively of the underlying social network. In the end, therefore, their formalization of diffusion is such that, contrary to what intuition suggests, a uniform configuration always arises in the long run independently of network structure![10]

---

[9] Gale and Kariv (2003) [118] study a related model where agents have local information on neighbors' actions but do *not* observe the latter's payoffs. In this context (which generalizes the classical herding model of Banerjee (1992) [23] and Bikhchandani *et al.* (1992) [30]), they obtain the same convergence of actions indicated below for the models of Bala and Goyal (1998) [20] and DeMarzo *et al.* (2003) [78].

[10] In general, of course, the common action or belief to which convergence obtains depends on the initial conditions and/or the network architecture.

1.2.3   Social Movements and Group Recruitment

Sociologists have long been concerned with understanding the relationship between networks and the dynamics of social movements – see Diani and McAdam (2003) [82] for an edited volume discussing a large collection of real-world cases. One important example is the triggering of mass protests (see, for example, Opp and Gern (1993) [227] on the East German revolution of 1989). Another example pertains to the processes of recruitment by which groups expand their ranks and thus attempt to gain influence (cf. Snow *et al.* (1980) [259], where a number of different religious and political movements are discussed).

In a sense, the mechanism involved in both of those cases is akin to the process of technological diffusion formerly discussed. A common feature is that the process starts to unfold and truly gain momentum only when a substantial number of individuals manage to coordinate effectively with enough of their closer neighbors. This certainly applies to the adoption of a new technology if, as it is often the case, compatibility is an important issue affecting payoffs. It is also true in group recruitment and the ignition of mass protests, a process formally studied by Chwe (2000) [63].

Chwe proposes a model where agents can only ascertain the behavior of (and thus coordinate with) those with whom they are directly connected. Postulating full rationality on the part of agents, he solves for the equilibrium of the induced game of incomplete information and identifies what network features are most conducive to collective action. Interestingly, he finds that an intermediate (low-dimensional) degree of connectivity facilitates the process. This is in line with the complex-network analysis of Watts (2002) [285], who finds a similar conclusion for diffusion processes with neighborhood effects. A complementary perspective is taken by Morris (2000) [207], who stresses the role of cohesiveness in processes of "contagion." These two latter contributions are discussed at some length in Chapter 4.

1.2.4   Informal Insurance

In some economic contexts – most significantly, in rural areas of less-developed countries – risk is an essential factor of everyday life but individuals cannot rely on market-based mechanisms to obtain insurance. Under these circumstances, it has been argued that non-market arrangements among households within a given village act as a common, albeit imperfect, insurance mechanism (see Townsend (1994) [269]). Often, the problem has been conceived and modeled as a collection of bilateral insurance contracts under limited commitment (Ligon *et al.* (2002) [190]). Recently, however, evidence has been gathered indicating that insurance arrangements are usually multilateral, although falling quite short of village-wide. More specifically, they are embedded in the prevailing social network, which is crucial for mitigating opportunistic incentives and thus relaxing enforceability constraints.

Interesting examples of this empirical research include the case of water insurance among households along two irrigation canals in Pakistan

(Murgai *et al.* (2002) [210]), informal credit in response to shocks within a disperse community of rice growers of a remote mountainous area of Philippines (Fafchamps and Lund (2003) [106]), or the insurance mechanisms against illness observed in a Tanzanian village (Dercon and de Weerdt (2002) [79]). A theoretical model attempting to understand the strategic factors involved in these situations has been recently proposed by Bloch *et al.* (2004) [32]. They focus on transfer schemes that satisfy a certain consistency requirement and then characterize what networks are strategically stable (in a quite strong sense). Their main conclusion is that network stability requires that the pattern of connections be sufficiently sparse.

1.2.5   Peer Effects In (Anti)Social Behavior

The general idea that neighborhood effects are important in shaping behavior is, of course, the central tenet underlying the whole field of social networks. One particularly important instance occurs when the relevant "neighbors" are peers, i.e. individuals in a similar ex-ante situation with whom there is close and frequent contact. A large body of empirical research has explored how such peer effects impinge on social and asocial behavior alike. On the positive side, interaction with peers may promote beneficial behavior such as, for example, good school performance (cf. Sacerdote (2001) [252] and Angrist and Lang (2002) [12] for some recent contributions). But, in an opposite negative vein, peer interaction may be decisive as well in inducing deleterious behavior such as dropping out of school and teenage pregnancy (see Crane (1991) [74] and Harding (2003) [150]).

Finally, peer effects are also well known to influence the rise and entrenchment of criminal behavior, a point already stressed in the nascent times of modern criminology by Edwin Sutherland and his controversial "differential association theory" (cf. Sutherland (1924, 1947) [267]). The core of Sutherland's theory is incorporated into many of the recent formalizations of the phenomenon, such as that of Glaeser *et al.* (1996) [128] and Calvó-Armengol and Zenou (2004) [53]. The first paper studies a model of one-dimensional local interaction inspired in the stylized *voter model* introduced by Clifford and Sudbury (1973) [65] and Holley and Liggett (1975) [153]. In contrast, the second paper allows for an arbitrary topology of interaction and analyzes matters by focusing on the (subgame perfect) equilibria of a suitably defined "crime game." In this two-stage game, agents first decide whether to become criminals and then choose their criminal efforts, under a correct anticipation of what the others (in particular, their neighbors) will choose to do. Both of these papers help to understand the mechanism by which peer effects and network structure can sustain substantial ex-post heterogeneities (i.e. inter-agent variance) in the crime levels displayed by *ex-ante* identical individuals.

1.2.6   Trade and Trust

It has become commonplace to contrast networks and markets as two opposing ways of carrying out transactions in an economic system. In general, of course, most real-world situations do not fall neatly into one or the other but display a mixture of market and network features. The relevance of the latter, however, is especially pronounced in many important cases.

There are two prime reasons promoting the reliance on networks in economic interaction – say, between buyers and sellers. One of them is that, in an uncertain environment, a rich pattern of nonmarket (i.e. personalized) relationships may afford flexibility, insurance, or bargaining power. Empirical support for the significance of these considerations is found, for example, in the well-known study by Uzzi (1996) [272] of the garment industry in New York, the analysis of Marseille fish market by Kirman *et al.* (2000) [172], or many of the contributions in the issue edited by Gulati *et al.* (2000) [147]. From a theoretical viewpoint, the problem has been modeled by Kranton and Minehart (2000, 2001) [183, 184] as part of a network formation game, and by Kirman *et al.* (2000) [172] as the outcome of a reinforcement learning dynamics. In both models, the primary emphasis is on understanding how the benefits and costs of diversification shape agents' networking decisions.

Another reason networks may have an important bearing on trade (or, for that matter, on any other economic interaction) revolves around the issue of trust. A key notion in this respect is that of "network closure", which was introduced by Coleman (1988) [70]. In essence, it reflects considerations analogous to what we called network clustering before.[11] Its empirical significance has been confirmed in a wide variety of different contexts: overseas trade in medieval times (Greif (1993) [141]), modern international trade (Rauch (2001) [246]), interfirm transactions in transition or developing economies (Radaev (2001) [242] and McMillan and Woodruff (1999) [199]), and online trade (Kollock (1999) [180]). Theoretically, there are some recent papers that shed light on the strategic issues involved, e.g. Buskens (1998) [47], Fafchamps (2002) [105], and Lippert and Spagnolo (2002) [191]. All of them address matters in a repeated-game context, where the opportunistic incentives in each separate interaction are modeled through a Prisoners' Dilemma (or a variation of it). Their equilibrium analysis, however, restricts to networks that are either homogenous (i.e. symmetric) or display a simple structure.

1.2.7 R&D Interfirm Partnerships

There is a large body of empirical research documenting the rise and increasing importance of interfirm R&D collaboration in many industries during the last decades of the 20th Century. For example, in a summary of trends and patterns since 1960, Hagedoorn (2002) [148] reports a steady rise in R&D partnerships throughout with a specially sharp increase in the 1980's. Interestingly, this phenomenon appears to be fastest among the most technologically dynamic

---

[11] In a trading network, for example, it could amount to the probability that two buyers of a particular seller may interact, and thus communicate, with each other. For an illuminating discussion of the role of "network closure" on restraining opportunistic incentives, see Coleman (1990, Ch 12) [71].

sectors of modern economies such as those of electronics, pharmaceuticals, information technology, and aerospace and defense (cf. Delapierre and Mytelka (1998) [76], Hagedoorn *et al.* (2000) [149], and Orsenigo *et al.* (2001) [228]).

Theoretical research on R&D collaboration among firms has a long tradition in the theory of industrial organization – see e.g. the influential papers of Katz (1986) [169], D'Aspremont and Jacquemin (1988) [75], and Kamien *et al.* (1992) [168]. Their approach, however, shuns interesting network issues by assuming that R&D collaboration must be organized by *partitioning* firms into disjoint (and completely connected) groups that *internally* coordinate their efforts. Recent work by Goyal and Moraga (2001) [133] and Goyal and Joshi (2002) [131] reconsider the problem in a genuine network setup, with firms being allowed to sustain *any* arbitrary pattern of *bilateral* R&D agreements. Their equilibrium analysis of the network-formation game leads, however, to simple network architectures. This contrasts with the evidence gathered from industries in which R&D collaboration is important, where very complex patterns of interaction are generally observed. A good illustration of this complexity is provided by the recent worldwide study of biotechnology firms conducted by Powell *et al.* (2005) [238]. Their exhaustive data show that R&D collaboration among firms in the biotechnology sector conforms to a very complex network, exhibiting an intricate structure and substantial internode heterogeneity (e.g. the distribution of connectivity appears to be scale-free).

1.2.8   Organizations, Networks, and "Network Organizations"

A central theme in the theory of organizations is that of "decomposition," i.e. the need to separate the overall decision problem of the organization into distinct tasks, whose solutions then need to be integrated in an efficient and feasible manner – see e.g. the survey by van Zandt (1999*b*) [296] for an excellent discussion. The implicit idea that motivates this perspective is one of bounded rationality. It stresses the fact that, given the limited capabilities of workers and managers, the organization cannot tackle tasks effectively by merging all of them into a single and compact decision problem. In turn, task decomposition raises implementation issues in at least three different spheres: communication, computation, and incentives. Indeed, most of the received literature on the theory of organizations can be seen as addressing at least one of these three concerns.

The essential objective of this theory has been normative. It has aimed at identifying what organizational structure (communication channels, acceptable messages, working protocols, etc.) best attains the organizational objectives. Once identified, this optimal structure is supposed to provide a map of how the organization must operate to achieve its best performance.

One of the key shortcomings of this approach to organizational design is that, well beyond the formal (often relatively simple) chart of the organization, there is its informal (usually complex) network of relationships. And, as it is amply recognized by contemporary researchers of the firm, "much of the real work in any company gets done through an informal organization, with complex networks of relationships that cross functions and divisions" (cf. Krackhardt and Hanson (1993) [182]). In fact, these informal networks are becoming increasingly important as modern organizations, facing growing volatility and the need for swift adaptations, move toward so-called network forms of organization (see van Alstyne (1997) [8] and Podolny and Page (1998) [237]).

Interesting empirical work attempting to identify such informal networks has been undertaken over the years by Ronald Burt and coauthors through personal surveys of managers working for different firms (see Burt (1992) [45], Burt *et al.* (2000) [46]). More recently, by relying on the computer logs that record internal email communication, this exercise has been extended to a large-scale comprehensive mapping of the informal networks of big firms. In this case, the focus has been on understanding what is the *actual* community structure that governs the everyday operation of those firms (cf. Tyler *et al.* (2003) [271]).[12]

In fact, it has been cogently argued (see e.g. Castells (1996) [58]) that entire economic sectors, industrial districts, or even large cities may be suitably regarded as a single "network organization." In this flexible setup, interpersonal connections are in continuous flux, cutting across formal boundaries as individuals try to learn and respond effectively to a quickly changing environment. Indeed, much of the vitality of successful industrial districts (e.g. Silicon Valley, as studied by Saxenian (1994) [253] and Castilla *et al.* (2000) [59]) or growing cities (see Jacobs (1984) [162] and Glaeser *et al.* (1992) [127]) has been largely attributed to the permeable boundaries and consequent rich flow of ideas afforded by a dense but adaptable social network underlying economic activity.

1.3 THE COMPLEXITY OF SOCIAL NETWORKS

The former section provides ample illustration of the rich range of socioeconomic phenomena that display an inherent network dimension and, therefore, are best conceived as embedded into some relevant social network. Our review has also provided a schematic account of the recent theoretical efforts devoted to understanding those phenomena from a network perspective. The bulk of this literature, however, does not properly account for an important feature of the problem, namely, the massive complexity of most social networks in the real world.

The problem affects theoretical and empirical research alike. Consider first that of a theoretical kind and, to fix ideas, let us return to the applications

---

[12] One natural way to identify the community structure underlying a certain network is provided by the algorithm proposed by Girvan and Newman (2002) [126]. This algorithm creates a progressively finer hierarchical segmentation of the nodes into groups by removing, in order, those links that display the highest "betweenness," i.e. are most crucial in connecting (directly or indirectly) the largest number of nodes – see Section 2.1 for a formal definition of betweenness.

outlined in Section 1.2. Typically, the theoretical attempts to understand, say, labor markets, technological diffusion, R&D partnerships, or organizations have been hampered by one of the two following shortcomings. The first one is that, quite often, a very simple network architecture is readily imposed on the model. This is done either exogenously (i.e. directly) or induced indirectly by the all too powerful implications of equilibrium analysis (alternatively, of convergent learning). But, even in those cases where network complexity is not *a priori* ruled out, the analysis focuses on properties that, although undoubtedly interesting, only hinge upon simple features of network structure. Thus, for example, a common concern is to understand whether basic connectedness of the network is enough to produce belief convergence, overall diffusion, or spatial and temporal correlations in wages and employment.

In empirical research, on the other hand, it is true that one generally finds an accent on the role of local effects but seldom an attempt to study how matters depend on the overall structure of the social network. Thus, for example, the aim is typically to confirm that peer effects are significant in school performance; or that workers often learn about job opportunities through contacts; or that peasants adopt new technologies based on neighbors' experience; or that informal insurance arrangements are preferentially observed within closely knit groups; or that managers' status largely depends on the size and nature of their (ego-centered) network within the firm. But, albeit a welcome first step, the mere evidence that such *local* network effects are significant is far from what could be regarded as a proper grasp of how network *structure* impinges on overall behavior. In general, one would expect that processes such as employment, diffusion, insurance, or organizational performance are a reflection of the *global* structure of the network, not just a juxtaposition or accumulation of local effects.

But what is a complex network? When are we to judge that a social network is indeed endowed with a complex structure? This is a slippery question, for which the answers found in the literature are only heuristic, suggestive, or partial. Unfortunately, we shall not be able to improve much on this state of affairs. Let us simply list some of the features that are generally viewed as a mark for complex networks:

1. To start with the most obvious, sheer size and sufficient diversity are natural prerequisites. Thus, the network must consist of a large number of entities (nodes) that display substantial heterogeneity.
2. The structure of node interaction (i.e. the array of links) ought to have an "intricate architecture", i.e. a configuration that involves many degrees of freedom and no recurrent or otherwise easily discernible patterns.[13]

---

[13] A situation where these features arise naturally is when the formation of the network is undertaken by a stochastic mechanism, e.g. when the network is random, in any of the various senses that will be explored in this monograph.

3. Indirectly, the complexity of the network may also be assessed by how different rules of local interaction operate on it. Specifically, in a complex network, even "simple" such rules should lead to an overall performance that goes well beyond a mechanical accumulation of local effects.[14]

4. Relatedly, local feedback effects will generally induce nonlinear, sometimes discontinuous, relationships between exogenous parameters (i.e. external conditions) and the global behavior of the system. This, in particular, must apply to the operation of network-based processes that shape the network itself over time.[15]

Admittedly, the above "check-list for complexity" is somewhat vague and perhaps too informal to be entirely useful in guiding research. It points, however, to some recognizable qualitative features of large social networks that could have significant implications on how these operate in the real world. Given our increasing ability to collect detailed and large-scale data on the structure of social networks, the near future is likely to witness a significant improvement in our ability to assess social complexity. In the meantime, the scant empirical evidence we do have on, say, networks of academic collaboration, R&D interfirm agreements, or email communication (cf. Sections 1.1 and 1.2) already seems to provide some support for items 1 and 2 above. Concerning 3 and 4, on the other hand, there is also some measure of support in the sharp transitions that are known to occasionally "punctuate" the dynamic evolution of various network phenomena. When these transitions occur, a chain of fast and self-reinforcing local changes unfolds that, within a short time lapse, leads to a substantial alteration of the global state of the system. The occurrence of such sharp adjustments has been highlighted, for example, in some of the empirical contexts already discussed in previous sections, e.g. in the rise of social pathologies studied by Crane (1991) [74], in the steep (twofold) increase of scientific collaboration among economists reported by Goyal et al. (2003) [132], or in the surge of interfirm R&D partnerships (tenfold in a mere decade) documented by Hagerdoorn (2002) [148].

Accepting, therefore, that many large social networks indeed qualify as complex, the next key issue is how we should model them. The standpoint defended here is that complex networks should be modeled as such, i.e. in ways that do

---

[14] By way of illustration, consider a simple process of diffusion in which a new technology is adopted by an agent (node) if 2/3 of its neighbors have already adopted. If the network displays some recurrent local pattern, the reach of diffusion can be anticipated from the study and extrapolation of this pattern. In contrast, if the network is genuinely complex, a detailed prediction requires a global (typically unfeasible) analysis of the situation.

[15] Again, a good illustration is provided by random networks. In the canonical framework used to study them (see Chapter 2), it can be shown that important properties such as overall connectedness or the rise of particular patterns arises "suddenly" (i.e. nonlinearly) when some key parameter (e.g. average connectivity) exceeds a certain threshold. On the other hand, for an elaboration on how similar nonlinearities may occur in the network-based process of formation of the network itself, see the discussion at the end of this section.

not belie their intrinsic complexity. This position is mainly justified by two distinct but complementary arguments. The first one is that, as we shall see amply confirmed throughout the monograph, complexity introduces novel and important considerations into the analysis. That is, it leads to insights that could *not* be gathered from a reductionist or otherwise simplified description of the situation. A good illustration is provided by the phenomena of *diffusion* and *search* in complex social networks with substantial internode heterogeneity. In these contexts, one finds that the presence of large "hubs" brings in possibilities – and also limitations – that do not arise, say, in regular networks. Pertaining to search, in particular, the access enjoyed by those hubs to many other agents (and their corresponding information) may prove invaluable in expediting the process. But, on the other hand, the very same fact that they have so many neighbors possibly "calling on their attention" could, under some circumstances, lead to congestion and even collapse in the overall search performance of the system.

A second reason supporting the need to account for the vast complexity of real-world social networks is a natural counterpart of the first one. To explain the argument, it is useful to refer to the traditional paradigm of economic theory, based on the twin postulates of (unbounded) rationality and equilibrium. This paradigm, of course, is not only ill-suited to model complex environments *as such* but, more importantly, is not geared to do so either. Implicitly, it is based on the assumption that, even if the context at hand is very complex, predictions that are inconsistent with the aforementioned postulates can represent only a transient state of affairs, or a superficial description of the problem. Introducing real complexity into the model, it is argued, would cloud the fundamental forces at work and conceal the core elements of the situation. A good model, therefore, should be relatively simple and, when analyzed in coherence with the principles of rationality and equilibrium, typically deliver a simple prediction as well.

In view of the complexity of most social environments of interest, one of the common justifications for this traditional approach relies on learning. It is argued that, even if agents can rely on just a very limited understanding of the environment, their adjustment over time should eventually make the system gravitate toward the theoretical prediction. In a sense, the implicit assumption being made is that learning will cut through the complexity of the situation and thus ultimately validate the simplified theory. There is, however, a key problem with this standpoint, which could render it substantially misleading in some cases. It is conceivable that, given agents' limited knowledge and abilities, their adjustment does not work toward simplifying the process. On the contrary, it could exacerbate the complexity of the situation, thus widening the "theoretical discrepancy" even further. In that case, the simplified model would fail to become a suitable anchor. Its predictions, in other words, would then always remain far from where the system, stubbornly complex, continues to lie in. This, in fact, will be one of the main insights to be gathered from some of the network-formation models studied in this monograph. Specifically, we shall find that when agents are allowed to adjust their links over time (with just a quite partial grasp of the whole situation), not only does the complex structure of the social network remain in place but new forms of complexity appear. For example, the system may come to display abrupt fast transitions in its global state in response to even slight parameter changes, as suggested in the last of the above items.

1.4 DIFFUSION, SEARCH, AND PLAY IN SOCIAL NETWORKS: AN OVERVIEW OF WHAT FOLLOWS

Hopefully, the reader is by now convinced about the rich scope of socioeconomic phenomena that can be studied from a network viewpoint. This vast diversity, however, renders it unwise to attempt a detailed coverage of even a representative fraction of those phenomena. This is why, in this monograph, we pursue a different strategy of discussion and analysis. We abstract from the modeling details of specific contexts (labor markets, technological diffusion, etc.) and instead concentrate on some of the key common forces that underlie agents' behavior in most of those cases. In particular, we focus on *diffusion, search, and play*, that are three essential forces at work in virtually all interesting network applications. By *diffusion*, we mean the process by which information (or, more generally, any kind of signal) travels along the network. In contrast, *search* refers to the somewhat polar process by which individuals actively look for information by exploring alternative network paths. Finally, the notion of *play* stands for the interaction that, mediated by the network, every agent undertakes with other (neighboring) members of the population.

Of course, no single process in this triad of diffusion, search, and play should be seen as operating in exclusion of the other two. Most economic phenomena in the real world embody an interplay of all of them, although the intensity, time-scale, and specific form with which each materializes varies greatly among specific instances. Given the essentially theoretical intent of the present monograph, it seems best to abstract from that interplay in a first stage, starting with a separate analysis of each of these three processes. However, some partial and yet preliminary integration will be later carried out, in which simple forms of search and play are brought to bear on the key phenomenon of network evolution.

Thus, to summarize, diffusion, play, and search are the central notions that help organize this monograph. A brief description of its contents is now advanced, through a schematic review of the material to be covered in each of the five ensuing chapters and the three final appendices.

We start in Chapter 2 with a self-contained presentation of the main concepts and basic tools of the modern theory of complex networks. The first step involves the introduction of the theoretical setup, certain key notions, and a collection of network characteristics of interest. Then, we discuss the framework that will act as a benchmark for our study of random networks: the so-called binomial model, which was intensively studied by Paul Erdös and Alfréd Rényi since the late 1950's. Next, this framework is generalized to allow for arbitrary degree distributions (i.e. not just binomial or Poisson), although maintaining the assumption that the network is random and has no "structure" (i.e. no correlations, clustering, etc.). We dispense with this assumption in the second half of the chapter, which turns to the discussion of some of the most prominently studied networks with specific structure. Starting with the simple lattice networks, the discussion then covers the stationary small-world networks introduced by Duncan Watts and Steven Strogatz, and ends with the *growing* scale-free networks studied by Albert-László Barabási and Réka Albert. In each case, our main concern is to understand what are the implications of the different structures on key network characteristics such as average internode distance, clustering, and the distribution of connectivities.

The analysis conducted in Chapter 2 uses for the first time some of the versatile techniques of statistical and dynamic analysis that will be repeatedly required in the rest of the monograph. Specifically, the study of generalized random networks relies on generating-function methods to characterize induced distributions, and the study of small-world and scale-free networks applies the so-called mean-field approach. While the essence of these methods is discussed in the main text, the more technical discussion is gathered in Appendices A and C.

Chapter 3 focuses on what we shall call *epidemic* diffusion. This refers to a type of diffusion that proceeds as biological infection, i.e. it is mediated by bilateral contact and grows with exposure but is unaffected by neighborhood (frequency-dependent) considerations. Depending on whether such "infection" is irreversible, may turn into recovery, or revert to the original susceptibility, we arrive at the SI, SIR, or SIS frameworks respectively. In the first two cases (SI and SIR), diffusion waves are unidirectional and the main questions of interest dwell on what is the range and resilience of their reach. These questions can be answered precisely (relating them, in particular, to the topology of the underlying network) by relying on a suitable adaptation of the generating-function techniques first used in Chapter 2.

Analogous questions can be addressed as well within the bidirectional SIS framework. In that context, however, we obtain only approximate results by resorting to mean-field dynamic analysis. The results thus attained again underscore the point that, in general, the underlying network topology crucially affects the process of diffusion. In particular, the threshold for the diffusion rate beyond which long-run prevalence of infection obtains turns out to be bounded above zero for networks with a well-defined characteristic scale (e.g. networks with a Poisson degree distribution) but is zero otherwise (say, for broad scale-free networks). The network topology also has an important bearing on the way different policies (e.g. the "immunization" of selected nodes) may impinge on diffusion.

Chapter 4 follows up on the topic of diffusion but studies it when an agent's adoption decision (of a product, technology, etc.) is frequency-dependent, i.e.

hinges upon the relative number of adopters in her neighborhood. In correspondence with the SI and SIS frameworks considered for epidemic diffusion in Chapter 3, the analysis is separated in two cases: permanent and temporary adoption, respectively. We also study how frequency-dependent diffusion is affected when the so-far maintained assumption that the underlying network displays no structure is dispensed with. In this respect, we focus on a model that, by allowing for local structure, highlights the important role played by some measure of network cohesion (or the lack thereof) in the reach of diffusion under neighborhood effects.

In many applications, the decision problem faced by agents is not merely one of adoption (temporary or not) but concerns what particular *behavior* to choose among several possible. Then, the considerations involved become "strategic" and, often, the problem is one of local coordination. A useful framework to address this latter case is provided by the so-called Potts model in statistical physics – an extension of the classical Ising setup to an arbitrary finite number of possible node states. In Chapter 4, we study that model both in the simplest scenario where the underlying network is a regular lattice and in the context where interaction occurs along an arbitrary (generalized) random network. Again, some of the technical details of this analysis are relegated to an appendix (Appendix B), which in particular discusses the canonical Gibbs approach to the analysis of spin systems and some of its key implications.

Chapter 4 also poses the question of how diffusion and play unfold when, in accordance with reality, they are continuously fuelled by persistent innovation. Some preliminary understanding on this issue is obtained through a simple model where agents are located along a regular one-dimensional network and interact with their immediate neighbors. In this context, the population adjustment is found to proceed in waves (or avalanches) of quite different sizes, distributed in a scale-free manner for a wide range of parameter values.

Chapter 5 addresses the problem of search, an issue of primary importance in large social networks. The need to search arises, for example, when a node/agent is confronted with a problem that can only be solved through the concourse of some other *specific* (yet unknown) node/agent in the network. What algorithms or protocols will work effectively for this purpose if, given the complexity of the setup, nodes can rely only on local, or otherwise limited, information? We study this general question under a number of different specifications of what is meant by information to be limited or local, and under different assumptions on the topology of the social network. For example, it turns out that if the network is scale-free and therefore includes a significant fraction of high-degree nodes, a search/communication protocol that biases the search path toward nodes with high degree is particularly effective. Or, if there is an underlying "geography" that can inform the direction of queries (e.g. a lattice network or some other coordinate system), search can take advantage of it to improve its performance substantially.

In general, one should conceive search in a network as involving many simultaneous quests, proceeding in parallel (i.e. simultaneously) along different paths and with different objectives. This then raises the question of congestion. What happens if a particular node faces many concurrent queries at some point in time? If, due to a limited ability to process information, not all of those queries can be handled simultaneously, congestion-induced delays on the search process might ensue. The last part of Chapter 5 addresses these questions formally and sheds some light on how the topology of the network impinges on the problem of congestion in search. This in turn leads to a corresponding network design problem that aims at identifying what topology of the network is optimal (minimizes delay), given the trade-offs involved (e.g. short distances versus low congestion).

Finally, Chapter 6 reconsiders the phenomena of search, diffusion, and play in social networks and brings them to bear on the crucial issue of (endogenous) network formation in a complex environment. Before setting on this course, however, we find it useful to compare this approach with the recent literature studying network formation from a game-theoretic viewpoint. The brief survey of this literature that opens the chapter is organized in two parts. First, we include a discussion of static models that are concerned with the characterization of the *equilibria* arising in suitably defined network-formation *games*. Then, we turn to reviewing the dynamic models that focus on the *long-run states* of network-formation *processes*. In both cases, the implicit presumption is that the underlying environment is stable and simple enough that agents are able to reach an equilibrium (or at least a well-defined pattern) in the configuration of the social network.

In contrast, when the environment is complex (say, because it is highly non-stationary), agents are best conceived as continuously groping for profitable links/opportunities. This search, of course, must then largely rely on the prevailing social network – it might be channeled, for example, through current neighbors. The bulk of Chapter 6 explores these issues through a collection of different dynamic models where the nonstationarity of the environment is made explicit and takes alternative forms. In one of these, the setup is a growing one, akin to the Barabási-Albert model studied in Chapter 2. In others, the change of the environment over time is caused by the "volatility" (i.e. recurrent update) that alters payoffs and opportunities. In all of these different contexts, our main concern is to understand how the details of the different processes (diffusion, play, and search) determine the long-run features of the social network, e.g. its distribution of connectivities, clustering, or component sizes.

In Chapter 6, the first approach to the problem of network evolution contemplates only quite basic considerations pertaining how payoffs and incentives bear on link formation. The last part of the chapter enriches this dimension by positing directly that players are involved in strategic interaction. In this respect, the more detailed analysis is carried out for a context where every pair of connected agents plays an $n \times n$-coordination game. Other scenarios discussed in less detail include one where agents play a one-shot Prisoner's Dilemma, another where they are involved in an infinitely repeated version of that same game, and a third setup where the network coevolves with a process of diffusion and growth. In all cases, we find an interesting interplay between network architecture and strategic choice that eventually determines whether or not the society manages to build up and maintain a high level of overall connectivity. If this occurs, the population is also able to sustain, respectively, a high level of coordination, cooperation, or growth.

CHAPTER 2

Complex Networks: Basic Theory

This chapter provides a systematic overview of the basic developments in the modern theory of complex networks. The first part is devoted to random networks, a construct that is consistent with any degree distribution but lacks any further structure such as clustering or internode correlations. The second part focuses on other network models (i.e. small worlds and growing scenarios) that result from alternative network-formation algorithms and generally enjoy significant structure. All these different network models provide the theoretical setup where we shall conduct most of our discussion of social phenomena (diffusion, search, and play) throughout the monograph.

2.1 PRELIMINARIES

We start by formalizing the idea of a network, providing some simple illustrations, and reviewing a number of key measures and network characteristics.

2.1.1 Networks: Definition and Representation

A network $\Gamma = (N, L)$ is given by a (finite) set of nodes $N = \{1, 2, \ldots, n\}$ and a set of links $L \subseteq N \times N$, which are assumed unweighted (i.e. all existing links have a fixed "strength"). Implicitly, we also assume that multiple links are absent, so that no more than one link can exist between two given nodes.[1] A convenient way to represent the network in this case is through its adjacency matrix, an $n \times n$-dimensional matrix denoted by A such that

$$a_{ij} = \begin{cases} 1 & \text{if } (i, j) \in L \\ 0 & \text{otherwise.} \end{cases}$$

Networks can be *directed* or *undirected*. If they are directed, the existence of a link (i, j) from i to j does not imply that the converse link (j, i) should necessarily exist. Some network applications presume or rely on directed links

---

[1] In the language of graph theory, the possibility of multiple links between two particular nodes gives rise to a *multigraph* – see, for example, Carré (1979) [55] or Clark and Holton (1991) [64].

(see e.g. some of the network formation models of Chapter 6). For the moment, however, we shall simplify matters and assume that links are undirected. This implies that if $(i, j) \in L$ then $(j, i) \in L$. The simpler notation ij is then used to denote the (undirected) link connecting i and j. Reflexive links are also ruled out, i.e. it is assumed that $ii \notin L$ for each $i \in N$.

The set of nodes that are connected to any given $i \in N$ define its *neighborhood* $\mathcal{N}^i \equiv \{j \in N : ij \in L\}$. Clearly, any network $\Gamma = (N, L)$ is characterized by the collection of neighborhoods for all nodes. Thus, still another equivalent way of describing a certain network is through the complete specification of those neighborhoods, $\{\mathcal{N}^i\}_{i \in N}$.

2.1.2 Some Types of Networks

Let us illustrate matters by outlining some archetypical classes of networks.

Lattice Networks

These are networks where the nodes are identified with points of a regular lattice of some finite dimension $m \in \mathbb{N}$, usually boundariless. Thus, if we consider the simplest case with $m = 1$, the underlying lattice may be conceived as a (discrete) ring, or if $m = 2$ as a torus. Given any such lattice and some distance function $\varphi(\cdot)$ appropriately defined on it, a corresponding network can be defined associated to some radius r. This parameter may be used to define the neighborhood (in the network) of any node i as follows:

$$\mathcal{N}^i \equiv \{j \in N : ij \in L\} = \{j \in N : \varphi(i, j) \leq r\}.$$

Tree Networks

Tree networks are characterized by the property of having no loops, i.e. no closed paths.[2] Or, equivalently, they are networks in which there is a unique path joining any two distinct nodes. Letting $\ell \equiv |L|$ stand for the number of links,[3] tree networks must satisfy

$$\ell = n - 1.$$

This follows, as a particular case, from a general expression that is applicable to *any* network that cannot be fragmented in disconnected parts (see below for a formal definition). In that case, we have

$$\ell = n - 1 + u,$$

where u stands for the number of minimal loops (closed paths) in the network.

---

[2] A path between two nodes, i and k, is simply a "connected" set of links $\{j_1 j_2, j_2 j_3, \ldots, j_{r-1} j_r\} \subset L$ such that $j_1 = i$ and $j_r = k$.

[3] In general, we will use the standard notation $|A|$ to represent the cardinality (i.e. the number of elements) of any given set A.

Random Networks

Typically, when using the term *random network*, we shall not refer to a specific network Γ but to a probabilistic construct (or statistical ensemble). Formally, a random network consists of two items:

- a family $\mathcal{G}$ of possible networks;
- a probability density P specifying the ex-ante probability $P(\Gamma)$ with which each network $\Gamma \in \mathcal{G}$ is selected.

In general, one can construct a wide variety of random networks by suitably choosing $\mathcal{G}$ and P. A classical example is the following setup, originally proposed by Erdös and Rényi (1959) [101].

There is a fixed set of nodes, $N = \{1, 2, \ldots, n\}$, and a fixed *number* of links, ℓ, that can be used to connect them. The set $\mathcal{G}$ is identified with the collection of *all* possible undirected networks that can be constructed by connecting the nodes in N with ℓ links. It is posited that every possible network is chosen with uniform probability. Therefore, since there are of course $\binom{n(n-1)/2}{\ell}$ different such networks, we have $P(\Gamma) = \binom{n(n-1)/2}{\ell}^{-1}$ for every $\Gamma \in \mathcal{G}$.

2.1.3   Network Characteristics

Any network, either deterministically given or random, can be studied from many different angles. Let us now review some of the main measures and network characteristics that will be repeatedly considered throughout.

Connectivity

A central feature in any network $\Gamma = (N, L)$ is, of course, the connectivity of its nodes. For any given node i, its *degree*

$$z^i \equiv |\mathcal{N}^i| = |\{j \in N : ij \in L\}|$$

is simply the number of its neighbors. These are the *first(-order)* neighboring nodes immediately connected to i, also denoted by $\mathcal{N}_1^i$. In addition, we might be interested in its *second(-order)* neighbors:

$$\mathcal{N}_2^i \equiv \{j \in N \backslash \{i\} : \exists k \in N \text{ s.t. } ik \in L \wedge kj \in L\} \backslash \mathcal{N}_1^i,$$

i.e. the set of nodes which are at a "geodesic" distance (exactly) equal to 2 from node i, i.e. the *shortest* path joining them to i consists of two links. The corresponding *second-order degree* of i is given by

$$z_2^i \equiv |\mathcal{N}_2^i|.$$

Recursively, we may define, for each r, the set of *rth-neighbors* and the *rth-order degree* as follows:

$$\mathcal{N}_r^i \equiv \left\{ \begin{array}{c} j \in N\backslash\{i\} : \exists k_0, k_1, \ldots, k_r \in N \text{ s.t.} \\ k_{s-1}k_s \in L \ (s = 1, 2, \ldots, r), \ k_0 = i, \ k_r = j \end{array} \right\} \backslash \left[\bigcup_{s=1}^{r-1} \mathcal{N}_s^i \right]$$

$$z_r^i \equiv |\mathcal{N}_r^i|.$$

For any network Γ, its (first-order) *degree distribution* $p(\cdot)$ specifies, for each $\kappa = 0, 1, \ldots, n-1$, the fraction of nodes

$$p(\kappa) = \frac{1}{n} \left| \{ i \in N : z^i = \kappa \} \right|$$

that display degree κ. Equivalently, we can view it as the probability that a randomly selected node has connectivity κ. This alternative interpretation is a natural one in cases where the network is random.

The degree distribution is a key characteristic of any network. Thus, in the specific context of random networks, it is common to pay special attention to statistical ensembles $(\mathcal{G}, P)$ that are defined in terms of a *given* degree distribution (see Section 2.3). As specific examples of degree distributions, the following ones will play a prominent role at different points in our discussion.

- *Binomial distribution*, with density

$$p(\kappa) = \binom{n-1}{\kappa} q^\kappa (1-q)^{n-\kappa-1} \qquad (\kappa = 0, 1, \ldots n-1), \quad (2.1)$$

  where q is the success probability of the $n-1$ independent Bernoulli trials. As explained in Section 2.2, this distribution arises for random networks within the so-called binomial model, i.e. a setup where, for every node i, each of its $n-1$ *a priori* possible links ij $(j \neq i)$ materializes with the same independent probability q.
- *Poisson distribution*, with density

$$p(\kappa) = \frac{1}{\kappa!} e^{-z} z^\kappa \qquad (\kappa = 0, 1, \ldots), \quad (2.2)$$

  where z, the single parameter of the distribution, coincides with the average degree. The Poisson distribution is well known to be approximated by the binomial distribution (2.1) when $n \to \infty$ and the expected connectivity $z = qn$ remains constant. Thus, in view of our previous discussion, it can also be regarded as the limit degree distribution of the binomial model when n is very large.
- *Geometric distribution*, with density

$$p(\kappa) = (1-a)a^{\kappa-1} \qquad (\kappa = 1, 2, \ldots), \quad (2.3)$$

where $a \in (0, 1)$. As we shall note in Section 2.5, this distribution emerges, for example, in growing networks if the entering nodes connect with existing ones fully at random (i.e. with no bias or preference).

- *Power-law distribution*, with density

$$p(\kappa) = A\kappa^{-\gamma} \qquad (\kappa = 1, 2, \ldots), \tag{2.4}$$

where $\gamma > 1$ is the parameter governing the rate at which probability decays with connectivity. Here $A = 1/\mathcal{R}(\gamma)$, where

$$\mathcal{R}(\gamma) \equiv \sum_{\kappa=1}^{\infty} \kappa^{-\gamma} \tag{2.5}$$

defines the Riemann Zeta function that normalizes the distribution. This degree distribution is said to be *scale-free* in the sense that $p(\alpha\kappa) = \alpha^{-\gamma} p(\kappa)$ for *any* κ and α (see Section 2.5 for an elaboration). It will also be seen to arise in growing networks, but only if new nodes display a "linear" preference for highly connected existing nodes.

Components and Component Sizes

In general, a network $\Gamma = (N, L)$ may be divided into different *components*. These are maximal subsets of nodes $\chi \subset N$ such that, for every $i, j \in \chi$, there is a path joining them. That is, there is a (finite) set of links $\{y_{u-1} y_u \in L\}_{u=1,\ldots,m}$ such that $y_0 = i$ and $y_m = j$. It is clear that the binary relationship "be connected by a network path" is an equivalence relationship. Therefore, the components induced by it define a *partition* of the set of nodes. If the network has just one component, it is said to be *connected*.

Let the *size* of a component be simply identified with the number of nodes it includes. We shall often be interested in the relative sizes of the network components. A useful way to summarize this information is through the distribution ϕ that, for each s, specifies the fraction $\phi(s)$ of nodes that are in a component of size s. Equivalently, one can think of $\phi(s)$ as the probability that a randomly selected node lies in a component of size s.

In the context of random networks, when the set of nodes becomes large (formally, when $n \to \infty$), we shall often find that any realized Γ has (almost surely) what is called a *giant component*. This is a *unique* component χ^0 whose relative size $|\chi^0|/n$ remains bounded *above* zero as the number of nodes $n \to \infty$. In those cases, therefore, any other component $\chi \neq \chi^0$ has its fractional size $|\chi|/n \to 0$.

Geodesic Distances

Another important characteristic of a network $\Gamma = (N, L)$ is the average *geodesic distance* $d(i, j)$ separating pairs of nodes i and j. This distance is simply defined as the minimum number of links that need to be used along some network path to connect i and j. If no such path exists, then we use the convention that $d(i, j) = +\infty$.

Assume, for simplicity, that there is a path between any two nodes. (Otherwise, the ensuing concepts can be defined component-wise.) Then, all pairwise distances are finite, and we can construct the distribution ϖ specifying the fraction $\varpi(r)$ of node pairs that are at distance r. That is,

$$\varpi(r) = \frac{|\{(i, j) \in N \times N : d(i, j) = r\}|}{n(n - 1)},$$

where, of course, $\sum_{r>0} \varpi(r) = 1$. Based on the distribution ϖ, the *average network distance* is computed as follows:

$$\bar{d} = \sum_{0<r<\infty} r\, \varpi(r),$$

while the *diameter* of the network is

$$\hat{d} = \max \{r : \varpi(r) > 0\},$$

i.e. the maximum geodesic distance prevailing across any pair of nodes.

Clustering

A feature of the network that, as advanced, will turn out to have important implications is its *clustering*. First, for each node i that has at least two neighbors, its clustering $\mathcal{C}^i$ is simply defined as the fraction of pairs of neighbors of i that are themselves neighbors. To introduce it formally, note that, for any such node i, the number of possible neighbor pairs is simply $\frac{z^i(z^i-1)}{2}$, where recall that z^i is its degree (i.e. its number of neighbors). Thus, its clustering is given by

$$\mathcal{C}^i \equiv \frac{|\{jk \in L : ij \in L \wedge ik \in L\}|}{\frac{z^i(z^i-1)}{2}}. \tag{2.6}$$

In terms of the adjacency matrix $A = (a_{ij})_{i,j=1}^n$, it can be succinctly rewritten as follows:

$$\mathcal{C}^i = \frac{\sum_{j<k} a_{ij}\, a_{ik}\, a_{jk}}{\sum_{j<k} a_{ij}\, a_{ik}}. \tag{2.7}$$

For a node j with less than two neighbors ($z^j < 2$), let us simply make $\mathcal{C}^j = 0$. Then, averaging over all nodes, we obtain the *clustering index* of the whole network as follows:

$$\mathcal{C} = \frac{1}{n} \sum_{i=1}^{n} \mathcal{C}^i. \tag{2.8}$$

Essentially, the clustering index reflects an average measure of the fraction of "triangles" actually in place out of all those possible. An alternative way to assess that fraction is to aggregate over all nodes i in both the numerator and denominator of (2.7). This gives rise to

$$\tilde{C} = \frac{\sum_{i<j<k} a_{ij} \, a_{ik} \, a_{jk}}{\sum_{i<j<k} a_{ij} \, a_{ik}}. \tag{2.9}$$

Both measures of network clustering, C and $\tilde{C}$, reflect similar considerations. The latter, however, gives more weight to high-degree nodes while the former treats all nodes equivalently.

The *informational* and *strategic* implications of clustering in networks may be all important. Concerning the *spread of information*, for example, it bears on the insightful dichotomy between weak and strong ties highlighted by Granovetter (1973) [136]. He proposed distinguishing between *strong* links that are typically transitive and *weak* ones for which transitivity is much less common (e.g. a friend of a friend is often a friend, in contrast with what happens for mere acquaintances). Strong links, he argued, will usually be informational redundant (i.e. what one knows through a strong link might have been equivalently learned through another strong link). Instead, weak links should be much more valuable in terms of contributing genuinely new information, since they are likely to represent the only (nonredundant) access to it. Network clustering, therefore, as induced by the strength/transitivity of the links, should have an important effect on the access to fresh information.

Clustering, on the other hand, could have *strategic implications* as well. This may happen, for example, if agents' cooperation is threatened by opportunistic incentives. In this case, the very same transitivity that could be detrimental concerning the access to new information might instead help in mitigating opportunism. For, as suggested by Coleman (1988) [70], "network closure" (analogous to clustering) may be important in supporting cooperative behavior through the threat that, if some agent takes advantage of any other, their common partners would swiftly punish this behavior – cf. Subsection 1.2.6.

Cohesiveness

Another important notion of network structure is cohesiveness. In contrast with clustering, however, it does *not* apply locally to a single node and its neighbors but to an arbitrary subset of nodes. Informally, we shall conceive some such set as cohesive if its nodes do *not* have a high proportion of "exogamous" links outside the set – or, reciprocally, if most of their links connect with other nodes in the set.

The following formal measure of cohesiveness can be found, among many others, in the network literature – cf. Wasserman and Faust (1994) [280].[4] Given

---

[4] This is the notion used by Morris (2000) [207] to define his notion of $(1-r)$-cohesive set (cf. Section 4.2). See also Young (1998, Ch. 6) [294] for the related concept of close-knitness.

a network $\Gamma = (N, L)$, let $M \subset N$ be some subset of nodes. First, for each node $i \in M$, we compute the fraction of its connections that lie within M, as given by:

$$\mathcal{H}^i(M) = \frac{|\{ij \in L : j \in M\}|}{z^i}. \qquad (2.10)$$

Then, the overall *cohesiveness* of the set M is defined as the minimum such fraction across all nodes $i \in M$, i.e.

$$\mathcal{H}(M) = \min_{i \in M} \mathcal{H}^i(M). \qquad (2.11)$$

The cohesiveness of a certain set M may be understood as an indication of how "shielded" it is (both for the good and the bad) from outside influence. Obviously, $\mathcal{H}(N) = 1$, so that the real interest here concerns the cohesiveness of strict (possibly small) subsets of N. More generally, note that if a subset M is a component, or a union of components, of Γ then $\mathcal{H}(M) = 1$ as well. This simply reflects the idea that a component, by definition, is totally insulated from external influence.

Betweenness

Finally, we introduce another characteristic of a node's position in the network, its centrality, that will be seen to have interesting implications on its role and performance. Intuitively, the centrality of a node measures the importance of this node in bridging the (indirect) connection – contact or access – between other nodes.

To have a concrete measure of centrality, let us assume, for simplicity, that the network is connected. Then, consider all the shortest paths joining any two nodes j and k ($j \neq k$) and denote by $v(j, k) (= v(k, j))$ their total number. Now let $v^i(j, k)$ stand for the number of those paths that, not only connect j and k, but also go through a particular node i ($i \neq j \neq k \neq i$). Then, the betweenness of node i is given by

$$b^i \equiv \sum_{j \neq k} \frac{v^i(j, k)}{v(j, k)}, \qquad (2.12)$$

where we rely on the notational convention that $v^i(i, k) = v^i(j, i) = 0$.

Note that, aggregating the betweenness over all nodes $i \in N$, we may write

$$\sum_{i=1}^{n} b^i = \sum_{i=1}^{n} \sum_{j \neq k} \frac{v^i(j, k)}{v(j, k)} = \sum_{j \neq k} \sum_{i=1}^{n} \frac{v^i(j, k)}{v(j, k)}.$$

Then, since for each pair of nodes j, k $(j \neq k)$ we have[5]

$$\sum_{i=1}^{n} \frac{v^i(j,k)}{v(j,k)} = d(j,k) - 1,$$

we obtain

$$\sum_{i=1}^{n} b^i = \sum_{j \neq k} [d(j,k) - 1]$$

$$= n(n-1) \left[\frac{\sum_{j \neq k} d(j,k)}{n(n-1)} - 1 \right] = n(n-1)(\bar{d} - 1),$$

i.e. the total betweenness is essentially proportional to average network distance, with the factor of proportionality being determined by the network size (specifically, by the number of possible node pairs). It is worth emphasizing that the notion of betweenness displayed in (2.12) is of an eminently topological nature since it considers only shortest paths between nodes – i.e. it abstracts from any specific mechanism that might be at work in *searching* for those paths.

Again, the notion of betweenness may have informational and strategic implications – recall the discussion of Subsection 1.2.8. On the *informational* side, a central node is crucial for widespread network communication. But this, in turn, raises some worries as well. For example, overall communication may be rendered too fragile if it can be crucially jeopardized by the malfunctioning of a single node. Or, relatedly, a highly central node could become so congested (or strained) that it might be unable to operate properly, thus affecting the overall performance of the network. Centrality, on the other hand, could also have *strategic* implications. This would occur, for example, if the very importance of a central node/agent may be translated into an exploitation of this position to its advantage *vis-á-vis* the remaining nodes.

2.2 POISSON RANDOM NETWORKS

The theoretical framework of random networks provides a natural setup for the study of large complex systems of interacting units. As advanced in Section 1.3, it allows for significant heterogeneities and intricate structures to arise, while many large-scale regularities can still be systematically studied through statistical analysis. One of the earliest precedents of this approach can be found in the paper by Solomonoff and Rapoport (1951) [262] that introduced the notion of *random nets* – a theoretical construct very close in spirit to the present-day formalization of random networks. Later developments along these lines by Rapoport and others (see e.g. Rapoport (1957) [244]) introduced the possibility

---

[5] To understand this, simply observe that, for every shortest path connecting some j and k, there are exactly $d(j,k) - 1$ intermediate nodes i that have their corresponding "counter" increase by one as they grow up to $v^i(j,k)$. After considering all of the possible $v(j,k)$ paths, the accumulated counter sum over all (intermediate) nodes is $v(j,k)(d(j,k) - 1)$.

of different sorts of "biases," leading to the concept of a *biased net*. A good summary of this approach, as well as an illustration of its potential for the study of social networks, is provided by Fararo and Skvoretz (1987) [108].

The modern theory of random networks (see Bollobás (1985, 2001) [37]) for a comprehensive account) is largely the outgrowth of work conducted by Paul Erdös and Alfréd Rényi through a period of fruitful collaboration in the 50's and 60's. It started with Erdös and Rényi (1959) [101], where they proposed the basic model outlined in Subsection 2.1.2, i.e. a context with n nodes and ℓ links where every possible network pattern is equiprobable. A different approach was proposed by Gilbert (1959) [125], and later by Erdös and Rényi (1960) [102], to study random networks: the binomial model. This alternative framework is essentially equivalent to the first one for large systems, but has proven to be more easily amenable to analysis. We focus on it, therefore, in what follows.

The model starts with a given set of nodes $N = \{1, 2, \ldots, n\}$ and no links among them. Then, it postulates that each possible (undirected) link ij is formed with independent probability $q > 0$. Typically, one is interested in the large-system properties of the resulting random network when the number of nodes grows unboundedly. In principle, n and q are independent parameters of the model. However, as one makes $n \to \infty$, the linking probability q is usually taken to adjust accordingly, as given by some function $q(n)$. One possibility, for example, may be to posit that $q(n)$ adjusts so that the expected connectivity $q(n)n \equiv z(n)$ remains approximately equal to a fixed value z.

Our first task is to determine the induced degree distribution $p(\cdot)$. Given the independent stochastic procedure determining the connectivity of each node, the probability that any one of them has degree κ is simply given by the binomial expression

$$p(\kappa) = \binom{n-1}{\kappa} q^{\kappa} (1-q)^{n-\kappa-1}. \tag{2.13}$$

For large networks, in view of the Law of Large Numbers, $p(\kappa)$ is also a good approximation of the *fraction* of nodes displaying degree κ. Moreover, the distribution becomes in that case essentially Poisson (cf. Subsection 2.1.3), and (2.13) can be approximated in the relevant range by

$$p(\kappa) = \frac{1}{\kappa!} e^{-z} z^{\kappa},$$

where

$$z \equiv qn \tag{2.14}$$

is (again with a very high probability for large n) the average degree of the network. Thus, since all of our "asymptotic" analysis will presume a large network, we shall directly speak of these networks as *Poisson networks*.

A first important question that arises is whether the average degree z is high enough to guarantee the overall connectedness of the network, at least with a very high probability, when $n \to \infty$. Quite remarkably, Erdös and Rényi were able to provide a "threshold" answer to this question – an approach that they were able to apply as well to the analysis of many other interesting properties of the network.[6] In general, given some property P under consideration, the aim then is to specify a certain function $q^P(n)$ that determines how the connection probability should evolve with n for this property to hold. In order for this function to be a *threshold function*, it must satisfy that, as $n \to \infty$,

$$\left[\frac{q(n)}{q^P(n)} \to \infty \right] \Rightarrow P \text{ holds, with a high probability;}[7]$$

$$\left[\frac{q(n)}{q^P(n)} \to 0 \right] \Rightarrow P \text{ does } not \text{ hold, with a high probability.}$$

It can be shown that, concerning the property C of connectedness, the following threshold function may be used (cf. Bollobás (1985, 2001: Ch. 7) [37]):

$$q^C(n) = \frac{\log n}{n},$$

which implies that the average connectivity must grow faster than logarithmically for connectedness to obtain.

Assume now that this requirement is met, i.e.

$$\lim_{n \to \infty} \frac{q(n)n}{\log n} = \lim_{n \to \infty} \frac{z(n)}{\log n} = \infty. \tag{2.15}$$

Then, with high probability (w.h.p.), there is a path between every two nodes in the network and its average distance $\bar{d}$ and diameter $\hat{d}$ can be suitably defined. Let us now outline an argument that allows us to estimate the order of magnitude of those measures, $\bar{d}$ and $\hat{d}$, as a function of the system size n.[8]

The key idea here is that, provided the average connectivity is high enough, a Poisson network is "spreading." That is, starting from any typical node, its successive-order neighborhoods encompass an exponentially growing number of nodes. Consider a typical node $i \in N$ and iterate the "neighbor operator" some r number of times to obtain the sets $\mathcal{N}_1^i, \mathcal{N}_2^i, \mathcal{N}_3^i, \ldots, \mathcal{N}_r^i$ consisting of first-, second-, third-, . . . , and rth-neighbors of i (recall Subsection 2.1.3). We are first interested in understanding the evolution of the *cardinality* of these sets,

---

[6] In particular, they found that such threshold answers are typically obtained when the property P under investigation is *monotone*. Essentially, this means that if P holds for some network $\Gamma = (N, L)$, then it must also hold for all $\Gamma' = (N, L')$ with $L' \supset L$, i.e. for all networks involving the same set of nodes and some additional links. Interesting monotone properties abound. Besides connectedness, of course, they include, for example, the occurrence of any kind of subgraphs (trees, cliques, etc.) or, say, the existence of a Hamiltonian cycle (i.e. a cycle involving every node).

[7] That is, it holds with limit probability 1, in the induced statistical ensemble.

[8] In fact, one may provide *exact* limit expressions of these magnitudes, in terms of the specific form of $q(n)$. See Theorem 10.10 in Bollobás (1985, 2001) [37].

$\{z_v^i\}_{v=1}^r$, where $z_v^i = |\mathcal{N}_v^i|$ for each $v = 1, 2, \ldots, r$ and r is the lowest natural number that satisfies[9]

$$z^r \sim n, \qquad (2.16)$$

where recall that z denotes the *average* degree of the network. Given some $v < r$, let j be a v-th neighbor of i in some network realization of the induced statistical ensemble (recall Subsection 2.1.2). What is the probability that any direct neighbor of j, say $k \in \mathcal{N}_1^j$, be a neighbor of order $(v + 1)$ of i and can only be accessed from i in $v + 1$ steps through node j? This is the probability that k *not* be a neighbor of some node $i' \in \mathcal{N}_u^i$ for $u = 1, 2, \ldots, v - 1$ or some $i'' \in \mathcal{N}_v^i \setminus \{j\}$. It is complementary, therefore, to the probability of the event

$$k \in \left[\bigcup_{u=1,2,\ldots,v} \mathcal{N}_u^i \right] \setminus \{j\}. \qquad (2.17)$$

But, in view of the assumption that $v < r$, it follows that $\sum_{u=1}^v z_u^i$ represents an infinitesimal fraction of the total number of nodes as the network becomes large. Hence the probability of the event given by (2.17) is arbitrarily close to zero. This implies, in turn, that a good estimate of the cardinality of $\mathcal{N}_{v+1}^i$ is

$$z_{v+1}^i = z \cdot z_v^i.$$

The same logic can be applied for all $v < r$ but not, of course, for $v = r$. For this case we know, by virtue of (2.16), that $z_r^i \sim n$. So happens, of course, for any other node ℓ, i.e. $z_r^\ell \sim n$. Therefore, for any such pair of nodes, i and ℓ, we must have w.h.p. that either $\mathcal{N}_r^i \cap \mathcal{N}_r^\ell \neq \varnothing$ or there is a link between some node in $\mathcal{N}_r^i$ and some other in $\mathcal{N}_r^\ell$. Thus we may conclude that the distance between i and ℓ is at most $2r + 1$ where, in view of (2.16), we have

$$r \sim \frac{1}{\log z} \log n.$$

It follows, therefore, that the diameter of the network grows at a rate that is no faster than logarithmic in network size n. But, as it should be clear from the above considerations, any node i has (w.h.p. for large n) *some* other node in the network that is at distance r. Thus, in fact, we can write that

$$\hat{d} \sim \frac{1}{\log z} \log n, \qquad (2.18)$$

i.e. the diameter of the network actually grows at the rate given by r. The same applies to average distance $\bar{d}$ since, given that the network is "spreading," most pairs of nodes are at a distance that is of order r.

The former discussion suggests that, in order for a Poisson network to be fully connected, the average degree z has to be sufficiently high. In fact, we

---

[9] Throughout, the standard notational convention $a \sim b$ is used to denote that, in the corresponding limit (here $n \to \infty$), $0 < \lim a/b < \infty$.

know from (2.15) that it must increase no slower than logarithmically with n. Thus, in particular, if the average connectivity remains constant but the network is large enough it must surely be fragmented into disjoint components. In this case, therefore, the focus must turn toward assessing the (fractional) sizes of these components. Are all of negligible size? Or, alternatively, is there a giant component that spans a significant (i.e. positive) fraction of all nodes? Interestingly, the answer to these questions again happens to be of a threshold nature, albeit not quite in the same format as before.

If we are solely concerned with the qualitative question of whether a giant component exists, everything hinges upon the average connectivity exceeding unity or not. Specifically, Erdös and Rényi (1960) [102] showed that, w.h.p. for large n, the following conclusions apply:[10]

- If $q > \frac{1}{n}$, a unique giant component arises that encompasses a non-negligible fraction of nodes and displays a complex topology.
- If $q < \frac{1}{n}$, all network components are of a negligible relative size and almost every node lies on a tree (i.e. is part of no cycle).

These sharp conclusions will be proven in Subsection 2.3 for the general framework of random networks, which encompasses the present model as a particular case. An illustration is provided in Figures 2.1 and 2.2 for a large network consisting of 5000 nodes and the average degree being slightly below and above the threshold of unity. In the first case, the largest component of the Poisson network is very small (relative to network size) and displays no cycles. In the second case, however, the component already includes a significant fraction (around 20%) of all nodes in the network and involves an intricate architecture.

Focusing on the case where a giant component exists (i.e. $z > 1$), an obviously important issue concerns the determination of its fractional size. In fact, this magnitude can be assessed quite easily through the following heuristic argument. Let w denote the fraction of nodes that belong to the giant component. Then, the probability that a randomly selected node i does *not* belong to this component is simply $(1 - w)$. But, by definition, it must also be true that there are no neighbors of node i that belong to the giant component (of course, a neighbor of a node in the giant component must belong to it as well). For each of these neighbors j, the corresponding (independent) probability that j does not belong to the giant component continues to be $1 - w$. Thus, if node i has, say, κ neighbors, the corresponding joint probability that none of them belongs to the joint component is $(1 - w)^\kappa$. The probability that node i has κ neighbors is given by $z^\kappa e^{-z}/\kappa!$ for large n. Therefore, on expected terms, averaging over all possible degrees of the node in question, we can write the following

---

[10] Essentially equivalent conclusions were derived earlier, in the context of random nets, by Solomonoff and Rapoport (1951) [262].

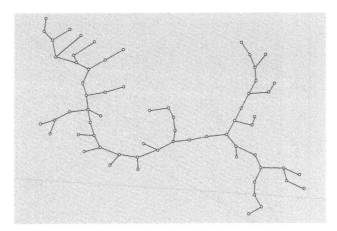

Figure 2.1. Largest component for a Poisson network with $n = 5000$ nodes and average degree $\bar{\kappa} = 0.9$ (Generated with *Pajek*, software package for large-network analysis, using the Kamada-Kawai algorithm for the layout)

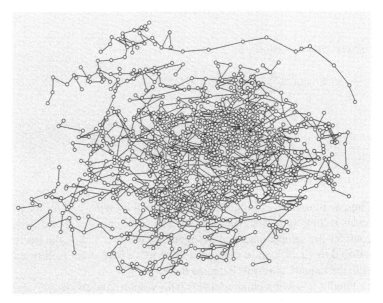

Figure 2.2. Largest ("giant") component for a Poisson network with $n = 5000$ nodes and average degree $\bar{\kappa} = 1.1$ (Generated with *Pajek*, software package for large-network analysis, using the Kamada-Kawai algorithm for the layout)

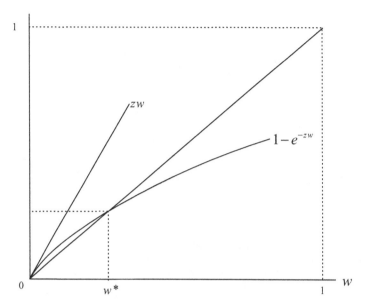

Figure 2.3. Self-consistency condition in the determination of the relative size of the giant component in a Poisson random network

self-consistency condition:

$$1 - w = \sum_{\kappa=0}^{\infty} (1-w)^{\kappa} \frac{1}{\kappa!} e^{-z} z^{\kappa}$$

$$= e^{-z} \sum_{\kappa=0}^{\infty} \frac{[(1-w)z]^{\kappa}}{\kappa!} = e^{-z} e^{(1-w)z} = e^{-zw}$$

or

$$w = 1 - e^{-zw}. \tag{2.19}$$

Thus, as illustrated in Figure 2.3, there is a solution $w^* > 0$ for the fraction of nodes belonging to the giant component whenever $z > 1$. For example, if we consider the setup considered in Figure 2.2 where $z = 1.1$, the fractional size induced by (2.19) can be computed to be $w^* \simeq 0.18$, very well in accordance with the numerical results depicted there.

Finally, it is worth emphasizing that the whole of the above analysis crucially relies on the assumption that internode connectivity is *stochastically indepen-dent* across different pairs. In a sense, this reflects a situation where the induced networks display "no local structure," i.e. the characteristics expected from any given node are largely unaffected by network-based (or structural) correlations. Such absence of correlations impinges most directly on the phenomenon of net-work clustering. In Poisson networks, the probability that two nodes be linked is always the same – roughly equal to z/n – independently of whether or not they share a common neighbor. Trivially, therefore, we have that network clustering in this case is simply given by $\mathcal{C} = z/n$ (cf. Subsection 2.1.3). Thus, unless the average connectivity grows very fast (at least linearly with n), the clustering index becomes vanishing small as the system gets large.

A similar line of reasoning may be used pertaining to cohesiveness. Consider any fixed set of nodes M and let the system grow in size by the addition of new nodes. Then, for any $i \in M$, the fraction of its links that connect to any other $j \in M$ must converge to zero w.h.p. (unless z grows at a rate no slower than system size). The cohesiveness of M, therefore, must fall to zero as the system grows. Again, this corresponds to a situation where the induced networks display essentially no structure. Since this stands in contrast with the empirical evidence gathered for social networks (recall Section 1.1), much of our ensuing efforts will be devoted to enriching the setup of Poisson networks to allow for such a structure to emerge. This will be done, specifically, in Sections 2.4 and 2.5, where we discuss small-world and growing scale-free networks. Before that, however, the following section explores a different generalization of Poisson random networks that still rules out internode correlations.

2.3 GENERAL RANDOM NETWORKS

Here we consider an extension of Poisson random networks that allows for an arbitrary degree distribution. Thus, even though the model presumes some given degree distribution, this distribution can *a priori* be of any kind, e.g. geometric, scale-free, etc. (cf. Subsection 2.1.3). With such a generalization, a diverse range of alternative scenarios may be accommodated within a common theoretical framework. For brevity, we shall label this framework as *general random networks*, and often simply refer to it as "random networks."

Consider the collection of all networks that consist of n nodes and display some given degree distribution $\{p(\kappa)\}_{\kappa=0}^{n-1}$. Denote this set of networks by $\mathcal{G}_p(n)$. Then, a *random network with degree distribution p* is simply the statistical ensemble in which every network $\Gamma \in \mathcal{G}_p(n)$ is selected with equal probability. Typically, we shall be interested in asymptotic results where $n \to \infty$ and p (as a function of n) converges to some well-defined distribution.

In general, it is difficult to define precise mechanisms for constructing general random networks. Alternatively, what is often done is to rely on indirect approximate methods to create them. Here we shall pursue the approach called the *configuration model*, which is based on the following simple and ingenious procedure originally proposed by Bender and Canfield (1978) [28].[11]

---

[11] See Bollobás (1980) [36], Wormald (1981) [292], or Molloy and Reed (1995) [202] for further elaboration on the configuration model.

Given the two (related)[12] parameters of the model, n and p, consider a *fixed* degree sequence $\{z^i\}_{i \in N}$ consistent with them. That is, a sequence that, for each $\kappa = 0, 1, \ldots$, satisfies

$$\frac{1}{n} \left| \{i \in N : z^i = \kappa\} \right| = p(\kappa).$$

Now construct the set W which includes z^i copies of every node i, with a total of $Z \equiv \sum_{i=1}^{n} z^i$ elements. Then, a *random configuration* is obtained by pairing the elements of W in a uniformly random fashion, each of the resulting pairs interpreted as a link in an induced network. In general, of course, it cannot be guaranteed that any realization of such a random configuration yields a proper network, in our restricted sense of Subsection 2.1.1 – i.e. it cannot be ruled out that several "links" in $W \times W$ join the same two nodes, or that there are loops connecting a node to itself. The configuration model is useful, however, because it can be shown that, under suitable conditions (cf. Molloy and Reed (1995) [202]), it displays essentially the same statistical properties as a "properly" specified general random network when n is large.[13]

In the configuration model, the correlation among node characteristics becomes vanishing small when n grows large, just as in the Poisson networks considered above. This is reflected, in particular, in the absence of any *degree correlations* between neighboring nodes. Essentially, that is, the degree z^i of any node i is stochastically independent of the degrees z^j of the nodes j that are connected to it. This, to be sure, does *not* mean that the distribution of those neighboring nodes j is equal to (or approximated by) $p(\cdot)$, even when the network is very large. The somewhat subtle reason for this is that the *ex-ante* probability that some node of degree κ be the *neighbor* of some particular node i is *not* independent of κ. In fact, it must be proportional to both $p(\kappa)$ *and* κ since, in the configuration model, the product $p(\kappa)\,\kappa$ determines the number of "copies" of nodes with connectivity κ lying in the set W. This implies that the degree distribution among *neighboring nodes* (i.e. the neighbors of any randomly selected node i) is given by a function $\zeta(\cdot)$ satisfying $\zeta(\kappa) \propto p(\kappa)\,\kappa$. Therefore, through normalization, we have

$$\zeta(\kappa) = \frac{p(\kappa)\,\kappa}{\sum_{\kappa'=0}^{\infty} p(\kappa')\,\kappa'}. \tag{2.20}$$

---

[12] Naturally, p and n cannot be treated as independent parameters since not all such pairs give rise to a well-defined and nonempty family of networks with that number of nodes and that degree distribution.

[13] Problems may arise when those conditions are not met – most prominently, in the case of very broad distributions. Alternative approaches have been proposed by Chung and Lu (2002) [62] and Caldarelli *et al.* (2002) [48] that are not afflicted by this problem. Nevertheless, in those cases the induced degree distribution is not fixed but stochastic and the desired match with the target distribution only occurs w.h.p. for large networks.

Based on this distribution, the average degree of a neighboring node can be computed as follows:

$$\sum_{\kappa=1}^{\infty} \kappa\, \zeta(\kappa) = \sum_{\kappa=0}^{\infty} \kappa\, \zeta(\kappa) = \frac{1}{\sum_{\kappa'=0}^{\infty} p(\kappa')\, \kappa'} \sum_{\kappa=0}^{\infty} p(\kappa)\, \kappa^2$$

$$= \frac{\langle \kappa^2 \rangle}{\langle \kappa \rangle},$$

where $\langle \cdot \rangle$ will always stand for averages, suitably defined from context (here, defined in terms of the degree distribution $p(\cdot)$).

Suppose now that, rather than the average degree of a neighboring node, we are interested in estimating the average number of *second* neighbors that may be accessed through it. Then, we have to exclude node i from the degree count of its neighboring node and obtain instead:

$$\sum_{\kappa=1}^{\infty} (\kappa - 1)\, \zeta(\kappa) = \frac{1}{\sum_{\kappa'=0}^{\infty} p(\kappa')\, \kappa'} \sum_{\kappa=0}^{\infty} (\kappa - 1)\kappa\, p(\kappa)$$

$$= \frac{\langle \kappa^2 \rangle - \langle \kappa \rangle}{\langle \kappa \rangle}. \tag{2.21}$$

The above expression specifies the expected number of second neighbors obtained through any *one* neighbor of a typical node. Such a typical node has on average $\langle \kappa \rangle$ links. Thus, taking into account the stochastic independence across nodes prevailing in random networks, we may compute the *total* number of second neighbors enjoyed, on average, by a typical node as follows:

$$z_2 = \frac{\langle \kappa^2 \rangle - \langle \kappa \rangle}{\langle \kappa \rangle} \langle \kappa \rangle = \langle \kappa^2 \rangle - \langle \kappa \rangle. \tag{2.22}$$

We arrive, therefore, at the simple conclusion that the average number of second neighbors is equal to the difference between the second- and first-order moments of the degree distribution $p(\cdot)$.

But, clearly, the number of rth-neigbors that arise, on average, from each $(r - 1)$th-neighbor of a node is also given by (2.21) for *any* $r \geq 2$ (i.e. not just for second neighbors). Thus, denoting by z_r the *total* number of rth-neigbors, we have:

$$z_r = \frac{\langle \kappa^2 \rangle - \langle \kappa \rangle}{\langle \kappa \rangle} z_{r-1}.$$

This equation can be iterated for $r = 2, 3, 4, \ldots, m$ to obtain:

$$z_m = \left[\frac{\langle \kappa^2 \rangle - \langle \kappa \rangle}{\langle \kappa \rangle} \right]^{m-1} z_1$$

$$= \left[\frac{z_2}{z_1} \right]^{m-1} z_1.$$

The above expression has a sharp implication: whether or not the network "spreads" unboundedly from any given node through the visit of its neighbors of successively higher orders depends on whether the ratio z_2/z_1 is larger or smaller than 1. That is, it only spreads indefinitely if

$$z_2 > z_1 \tag{2.23}$$

or

$$\langle \kappa^2 \rangle - 2 \langle \kappa \rangle > 0.$$

This condition was first derived by Molloy and Reed (1995) [202], who also provided the following intuition for it. Suppose that, starting from a particular node, one begins exploring its component by means of a branching process that, at each juncture, chooses randomly the link along which to proceed. When a particular node j with connectivity κ^j is visited, the number of nodes that are "recorded but yet unknown" in the component changes as follows. On one hand, it decreases by one since j is no longer unknown. On the other hand, a new set of $\kappa^j - 1$ nodes may be registered as existing but yet unknown. Thus, in total, the number of unknown nodes increases by $\kappa^j - 2$. What is then the expected increase in the number of unknown nodes? Since a node of degree κ is visited with probability $\zeta(\kappa)$, it is

$$\frac{1}{\langle \kappa \rangle} \sum_{\kappa=0}^{\infty} (\kappa - 2)\kappa \, p(\kappa). \tag{2.24}$$

An unbounded component requires that the number of unknown nodes increases along the branching process. That is, it requires that (2.24) is positive, which is obviously equivalent to condition (2.23). The threshold where (2.24) vanishes is precisely the point where the largest component of the network becomes "giant" – i.e. of positive fractional size – as $n \to \infty$.

Assume now that $z_2 \gg z_1$ (i.e. z_2 is much larger than z_1) so that the giant component essentially includes all nodes. Then, we can suitably estimate the network diameter $\hat{d}$ (as a function of n) from the following expression:

$$\left[\frac{z_2}{z_1} \right]^{\hat{d}-1} z_1 \sim n,$$

which leads to

$$\hat{d} \sim \frac{\log(n/z_1)}{\log(z_2/z_1)} + 1. \tag{2.25}$$

Here, we rely on the same considerations that were used in Section 2.2 to compute the diameter of large and connected Poisson networks. And, again, since most pairs of nodes are at the maximum (diameter) distance, it follows that (2.25) also represents a good estimate of $\bar{d}$, the average distance in the network.

It is instructive to see how the former derivations (which are valid for any general random network) particularize to the case of a large Poisson network. In this case, we have

$$\frac{z_2}{z_1} = \frac{\langle \kappa^2 \rangle - \langle \kappa \rangle}{\langle \kappa \rangle} = \langle \kappa \rangle,$$

since, for a Poisson distribution, $\langle \kappa^2 \rangle - \langle \kappa \rangle = \langle \kappa \rangle^2$. Then, the condition for "unbounded spread" becomes

$$\langle \kappa \rangle > 1,$$

which is the condition referred (but not proven) in our discussion of Poisson networks. That is, nodes must enjoy, on average, more than one neighbor if a giant component is to exist. On the other hand, particularizing (2.25) for a Poisson degree distribution, the diameter of the network is found to be:

$$\hat{d} \sim \frac{\log(n/z_1)}{\log(z_2/z_1)} + 1 = \frac{\log n - \log z}{\log z} + 1 = \frac{\log n}{\log z}, \tag{2.26}$$

where again we use that, in the present case, $z_2/z_1 = z_1 \equiv z$. This recovers expression (2.18) obtained above for Poisson networks.

So far, we have focused our discussion on the case where the network connectivity is high enough so that, at least, it displays a giant component. But what happens if the ratio $z_2/z_1 < 1$, i.e. it is below the threshold required? In this case, one expects to find the network fragmented into a large set of finite components with a wide size distribution. A key concern is then to characterize this distribution, or at least to compute its more relevant moments. For this task, Newman *et al.* (2001) [223] have developed a powerful method that involves the use of generating functions, a classical tool in statistics to characterize any distribution. A brief tutorial on this tool, tailored to our purposes, is presented in Appendix A. The reader less than fully familiar with it is advised to read that appendix before proceeding with the ensuing discussion.[14]

Provided the random network is below the threshold required for a giant component to arise, it may be assumed that its (bounded) components display essentially no closed loops. The reason is that, for any two nodes already connected in a component, either directly or indirectly, the probability that they are further connected through some other path is of infinitesimal order $1/n$. In essence, therefore, we may regard those components as trees. This then allows us to assess their size distribution through a procedure that explores the likely "depth" of their branches. The gist of this procedure is explained next.

---

[14] The reader may also consult the excellent surveys in Newman (2003*a*) [215] and Newman (2003*b*) [216].

Consider any typical nonisolated node i and follow one of its links to some node j. The following possibilities arise.

- With probability $\zeta(1)$, node j has no further neighbors other than i and the advance along i's component ends there.
- With probability $\zeta(2)$, node j has one more neighbor k and then the link jk must be explored to check whether a further advance along the component is possible. This exploration, of course, is facing *ex-ante* the *same* considerations that applied originally to the link ij.
- With probability $\zeta(3)$, node j has two neighbors, say k and ℓ, and the advance must proceed *independently* along the corresponding links, jk and $j\ell$. For each of these links, again the situation is analogous to that of the original link ij.

The above chain of contingencies can be extended to all of the successive $\kappa = 4, 5, \ldots$, where each of these cases occurs with respective probability $\zeta(\kappa)$. When the problem is formulated *ex-ante,* prior to "visiting" node j, it embodies a probabilistic assessment of the conditions (i.e. degree) that will be encountered for this node. A key point to note is that, no matter how many other links node j might be found to have, the ensuing (and independent) exploration along any of those links is *ex-ante identical* to the original situation (i.e. to the situation prevailing before visiting node j). This introduces a *self-referential* element into the problem, which in turn requires that its solution should satisfy a corresponding criterion of *self-consistency*.

In imposing such a criterion of self-consistency, a natural way to proceed is to formulate it on the generating functions that characterize the distributions of interest. Let $H_1(x)$ be the generating function associated to the distribution of the number of nodes that can be reached, directly and indirectly, by following one randomly chosen link in a certain direction. This process starts, first, by visiting one of the nodes at the end of the chosen link; secondly, it visits each of the additional nodes that can be reached through the links springing from that first node; thirdly, it visits the additional nodes that can be reached from the second set of nodes; and so on until we come to a "dead end" along any of the induced paths.

If the first visited node (node j) has, say, κ links, the distribution on component sizes induced by the *joint* exploration of these links is characterized by the generating function $[H_1(x)]^\kappa$ (cf. Appendix A). Thus, when all the different possibilities $\kappa = 0, 1, 2, \ldots$ are taken into account, the self-consistency (or "fixed-point") condition that must be satisfied by the generating function $H_1(x)$ may be written as follows:

$$H_1(x) = x \sum_{\kappa=1}^{\infty} \zeta(\kappa) [H_1(x)]^{\kappa-1}, \tag{2.27}$$

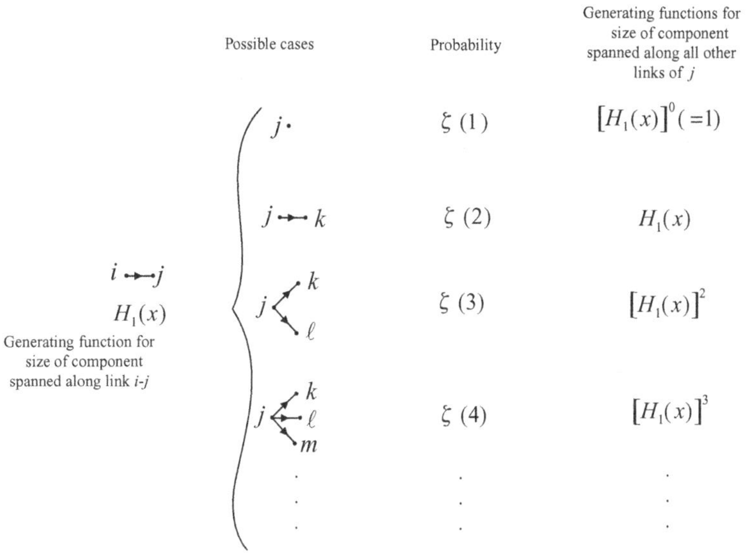

Possible cases	Probability	Generating functions for size of component spanned along all other links of j
$j \bullet$	$\zeta(1)$	$\left[H_1(x)\right]^0 (=1)$
$j \rightarrowtail k$	$\zeta(2)$	$H_1(x)$
$j <^{k}_{\ell}$	$\zeta(3)$	$\left[H_1(x)\right]^2$
$j <^{k}_{\ell}_{m}$	$\zeta(4)$	$\left[H_1(x)\right]^3$

$i \rightarrowtail j$

$H_1(x)$

Generating function for size of component spanned along link $i\text{-}j$

Figure 2.4. Illustration of the self-consistency condition to be satisfied by the generating function that characterizes the distribution of component sizes below the giant-component threshold

where the leading factor x merely accounts for the first node visited along the first link (cf. the similar feature displayed by the generating function in (A.1)). A schematic illustration of the approach is provided in Figure 2.4.

The degree distribution used to weigh the different terms in the right hand side of (2.27) has to be $\{\zeta(\kappa)\}_{\kappa=1}^{\infty}$ since the accessed node (node j in Figure 2.4) is, by construction, a neighboring node. In effect, our interest is on the additional links this node has in excess of the one used to access it. Of course, such excess-degree distribution $\left\{\hat{\zeta}(\kappa)\right\}_{\kappa=0}^{\infty}$ is simply given by

$$\hat{\zeta}(\kappa) = \zeta(\kappa + 1) \qquad (\kappa = 0, 1, \dots), \tag{2.28}$$

while its generating function is[15]

$$\hat{G}_1(x) = \sum_{\kappa=0}^{\infty} \hat{\zeta}(\kappa) x^{\kappa} = \sum_{\kappa=1}^{\infty} \zeta(\kappa) x^{\kappa-1}. \tag{2.29}$$

---

[15] The following conventions will be used throughout. The notation G and H refer to generating functions corresponding to distributions of degree and component size, respectively. A subindex 0 or 1 appended to a generating function specifies whether it is associated to a randomly selected node or to a link/neighboring node, respectively. The symbol ^ attached to the function G_1 generating a degree distribution of a neighboring node indicates that excess (rather than total) degree is considered. Finally, note that the symbol ^ is also used to distinguish between the excess and total degree distributions themselves, as in (2.28).

This allows us to rewrite (2.27) more compactly as follows:

$$H_1(x) = x\hat{G}_1(H_1(x)). \tag{2.30}$$

In general, it may be difficult to solve the previous functional equation for a complete and explicit determination of H_1. We always have, however, an easy method to approximate it to an arbitrary extent through the following inductive procedure.

Let H_1^r be an approximation of H_1 that is exact up to all terms of order r. That is, letting the true generating function be given by[16]

$$H_1(x) = \sum_{\kappa=1}^{\infty} \nu(\kappa)\, x^\kappa,$$

we make the following

induction hypothesis: the first r terms $\{\nu^r(\kappa)\}_{\kappa=1}^r$ in

$$H_1^r(x) = \sum_{\kappa=1}^{\infty} \nu^r(\kappa)\, x^\kappa$$

are such that $\nu^r(\kappa) = \nu(\kappa)$ for all $\kappa = 1, \ldots, r$.

Now, given $H_1^r(x)$, insert it into the right-hand side of (2.27) to define

$$H_1^{r+1}(x) = x\sum_{\kappa=0}^{\infty} \hat{\xi}(\kappa)\left[H_1^r(x)\right]^\kappa = x\sum_{\kappa=0}^{\infty} \hat{\xi}(\kappa)\left[\sum_{\kappa'=1}^{\infty} \nu^r(\kappa')\, x^{\kappa'}\right]^\kappa. \tag{2.31}$$

Then, we want to establish the following

induction step: the function

$$H_1^{r+1}(x) = \sum_{\kappa=1}^{\infty} \nu^{r+1}(\kappa)\, x^\kappa$$

has its first $r + 1$ coefficients equal to those of the true H_1.

The validity of the induction hypothesis is clear for $r = 1$ if we choose

$$H_1^1(x) = \hat{\xi}(0)\, x,$$

which is correct up to its first (and only) term. Next, the validity of the induction step derives from the following simple observation. In view of the leading factor x in (2.31), the terms

$$\nu^{r+1}(\kappa), \qquad \kappa = 1, 2, \ldots, r + 1$$

---

[16] Note that, by construction, $\nu(0) = 0$ since the number of nodes encountered by following an edge must include at least the end node. This means that the summatory defining $H_1(x)$ can be made to start at $\kappa = 1$.

only depend on $\{v^r(\kappa)\}_{\kappa=1}^r$ and the distribution $\{\hat{\zeta}(\kappa)\}_{\kappa=0}^{\infty}$. That is, we have

$$v^{r+1}(1) = v^r(1) = \hat{\zeta}(0)$$
$$v^{r+1}(2) = \hat{\zeta}(1) \, v^r(1)$$
$$v^{r+1}(3) = \hat{\zeta}(1) \, v^r(2) + \hat{\zeta}(2) \, (v^r(1))^2$$
$$v^{r+1}(4) = \hat{\zeta}(1) \, v^r(3) + 2 \, \hat{\zeta}(2) \, v^r(1) \, v^r(2) + \hat{\zeta}(3) \, (v^r(1))^3$$
$$\vdots$$

Thus, if $H_1^r(x)$ and $H_1(x)$ coincide in their first r coefficients, then $H_1^{r+1}(x)$ and $H_1(x)$ must coincide in their first $(r + 1)$ coefficients, as claimed.

Repeated application of the inductive procedure converges to the true generating function H_1. In the limit, that is, we have $\lim_{r\to\infty} H_1^r = H_1$. But, short of this limit, one may of course proceed only some finite number of steps along the sequence $\{H_1^r\}$ and still obtain as good an approximation of H_1 as desired.

The size distribution generated by H_1 is *link-based* and *directional*, in the sense that it considers moving along a randomly chosen link in one of the two directions. Building upon it, we now consider a typical node and consider all possible paths that can be spanned from it in every direction, i.e. along each of its links. The induced distribution has a generating function H_0 which builds upon H_1 as follows:

$$H_0(x) = x \sum_{\kappa=0}^{\infty} p(\kappa) \, [H_1(x)]^\kappa = x G_0(H_1(x)), \tag{2.32}$$

where, again, there is a leading factor x that accounts for the starting node. Note that, in this case, we use the original degree distribution $p(\cdot)$, or its corresponding generating function G_0 given by

$$G_0(x) = \sum_{\kappa=0}^{\infty} p(\kappa) \, x^\kappa.$$

The reason is that the original random choice concerns an arbitrary node (not a neighboring node or a link).

Once the generating functions H_0 and H_1 are obtained, it is straightforward to use them to compute any magnitude of interest such as the average component size (when z_2/z_1 is below the threshold of 1) or the relative size of the giant component (when $z_2/z_1 > 1$). Assume first that $z_2 < z_1$ and denote the (finite) average component size by ϱ. Then, due to a basic property of generating functions (cf. Appendix A), we have

$$\varrho = H_0'(1),$$

which, relying on (2.32), can be rewritten as

$$\varrho = G_0(H_1(1)) + G_0'(H_1(1)) \, H_1'(1) = 1 + G_0'(1) \, H_1'(1), \tag{2.33}$$

where we use that $H_1(1) = G_0(1) = 1$. Then, differentiating (2.30), we find

$$H_1'(x) = \hat{G}_1(H_1(x)) + x\hat{G}_1'(H_1(x)) \, H_1'(x),$$

which evaluated at $x = 1$ yields

$$H_1'(1) = 1 + \hat{G}_1'(1) \, H_1'(1),$$

or

$$H_1'(1) = \frac{1}{1 - \hat{G}_1'(1)},$$

which can then be inserted in (2.33) to find

$$\varrho = 1 + \frac{G_0'(1)}{1 - \hat{G}_1'(1)}.$$

Now if we use $G_0'(1) = z_1$ and (2.22), we may write:

$$G_0'(1)\hat{G}_1'(1) = z_1 \frac{\sum_{\kappa=0}^{\infty}(\kappa - 1)\kappa \, p(\kappa)}{z_1} = \langle \kappa^2 \rangle - z_1 = z_2,$$

and therefore

$$\varrho = 1 + \frac{z_1}{1 - z_2/z_1}.$$

The above expression indicates that as $z_2/z_1 \nearrow 1$, the value of ϱ diverges and thus the average component size grows unboundedly. When the ratio z_2/z_1 has exceeded the threshold of unity, a giant component exists that encompasses a positive fraction of all nodes. To obtain a quantitative assessment of the fractional size w of the giant component, we can rely on the following adaptation of the argument outlined in Section 2.2 for a Poisson random network.[17]

Let w stand for the fraction of *nodes* in the giant component and denote by $\hat{w}$ the fraction of existing *links* that connect such nodes. Thus, if we consider a randomly selected link and any one of the nodes connected by it, the probability that this node does *not* connect to the giant component through that link is simply $1 - \hat{w}$. But, of course, self consistency requires that the remaining links leaving such a node should not lead into the giant component either. So, in expected terms, we must have[18]

$$1 - \hat{w} = \sum_{\kappa=0}^{\infty} \hat{\zeta}(\kappa) \, (1 - \hat{w})^{\kappa} = \hat{G}_1(1 - \hat{w}). \tag{2.34}$$

---

[17] A fully rigorous result for large n may be found in Molloy and Reed (1998) [203].

[18] Recall that, in Section 2.2, when we discussed this issue for Poisson networks, we did not approach matters in terms of edges (or neighboring nodes) in the giant component but in terms of randomly chosen nodes. This, however, turns out to be inconsequential for that case. The reason is that, in Poisson networks, the degree distribution of randomly selected nodes and the excess degree distribution of randomly chosen neighboring nodes coincide. Or, in terms of their corresponding generating functions:

$$\hat{G}_1(x) = \frac{G_0'(x)}{G_0'(1)} = \frac{ze^{z(x-1)}}{z} = e^{z(x-1)} = G_0(x).$$

From the former equation, we may solve for the probability $\hat{w}$ that a randomly selected *link* leads into the giant component. Hence we can readily obtain the probability that a *node* does *not* lie in the giant component, which is simply the probability that none of its links should connect to the giant component. Averaging over all possible connectivities, it becomes equal to

$$\sum_{\kappa=0}^{\infty} p(\kappa)\,(1-\hat{w})^{\kappa} = G_0(1-\hat{w}),$$

so that the probability w that a randomly selected node belongs to the giant component is given by

$$w = 1 - G_0(1-\hat{w}), \tag{2.35}$$

a direct counterpart of the analogous self-consistency condition (2.19) used in our former analysis of Poisson networks.

Indeed, random networks not only extend many of the ideas and insights gathered from our former study of Poisson networks but also some of its key properties. One of these properties, the lack of *degree correlations* among neighboring nodes, was already highlighted before. Another important one, concerning (the absence of) "linkage correlations" between neighboring nodes, follows as well from similar considerations. It can be shown, more specifically, that such linkage correlations – as measured by the notion of *network clustering* (cf. (2.8)) – always vanish for any large random network, provided its degree distribution has a bounded variance.

To check precisely this claim, let us remain, for simplicity, within the framework provided by the configuration model. Consider any node i and two of its neighbors, say j and k, with respective degrees z^j and z^k. What is the probability that nodes j and k be connected? First note that the probability that any *one* of the remaining links of j (other than the one connecting to i) be matched to at least one of the remaining $(z^k - 1)$ links of node k is approximately equal to $(z^k - 1)/(nz)$ for large n. Therefore, since there is a total of $z^j - 1$ remaining "copies" of node j that can be connected in this fashion, the overall probability for a connection between j and k is $(z^k - 1)(z^j - 1)/(nz)$. To compute the clustering index $\mathcal{C}$, we simply have to compute the average

$$\left\langle (z^k - 1)(z^j - 1)/(nz) \right\rangle_{j,k},$$

where j and k are *not* just any two nodes but they are both *neighbors* of some arbitrary node i. The latter implies that the suitable degree distribution to be used in computing the average is that corresponding to a neighboring node, $\zeta(\cdot)$, as given by (2.20). Using (2.21), we obtain

$$\mathcal{C} = \left\langle (z^k - 1)(z^j - 1)/(nz) \right\rangle_{j,k}$$
$$= \frac{1}{nz}\left[\sum_{\kappa=1}^{\infty} (\kappa - 1)\,\zeta(\kappa)\right]^2 = \frac{1}{nz}\left[\frac{\langle \kappa^2 \rangle}{z} - 1\right]^2. \tag{2.36}$$

If the above expression is particularized to a Poisson network (where $\langle\kappa^2\rangle/z = z + 1$), the clustering index $\mathcal{C} = z/n$ derived in Section 2.2 is readily recovered. In that case, therefore, for any given value of z, clustering vanishes as the network size grows. Obviously, an analogous conclusion directly follows from (2.36) for any degree distribution, as long as the second-order moment remains bounded (or does not grow too fast with n).

In sum, we find that large random networks tend to be fundamentally devoid of "local structure."[19] In the real world, however, prevailing networks do often display that structure. For social networks, in particular, the empirical relevance of linkage correlations (clustering) was already discussed at length in Section 1.1, so it does not need to be stressed here again. Degree correlations, on the other hand, have received somewhat less attention in the study of social networks, but are undoubtedly significant in many cases. For example, Newman (2003c) [217], and Newman and Park (2003) [222] report that a number of social networks (sexual contacts, email communication, or scientific coauthorship) display positive assortativeness, i.e. highly connected nodes tend to be linked among themselves.[20]

In general, the local structure of a network may have a significant bearing on the phenomena that unfold on it. This is why it is important to have network models that allow for some such structure to emerge. In the last part of this chapter, we consider two models of this sort that have become paradigmatic in the modern network literature. First, in Section 2.4, we study the so-called small worlds, a model proposed by Watts and Strogatz (1998) [288]. These are networks designed to reconcile both high clustering and short distances with a low internode variance in connectivity. Next, in Section 2.5, we shall discuss the model introduced by Barabási and Albert (1999) [24] that produces instead a broad (scale-free) distribution of connectivities and low clustering. Its dynamic (growing) framework will be seen to introduce, however, a different manifestation of local structure: significant degree correlations among neighboring nodes.

2.4 SMALL WORLDS

A small world, in the sense of Watts and Strogatz (1998) [288], is a setup that results from a one-parameter interpolation between a random and a lattice network. While random networks have been the object of the previous two

---

[19] Similar conclusions arise if we focus on other measures of network structure such as cohesiveness. Recall the discussion on this notion conducted for Poisson networks at the end of Section 2.2.

[20] In contrast, the empirical evidence available in other contexts (biological networks or the internet) appears to point in the opposite direction. For example, *disassortative* degree correlations have been found by Pastor-Satorras, Vázquez, and Vespignani (2001) [232] in the internet network, or by Maslov and Sneppen (2002) [197] in protein-interaction and genetic-regulatory networks. In these cases, therefore, highly connected nodes tend to be linked to those that are little connected.

sections, lattice networks were only sketchily introduced in Subsection 2.1.2. Thus, before proceeding with our study of small worlds, let us start by providing a more detailed discussion of lattice networks.

A *lattice network* Γ has its set of nodes N associated to the points in a regular lattice. To fix ideas, we shall think of this underlying lattice as an m-dimensional *square grid* without boundaries. To construct the network, a link is established between every pair of nodes that are within a certain lattice distance $r \in \mathbb{N}$. Therefore, for any given node $i \in N$, its neighborhood $\mathcal{N}^i$ is given by

$$\mathcal{N}^i = \{ j \in N : \varphi(i, j) \le r \},$$

where $\varphi(\cdot)$ denotes the lattice distance under consideration. Here, for concreteness,[21] we shall consider the usual distance on the square-grid lattice. Thus, if i and j are nodes with lattice coordinates $x^i = (x^i_1, x^i_2, \ldots, x^i_m)$ and $x^j = (x^j_1, x^j_2, \ldots, x^j_m)$, we define

$$\varphi(i, j) = \sum_{u=1}^{m} |x^i_u - x^j_u|,$$

where, for each u, the one-dimensional distance $|x^i_u - x^j_u|$ is taken to account for the identification of endpoints that eliminates boundaries. If $r = 1$ the network can be viewed as coinciding with the underlying lattice, while for larger values of r the neighborhood of any particular node i spans a progressively larger fraction of the set of nodes "around" it.

Let us now consider more closely how the different characteristics of a lattice network depend on its parameters, m and r. First, fix $m = 1$ and consider changes in r (cf. Figure 2.5). Concerning the average degree, we obviously have

$$z = 2r \tag{2.37}$$

since all nodes have the same degree $2r$.

Next, we turn to the network diameter $\hat{d}$ and the average distance $\bar{d}$. It is easy to see that

$$\hat{d} = \frac{n-1}{2r} = \frac{n-1}{z} \tag{2.38}$$

$$\bar{d} = \frac{1}{2}(1 + \frac{n-1}{2r}) = \frac{1}{2} + \frac{n-1}{2z}, \tag{2.39}$$

where, to simplify matters, we are implicitly assuming that z divides $n - 1$. From (2.38)–(2.39), we observe that $\hat{d}$ and $\bar{d}$ increase *linearly* with respect to the number of nodes. This, of course, is specific to the one-dimensional lattice ($m = 1$). For $m > 1$, the corresponding increases in $\hat{d}$ and $\bar{d}$ proceed at the slower rate embodied by $n^{\frac{1}{m}}$.

---

[21] Other distance functions could be defined as well, as considered for example in Section 4.2 (cf. (4.27)).

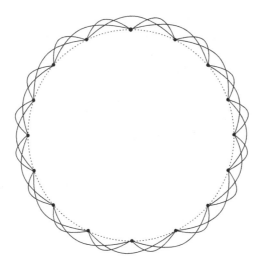

Figure 2.5. A one-dimensional regular lattice ($m = 1$) with neighborhood radius $r = 2$

On the other hand, concerning clustering we may readily compute that, if $m = 1$,

$$C = \frac{3(r-1)}{4(r-\frac{1}{2})},$$ (2.40)

which is positive as long as $r > 1$, i.e. provided the neighborhood of a node spans more than the immediately adjacent nodes in the lattice. In that case ($r > 1$), we have that $C \geq 1/2$ and, as the neighborhood radius r increases, C grows up to the maximum value of $3/4$. It is important to emphasize the obvious fact that these considerations are independent of population size.[22] In general, if we allow for any dimension of the underlying lattice $m \geq 1$, it can be shown that the above expression generalizes to

$$C = \frac{3(r-m)}{4(r-\frac{1}{2}m)},$$ (2.41)

and the former discussion and conclusions extend naturally.

As advanced, the model of small worlds proposed by Watts and Strogatz (1998) [288] results from an interpolation between a lattice network and a random network. Their simple constructive procedure can be described as follows. Start with a one-dimensional lattice network Γ such as that depicted in Figure 2.5, with n nodes and $z(= 2r)$ links per node. Then proceed in turn with nodes $i = 1, 2, \ldots, n$ and "rewire" the link that connects i to node $i + 1$ (modulo n)

---

[22] So long as $r < n/3$, i.e. the neighborhood is not so large that it spans at least $2/3$ of the whole population. For large networks, this caveat is inconsequential since we want to think of r as fixed independently of n.

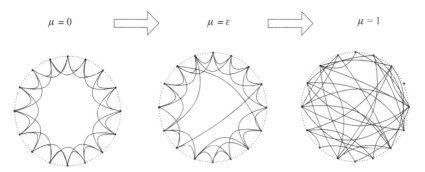

$\mu = 0$ $\mu = \varepsilon$ $\mu = 1$

Figure 2.6. An originally regular lattice modified by an increasing rewiring probability μ

with a fixed probability μ, independently across links. If any such rewiring does take place for some node i, then its link to $i + 1$ is deleted and a new link is created between i and some other node randomly chosen (with uniform probability) among the set of nodes that are *not* already connected to i. Once such round has been completed, an analogous subsequent round is performed, but now considering the links between i and $i + 2$ for each $i = 1, 2, \ldots, n$. This is repeated up to r rounds, the last one of them considering the links between each i and $i + r$ for every $i = 1, 2, \ldots, n$.

The outcome of the "rewiring mechanism" considered gives rise to a network Γ' with the same number of nodes as Γ and the same number of links (i.e. nr of them). If μ is low, most of the links in Γ' are just as in Γ and remain "local." A fraction of them, however (approximately μnr if n is large), are global and must typically display a pattern analogous to that of a random network. The rewiring probability μ is a way of continuously parametrizing a collection of networks ranging from the lattice ($\mu = 0$) to the random network ($\mu = 1$) – cf. Figure 2.6. The primary concern is then to understand how the characteristics of the network change with μ. In particular, an important question is whether, even for small μ, there emerge some new qualitative features that were not present in the original lattice network.

A natural way to approach this issue is to trace the change of some of the leading characteristics of the network (cf. Section 2.1.3) when μ grows in the range $[0, 1]$. First, concerning the average degree, it clearly remains equal to $z = 2r$ for *all* values of μ since the rewiring procedure does not alter either the number of nodes or links of the originally regular network. Of course, the degree for particular nodes should generally differ from z, since some nodes are now likely to display more (and then others fewer) links than average. This internode heterogeneity, however, has to be small if μ is correspondingly low.

As long as μ remains low, the levels of clustering must also be close to that of the regular network. In that case, the local environment of most nodes stays largely unchanged since only a few of the links are rewired. It follows, therefore, that the corresponding clustering index C_μ satisfies

$$C_\mu \simeq C_0$$

for μ low where (cf. (2.40))

$$C_0 \equiv \frac{3(r-1)}{4(r-\frac{1}{2})}$$

is the clustering index of the lattice network (i.e. for $\mu = 0$). As μ rises, however, the induced network starts losing its local structure and approaches a global topology akin to that of a Poisson network. Eventually, for high enough μ,

$$C_\mu \simeq C_1,$$

where, from a direct adaptation of the ideas discussed in Section 2.2, we have

$$C_1 \sim \frac{z}{n}$$

for large n.

Turning now to the study of the average network distance $\bar{d}_\mu$, as a function of μ, we may also arrive at corresponding approximate estimates of it at both ends of the interval $[0, 1]$. Thus, for low μ we have

$$\bar{d}_\mu \simeq \bar{d}_0,$$

where

$$\bar{d}_0 = \frac{1}{2} + \frac{n-1}{2z}$$

is the average distance of the lattice network (cf. (2.39)). On the other hand, if μ is close to 1,

$$\bar{d}_\mu \simeq \bar{d}_1,$$

and bear in mind that, for large n, we have[23]

$$\bar{d}_1 \sim \ln n$$

i.e. the average distance is of logarithmic order in n since $\mu = 1$ yields a fully random network.

Now, given any ε (to be conceived as small), we can combine the previous considerations and, invoking continuity in μ, make the following assertions:

1. There is an *upper bound* $\hat{\mu}(\varepsilon) < 1$ on the rewiring probability μ such that if $\mu < \hat{\mu}(\varepsilon)$, the clustering coefficient C_μ of the induced network remains w.h.p. ε-close to C_0 in the following sense:

$$\frac{C_\mu}{C_0} \geq 1 - \varepsilon.$$

---

[23] Here, of course, we implicitly assume that the average connectivity is high enough so that the random network induced by complete rewiring is essentially connected.

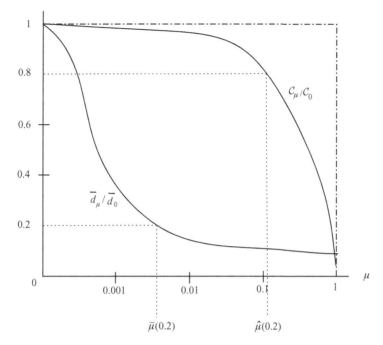

Figure 2.7. Average distance and clustering index (normalized by the corresponding values for a regular one-dimensional lattice) as the rewiring probability μ changes in the small-world model of Watts and Strogatz (1998) [288]. The diagram provides an illustration of their reported results for numerical simulations with 1000 nodes and $z = 10$ (Notice that μ is measured along a logaritmic scale)

2. There is a *lower bound* $\breve{\mu}(\varepsilon)$ on the rewiring probability μ such that, if $\mu > \breve{\mu}(\varepsilon)$ (and n is large), the induced average distance $\bar{d}_\mu$ is w.h.p. ε-smaller than $\bar{d}_0$, i.e.

$$\frac{\bar{d}_\mu}{\bar{d}_0} \le \varepsilon.$$

The key question then hinges upon comparing $\hat{\mu}(\varepsilon)$ and $\breve{\mu}(\varepsilon)$. In particular, one would like to ask the following questions. Are there "reasonably small" values of ε for which $\hat{\mu}(\varepsilon) > \breve{\mu}(\varepsilon)$? And, if so, is the interval $[\breve{\mu}(\varepsilon), \hat{\mu}(\varepsilon)]$ of sizable measure? As it turns out, both questions were answered in the affirmative by Watts and Strogatz (1998) [288] through extensive numerical simulations – cf. Figure 2.7.

Figure 2.7 depicts a situation where for $\varepsilon = 0.2$ the interval $[\breve{\mu}(\varepsilon), \hat{\mu}(\varepsilon)]$ spans more than an order of magnitude. This suggests that if a regular network with strong local clustering is enriched (or perturbed) with a few global links, there is a substantial scope for attaining *both* a significant extent of clustering and a rather low average distance. The combination of these two features is what characterizes the networks known as *small worlds*, whose empirical significance was highlighted in Section 1.1.

Further light on the model has been shed by the elegant analytical approach of Newman, Moore, and Watts (2000) [221]. They formulate what is known as a *mean-field theory* in statistical physics. In essence, it embodies the idea that, in a network with a large set of nodes, the overall impact of the stochastic process of link rewiring on internode distances may be suitably modeled through its mean (or expected) effects. The mean-field approach will be a method of analysis repeatedly used in different parts of the present monograph. In general, it amounts to studying a stylized model of the situation (i.e. a "model" of the original model) where the overall effect resulting from the stochastic forces impinging on a large set of individual entities/processes is identified with the mean (or expected) field. See Appendix C for further elaboration on this approach and an illustration of it through a pair of applications.

Newman *et al.* (2000) [221] start with the following variation of the original Watts-Strogatz setup:

(a) There is a set of n nodes placed equidistantly along a one-dimensional ring of length L and linked to the r closest nodes on either side.

(b) Given a ring as indicated above, *additional* long-range links (shortcuts) are created independently with probability μ at each node. These links do *not* replace any "local" link but connect the node in question to some other node in the ring, uniformly selected.

Thus, the main contrast with the original small-world model is that long-range links now represent net additions to the links of the network. It is intuitively clear, however, that the qualitative role of these shortcuts should be analogous in both contexts.

Formally, the analysis is undertaken in an idealized representation of the former setup where there is a *continuum* set of nodes arranged in a ring, with a total measure of L. In this context, the geodesic distance between any two points is simply identified with their Euclidean distance along the ring. The parameter r, on the other hand, is conceived as a reflection of "network density," specifying the rate at which new nodes are accessed as one moves along the ring.

Let us now focus on some typical node i. The aim then is to trace how the number (measure) of nodes reached by i increases when the radius of its (geodesic) neighborhood, denoted by ρ, grows. Of course, in the absence of shortcuts, this measure just increases linearly with ρ along the ring. But, in the presence of shortcuts – which are assumed of zero length – the neighborhood also stretches through them to possibly distant points in the original ring. See Figure 2.8 for an illustration.

As we move from node i at growing distances ρ, two key magnitudes are of interest to us. First, we are concerned with the (expected)[24] measure of

---

[24] Throughout, the magnitudes involved are to be interpreted as given in expected terms. As explained, the mean-field approach operates on them as if they had been effectively realized.

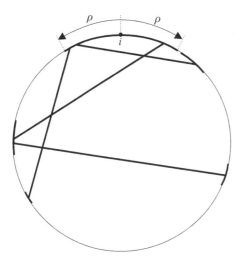

Figure 2.8. The ρ-neighborhood of a typical node i in the continuum model
of a small world network, as proposed and illustrated in Newman *et al.* (2000)
[221]. The *neighborhood* consists of the arcs marked with a thick line while
the *gaps* are identified with the intervening sections along the circle

nodes covered by the corresponding ρ-neighborhood – or, alternatively, the
measure of those still remaining outside. For convenience, we focus on the
latter magnitude and denote it by $a(\rho)$. Second, we are also interested in
the expected number $b(\rho)$ of "gaps" that exist in the induced ρ-neighborhood.
Here, we speak of a *gap* in the neighborhood as any maximally connected subset of nodes in the ring that are not part of that neighborhood (refer again to
Figure 2.8).

Concerning now $a(\rho)$, its rate of change as ρ grows is given by

$$\frac{da(\rho)}{d\rho} = -2rb(\rho). \tag{2.42}$$

This follows from the observation that, given the number of gaps $b(\rho)$ currently "open," the neighborhood advances at a rate r at each of the two ends of
every gap.

Turning now to the change in the number of these gaps, note that there are two
possible sources of variation. First, of course, new gaps may be opened when a
shortcut is encountered. As ρ increases, shortcuts appear at an independent rate
of 2μ at each end of every gap, since the density of shortcut ends is twice the
rewiring rate (each node can be at either end of a shortcut). Thus, since there are
$b(\rho)$ gaps and each has two ends, the aggregate rate at which shortcuts appear
throughout the network is $4\mu b(\rho)$. But, of course, not all of these shortcuts
increase the number of existing gaps. This only occurs when the outward end
attaches to a node that happens to lie in some existing gap. Since the choice
of this end node is made uniformly over all those possible, the probability

of such an event is simply $a(\rho)/L$. Combining the former considerations, it follows that new gaps are opened as ρ increases at an aggregate rate equal to $4\mu b(\rho)a(\rho)/L$.

The number of gaps, on the other hand, may also change – now decrease – when a preexisting gap is closed because its two ends merge. To estimate the probability of this event, consider any one of the gaps existing for a certain value of ρ. As the radius increases from ρ to $\rho + d\rho$, this gap will close if its width is no higher than $2r d\rho$. Given the random fashion in which the prevailing configuration has been reached, the question we need to ask can be phrased as follows: among all possible configurations consistent with the current $(a(\rho), b(\rho))$, what is the probability that any one of its $b(\rho)$ gaps has a width lower or equal than $2r d\rho$? It can be shown that the width distribution of those gaps (resulting from the different ways in which one can fit $a(\rho)$ nodes into $b(\rho)$ gaps) coincides with the distribution of the smallest of $b(\rho) - 1$ numbers that are independently drawn uniformly from 0 to $a(\rho)$ – see the preprint by Newman *et al.* (1999) [220] for the details.[25] Therefore, the probability of the event under consideration (i.e. that any particular gap has a width less than $2r d\rho$) is given by

$$1 - \left(1 - \frac{2r d\rho}{a(\rho)}\right)^{b(\rho)-1} \equiv f(d\rho).$$

For small $d\rho$, the above expression can be approximated by

$$f'(0)d\rho = \frac{2r(b(\rho) - 1)}{a(\rho)} d\rho.$$

Thus, since there are a total of $b(\rho)$ gaps, the combined probability *rate* at which one of them closes is given by $2r b(\rho)(b(\rho) - 1)/a(\rho)$.

Bringing together the total rates at which gaps open and close, the net change in the number of gaps is governed by the following differential equation:

$$\frac{db(\rho)}{d\rho} = \frac{4\mu b(\rho)a(\rho)}{L} - \frac{2r b(\rho)(b(\rho) - 1)}{a(\rho)}. \tag{2.43}$$

For every ρ, let $\phi(\rho)$ denote the density of nodes that lie at precisely distance ρ from the typical node i. Then, in the continuum model, the average distance of the network, $\bar{d}_\mu$, may be defined as follows:

$$\bar{d}_\mu = \frac{1}{L} \int_0^\infty \rho\phi(\rho)\, d\rho.$$

---

[25] Note, specifically, that the probability $p(y)$ that any particular gap includes y nodes is given by $p(y) = \binom{a(\rho)-y-1}{b(\rho)-2} \Big/ \binom{a(\rho)-1}{b(\rho)-1}$.

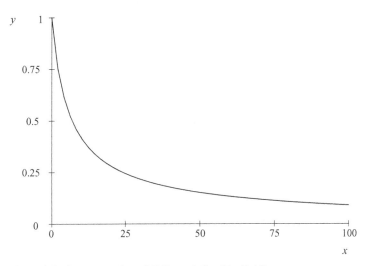

Figure 2.9. Representation of $F(\cdot)$, as defined in (2.45)

But, of course, $\phi(\rho)$ is simply the rate at which new nodes enter the neighborhood of i, i.e.

$$\phi(\rho) = -\frac{da(\rho)}{d\rho},$$

and thus can be directly determined from the solution of the system (2.42)–(2.43). This is used by Newman *et al.* (2000) [221] to obtain an expression for $\bar{d}_\mu$ of the form

$$\bar{d}_\mu = \frac{L}{2z}F(\mu z L), \qquad (2.44)$$

where $z \equiv 2r$ denotes the average degree of the original lattice network (without shortcuts) and the function $F(\cdot)$ is given by (cf. Figure 2.9):

$$F(x) = \frac{4}{\sqrt{x^2 + 4x}}\tanh^{-1}\left(\frac{x}{\sqrt{x^2 + 4x}}\right). \qquad (2.45)$$

The above expression for the average network distance has important and insightful implications. It indicates that the "correction factor" that must be applied to $L/2z$ (the average distance of the original lattice network) to arrive at $\bar{d}_\mu$ only depends, through the function $F(\cdot)$, on the product $\mu z L$ of the three parameters of model. This product coincides with twice the expected number of shortcuts. Thus, quite naturally, the model yields the prediction that, in a large network, the prevailing number of shortcuts should be the *only* magnitude relevant in the determination of the average network distance.

The function $F(\cdot)$ depicted in Figure 2.9 shows a quite fast decay. Thus, for *any* given μ, arbitrarily small, if the network size is large enough so that

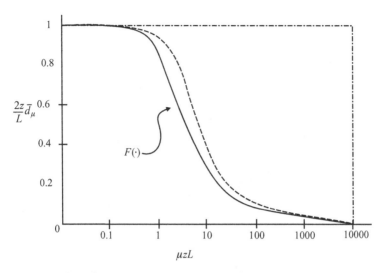

Figure 2.10. The solid line represents $F(\cdot)$, as defined in (2.45) and depicted in Figure 2.9, with the argument now measured in logarithmic scale. The dashed line, on the other hand, provides an approximate illustration of the simulation results reported by Newman *et al.* (2000) [221]. These involve a large context with $L = 10^6$ nodes, an average degree $z = 2$, and different values of μ

$\mu z L \gg 1$, the average distance resulting from (2.44) turns out to be substantially lower than in the original lattice. Indeed, for large values of the argument x, it can be seen that the function F satisfies

$$F(x) \sim \frac{\log x}{x}.$$

This implies that, when $\mu z L$ is large,

$$\bar{d}_\mu \sim \log L,$$

which is comparable to the situation prevailing for a random network. In contrast, when $\mu z L \ll 1$, we have that $F(x) \simeq 1$ (cf. Figure 2.9). Then, the average distance of the network is roughly equal to that of the original lattice network, growing linearly with L. These predictions of the model are in good accord with the large-scale numerical simulations conducted by Newman *et al.* (2000) [221], whose qualitative features are depicted in Figure 2.10. The predictions are less accurate for the intermediate regime where $\mu z L \simeq 1$, which is the "critical point" at which the small-world effects start to emerge.

2.5 SCALE-FREE NETWORKS

The model of a "small world" proposed by Watts and Strogatz (1998) [288] introduces some important new features that are absent from the theoretical framework of random networks – most importantly, it reconciles local structure (high clustering) and typical internode proximity (low average distances). That model, however, does not account for the heterogeneity encountered in many real-world networks. Social networks, in particular, often display wide differences in the network characteristics of nodes/agents that affect, most crucially, both individual and overall performance. The Watts–Strogatz model cannot accommodate such diversity since, for low values of the "rewiring probability", most nodes enjoy very similar properties, e.g. a degree that is close to the average (characteristic) value in the network.

Influential work by Barabási and Albert (1999) [24] has addressed in part these concerns.[26] As we shall see, their model not only gives rise to a broad distribution of connectivity but also yields short average distances. Its clustering, however, still declines sharply as the network size grows to infinity but remains significantly higher than that of Poisson random networks for large finite setups.

The model put forward by Barabási and Albert embodies an explicit dynamic process of network formation. The two essential features that underlie this process are *growth* and *preferential attachment*, in the following senses.

(1) *Growth.* The network is formed, becoming ever larger, through the successive arrival of new nodes that, upon entry, link to some of the preexisting nodes.

(2) *Preferential attachment.* The (stochastic) mechanism used by new nodes in establishing their links is biased in favor of those that are more highly connected at the time of their entrance.

To understand the different implications of each of these two features, it is useful to decouple them and study in turn the implications of considering only (1) or (2), alternatively.[27]

First, consider the following simple model with growth but *no* preferential attachment. The process starts at $t = 1$ with two nodes linked to each other. As t grows ($t > 1$), a new node is added and linked to one of the preexisting nodes, each of these chosen with uniform probability. Thus, at the end of stage t of the process, we have $t + 1$ nodes and t links. For simplicity, let us label the nodes by their time of birth, so that node s ($s > 1$) is the node that enters at time s, while the two initial nodes have indices $s = 0, 1$.

Now let $q_t(s, \kappa)$ stand for the probability that any particular node s has degree κ at t, where naturally $s \leq t$ (i.e. node s has already entered at t). These are *ex-ante* probabilities that reflect the dynamic evolution of the whole *statistical ensemble* of networks induced by the process at every t. Since only one change occurs at every point in time, we may analyze the stochastic network dynamics

---

[26] There is an early precedent in the work of Price (1965) [239], who found that scientific citation is conducted in ways that lead to power-law distributions for the number of cited articles. Later on, Price (1976) [240] elaborated upon ideas put forward by Simon (1955) [257] in order to shed light on this phenomenon along lines quite similar to those explained here.

[27] The approach pursued here largely follows that of Dorogovstev *et al.* (2000) [88] – see also Dorogovtsev and Mendes (2001, 2002) [86, 87].

through the set of master equations that govern the probabilities $q_t(s, \kappa)$ for each κ, s, and t (cf. Appendix C.2). As we explain below, these master equations are of the following form:

$$q_{t+1}(s, \kappa) = \frac{1}{t+1} q_t(s, \kappa - 1) + (1 - \frac{1}{t+1}) q_t(s, \kappa) \qquad (s \leq t),$$

$$(2.46)$$

subject to the boundary conditions:

$$q_1(0, \kappa) = q_1(1, \kappa) = \delta_{\kappa,1} \qquad (2.47)$$
$$q_t(t, \kappa) = \delta_{\kappa,1} \qquad (t = 2, 3, \ldots), \qquad (2.48)$$

where $\delta_{\kappa,1}$ is a Kronecker delta, i.e.

$$\delta_{\kappa,1} = \begin{cases} 1 & \text{if } \kappa = 1 \\ 0 & \text{if } \kappa \neq 1. \end{cases} \qquad (2.49)$$

The interpretation of (2.46) is as follows. Any existing node s enjoys degree $\kappa \geq 1$ at $t + 1$ ($s \leq t$) if, and only if, one of the following two (exclusive) events occur:

(a) it had degree $\kappa - 1$ at t (an event with probability $q_t(s, \kappa - 1)$) and is chosen to be linked by the node entering at t (something which occurs with probability $1/(t + 1)$ since there are $t + 1$ nodes), or
(b) it already had degree κ at t (which has probability $q_t(s, \kappa)$) and is *not* chosen to be linked by the node entering at t (something which occurs with probability $1 - 1/(t + 1)$).

The two terms in (2.46) simply reflect the respective probabilities of these two events.

Based on $\{q_t(s, \kappa)\}_{s,\kappa}$, one may derive the overall degree distribution induced at t. This distribution specifies the probability $p_t(\kappa)$ that a randomly selected node has any given degree κ at t. Since the processes impinging on different nodes are stochastically independent, that probability can be obtained by averaging $q_t(s, \kappa)$ across all nodes $s = 0, 1, 2, \ldots$, i.e.

$$p_t(\kappa) = \frac{1}{t+1} \sum_{s=0}^{t} q_t(s, \kappa). \qquad (2.50)$$

Thus, adding (2.46) across all nodes $s \leq t$, we obtain

$$\sum_{s=0}^{t} q_{t+1}(s, \kappa) = \frac{1}{t+1} \sum_{s=0}^{t} q_t(s, \kappa - 1) + \left(1 - \frac{1}{t+1}\right) \sum_{s=0}^{t} q_t(s, \kappa),$$

and further adding the term $q_{t+1}(t+1, \kappa)$ to both sides:

$$\sum_{s=0}^{t+1} q_{t+1}(s, \kappa) = \frac{1}{t+1} \sum_{s=0}^{t} q_t(s, \kappa - 1)$$

$$+ \left(1 - \frac{1}{t+1}\right) \sum_{s=0}^{t} q_t(s, \kappa) + \delta_{\kappa,1}$$

$$= p_t(\kappa - 1) + t \, p_t(\kappa) + \delta_{\kappa,1}, \qquad (2.51)$$

where the term $\delta_{\kappa,1}$ above simply reflects the fact that, in every period $t + 1$, the entering node $t + 1$ always represents a unit contribution to the set of nodes with degree 1 (and only to these nodes). Then, using the fact that

$$(t + 2)\frac{1}{t+2} \sum_{s=0}^{t+1} q_{t+1}(s, \kappa) = (t + 2) \, p_{t+1}(\kappa)$$

we may rewrite (2.51) as follows:

$$(t + 2) \, p_{t+1}(\kappa) - t \, p_t(\kappa) = p_t(\kappa - 1) + \delta_{\kappa,1},$$

which is the law of motion of the degree distribution. In the limit, as $t \to \infty$ and $p_t(\cdot) \to p(\cdot)$, the long-run stationary distribution satisfies

$$2p(\kappa) = p(\kappa - 1) + \delta_{\kappa,1}$$

whose solution is

$$p(\kappa) = 2^{-\kappa} \qquad (\kappa = 1, 2, \dots),$$

i.e. the long-run degree distribution is geometric.

Thus, if the aim is indeed to understand how a broad distribution of connectivities might come about, the above analysis clarifies that growth alone cannot be the only factor at work. For, if random linking is unbiased, the induced networks display a geometric degree distribution, i.e. are so-called *exponential networks*, exhibiting a sharp (exponential) decay for high degrees. In this sense, they are not qualitatively very different from the *Poisson networks* obtained in a stationary context (recall Section 2.2). In both cases, a narrow degree distribution obtains, with a well-defined characteristic scale.

Next, as a polar alternative to the former scenario (unbiased linking, growing set of nodes), consider a situation where the network is formed over time with preferential (i.e. biased) attachment but the set of nodes N is fixed. That is, at each time step t, one of the n nodes, say i, is picked at random and a new link is established between this node and one of the other nodes in the system. The novel feature now is that the node to be linked to i is chosen with a "preference" in favor of the more connected nodes. More specifically, suppose that such a preference is linear, in the sense that the probability with which node j is chosen at t is *proportional* to its current degree, denoted by z_t^j. Hence the selection probability, represented by π_t^j, is simply given by

$$\pi_t^j = \frac{z_t^j}{\sum_{k \in N \setminus \{i\}} z_t^k}. \tag{2.52}$$

Naturally, if i happens to select a node j with which there is already a link, the network is merely left unchanged. Otherwise, the link ij is formed.

Clearly, the setup just described leads to a trivial situation in the long run: the complete network is eventually established, with all possible links finally in place. This underscores the fact that if preferential attachment is to yield interesting insights, it must take place in a growing environment. It suggests, in other words, that preferential attachment can only deliver interesting insights in a scenario where the set of nodes increases unboundedly over time.

This is precisely the scenario proposed by Barabási and Albert (1999) [24]. In it, one *new* node enters the system at each stage and establishes links to preexisting nodes with a *linear preferential* bias toward more connected ones. As before, at $t = 1$, the process starts with two nodes linked to each other. Then, at every further t, the node that enters at that stage creates a link to *one*[28] of the t nodes already in place through a mechanism that is the counterpart of that embodied by (2.52). That is, the probability that the link be established with any particular incumbent s is

$$\pi_t^s = \frac{z_t^s}{\sum_{s'=0}^{t-1} z_t^{s'}}, \tag{2.53}$$

where we continue to rely on the useful convention of labeling the nodes by their time of birth – therefore, node s ($s > 1$) refers to the node that entered at time s. Clearly, at every time t in the process, there are $t + 1$ nodes and t links.

The analysis of the dynamics is again based on the study of the suitable master equations governing the probabilities $q_t(s, \kappa)$ that any node s has degree $\kappa \geq 1$ at time t ($s \leq t$). They can be written as follows:

$$q_{t+1}(s, \kappa) = \frac{\kappa - 1}{2t} q_t(s, \kappa - 1) + \left(1 - \frac{\kappa}{2t}\right) q_t(s, \kappa) \tag{2.54}$$

with the same initial conditions described in (2.47)–(2.48). Along the lines of (a)–(b) above, the two terms in (2.54) correspond to the two exclusive events that may lead a node s to have degree κ in stage $t + 1$. These are as follows:

(a′) Node s had degree $\kappa - 1$ at t and the new node $t + 1$ (i.e. the one entering at $t + 1$) establishes a link to it.

---

[28] Here, for simplicity, we restrict to the case where each new node forms just one link. This, of course, implies that the induced network must be a tree (i.e. have no cycles) – see Subsection 2.1.2. The model studied by Barabási and Albert (1999) [24] admits any *fixed* number of nodes, $m \in \mathbb{N}$, to be created at each stage. Naturally, this allows for a richer set of network architectures to arise along the process. It also introduces subtle issues that impinge on what is the precise specification of the process, as explained by Bollobás and Riordan (2003) [38]. See Footnote 31 in this chapter for further elaboration on these matters.

(b′) Node s had degree κ at t and the new node $t + 1$ does *not* form a link with it (hence the degree of s remains unchanged).

In view of (2.53), the probability of the event described in (a′) is given by $q_t(s, \kappa - 1)$ multiplied by the ratio of the prior connectivity of node s (i.e. $\kappa - 1$) to the total degree of the system (which is $2t$, since the total number of existing links is t). On the other hand, the probability of the event in (b′) is $q_t(s, \kappa)$ multiplied by $1 - \kappa/(2t)$, which is simply the complement of the probability that any incumbent node with degree κ be linked to the new node. Aggregating again (as in (2.51)) across all nodes $s \leq t + 1$, we arrive at the law of motion for the degree distribution. First, note that

$$\sum_{s=0}^{t+1} q_{t+1}(s, \kappa) = \frac{\kappa - 1}{2t} \sum_{s=0}^{t} q_t(s, \kappa - 1)$$

$$+ \left(1 - \frac{\kappa}{2t}\right) \sum_{s=0}^{t} q_t(s, \kappa) + \delta_{\kappa, 1},$$

where the term $\delta_{\kappa, 1}$ has the same interpretation as before. Then, straightforward algebraic manipulations yield

$$\sum_{s=0}^{t+1} q_{t+1}(s, \kappa) = \frac{1}{2} \frac{t+1}{t} \left\{ (\kappa - 1) \left[\frac{1}{t+1} \sum_{s=0}^{t} q_t(s, \kappa - 1) \right] \right.$$

$$\left. - \kappa \left[\frac{1}{t+1} \sum_{s=0}^{t} q_t(s, \kappa) \right] \right\}$$

$$+ (t+1) \left[\frac{1}{t+1} \sum_{s=0}^{t} q_t(s, \kappa) \right] + \delta_{\kappa, 1}$$

$$= \frac{1}{2} \frac{t+1}{t} \left[(\kappa - 1) \, p_t(\kappa - 1) - \kappa \, p_t(\kappa) \right]$$

$$+ (t+1) \, p_t(\kappa) + \delta_{\kappa, 1}.$$

Using the fact that

$$\sum_{s=0}^{t+1} q_{t+1}(s, \kappa) = (t+2) \left[\frac{1}{t+2} \sum_{s=0}^{t+1} q_{t+1}(s, \kappa) \right] = (t+2) \, p_{t+1}(\kappa)$$

the above expression can be rewritten as follows:

$$(t+2) \, p_{t+1}(\kappa) = \frac{1}{2} \frac{t+1}{t} \left[(\kappa - 1) \, p_t(\kappa - 1) - \kappa \, p_t(\kappa) \right]$$

$$+ (t+1) \, p_t(\kappa) + \delta_{\kappa, 1}.$$

In the limit, as $t \to \infty$ and each $p_t(\kappa)$ converges to the limit $p(\kappa)$, we obtain

$$p(\kappa) = \frac{1}{2} \left[(\kappa - 1) \, p(\kappa - 1) - \kappa \, p(\kappa) \right] + \delta_{\kappa, 1}, \tag{2.55}$$

whose solution is readily seen to be given by

$$p(\kappa) = \frac{4}{\kappa(\kappa + 1)(\kappa + 2)} \qquad (\kappa = 1, 2, \ldots).$$

For large systems, it is often convenient to approximate the theoretical framework by its continuum counterpart, where node degree κ is measured continuously in the range $[1, \infty)$. Then, the difference equation in (2.55) can be recast in the format of the following differential equation:

$$p(\kappa) = -\frac{1}{2} \frac{\mathrm{d}\,[\kappa\,p(\kappa)]}{\mathrm{d}\kappa},$$

whose unique solution is given by

$$p(\kappa) = A\,\kappa^{-3} \tag{2.56}$$

for some constant A which, from the density normalization condition

$$\int_1^\infty A\,\kappa^{-3}\,\mathrm{d}\kappa = 1,$$

is readily computed to be $A = 2$.

We find, therefore, that the combination of growth and linear preferential attachment yields a degree distribution that satisfies a "power law"

$$p(\kappa) \propto \kappa^{-\gamma}$$

with a decay parameter (also called scaling exponent) $\gamma = 3$. The fact that $p(\cdot)$ embodies a power law implies that the distribution is scale-free in the following sense. Consider *any* value of κ and *any* $\alpha > 0$. Then, the frequencies/ probabilities of nodes with degree κ and those of degree $\alpha\kappa$ satisfy the relationship

$$p(\kappa) \propto p(\alpha\kappa),$$

where the precise constant of proportionality naturally depends on α (and, for general γ, on this decay parameter as well). This leads us to saying that the degree distribution displays "no well-defined scale" since, *independently* of the "benchmark" degree κ under consideration, the ratio $p(\kappa)/p(\alpha\kappa)$ is always the same.[29]

In the present case, the fact that γ is relatively small (in this respect, the relevant criterion is that $\gamma \leq 3$) has further consequences concerning issues of scale. Specifically, it implies that the second-order moment of the degree distribution is unbounded. Hence the average degree can hardly be conceived as a suitable estimate of the typical node connectivity found in the network. It is in this sense that one says that the network displays no characteristic degree (or

---

[29] Also notice that, graphically, the distinctive mark of a scale-free distribution is that when depicted in a logarithmic ("log–log") scale, the function appears linear (with a slope equal to the decay parameter).

that its degree has no characteristic scale). Despite terminological similarities, note that there are meaningful conceptual differences between the following two notions: (i) the *degree distribution* is scale free, and (ii) the *network degree* displays no characteristic scale. Both apply only in the case when the degree distribution is given by a power law *and* the corresponding decay parameter $\gamma \leq 3$.

Finally, we turn to discussing the "structural" properties of the scale-free networks resulting from the Barabási–Albert (BA) model. In particular, we are interested in a comparison with the counterpart "static" networks that are both random (in the sense of Section 2.3) and display scale-free (power-law) distributions. To this end, it is appropriate to extend the simplified version of the BA model considered so far and suppose (in line with Barabási and Albert (1999) [24]) that entering nodes can create any *given* number m of new links with different incumbents. This can be seen to have no important implications on the induced degree distribution (cf. Subsection 6.2.1) but does have an important effect on other structural properties. For example, note that if $m = 1$, the induced network remains a tree and, therefore, displays zero clustering throughout the process.

First, let us contrast matters for the induced average distances. Early numerical results reported by Albert and Barabási (2002) [4] suggest that the BA model has the average distance grow logarithmically with network size, which is in line with the situation prevailing for general random networks – cf. (2.25).[30] Analytically, the issue has been rigorously studied by Bollobás and Riordan (2003) [38] in the context of a particular formalization of the BA model called the Linearized Chord Diagram (LCD).[31] They establish, in contrast, that the diameter $\hat{d}$ of the LCD model satisfies (cf. Theorem 18, *op. cit.*)

$$\hat{d} \sim \frac{\log n}{\log \log n}.$$

Pertaining now to clustering, numerical results also reported by Albert and Barabási (2002) [4] suggest that, while their model has the clustering index $\mathcal{C}$

---

[30] Chung and Lu (2002) [62] have studied the average distance (as well as the diameter) of power-law random graphs in a model of random networks somewhat different from the configuration model (cf. Footnote 13). They show that, as the network size n increases, average distance grows as $\log n$ if the decay parameter is higher than 3 but at the slower rate of $\log \log n$ if this parameter is lower than this. See also Cohen and Havlin (2003) [68] for similar results.

[31] Bollobás and Riordan (2003) [38] explain that the BA model is not well (i.e. uniquely) defined if the number of links m established at each stage by the corresponding new node has $m \geq 2$. The essential problem is that the Barabási–Albert description of the network formation specifies only *marginal* linking probabilities, but these are consistent with widely different *joint* linking probabilities. In fact, they prove that one can choose alternative specifications consistent with the same linking marginals that yield drastically different conclusions for some features of network topology (see e.g. their Theorem 5). In response to this state of affairs, the LCD formalization considers a version of the BA framework where each separate link is chosen in sequence and every previous choice (even an immediately previous one by the same entering node) affects the subsequent linking probabilities.

vanish in the limit (i.e. for very large networks), the rate at which this happens is slower than for general random networks with bounded second moment.[32] For the latter (cf. (2.36)), we know that $C \sim n^{-1}$. In contrast, the aforementioned numerical results appear to support the idea that, in the BA model, $C \sim n^{-3/4}$. Again, Bollobás and Riordan (2003) [38] have studied the problem in the LCD framework and arrive at the following result (cf. Theorem 14, *op. cit.*):

$$C \sim \frac{m-1}{8} \frac{(\log n)^2}{n},$$

where m is the number of links created by each entering node. This indeed indicates a slower decay than for random networks, although the rate differs significantly from that gathered by Albert and Barabási (2002) [4] from their numerical simulations.

Specific details notwithstanding, the above discussion generally points to the fact that the BA model induces significantly more structure than that present in random networks. This, in fact, must be a key factor underlying the shorter distances and higher clustering that have been found in this model (see below for an elaboration). Intuitively, much of the structure unfolding in the BA model should derive from the inherent asymmetry among nodes established by the formation process itself. Some nodes arrive early and thus have a long exposure as targets for newcomers. Others, instead, arrive relatively late and thus face very different conditions, i.e. they come up against a markedly "uphill" struggle to become visible and thus succeed in being linked by entering nodes. This asymmetry, in turn, should introduce substantial correlations in the degrees of neighboring nodes. For example, if a node has a high degree it will tend to be old and thus connected to old (and high-degree) nodes as well.

The important issue of internode degree correlations has been studied in some detail by Krapivsky and Redner (2001) [185] within the BA model – see also Krapivsky and Redner (2003) [186]. Their approach is, in essence, a continuous-time variant of that pursued in our former analysis of the BA model. They also restrict to the case where $m = 1$, so that each entering node connects to only one of the existing nodes. For each link, a distinction is made between the node that "initiates" the link at the time of entrance and the incumbent node that is selected for attachment. While the former is called the *descendant*, the latter is labelled the *ancestor*.[33]

---

[32] For a model of an infinitely growing population where a scale-free degree distribution is reconciled, even in the limit, with positive clustering see Klemm and Eguíluz (2002a, 2002b) [177, 178] and Dorogovtsev *et al.* (2000, 2001) [89, 86]. The latter model is discussed in some detail in Subsection 6.2.1. Finally, for quite different approaches to constructing complex networks with high clustering in nongrowing environments, see Jin *et al.* (2001) [167] or Newman (2003d) [218].

[33] Note that even if we think of the network as directed (as a reflection of the dichotomy between ancestors and descendants), this should not affect the large-system properties of the (in)degree distribution. The simple reason is that the difference between the indegree (number of ingoing links or descendants) and the total degree (number of links, ingoing and outgoing) is uniformly equal to 1 for every node.

At any given t and for every pair of possible degrees, κ and ℓ, let $N_t(\kappa, \ell)$ denote the number of nodes that have degree κ at t and whose ancestor (unique, since $m = 1$) currently has degree ℓ. In a continuous-time version of the model, the rate at which these numbers (measures) change over time is given by the following mean-field rate equations:

$$\frac{\mathrm{d}N_t(\kappa, \ell)}{\mathrm{d}t} = \frac{1}{2t}\left[(\kappa - 1)N_t(\kappa - 1, \ell) + (\ell - 1)N_t(\kappa, \ell - 1)\right]$$
$$-\frac{1}{2t}\left[\kappa N_t(\kappa, \ell) + \ell N_t(\kappa, \ell)\right]$$
$$+\frac{1}{2t}(\ell - 1)N_t(\ell - 1)\,\delta_{\kappa,1}, \tag{2.57}$$

where $N_t(\kappa)$ simply denotes the total number of nodes with degree κ. To understand the former expression, note that the number of links connecting nodes of degree κ with ancestors of degree ℓ can change for any of the following different reasons:

- It can increase if either
  - a node of degree $\kappa - 1$ whose ancestor node has degree ℓ, or
  - a node of degree $\ell - 1$ that has a descendant of degree κ
  is selected by an entering node (an event that occurs with respective probabilities $(\kappa - 1)/(2t)$ or $(\ell - 1)/(2t)$, respectively).
- It can decrease if either
  - a node of degree κ whose ancestor node has degree ℓ, or
  - a node of degree ℓ that has a descendant of degree κ
  is selected by an entering node (something that occurs with respective probabilities $\kappa/(2t)$ or $\ell/(2t)$, respectively).
- For $\kappa = 1$, it can increase if the entering node (that of course has a unit degree) selects a node (its ancestor) of degree $\ell - 1$. This event occurs with probability $(\ell - 1)/(2t)$.

The above three cases correspond, in turn, to each of the three terms in (2.57). Naturally, we can express the variables involved through their counterpart frequencies, $v_t(\kappa, \ell)$ and $v_t(\kappa)$, where

$$N_t(\kappa, \ell) = t\, v_t(\kappa, \ell)$$
$$N_t(\kappa) = t\, v_t(\kappa).$$

In the limit of $t \to \infty$, we have $v_t(\kappa, \ell) \to v(\kappa, \ell)$, $v_t(\kappa) \to v(\kappa)$, and

$$\frac{\mathrm{d}N_t(\kappa, \ell)}{\mathrm{d}t} \to v(\kappa, \ell)$$

for all κ and ℓ. This implies that, in the limit, the following condition must hold for all κ and ℓ:

$$(\kappa + \ell + 2)\,v(\kappa, \ell) = (\kappa - 1)\,v(\kappa - 1, \ell) + (\ell - 1)\,v(\kappa, \ell - 1)$$
$$+ (\ell - 1)\,v(\ell - 1)\,\delta_{\kappa,1}.$$

The above expressions are solved recursively by Krapivsky and Redner (2001) [185] to yield

$$
v(\kappa, \ell) = \frac{4(\ell - 1)}{\kappa(\kappa + 1)(\kappa + \ell)(\kappa + \ell + 1)(\kappa + \ell + 2)}
$$
$$
+ \frac{12(\ell - 1)}{\kappa(\kappa + \ell + 1)(\kappa + \ell)(\kappa + \ell + 1)(\kappa + \ell + 2)}. \tag{2.58}
$$

The essential point to get from these expressions is that the joint frequencies $v(\kappa, \ell)$ do not factorize, i.e. $v(\kappa, \ell) \neq v(\kappa) v(\ell)$. There are, therefore, discernible stochastic correlations in the degree of neighboring nodes, at least between any given node and its ancestor. The former cumbersome expression becomes more transparent if we restrict attention to nodes with large connectivity. Making $\kappa, \ell \to \infty$ in (2.58) with the ratio $y \equiv \ell/\kappa$ constant, we find that

$$
v(\kappa, \ell) \to \frac{4y\kappa}{\kappa^5(1 + y)^3} + \frac{12y\kappa}{\kappa^5(1 + y)^4} = \frac{4y(y + 4)}{\kappa^4(1 + y)^4}.
$$

For given κ, the previous expression attains a maximum at a value $y^* = (\sqrt{33} - 5)/2 \simeq 0.372$. This indicates that a highly linked node has the typical degree of its ancestor also being large, somewhat above $1/3$ of its own degree. In general, therefore, we expect that high-degree nodes tend to be connected among themselves, as intuitively argued above. This, in turn, must be partly responsible for the structure displayed by the resulting network. In particular, it is apparent that such a tendency for "hubs" to be connected should both decrease the average distance across the whole network and enhance clustering.

CHAPTER 3

Epidemic Diffusion

This chapter initiates our study of diffusion and models it as a process whose spreading mechanism is independent of any neighborhood considerations. This means that the procedure by which the process propagates from a certain node to any one of its neighbors is unaffected by the conditions prevailing in the neighborhoods of those two nodes – thus, in particular, it is unrelated to the states displayed by their other neighboring nodes. In this sense, one can conceive the phenomenon as akin to biological infection, a process that is often mediated through local contact at a rate that depends on the *aggregate* exposure to infected neighbors. With this analogy in mind, we shall label such a process as epidemic diffusion. But, of course, diffusion in socioeconomic environments is often different, subject to neighborhood (as well as payoff-related) considerations. To study it under these conditions, therefore, we need a different framework of analysis, which is introduced in Chapter 4.

3.1 ALTERNATIVE THEORETICAL SCENARIOS

Epidemiology is an old and well-established field of research, both empirical and theoretical. Its canonical models fall into two categories:[1]

- *SIR* (*susceptible-infected-recovered*), where the life history of each node (or agent) passes from being susceptible (S), to becoming infected (I), to finally being recovered (R), always moving in a unidirectional fashion.
- *SIS* (*susceptible-infected-susceptible*), where each node passes from being susceptible (S) to turning infected (I), to becoming again susceptible (S), thus allowing for a bidirectional transition between the two possible states.

---

[1] See Bailey (1975) [16] and Anderson and May (1991) [11] for the classical approach pursued in mathematical epidemiology. On the other hand, for the perspective adopted by the recent network literature, the reader may refer to the survey by Pastor-Satorras and Vespignani (2003) [235].

In addition to the former two frameworks, it is also natural to consider a third simpler context that may be labeled the *SI* (*susceptible-infected*) model. In it, there is a single transition from susceptible to infected, the latter being an absorbing state once any given node enters into it. In the SI and SIR models, the transitions into infection and (in the SIR case) recovery are irreversible, i.e. have no way back. Thus, it is natural to conceive the epidemics as a "wave" in which, in the long run, the key question is how many nodes are (or have become) infected all along the process (even if they eventually recover). In contrast, in the SIS framework, the system must always remain in continuous flux, even in the long run, and the relevant question should be of a different nature. Clearly, the best one can hope in this case by way of definite prediction is convergence to some population profile where the frequency of infected and healthy/susceptible nodes remains stable over time. In the SIS setup, therefore, the analysis has to center on understanding, and possibly predicting, the extent of prevalence of the infection in the long run, while the particular identity of susceptible and infected nodes is continuously changing.

The above considerations suggest that the SI(R) and SIS frameworks not only raise different questions but also require a different theoretical approach. It is advisable, therefore, to study them separately, as we indeed do in what follows. First, we shall consider the SI and SIR models, embedding them in the general framework of random networks discussed in Section 2.3. As we shall see, the results and techniques developed in Chapter 2 will prove markedly pertinent and useful in the analysis. Next, we shall turn to the SIS models, again studied within the general scenario of random networks. In this case, the primary theoretical approach used in the endeavor will instead be mean-field analysis, analogous to that already used in Section 2.4.

3.2   THE SI MODEL: RESILIENT DIFFUSION

Consider some random network $(\mathcal{G}, P)$, where $\mathcal{G}$ is the collection of admissible networks defined over a given set of nodes N and $P(\Gamma)$ is the probability with which each $\Gamma \in \mathcal{G}$ is selected. Given any such (undirected) network $\Gamma = (N, L)$ in place, the process of diffusion (or infection) is taken to proceed in continuous time $t \in [0, \infty)$ as follows.

At every t, the state of the system consists of a partition of the nodes N into three subsets:

- the set $S(t)$ of susceptible nodes;
- the set $I(t)$ of infected nodes;
- the set $R(t)$ of recovered (or "removed")[2] nodes.

---

[2] An alternative interpretation for recovered nodes is that they are merely removed from the network (say, because they die or become nonoperational due to infection), which in turn implies that they can no longer be a channel for the infection of other nodes.

Of course, all the three classes of nodes arise along the process only in the SIR setup where the infected nodes may eventually recover (or be removed). Instead, in the SI framework the set of recovered nodes remains empty throughout. Both setups, however, have in common the same mechanism of transition from susceptibility into infection, which will be formulated as follows:

Infection. At every t, each susceptible node $i \in S(t)$ may become infected if a neighbor is so. Infection happens at an independent rate $v > 0$ for each of the neighboring nodes j that is infected, i.e. for each $j \in I(t) \cap \mathcal{N}^i$.

This formulation of infection is flexible enough to accommodate a wide range of different phenomena. An obvious one is the contagion of a certain illness through bilateral contact. Another problem that has received much attention lately is the spread of computer viruses through internet (e.g. by email communication) – cf. Pastor-Satorras and Vespignani (2004) [236]. Finally, in a social context, the process could be interpreted as the diffusion of fads, fashion, or behavior through local imitation of neighbors. In this case, the behavioral adjustment may be conceived as resulting from the observation (possibly noisy) of own and neighbor's actions, as in e.g. Ellison and Fudenberg (1993, 1995) [99, 100] and Bala and Goyal (1998) [20].

Modeling matters in this way, let us consider first the *SI scenario* where infection is the sole driving force fueling the epidemics. Then, if our main concern is simply to assess the reach of a *diffusion wave* that is initiated by some seed $I(0)$ of originally infected nodes, the answer is immediately clear: eventually, with probability 1, the set of infected nodes will include exactly those that are in the network component of at least one of the nodes in $I(0)$ (cf. Subsection 2.1.1). Thus, if we denote by $\chi(i)$ the component to which any given node i belongs, the *reach* (or size) of the diffusion wave is

$$D(I(0)) = \{ j \in N : j \in \chi(i), \, i \in I(0) \}.$$

Consider, for simplicity, the case where $I(0)$ is a singleton, i.e. consists of just one node. Then, if this node is chosen at random, the induced probability distribution over the reach of the entailed diffusion wave coincides with the distribution of component sizes. Thus, when the random network is characterized by a degree distribution, we can rely on the approach pursued in Section 2.3 to readily estimate the likely reach of diffusion waves. We may assert, in particular, that in order for the diffusion process to have a positive probability of reaching an unbounded number of nodes as $n \to \infty$, the random network must satisfy $z_2 > z_1$ (cf. (2.23)). In this canonical case, therefore, it all depends on whether the expected number of second-order neighbors exceeds that of first-order ones.

The situation, however, is less straightforward if local contact is not always effective in advancing the process. To fix ideas, suppose that the object of diffusion is a certain piece of information that arrives at some randomly chosen node of the network. Further assume that, subsequently, if a node ever happens to be informed at some point in the process, it transmits the information to each of its neighbors, say immediately. If this transmission were never faulty, the fraction of nodes eventually becoming informed (i.e. the diffusion wave) would indeed coincide with the size of the component of the initially informed node. But suppose that, instead, along the diffusion wave, there is a certain probability that informed nodes might break down before they are able to transmit any information. How is the final outcome affected by this perturbation? The key point here, of course, is to understand how the configuration of the network affects the fragility of the information dissemination process. Or, expressed differently, the question is whether the network is robust enough so that, even in the face of those perturbations, we may still be assured that the information can spread with positive probability to a sizable number of nodes.

To address the problem precisely, let us follow Callaway *et al.* (2000) [49] and assume that the underlying random network is of the sort introduced in Section 2.3, i.e. it is characterized by some degree distribution $\{p(\kappa)\}_{\kappa=0}^{\infty}$ for some very large number of nodes, formally infinite. With some probability, each node may end up malfunctioning, thus failing to pass on the information received. In principle, let us allow this to depend on the degree of the node in question, denoting by q_κ the probability that a node of degree κ is operational (thus with probability $1 - q_\kappa$ it is faulty). Our interest is to characterize the so-called percolation clusters. These are the network components obtained when, independently across nodes, any particular one of degree κ is operative (i.e. able to transmit information) only with probability q_κ.

As before, we rely on generating-function methods. First, consider the (pseudo)[3] generating function

$$F_0(x) = \sum_{\kappa=0}^{\infty} p(\kappa)\, q_\kappa\, x^\kappa,$$

characterizing the probability distribution that a randomly chosen node display any given degree $\kappa = 0, 1, 2, \ldots,$ *and* be well-functioning. On the other hand, if we consider neighboring nodes (i.e. nodes found by following a randomly chosen link), their degree distribution is given by (2.20) and therefore the degree distribution of well-functioning nodes is characterized by

$$F_1(x) = \sum_{\kappa=0}^{\infty} \zeta(\kappa)\, q_\kappa\, x^\kappa = \frac{1}{\sum_{\kappa'=0}^{\infty} \kappa'\, p(\kappa')} \sum_{\kappa=0}^{\infty} \kappa\, p(\kappa)\, q_\kappa\, x^\kappa.$$

Now we follow a procedure analogous to that used in Section 2.3 for the analysis of large random networks. Suppose that the underlying conditions are such that *no* giant component of operational (i.e. well-functioning) nodes exists. Then, let us denote by $H_1(x)$ the function generating the probability distribution

---

[3] Note that this function is not normalized. That is, unless $q_\kappa = 1$ for all κ, we have $F_0(1) \neq 1$. Normalization would require dividing all its terms by $F_0(1)$. This would render these terms suitably normalized conditional probabilities and the induced function a well-defined generating function. A similar comment applies to the function $F_1(x)$ pertaining to neighboring nodes.

of the (finite) sizes of "operational components" (i.e. components consisting of operational nodes), as they are reached through a randomly chosen link followed in either direction.[4] Of course, any such component may be empty if the node at the end of the link is not operative – something which occurs with the probability

$$1 - \sum_{\kappa=0}^{\infty} \zeta(\kappa) \, q_{\kappa} = 1 - F_1(1).$$

But, with the complementary probability, the link in question leads to an operational node of some degree $\kappa = 1, 2, \ldots$, in which case analogous considerations are faced in following each of its $\kappa - 1$ additional links. This means that, as a counterpart of (2.27) for the present case, the generating function H_1 must satisfy the following self-consistency condition:

$$H_1(x) = 1 - F_1(1) + x \, \hat{F}_1(H_1(x)), \tag{3.1}$$

where

$$\hat{F}_1(x) = \sum_{\kappa=1}^{\infty} \zeta(\kappa) \, q_{\kappa} \, x^{\kappa-1} = \sum_{\kappa=0}^{\infty} \hat{\zeta}(\kappa) \, q_{\kappa+1} \, x^{\kappa} \tag{3.2}$$

is the generating function (counterpart of F_1) that pertains to the distribution $\{\hat{\zeta}(\kappa)\}_{\kappa=0}^{\infty}$ given by (2.28). As it will be recalled, this distribution concerns the excess degree of a neighboring node – i.e. its number of links, in excess of the one used to arrive to it. As usual, the factor x multiplying $\hat{F}_1$ in (3.1) simply accounts for the initial (operational) node from which the component spans. Figure 3.1 provides a schematic illustration of the approach (which may be contrasted with that presented in Figure 2.4 for the case where, in a sense, all nodes may be conceived as "operational" with probability one).

Now, on the basis of H_1, we may define the function H_0 that generates the distribution of component sizes associated to a randomly chosen node (functioning or not). Since the probability that a randomly selected node does *not* function is $1 - F_0(1)$, the generating function H_0 must satisfy

$$H_0(x) = 1 - F_0(1) + x \left[\sum_{\kappa=0}^{\infty} p(\kappa) \, q_{\kappa} \, (H_1(x))^{\kappa} \right]$$
$$= 1 - F_0(1) + x \, F_0(H_1(x)), \tag{3.3}$$

where the probabilities (and corresponding generating function) involved are those corresponding to the degree distribution of a randomly selected node, i.e. $\{p(\kappa)\}_{\kappa=0}^{\infty}$. Hence we can compute the average component size in the customary way:

$$\varrho = H_0'(1).$$

---

[4] Note that, for the sake of simplicity, we rely on the same notational convention used in Chapter 2 when no issue was raised concerning the operational status of nodes.

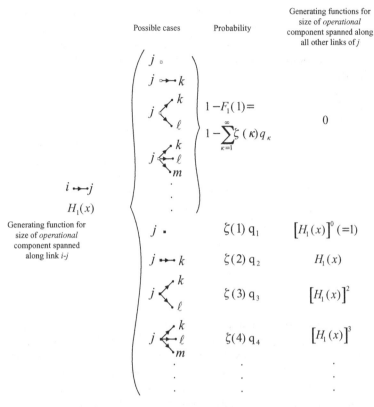

Figure 3.1. Illustration of the self-consistency condition to be satisfied (below the giant-component threshold) by the generating function that characterizes the size distribution of operational components. Circles stand for general nodes, whereas squares represent nodes with specific operational status. In the latter case, while filled squares symbolize operational nodes, empty squares represent nonoperational ones

Differentiating (3.3), we find

$$H_0'(x) = F_0(H_1(x)) + x\, F_0'(H_1(x))\, H_1'(x)$$

which, evaluated at $x = 1$, yields[5]

$$\begin{aligned} H_0'(1) &= F_0(H_1(1)) + F_0'(H_1(1))\, H_1'(1) \\ &= F_0(1) + F_0'(1)\, H_1'(1). \end{aligned} \tag{3.4}$$

Now derivating (3.1) we have

$$H_1'(x) = \hat{F}_1(H_1(x)) + x\, \hat{F}_1'(H_1(x))\, H_1'(x)$$

---

[5] Note that, unlike F_0 or F_1 (cf. Footnote 3), H_1 is a suitably normalized generating function and thus $H_1(1) = 1$.

or

$$H_1'(x) = \frac{\hat{F}_1(H_1(x))}{1 - x\hat{F}_1'(H_1(x))},$$

so that, at $x = 1$,

$$H_1'(1) = \frac{\hat{F}_1(1)}{1 - \hat{F}_1'(1)},$$

which can be inserted in (3.4) to obtain

$$\varrho = H_0'(1) = F_0(1) + \frac{F_0'(1)\hat{F}_1(1)}{1 - \hat{F}_1'(1)}. \tag{3.5}$$

We find, therefore, in analogy with the discussion of Section 2.3, that a giant operational component arises (i.e. one that spans a significant fraction of nodes) as $\hat{F}_1'(1) \nearrow 1$. Beyond the threshold of unity, the fractional size w of the giant component can be computed, adapting the usual approach, through the condition

$$1 - w = 1 - F_0(1) + F_0(1 - \hat{w})$$

or

$$w = F_0(1) - F_0(1 - \hat{w}), \tag{3.6}$$

where $\hat{w}$ represents the fraction of edges in the component that is the solution to the equation

$$1 - \hat{w} = 1 - \hat{F}_1(1) + \hat{F}_1(1 - \hat{w}). \tag{3.7}$$

In contrast with the analogous expressions (2.34)–(2.35), those above introduce the following changes. First, (3.6) replaces the full relative measure of nodes (i.e. unity) by $F_0(1)$, since some nodes simply do not span even a singleton component because they themselves are not functional. On the other hand, (3.7) contemplates the possibility that a randomly chosen edge leads to a nonfunctional node by including the probability $1 - \hat{F}_1(1)$.

To further understand the implications of the former derivations, it is useful to focus first on the case where the prior probability of being operational is the same for all nodes, i.e. there is a common q such that, for all $\kappa = 0, 1, 2, \ldots,$

$$q_\kappa = q. \tag{3.8}$$

Then, we have

$$\hat{F}_1'(1) = q\,\hat{G}_1'(1),$$

where $\hat{G}_1(x)$ is the ordinary generating function (2.29) for a neighboring node in the underlying network (i.e. abstracting from node functionality). In this case, the threshold probability q_c that marks the rise of a giant operational component is[6]

$$q_c = \frac{1}{\hat{G}_1'(1)}. \tag{3.9}$$

That is, if (and only if) the operating probability q is higher than such q_c will there be an operational component of infinite size. Under these conditions, therefore, there is a positive probability that the (perturbed) diffusion process originating in some randomly selected node may reach a significant fraction of the set of nodes.

In general, of course, the threshold probability given by (3.9) depends on the degree distribution. To illustrate the point, assume that the random network under consideration displays a scale-free degree distribution and let us approximate it by the continuous density

$$p(\kappa) = (\gamma - 1)\,\kappa^{-\gamma} \qquad (\kappa \geq 1)$$

with $\gamma > 2$. Then, since

$$
\begin{aligned}
\hat{G}_1(x) &= \frac{1}{\int_{\kappa=1}^{\infty} \kappa\, p(\kappa)\, d\kappa} \int_{\kappa=1}^{\infty} \kappa\, p(\kappa)\, x^{\kappa-1}\, d\kappa \\
&= \frac{1}{(\gamma-1)/(\gamma-2)} \int_{\kappa=1}^{\infty} \kappa\, (\gamma-1)\kappa^{-\gamma}\, x^{\kappa-1}\, d\kappa
\end{aligned}
$$

it follows that

$$
\begin{aligned}
\hat{G}_1'(1) &= \frac{(\gamma-1)(\gamma-2)}{(\gamma-1)} \int_{\kappa=1}^{\infty} \kappa^{1-\gamma}\,(\kappa-1)\, d\kappa \\
&= (\gamma-2)\left\{ \left[\frac{\kappa^{3-\gamma}}{3-\gamma}\right]_1^{\infty} - \left[\frac{\kappa^{2-\gamma}}{2-\gamma}\right]_1^{\infty} \right\}.
\end{aligned}
$$

Let us make the assumption that $2 < \gamma \leq 3$, which means that the degree distribution is so broad that it displays unbounded second moments but still enjoys a well-defined average degree. Then, since $\hat{G}_1'(1)$ diverges in this case, (3.9) induces a critical operating probability $q_c = 0$. This implies that a diffusion component spanning a large (infinite) set of nodes exists almost surely whenever there is *any* positive probability, no matter how low, that each node operates correctly.

Such a striking conclusion represents the first manifestation of a general and multifaceted insight that will be encountered repeatedly throughout: the global performance of processes mediated by network-based (local) contact may be greatly enhanced by internode heterogeneity. The same idea turns out to be important, for example, to understand the effectiveness of processes of search, as will be discussed at length in Chapter 5. Here, concerning processes of diffusion, we have just seen its analogous implications for the SI framework

---

[6] The same threshold is derived by Cohen *et al.* (2000) [66] using other analytical methods.

in the form of improved robustness. Within the SIR scenario (Section 3.3), it will appear again in the form of a wider diffusion range, and within the SIS context (Section 3.4) in the form of higher prevalence of infection.

In all these contexts, however, there is an important assumption on the nature of the perturbation that crucially underlies the analysis. It is being supposed (cf. (3.8)) that all nodes enjoy the same probability of being operational – thus, reciprocally, they are all subject to the same probability as well of turning faulty. But this, in turn, implicitly presumes that whatever may affect the operativeness of nodes is governed by random and unguided forces. It rules out, therefore, that the network may in fact be facing targeted perturbations that aim preferentially at certain nodes by virtue of their special role and/or position. Such an alternative scenario would be one where, in the language of Albert *et al.* (2000) [6], the concern should not be the *error tolerance* displayed by the network but its robustness to *targeted attacks* (see also Broder *et al.* (2000) [43]).

To be more specific, consider that the "attack" in question proceeds by disrupting *all* nodes that would intuitively seem to be most crucial in ensuring global diffusion, i.e. the highest-degree nodes. For example, suppose that it succeeds in disrupting all those whose degree is above a certain threshold, say κ_0. How does this affect the size of operational components?

Again, this question can be addressed by a suitable particularization of the general approach of Callaway *et al.* (2000) [49] introduced here. In effect, it amounts to positing that the probabilities q_κ that govern node reliability, rather than constant, are given by

$$q_\kappa = \begin{cases} 1 & \text{if } \kappa \le \kappa_0 \\ 0 & \text{if } \kappa > \kappa_0. \end{cases}$$

Although analytically more cumbersome, the same generating-function methods can be applied in this case to check for the existence of a giant operational component. And, if it exists, one can estimate its fractional size through (3.6)–(3.7), just as explained for the general case.

This issue has been studied in detail by Callaway *et al.* (2000) [49] themselves – and, independently, by Cohen *et al.* (2001) [67] – for the case of scale-free networks with decay exponent $\gamma > 2$. They find that, in marked contrast with the strong resilience these networks enjoy under uniform (i.e. nontargeted) disruption, scale-free networks are extremely fragile in the face of attacks that target the highest-degree nodes. Specifically, they show analytically (and in full accordance with numerical simulations) that it is *never* necessary to disrupt more that 3% of the total nodes for the giant operational component to vanish. And, in fact, even less than a meager 1% will do when, approximately, $\gamma \ge 2.7$. The required fraction decreases monotonically beyond this point. The caveat, however, is that as γ grows, the threshold κ_0 that needs to be used to account for, say, 1% of all highest-degree nodes also falls as given by

$$\kappa_0 \simeq 10^{2/(\gamma-1)}.$$

This indicates that it may also be more difficult to "find" the right nodes as γ grows. In any case, what our overall discussion should render clear is that, in general, there is a subtle interplay between the topology of the network and the particular details of the perturbation process in shaping the resulting global properties of the network. This concerns, specifically, its potential for extensive diffusion, as explained here.

3.3 THE SIR MODEL: THE REACH OF DIFFUSION WAVES

The SIR framework models infection in the same way as the SI context but contemplates an additional state for nodes and, correspondingly, an additional transition in the law of motion. The new possible state for a node is that of *recovery*, whose interpretation is simply a situation in which the node in question can no longer be infected nor pass the infection to its neighbors. In a biological scenario, this state could represent complete immunization from a disease, once having experienced and recovered from it. Alternatively, as explained, it could also mean "removal" – i.e. an outright elimination of the node from the network due to, say, death or some other incapacitating condition. In a social context, of course, the appropriate interpretation should depend on what is the nature of the phenomenon considered. Suppose, for concreteness, that the object of diffusion is a certain type of behavior that is spread through local imitation, e.g. the consumption of a conspicuous good. Then, recovery could simply signify that such a behavior (consumption) is irreversibly abandoned (or looses visibility) due to obsolescence, reduced salience, or depreciation of some sort.

Since infection is no longer an absorbing state for nodes in the SIR model (but recovery is), an additional law of motion is required to govern the transition from infection to recovery. Resorting again to biologically inspired terminology, let us label this transition as (irreversible) "cure" and formulate it as follows:

Cure (SIR model). At every t, each infected node $I(t)$ irreversibly recovers at the (independent) rate $\delta > 0$. When this event happens, the node in question can never again transmit the infection to its neighbors.

Abstracting from the robustness issues that concerned us before in the study of the SI framework, our objective here will be to obtain a precise assessment of when the (unperturbed) diffusion in the SIR scenario may have a significant reach. The problem is now complicated by the fact that the infection of a node does not by itself guarantee that the process keeps moving to its noninfected neighbors. This only happens if such a contagion occurs *before* the infected node (irreversibly) recovers.

A natural way to integrate this feature into the analysis is simply to account for the *ex-ante* probability that, after a node becomes infected, it recovers *before* a particular neighbor becomes infected. This approach, proposed by Grassberger (1983) [140], allows us to conceive and model the SIR process very much like a *perturbed* SI process. In this case, of course, the "perturbation" is given by the possibility that the node ends up recovering before the actual contagion of a neighbor takes place.

Our formulation of recovery prescribes that every infected node recovers at the same independent rate δ and, until this happens, it infects every neighboring susceptible node at the common rate v.[7] Thus, the probability that, upon contagion, a given node ends up infecting any one of its neighboring susceptible nodes is

$$\vartheta = 1 - e^{-v/\delta}.$$

In a large network, we can use ϑ as the transmission/diffusion probability bearing on susceptible nodes when assessing the extension of an epidemic outbreak. The essential difference with the approach undertaken in Section 3.2 for the perturbed SI model is that, in the present case, the perturbation affects each of the *links* springing from an infected node rather than this node itself.

Bearing this in mind, let us now study the size distribution of an epidemic wave, our aim being to identify the point at which it may come to include a set of nodes with a significant fractional measure. Assuming that we are below that point (thus all waves are almost surely of finite size), the relevant generating functions involved in the analysis are

- the function W_1 that generates the size distribution for the "components" of *links* (not nodes) that would be expected to pass the infection if they connect an infected node to a susceptible one;
- the function H_0 that generates the size distribution for the components of *ever* infected *nodes* associated to an *originally infected node* that is randomly selected.

These generating functions may be obtained from the following adaptation of the customary self-consistency conditions (cf. Newman (2002a) [213]):

$$W_1(x) = 1 - \vartheta + \vartheta \, x \, \hat{G}_1(W_1(x)) \tag{3.10}$$
$$H_0(x) = x \, G_0(W_1(x)), \tag{3.11}$$

where recall that

- G_0 is the generating function for the degree distribution of the underlying network,
- $\hat{G}_1$ is the generating function for the excess degree of a neighboring node.

Here, to repeat, the sole difference with our previous approach is that we consider a *dual* generating function W_1 characterizing the distribution of "functioning" links, i.e. the links that *would be* operative in spreading the infection.

---

[7] To keep things simple, we maintain the assumption that all nodes are *ex-ante* symmetric in every respect concerning not only recovery but also contagion. However, Newman (2002a) [213] shows that heterogeneity in recovery and infection rates can be allowed, as long as these are determined in a stochastically independent manner across all nodes.

Note, on the other hand, that the nodes labeled "infected" are those that *ever* get so (and thus *may* possibly transmit the disease sometime along the process). Eventually, of course, there are no infected nodes left since, in the long run, all nodes are either in the state of *recovered* (if once infected) or *susceptible* (if never infected).

In view of the former considerations, the interpretation of (3.10) should be by now clear. By proceeding along a randomly selected link, we may find that one of the following two events materializes:

- the link in question is *not* operative (with probability $1 - \vartheta$) and the diffusion component stops there; or
- it is operative and then the same considerations are repeated for *each* of the *additional* links that springs from the node thus reached (each of those links being operative with *independent* probability ϑ).

Building upon the distribution of operative links characterized by W_1, the generating function H_0 given in (3.11) is obtained by simply accounting for the number of operative links that may spring from a randomly selected infected node. This function generates the size distribution for the set of nodes that may be eventually reached from that originally infected node. As we know, the induced average size is given by $H_0'(1)$. Straightforward computations, fully analogous to those repeatedly performed before, lead to

$$H_0'(1) = 1 + \frac{\vartheta G_0'(1)}{1 - \vartheta \hat{G}_1'(1)}.$$

Therefore, the threshold of divergence at which an infinite epidemic wave starts to be possible is

$$\vartheta_c = \frac{1}{\hat{G}_1'(1)}.$$

This threshold for ϑ is exactly the same as (3.9), the one derived for q in the perturbed SI framework.[8] This underscores the parallelisms between the two frameworks. Again, therefore, we arrive at the conclusion that the broadness of the degree distribution helps to extend the reach of a diffusion wave. In particular, if the degree distribution is scale-free with an exponent $\gamma \in (2, 3]$, the analysis performed in Section 3.2 implies, *mutans mutandis*, that there is a positive probability that the infection may expand to a significant fraction of the (infinite) population for any arbitrary small $\vartheta > 0$.

---

[8] Again, we could introduce considerations of robustness into the SIR framework, in ways analogous to how they were approached in the SI model. This would simply amount to an adjustment of the infection probability ϑ, which would have to be scaled by the corresponding probability that the node in question is operational. Then, of course, the threshold for divergence would apply to the resulting "net" probability.

3.4   THE SIS MODEL: LONG-RUN PREVALENCE

In some applications, it is natural to posit that when a node recovers from infection it reverts to a susceptible state, i.e. it may be infected again later on if any of its neighbors happens to be infected. In biological contexts, this occurs when, for example, the recovery from a disease does not bring permanent immunity. In social environments, on the other hand, an analogous situation arises when the behavior that was triggered by local stimulus (e.g. the consumption of a certain good due to imitation of neighbors) can be abandoned, and then readopted again, depending on neighborhood conditions. In essence, this amounts to positing that "cure" is a reversible phenomenon. But then its previous formulation in the SIR scenario must be replaced by the following alternative.

Cure (SIS model). At every t, each infected node $I(t)$ recovers at the (independent) rate $\delta > 0$. When this event happens, the node in question becomes susceptible, i.e. exposed to future contagion as formulated in Section 3.2.

Under the previous formulation, the state of infection is no longer absorbing and the life-history of a node does not move in only one direction. Typically, therefore, nodes must display recurrent phases of infection and susceptibility that translate into continuous variability in the overall configuration of the system. Despite this variability, one expects that the population profile (i.e. the *fraction* of infected and susceptible nodes) should eventually reach a stable situation. And then, the central question is whether such long-run profile will display positive *prevalence*, i.e. a positive fraction of infected nodes. If this indeed happens, infection is bound to become an entrenched phenomenon that is unlikely to disappear from the system in a reasonable time horizon (at least if the system is large).[9]

Our analysis of the SIS model will be based on a mean-field theory of the induced epidemics.[10] Naturally, this theory must be adapted to the characteristics of the underlying framework. It is simplest in the case of homogenous (say, lattice) networks, which is the setup studied first in Subsection 3.4.1. Then, in Subsection 3.4.2, we address the SIS model in random networks. Finally, Subsection 3.5 studies issues of robustness and how policies of targeted cure or immunization may impinge on the outcome.

---

[9] Note that, in any finite system, the process must eventually converge, with probability 1, to an *absorbing* situation where no node is infected. (This simply follows from the fact that the probability of cure is positive and independent across all infected nodes.) Such an outcome, however, depends on a coincidence of events (i.e. all infected nodes being cured before infection spreads further) that is extremely improbable (and thus subject to astronomical expected waiting times) if the population is very large. This is why that possibility is implicitly ignored by our ensuing mean-field approach to the study of the model.

[10] Again, see Appendix C for further discussion of this approach, and recall how this methodology was first applied in Section 2.4.

3.4.1   Long-Run Prevalence in Regular Networks

Firstly, we study how the epidemics evolves if the underlying network is regular, in the sense that all nodes $i \in N$ have the same degree $\kappa_i = z$. (It could be, for example, that it is a lattice network or, alternatively, that it is *ex-ante* random with the set $\mathcal{G}$ of possible networks all having the required degree homogeneity.) The key assumption that underlies the customary mean-field theory of the epidemics is labelled *homogenous mixing* (cf. Anderson and May (1991) [11]). It embodies the postulate that nodes are, on average, subject to the same exposure to infection and, therefore, there are *no systematic* differences across susceptible nodes. Thus, all of them (even if we allowed for different degrees) face the same expected probability of becoming infected through *each one* of their neighbors.

The homogenous-mixing assumption is undoubtedly "unrealistic." Even if the initial state did indeed display such homogenous mixing, significant correlations should be expected to develop over time by the sheer operation of the dynamics. Such correlations, in turn, would alter the idealized mixing presumed by the theory throughout. The previous comments notwithstanding, it may be hoped that the deviations from the theory are not crucial and therefore some of its predictions still approximately valid, at least qualitatively. This is indeed confirmed by numerical simulations (cf. Pastor-Satorras and Vespignani (2004) [236]), which suggest that the mean-field approach does capture much of the essential gist of the dynamics, both for regular networks as well as for the other random contexts studied below. In particular, it turns out to predict quite well the inception of a persistent state of infection as a function of the underlying parameters (see below).

Denote by $\rho(t)$ the fraction of nodes that are infected at any given t, i.e. the infection *prevalence*. Then, for a large population of nodes arranged in a regular network of degree z, the *mean-field dynamics* of $\rho(t)$ is written as follows:

$$\dot{\rho}(t) = -\delta \rho(t) + \nu z \rho(t) [1 - \rho(t)], \qquad (3.12)$$

where recall that δ and ν stand for the rates of cure and infection, respectively (cf. Sections 3.2 and 3.3).

The law of motion (3.12) embodies the *expected* evolution of ρ under the assumption of homogenous mixing. For a large network, the differential equation is conceived as a good approximation of the *actual* dynamics of the system. Its first term reflects the process of cure, which impinges on the fraction $\rho(t)$ of infected nodes. It cures them at the rate δ, thus decreasing their numbers. The second term of (3.12), on the other hand, represents the infection process by which the susceptible nodes (their frequency is $1 - \rho(t)$) become infected at the rate ν for each of its infected neighbors. To understand this term, note that, by virtue of homogenous mixing, the expected number of infected neighbors is $z\rho(t)$. Thus, the probability that a susceptible node is infected in the small time

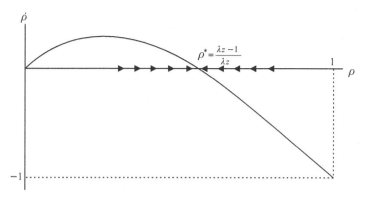

Figure 3.2. Representation of the law of motion given in (3.13)

interval $[t, t + dt]$ is simply given by $[1 - (1 - \nu dt)^{z\rho(t)}]$. For infinitesimal dt, it induces the following rate:

$$\lim_{dt \to 0} \frac{[1 - (1 - \nu dt)^{z\rho(t)}]}{dt} = \nu z \rho(t)$$

as specified in (3.12).

By an appropriate scaling of (continuous) time, we may normalize the rate of cure to unity and thus deal with the relative rate of infection $\lambda \equiv \nu/\delta$, often called the (effective) *spreading rate*. This leads to rewriting (3.12) as follows:

$$\dot{\rho}(t) = -\rho(t) + \lambda z \rho(t)[1 - \rho(t)]. \tag{3.13}$$

We are interested in the stationary long-run rate of prevalence ρ^* obtained by setting

$$\dot{\rho}(t) = 0$$

in (3.13). This gives rise to

$$\rho^* \left[-1 + \lambda z (1 - \rho^*) \right] = 0$$

so that the state with zero prevalence,

$$\rho^* = 0,$$

is always a stationary state. But if λ is above the critical value

$$\lambda_c = 1/z, \tag{3.14}$$

there is also a stationary state with positive prevalence

$$\rho^* = \frac{\lambda z - 1}{\lambda z}. \tag{3.15}$$

In fact, if $\lambda > \lambda_c$, (3.15) specifies the (unique) globally stable state for the mean-field dynamics (3.13), as illustrated in Figure 3.2.

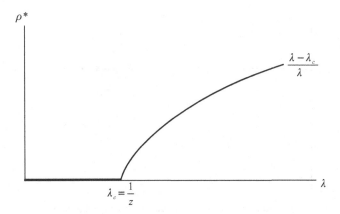

Figure 3.3. The long-run prevalence of infection as a function of the spreading rate in a regular network

As we change the spreading rate λ, we may trace the unique stable long-run state $\rho^*(\lambda)$ as follows (cf. Figure 3.3):

$$\rho^*(\lambda) = \begin{cases} 0 & \text{if } \lambda < \lambda_c = 1/z \\ \frac{\lambda z - 1}{\lambda z} = \frac{\lambda - \lambda_c}{\lambda} & \text{if } \lambda \geq \lambda_c = 1/z \end{cases}.$$

3.4.2   Long-Run Prevalence in Random Networks

Now assume that the underlying context is a general random network of the sort studied in Section 2.3. We face, that is, a *statistical ensemble* consisting of the equiprobable selection of a specific network within the collection of possible networks $\mathcal{G}_p$ that display a fixed degree distribution $p \equiv \{p(\kappa)\}_{\kappa=0}^{\infty}$. Since, in general, the connectivity will no longer be homogenous across nodes (i.e. p will not be degenerate), the model must take this into account and should differentiate among nodes depending on their degree. In what follows, we discuss the mean-field approach proposed by Pastor-Satorras and Vespignani (2001) [233] that accommodates for such internode heterogeneity.

Let $p \equiv \{p(\kappa)\}_{\kappa=0}^{\infty}$ represent the degree distribution of a large random network. Denote by $\rho_\kappa(t)$ the average prevalence of infection at t among the collection of nodes with degree $\kappa = 0, 1, 2, \ldots$. Then, as a counterpart of the law of motion (3.13) for regular networks, we may write separate mean-field expressions governing the expected dynamics of each ρ_κ as follows:

$$\dot{\rho}_\kappa(t) = -\rho_\kappa(t) + \lambda \, \kappa \, \left[1 - \rho_\kappa(t)\right] \theta \left[\{\rho_{\kappa'}(t)\}_{\kappa'=1}^{\infty}\right] \qquad (\kappa = 0, 1, 2, \ldots). \tag{3.16}$$

The contrast with (3.13) is twofold. First, the process of infection affecting a susceptible node of degree κ is adjusted in order to take into account the number of "routes" it can rely upon (i.e. the number of links κ). Second, the probability that any given link connects to an infected node is no longer made equal to the fraction of infected nodes

$$\rho(t) = \sum_{\kappa=0}^{\infty} \rho_\kappa(t)\, p(\kappa),$$

but is identified with some other function $\theta(\cdot)$ of the profile of infected nodes across the different degrees. The reason for this change is that, as explained in Section 2.3, the degree distribution across *neighbors* of a particular node is not p but instead (recall (2.20)) given by

$$\zeta(\kappa) = \frac{p(\kappa)\,\kappa}{\sum_{\kappa'=0}^{\infty} p(\kappa')\,\kappa'} = \frac{1}{\langle \kappa \rangle}\, p(\kappa)\,\kappa. \tag{3.17}$$

Therefore, the probability that any one neighbor of a randomly selected node be infected is given by

$$\theta\left[\{\rho_\kappa(t)\}_{\kappa=0}^{\infty}\right] = \sum_{\kappa=1}^{\infty} \rho_\kappa(t)\, \zeta(\kappa). \tag{3.18}$$

At a stationary point of the dynamics we have

$$\dot\rho_\kappa(t) = 0 \qquad (\kappa = 0, 1, 2, \ldots),$$

which implies that the infection prevalence ρ_κ^* among nodes of degree κ must satisfy

$$\rho_\kappa^* = \frac{\lambda\kappa\,\theta^*}{1 + \lambda\,\kappa\,\theta^*} \qquad (\kappa = 0, 1, 2, \ldots), \tag{3.19}$$

so that, using (3.18), the long-run stationary probability θ^* that any one of the links of a randomly chosen node be connected to an infected node is computed as follows:

$$\theta^* = \sum_{\kappa=1}^{\infty} \rho_\kappa^*\, \zeta(\kappa). \tag{3.20}$$

In fact, introducing (3.19) into the above expression, the value of θ^* may be derived from the following self-consistency condition:

$$\theta^* = \sum_{\kappa=1}^{\infty} \zeta(\kappa)\frac{\lambda\kappa\,\theta^*}{1 + \lambda\kappa\,\theta^*} \tag{3.21}$$

$$= \frac{1}{\langle \kappa \rangle} \sum_{\kappa=1}^{\infty} p(\kappa)\kappa\,\frac{\lambda\kappa\,\theta^*}{1 + \lambda\kappa\,\theta^*}. \tag{3.22}$$

Clearly, the previous equation always has a solution $\theta^* = 0$, where no node is infected. But, as in Subsection 3.4.1, we are interested in knowing under what conditions such a corner solution is unstable and there is another (stable) solution where $\theta^* > 0$. The answer turns out to be especially simple, as a consequence of the fact that the function

$$\phi_\lambda(\theta) \equiv \frac{1}{\langle \kappa \rangle} \sum_{\kappa=1}^{\infty} p(\kappa)\kappa \, \frac{\lambda\kappa\,\theta}{1+\lambda\kappa\,\theta} \qquad (3.23)$$

is strictly concave in θ and, moreover,

$$\phi_\lambda(1) = \frac{1}{\langle \kappa \rangle} \sum_{\kappa=1}^{\infty} p(\kappa)\kappa \, \frac{\lambda\kappa}{1+\lambda\kappa} < 1.$$

In view of these considerations, we may conclude that $\theta^* > 0$ if, and only if,

$$\left.\frac{d\phi_\lambda(\theta)}{d\theta}\right|_{\theta=0} = \frac{1}{\langle \kappa \rangle} \sum_{\kappa=1}^{\infty} p(\kappa)\kappa \, \lambda\kappa > 1. \qquad (3.24)$$

Rearranging terms, the above condition can be written as follows:

$$\lambda > \frac{\langle \kappa \rangle}{\langle \kappa^2 \rangle}, \qquad (3.25)$$

where the average $\langle \cdot \rangle$ is computed for the degree distribution $\{p(\kappa)\}_{\kappa=0}^{\infty}$. The value

$$\lambda_c \equiv \langle \kappa \rangle / \langle \kappa^2 \rangle \qquad (3.26)$$

is the *critical spreading rate* that marks the threshold for long-run prevalence. That is, given any spreading rate λ, we have

$$\rho^* \equiv \sum_{\kappa=0}^{\infty} \rho_\kappa^* \, p(\kappa) > 0 \Leftrightarrow \lambda > \lambda_c. \qquad (3.27)$$

Therefore, at the uniquely stable solution of the mean-field model, the induced long-run prevalence is positive if, and only if, the spreading rate exceeds the ratio of the first and second moments of the degree distribution.

Networks with a Characteristic Scale

Note that (3.27) leads to the threshold derived in Section 3.4.1 for regular networks as a particular case. If all nodes display the same degree (i.e. the distribution is degenerate and has all its mass concentrated at the mean), then $\langle \kappa^2 \rangle = \langle \kappa \rangle^2$ and therefore

$$\lambda_c = \langle \kappa \rangle / \langle \kappa^2 \rangle = 1/ \langle \kappa \rangle ,$$

which coincides with (3.14). In general, of course, it always holds that

$$\langle \kappa^2 \rangle \geq \langle \kappa \rangle^2 ,$$

which indicates that degree heterogeneity (a broader degree distribution) favours the spread of infection. Thus, among all networks with a given connectivity (average degree), the higher threshold on the spreading rate required for long-run prevalence occurs precisely for those networks where there is no internode variability in degree. As long as this variability remains limited, i.e. if the variance

$$\sigma^2 = \langle \kappa^2 \rangle - \langle \kappa \rangle^2$$

is bounded, there is a *positive* threshold for long-run prevalence:

$$\lambda_c = \frac{\langle \kappa \rangle}{\sigma^2 + \langle \kappa \rangle^2} = \frac{1}{\langle \kappa \rangle} \frac{1}{(c_v)^2 + 1},$$

where c_v stands for the coefficient of variation (i.e. the ratio between the standard deviation and mean of the degree distribution). If c_v is finite, the average degree acts a meaningful representation (or benchmark) of the overall connectivity and the network degree may be said to display a characteristic scale – recall our discussion in Section 2.5. An opposite paradigmatic case is provided by scale-free networks with a low decay parameter ($\gamma \leq 3$) and thus no characteristic degree. This is the context studied in what follows.

Scale-Free Networks

Assume that the *random* network displays a scale-free degree distribution with the same decay parameter, $\gamma = 3$, that results from the Barabási-Albert (BA) model studied in Chapter 2 (i.e. a growing network under linear preferential attachment).[11] Focusing, for simplicity, in the continuum approximation of the model (cf. Section 2.5), the induced degree distribution $p(\cdot)$ is given by

$$p(\kappa) = 2\kappa^{-3} \tag{3.28}$$

for each $\kappa \in [1, \infty)$. This distribution has

$$\langle \kappa^2 \rangle = 2 \int_{\kappa=1}^{\infty} \frac{1}{\kappa} d\kappa = +\infty,$$

which implies, in view of (3.25), that there is positive long-run prevalence for *any* spreading rate $\lambda > 0$. In a sense, this reflects, for the present SIS context, the same insight that was gathered in Sections 3.2 and 3.3 for the SI and SIR scenarios. Namely, it indicates that diffusion is greatly enhanced, and can attain an infinite reach, whenever the underlying random network displays wide degree heterogeneity.

Given the specific degree distribution given in (3.28), it is possible to go beyond the mere "qualitative" concern for long-run prevalence and obtain a full-fledged solution of the model. That is, we may arrive at an explicit determination

---

[11] Recall, however, that internode correlations arise in networks formed through growth, as discussed in Section 2.5. These correlations are assumed absent here since we study a *random* (scale-free) network.

of how the stationary level ρ^* depends on the spreading rate λ. To this end, let us start by rewriting (3.21)–(3.22) in its continuum version as follows:

$$\theta^* = \frac{1}{\langle \kappa \rangle} \int_{\kappa=1}^{\infty} 2\kappa^{-3} \, \kappa \, \frac{\lambda \kappa \, \theta^*}{1 + \lambda \kappa \, \theta^*} \mathrm{d}\kappa$$

$$= \lambda \theta^* \int_{\kappa=1}^{\infty} \frac{1}{\kappa \, (1 + \lambda \kappa \, \theta^*)} \mathrm{d}\kappa, \tag{3.29}$$

where note that, in this case,

$$\langle \kappa \rangle = \int_{\kappa=1}^{\infty} 2\kappa^{-3} \, \kappa \, \mathrm{d}\kappa = 2.$$

By integrating the right-hand side of (3.29), we have[12]

$$\theta^* = \lambda \theta^* \log \left(1 + \frac{1}{\lambda \theta^*} \right),$$

hence we may solve for $\theta^* (> 0)$ and find

$$\theta^* = \frac{1}{\lambda(e^{1/\lambda} - 1)}. \tag{3.30}$$

Now, in order to compute the extent of long-run prevalence

$$\rho^* = \int_{\kappa=1}^{\infty} p(\kappa) \, \rho_\kappa^* \, \mathrm{d}\kappa$$

use (3.19) to write

$$\rho^* = \int_{\kappa=1}^{\infty} p(\kappa) \, \rho_\kappa^* \, \mathrm{d}\kappa = \int_{\kappa=1}^{\infty} 2\kappa^{-3} \frac{\lambda \kappa \, \theta^*}{1 + \lambda \, \kappa \, \theta^*} \mathrm{d}\kappa$$

which, after integration, becomes

$$\rho^* = 2\lambda \theta^* \left[1 - \lambda \theta^* \log \left(1 + \frac{1}{\lambda \theta^*} \right) \right].$$

Then, replacing θ^* in the above expression by its equilibrium value (3.30), we arrive at the following explicit expression for the dependence of ρ^* on λ:

$$\rho^* = \frac{2}{e^{1/\lambda} - 1} \left[1 - \frac{1}{\lambda(e^{1/\lambda} - 1)} \right]. \tag{3.31}$$

This reconfirms that prevalence is indeed positive as long as the spreading rate is not zero. However, it also shows that, for low values of λ just above the zero threshold of infection (i.e. as $\lambda \searrow 0$), we have

$$\rho^* \sim e^{-1/\lambda},$$

---

[12] Simply write $\int_{\kappa=1}^{\infty} \frac{1}{\kappa(1+\lambda\kappa\,\theta^*)} \mathrm{d}\kappa = \int_{1}^{\infty} \frac{A}{\kappa} \mathrm{d}\kappa + \int_{1}^{\infty} \frac{B}{1+\lambda\,\kappa\,\theta^*} \mathrm{d}\kappa$ and, through suitable identification, obtain $A = 1$, $B = -\lambda\theta^*$.

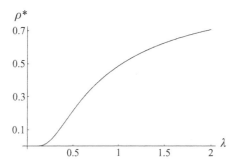

Figure 3.4. The long-run prevalence of infection in a scale-free network with degree distribution (3.28), as given by (3.31)

which reflects a very slow growth in ρ^* – in particular, slower than λ^m for any $m \in \mathbb{N}$ (cf. Figure 3.4).

3.5 DIFFUSION POLICY

Once we have a better grasp of some of the key factors underlying epidemic processes, it is natural to consider the possibility of affecting their evolution. In general, of course, the form of the intervention should depend on the specific forces governing the process (e.g. whether "infection" is reversible or not) and on whether the object of diffusion leads to positive or negative consequences (e.g. whether it concerns, say, some valuable information or a deleterious disease).

Since many of the insights to be gained for the different possible scenarios are quite similar, an exhaustive discussion of all those cases would be largely redundant. In what follows, therefore, we focus on the SIS framework alone and consider the case where the policy objective is to *reduce* (harmful) infection. We consider, specifically, two different sorts of policies: (permanent) immunization and (temporary) cure. The effectiveness of each of them in reducing the prevalence of infection is studied, in turn, in the following subsections. If the underlying framework were different (e.g. irreversible diffusion) or the object of diffusion were valuable (and thus should be promoted rather than hampered), the key insights that will be obtained may be adapted quite readily.

3.5.1 Immunization

First, suppose that it is possible to immunize a random fraction g ($0 < g < 1$) of the whole population, who then becomes permanently protected from infection. If we continue to make the assumption that the underlying network is random with a given degree distribution $p \equiv \{p(\kappa)\}_{\kappa=0}^{\infty}$, how is the epidemic process affected by this intervention? Formally, the only change required from the original SIS model is a replacement of the benchmark spreading rate λ by

$$\tilde{\lambda} = \lambda(1 - g). \tag{3.32}$$

This reflects the fact that only if a node is not immune (an event that has probability $1 - g$) can it be infected by a neighboring infected node. If we then want to determine the induced threshold for long-run prevalence, this results from the following simple adaptation of the former analysis (cf. Pastor-Satorras and Vespignani (2002) [234]).

Let λ_c^g denote the critical spreading rate when the degree of immunization is g, so that $\lambda_c^0 = \lambda_c$ is the critical threshold in the absence of any immunization – a threshold that depends on the topology of the network, as captured by p. In general, one can readily solve λ_c^g from the equation

$$\lambda_c^g(1 - g) = \lambda_c, \tag{3.33}$$

which yields

$$\lambda_c^g = \frac{\lambda_c}{1 - g}. \tag{3.34}$$

If λ_c is positive, then $\lambda_c^g > \lambda_c$, which is merely a reflection of the trivial fact that immunization always works against the long-run prevalence of infection if the latter is at all positive.

Reciprocally, we may ask the question of what is the minimum degree of immunization g^λ required to ensure zero prevalence for any given (immunization-free) spreading rate λ. If $\lambda > \lambda_c$ and λ_c is positive, such a g^λ is obtained from the following counterpart of (3.33):

$$\lambda(1 - g^\lambda) = \lambda_c,$$

which leads to

$$g^\lambda = 1 - \frac{\lambda_c}{\lambda} > 0. \tag{3.35}$$

Of course, if $\lambda \leq \lambda_c$ then $g^\lambda = 0$, since even in the absence of immunization there is zero infection prevalence.

The former considerations indicate that immunization is a useful policy in reducing, or eliminating, long-run prevalence as long as $\lambda_c > 0$. If this is the case, *any* positive immunization rate g narrows down the range in which longrun infection persists by increasing the threshold for positive prevalence (cf. (3.34)), or may even eliminate it altogether if chosen large enough (cf. (3.35)).

As we know (cf. (3.26)), the critical λ_c is positive whenever the underlying degree distribution is such that $\langle \kappa^2 \rangle < +\infty$, i.e. it has a finite variance and thus displays a characteristic degree. This condition is satisfied in some cases (e.g. Poisson networks) but is violated in others – e.g., most prominently, in scale-free networks with a decay exponent $\gamma \leq 3$. In the latter cases, random immunization of the sort contemplated above is *never* successful in eradicating long-run infection. That is, no matter how low the spreading rate λ might be, long-run prevalence occurs under *any* policy short of complete immunization. Or, equivalently expressed, the induced critical value $\tilde{\lambda}_c$ is always zero as long as $g < 1$.

The above discussion suggests that, in random networks with a broad degree distribution (i.e. with diverging second moments), immunization can only have long-run effects on removing infection from the population if it is a *targeted* mechanism, i.e. it discriminates among nodes depending on their connectivity. Intuitively, of course, what such a policy should do is aim at "protecting" those nodes with the highest degree, whose infection potential is also highest. In fact, the essential bottom line here can be stated quite simply. At a minimum, selective immunization must ensure that across all nonimmunized nodes (i.e. all those that can ever get and transmit the infection), the following condition is met (cf. (3.25)):

$$\langle \tilde{\kappa} \rangle / \langle \tilde{\kappa}^2 \rangle > 0,$$

where $\langle \cdot \rangle$ represents the average restricted to those nodes. Only then will the induced epidemics display a *positive* threshold for long-run prevalence.

In general, of course, given the resources available for immunization, the objective should be to minimize $\langle \tilde{\kappa} \rangle / \langle \tilde{\kappa}^2 \rangle$. Consider, for concreteness, the case where the degree distribution is scale-free with a decay exponent $\gamma = 3$. Then, if it is feasible to immunize all those nodes that exceed some given degree κ_0 (possibly very large but finite), we have

$$\langle \tilde{\kappa}^2 \rangle = \tilde{A} \int_1^{\kappa_0} \kappa^{-1} \, d\kappa$$
$$= \tilde{A} \, \log \kappa_0 < +\infty,$$

for a normalization constant $\tilde{A} = 2(1 - \kappa_0^{-2})^{-1}$. This will be enough to fully eradicate infection if the prevailing spreading rate λ satisfies

$$\lambda \leq \langle \tilde{\kappa} \rangle / \langle \tilde{\kappa}^2 \rangle = \frac{(\kappa_0 - 1)/\kappa_0}{\log \kappa_0}. \tag{3.36}$$

Naturally, as λ falls, the fraction of nodes that need to be immunized:

$$2 \int_{\kappa_0}^{\infty} \kappa^{-3} \, d\kappa = \kappa_0^{-2},$$

decreases steeply. Indeed, from (3.36), we find that the lowest degree κ_0 marking the set of nodes affected by the policy increases exponentially in $1/\lambda$.

There is an important insight that transpires from the former analysis. In very broadly distributed networks, the only way of implementing a successful immunization policy is by taking into account the overall features of the network and the degree characteristics of the different nodes. It is necessary, in particular, to gear the efforts toward the more connected nodes, since these play a crucial role in diffusion within such heterogenous networks.

A fair criticism, however, can be raised concerning the real applicability of such targeted policies. They presume a detailed knowledge of the network, which will often be impossible to muster in complex real-world contexts. How, for example, is one to find the most highly connected nodes? The implicit assumption that such detailed information of the network might be available runs against our basic tenet that, indeed, networks in the real world are often too complex to allow "microscopic" description or analysis. We are then led to the following question: Is it still possible to devise effective policies when only imperfect information on the network is available?

One possible approach that does render a positive answer is outlined in Subsection 3.5.2. This approach, however, changes the focus from a policy of (permanent) immunization to a less ambitious one of (temporary) cure. But remaining within the present context of immunization, an indirect and ingenious way of addressing the problem has been proposed by Cohen et al. (2003) [69]. They call it *acquaintance immunization* and, as we explain next, requires no detailed (global) information on the network.

Their procedure starts by independently selecting, fully at random, a certain fraction g of individuals in the whole population. In this sense, the informational demands are identical to those of the random immunization considered at the beginning of this subsection. The key novelty is that, rather than immunizing each of the individuals so selected, the immunization is *redirected* to one of her randomly selected neighbors.

Focusing on a SIR scenario, Cohen et al. (2003) [69] show that, even for scale-free networks with a decay parameter $\gamma \in (2, 3]$, zero prevalence can be ensured for a value of $g < 1$. Indeed, the fraction of actually immunized individuals $\tilde{g}$ – which is in general less than g, due to the possibility of redundancies – is found to be well below $1/4$ for all values of γ within that range. The intuition for this state of affairs should be clear. Immunization through acquaintances introduces a preferential bias in favor of highly connected nodes that, in the end, is analogous to that which could be implemented *directly* through node selection.

In fact, as we shall see in Subsection 6.2.1, these same considerations yield an analogous bias in processes of network formation when new partners are found through network-based search. In that case, "networking through acquaintances" becomes an indirect way of introducing a preferential bias for high-degree nodes. The resulting degree distribution then turns out to be scale-free for reasons essentially the same as in the model proposed by Barabási and Albert (1999) [24], where such a bias is posited directly.

3.5.2   Cure

Immunization, as formulated above, attempts to control infection by operating on the contagion process and blocking it for some particular nodes. Now, we consider the dual procedure that impinges on the process by which nodes "cure" (and, in the SIS framework, become susceptible again). To start analyzing the problem in the simplest possible way, suppose that there is a policy available that improves the healing rate of infected nodes by a factor $\chi > 1$. Under the maintained assumption that the underlying network is large and random (and characterized by a given degree distribution), this merely modifies the mean-field law of motion (3.16) as follows:

$$\dot{\rho}_\kappa(t) = -\delta \chi \rho_\kappa(t) + \nu \, \kappa \, \left[1 - \rho_\kappa(t)\right] \, \theta \left[\{\rho_{\kappa'}(t)\}_{\kappa'=1}^\infty\right] \qquad (\kappa = 0, 1, \dots)$$

so that, applying the usual normalization, we have

$$\dot{\rho}_\kappa(t) = -\rho_\kappa(t) + \frac{1}{\chi} \lambda \, \kappa \, \left[1 - \rho_\kappa(t)\right] \, \theta \left[\{\rho_{\kappa'}(t)\}_{\kappa'=1}^\infty\right] \qquad (\kappa = 0, 1, \dots),$$

where we continue to denote $\lambda \equiv \nu/\delta$. This highlights the obvious fact that a more effective way of curing infected nodes plays a role that is formally equivalent to uniform immunization. That is, it changes the effective spreading rate to

$$\tilde{\lambda} = \frac{1}{\chi} \lambda,$$

an equation that is identical to (3.32) if we identify $(1 - g)$ and $1/\chi$. Therefore, the whole analysis conducted above for the immunization rate g can be suitably reproduced here for the ratio $(\chi - 1)/\chi$. In particular, we arrive at the same conclusion on the ineffectiveness of unbiased diffusion policy when the underlying degree distribution has an unbounded second-order moment. Under these conditions long-run prevalence cannot be forestalled by any (finite) increase in the rate of cure that applies *uniformly* to all nodes.

And what can one do in that case if, as before, we instead allow the mechanism (cure in the present case) to be tailored appropriately to node degree? Of course, if we could be sure to heal "instantaneously" all nodes whose degree is above a suitably low threshold κ_0, the effect would be indistinguishable from immunization of these nodes and long-run prevalence could be averted. But, again, this raises major conceptual problems since, as explained, it seems hardly applicable in real-world networks.

What then if, rather than a perfect selection of high-connectivity nodes, the curing efforts may be directed only imperfectly to them? Dezsö and Barabási (2002) [81] propose a simple model that addresses this possibility. They posit that nodes, effectively, display a different healing rate that increases with their connectivity. The idea here is that, even though healing efforts cannot be concentrated on high-degree nodes alone, these nodes do enjoy a higher probability of being identified (and thus cured). Such a bias may reflect a conscious aim in the design of the policy, which can nevertheless not be sure to "hit" only nodes that exceed a certain connectivity.

Formally, Dezsö and Barabási suppose that any node with degree $\kappa \geq 1$ is cured at the rate $\delta \kappa^\alpha$ where $\alpha \geq 0$ measures the strength of the high-degree bias. If $\alpha = 0$, there is no bias and we are in the uniform case discussed above. Naturally, we are interested in the case where

$$0 < \alpha < +\infty,$$

i.e. high-degree nodes enjoy some preference for cure but not an extreme one.[13]

With this formulation (and the usual normalization), the counterpart of the law of motion (3.16) for nodes with degree $\kappa \geq 1$ can be written as follows:

$$\dot{\rho}_\kappa(t) = -\rho_\kappa(t)\,\kappa^\alpha + \lambda\,\kappa\,\left[1 - \rho_\kappa(t)\right]\,\theta\left[\{\rho_{\kappa'}(t)\}_{\kappa'=1}^\infty\right] \qquad (\kappa = 1, 2, \ldots),$$

$$(3.37)$$

where $\theta(\cdot)$ has the same interpretation as in Section 3.4.2, i.e. the probability that an arbitrary link connects to an infected node (cf. (3.18)). As usual, we are interested in the long-run stationary value

$$\theta^* = \sum_{\kappa=1}^\infty \rho_\kappa^* \, \zeta(\kappa), \qquad (3.38)$$

where recall that $\zeta(\kappa)$ denotes the probability that a *neighboring* node has degree κ and $\{\rho_\kappa^*\}_{\kappa=1}^\infty$ stand for the stationary frequencies of infected nodes of every degree $\kappa \geq 1$. These long-run values are obtained by imposing on (3.37) the conditions of stationarity:

$$\dot{\rho}_\kappa(t) = 0 \qquad (\kappa = 1, 2, \ldots),$$

which lead to

$$\rho_\kappa^* = \frac{\lambda \kappa\,\theta^*}{\kappa^\alpha + \lambda\,\kappa\,\theta^*} \qquad (\kappa = 1, 2, \ldots). \qquad (3.39)$$

The above expression may be compared with its counterpart (3.19), obtained in the benchmark context where no policy whatsoever interferes with the epidemics.

Combining (3.38) and (3.39), we are interested in whether the resulting equation,

$$\sum_{\kappa=1}^\infty \frac{\lambda \theta^*}{\kappa^{\alpha-1} + \lambda\,\theta^*} \, \zeta(\kappa) = \theta^*, \qquad (3.40)$$

has a stable solution $\theta^* > 0$, i.e. one with positive prevalence. To gain the sharpest contrast with previous analysis, let us address this question in our leading scenario where the degree distribution is scale-free with the same decay exponent $\gamma = 3$ arising in the BA model. Furthermore, we shall simplify matters by carrying out the analysis in the continuum version where the degree

---

[13] Heuristically, the limit case $\alpha \to +\infty$ can be understood as one where cure is done "hierarchically," with higher-degree nodes being cured always before those of lower degree. In a sense, therefore, it is just like the policy that is able to accurately target all nodes above a certain degree.

distribution is given by (3.28). Then, the induced distribution $\zeta(\cdot)$ has the form (cf. (3.17))

$$\zeta(\kappa) = \frac{1}{\langle \kappa \rangle} p(\kappa) \kappa = \kappa^{-2},$$

and (3.40) can be rewritten as follows:

$$\int_{\kappa=1}^{\infty} \frac{\lambda \theta^*}{\kappa^2 \left(\kappa^{\alpha-1} + \lambda \, \theta^* \right)} d\kappa = \theta^*.$$

Define

$$\psi_\lambda(\theta) \equiv \int_{\kappa=1}^{\infty} \frac{\lambda \theta}{\kappa^2 \left(\kappa^{\alpha-1} + \lambda \, \theta \right)} d\kappa = \int_{\kappa=1}^{\infty} \frac{\lambda \theta}{\left(\kappa^{\alpha+1} + \lambda \kappa^2 \theta \right)} d\kappa,$$

so that

$$\frac{d\psi_\lambda(\theta)}{d\theta}\bigg|_{\theta=0} = \int_{\kappa=1}^{\infty} \frac{\lambda}{\kappa^{\alpha+1}} d\kappa = \frac{\lambda}{\alpha}.$$

It follows that $\theta^* > 0$ if, and only if, the following counterpart of (3.24) holds:

$$\frac{\lambda}{\alpha} > 1.$$

Thus, in contrast with the benchmark case, we find that positive prevalence obtains in the long run if, and only if, the spreading rate exceeds the critical value $\lambda_c^\alpha \equiv \alpha$.

When $\alpha = 0$ (and therefore there is no curing bias in favor of higher-degree nodes), we recover the conclusion that $\lambda_c^\alpha (= \lambda_c) = 0$ – that is, any spreading rate $\lambda > 0$ leads to positive long-run prevalence. However, when there is some bias, no matter how small, and $\alpha > 0$ the critical rate $\lambda_c^\alpha = \alpha$ becomes positive. In the range where $\lambda \in (0, \alpha]$ no prevalence of infection may persist in the long run. As $\alpha \to \infty$, this range grows unboundedly, a reflection of the fact that, in this case, the bias in favor of high degree nodes is so strong that the spread of infection can be checked even for arbitrarily high spreading rates.

3.6 STRUCTURED NETWORKS

The analysis conducted so far in this chapter has assumed that the diffusion process takes place in a large random network. This implies, in particular, that the topology of node interaction is bound to display little local structure, in the sense that correlations between neighboring nodes (in, say, degrees or linkage with other nodes) is largely absent.[14] Since the presence of such local

---

[14] Recall our discussion at the end of Section 2.3, where we argue that the canonical (configuration) model of random networks induces vanishing correlations between neighboring nodes. This absence of correlation pertains not only to their respective degrees but also has implications on clustering (i.e. the probability that either of them may be linked to a third node is independent of the links of the neighboring node).

structure is a salient empirical feature in many social networks (cf. Section 1.1), it is undoubtedly of interest to explore how our former conclusions on long-run diffusion might be affected by changes in that assumption. We end this chapter by briefly sketching how the recent literature has adapted the benchmark approach used for random networks to address these concerns.

Consider first the case where the network displays *degree correlations* between neighboring nodes. Most simply, suppose that these correlations can be modeled in a "Markovian" fashion, so that the network (still to be conceived as a "uniform" statistical ensemble) can be characterized by the *symmetric* distribution $\{\xi(\kappa, \kappa')\}_{\kappa, \kappa'=1}^{\infty}$ where, for each κ and κ', $\xi(\kappa, \kappa')$ stands for the probability that a randomly selected link connects nodes with degrees κ and κ'. (For notational convenience, let $\xi(0, 0)$ stand for the fraction of isolated nodes.) Given such a distribution, we can define the marginal distribution $\{\zeta(\kappa)\}_{\kappa=1}^{\infty}$ by

$$\zeta(\kappa) = \sum_{\kappa'=1}^{\infty} \xi(\kappa, \kappa') \qquad (\kappa = 1, 2, \dots), \tag{3.41}$$

which, as usual (cf. (2.20)), represents the degree distribution of a neighboring node, i.e. a node encountered at one end of a randomly selected link. Then, since $\zeta(\kappa) \propto p(\kappa)\kappa$, we can readily recover the basic degree distribution $\{p(\kappa)\}_{\kappa=0}^{\infty}$, given the knowledge of $p(0) = \xi(0, 0)$.

From the above specification, one can also obtain the collection of conditional probability distributions

$$\{p(\kappa'|\kappa)\}_{\kappa'=1}^{\infty} \qquad (\kappa = 1, 2, \dots),$$

where, for each κ, $p(\kappa'|\kappa)$ simply denotes the (conditional) probability that a node of degree κ be connected to a node of degree κ'. It has the following form:

$$p(\kappa'|\kappa) = \frac{\xi(\kappa, \kappa')}{\sum_{\kappa''=1}^{\infty} \xi(\kappa, \kappa'')} = \frac{\xi(\kappa, \kappa')}{\zeta(\kappa)}. \tag{3.42}$$

If internode degree correlations are absent, then $\xi(\kappa, \kappa') = \zeta(\kappa)\zeta(\kappa')$ and therefore we have, as we should, that

$$p(\kappa'|\kappa) = \zeta(\kappa').$$

The effect of degree correlation on epidemics has been studied by several authors – e.g. Boguñá and Pastor-Satorras (2002) [34] for the SIS model, and Newman (2002*b*) [214] for the SI(R) setup. We take each of these two contexts in turn.

In the SIS model, when the degrees of neighboring nodes may be correlated, the key modification that needs to be introduced into the mean-field analysis pertains to the probability that a link of a particular node connects to an infected neighbor – i.e. the counterpart of the variable $\theta(\cdot)$ defined in (3.18). Now, it can no longer be specified independently of the degree κ of the node in question. Thus, we have to define the corresponding probabilities

$$\theta_\kappa \left[\{\xi(\kappa', \kappa'')\}_{\kappa',\kappa''=1}^\infty \right] = \sum_{\kappa'=1}^\infty \rho_{\kappa'}(t)\, p(\kappa'|\kappa)$$

and insert them into a modified version of the mean-field law of motion for each $\rho_\kappa(t)$ as follows:

$$\dot\rho_\kappa(t) = -\rho_\kappa(t) + \lambda\,\kappa\,\left[1 - \rho_\kappa(t)\right]\,\theta_\kappa\left[\{\xi(\kappa', \kappa'')\}_{\kappa',\kappa''=1}^\infty\right] \qquad (\kappa = 0, 1, \dots),$$

which is to be contrasted with (3.16) for the scenario without correlations.

Recall that when there are no correlations and the random network is characterized by the degree distribution p alone, long-run prevalence requires (cf. (3.25)) that the effective spreading rate λ satisfies

$$\lambda > \langle \kappa \rangle / \langle \kappa^2 \rangle. \tag{3.43}$$

But note that

$$\sum_{\kappa=1}^\infty \zeta(\kappa)\kappa = \frac{1}{\langle \kappa \rangle} \sum_{\kappa=1}^\infty p(\kappa)\kappa\,\kappa = \frac{\langle \kappa^2 \rangle}{\langle \kappa \rangle}$$

and, therefore, the ratio of second and first moments of the distribution p can be simply conceived as the average degree of a neighboring node. Denote this magnitude by $\breve{z}$. Again, its counterpart in the scenario with degree correlations can no longer be defined independently of the degree of the node in question. Thus, for each possible degree κ, we must consider the corresponding averages:

$$\breve{z}_\kappa \equiv \sum_{\kappa'=1}^\infty p(\kappa'|\kappa)\,\kappa' = \sum_{\kappa'=1}^\infty \frac{\xi(\kappa, \kappa')}{\zeta(\kappa)}\,\kappa' \qquad (\kappa = 0, 1, \dots).$$

By analogy with (3.43), the natural conjecture is that, in a scenario with degree correlations, long-run prevalence should depend on the above magnitudes. Indeed, this has been confirmed by Boguñá and Pastor-Satorras (2002) [34] and applied to random scale-free networks by Boguñá et al. (2003) [35]. The key observation derives from the following "accounting identity":

$$\kappa\,p(\kappa'|\kappa)\,p(\kappa) = \kappa'\,p(\kappa|\kappa')\,p(\kappa') \qquad (\kappa, \kappa' = 1, 2, \dots), \tag{3.44}$$

which simply expresses the obvious requirement that, for every κ and κ', the number of links that connect nodes of degree κ to those of degree κ' must be the same as the other way around. Multiplying each of the expressions in (3.44) by the corresponding κ and adding all of them for every κ and κ', we have

$$\left[\sum_{\kappa=1}^\infty \kappa^2\,p(\kappa)\right]\sum_{\kappa'=1}^\infty p(\kappa'|\kappa) = \langle \kappa^2 \rangle = \sum_{\kappa'=1}^\infty \left\{ \kappa'\,p(\kappa')\left[\sum_{\kappa=1}^\infty \kappa\,p(\kappa|\kappa')\right]\right\}. \tag{3.45}$$

Suppose now that the random network displays a wide enough scale-free distribution, i.e. the induced degree distribution (in a continuum framework) satisfies

$$p(\kappa) = (\gamma - 1)\,\kappa^{-\gamma} \qquad (\kappa = 1, 2, 3, \ldots),$$

for $2 < \gamma \le 3$. Then, since $\langle \kappa^2 \rangle = +\infty$ and $\sum_{\kappa'=1}^{\infty} \kappa'\, p(\kappa')$ is summable, it follows from (3.45) that $\sum_{\kappa=1}^{\infty} \kappa\, p(\kappa|\kappa')$ cannot possibly be uniformly bounded in a set of degrees κ' of full measure. This is the key observation that has been used by Boguñá et al. (2003) [35] to show that, in scale-free networks with $2 < \gamma \le 3$, SIS epidemics lead to the same threshold for long-run prevalence as in the benchmark case. That is, it continues to display a critical $\lambda_c = 0$, and positive long-run prevalence obtains for any $\lambda > 0$ irrespectively of the nature[15] and magnitude of the degree correlations.

The implications of degree correlations can also be studied in the one-directional SI and SIR setups. For example, Newman (2002b) [214] again relies on the generating-function methodology described in Section 2.3 to study some of their important stochastic regularities – in particular, the threshold of divergence for component size, and the fractional size of the giant component above that threshold.

To fix ideas, let us consider the basic SI framework[16] and, adapting previous constructs and notation (cf. Footnote 15 of Chapter 2), denote by $H_1(x\,|\kappa)$ the function generating the probability distribution for the number of nodes that are accessed, directly and indirectly, when a randomly selected link is followed in one direction and at the other end of that link there is a node of degree κ. Then, if we assume that we are at a point where all components are almost surely of finite size (i.e. no giant component exists), familiar considerations allow us to write the following self-consistency conditions for all $\kappa = 1, 2, \ldots$:

$$H_1(x|\kappa) = x \frac{1}{\zeta(\kappa)} \sum_{\kappa'=1}^{\infty} \xi(\kappa, \kappa') \left[H_1(x|\kappa') \right]^{\kappa'-1}, \qquad (3.46)$$

where we use (3.42). Or, letting

$$\hat{H}_1(x|\kappa) \equiv H_1(x|\kappa + 1)$$

be the counterpart generating function for the case when the original node has excess degree κ, it is convenient to rewrite (3.46) as follows:

$$\hat{H}_1(x|\kappa) = x \frac{1}{\hat{\zeta}(\kappa)} \sum_{\kappa'=0}^{\infty} \hat{\xi}(\kappa, \kappa') \left[\hat{H}_1(x|\kappa') \right]^{\kappa'} \qquad (\kappa = 0, 1, 2, \ldots),$$

$$(3.47)$$

---

[15] Note that the same line of argument applies whether the degree correlation is positive (assortative networks) or negative (disassortative networks).

[16] As before (cf. Section 3.3), one may study the epidemics of a SIR scenario by simply reinterpreting the linking probabilities as probabilities of connection *cum* infection (before irreversible cure).

where $\{\hat{\xi}(\kappa, \kappa')\}_{\kappa,\kappa'=0}^{\infty}$ stands for the distribution on excess degree of two nodes connected by a randomly selected link and, as usual, $\hat{\zeta}(\kappa)$ denotes the marginal frequency of neighboring nodes with *excess* degree κ. The interpretation of (3.47) should be clear by now. When following the randomly chosen link, one first encounters a node – this is the interpretation of the factor x that premultiplies its right-hand side. This node displays excess degrees κ' with respective probabilities $\hat{\xi}(\kappa, \kappa')$. For each of these possibilities and *independently* for each of the κ' links, we have a situation analogous to the original one, which again may be characterized by the generating function $\hat{H}_1(x|\kappa')$ (now conditioned on the degree κ' displayed by the encountered node).

In general, it may be difficult to solve for the different functions $\hat{H}_1(x|\kappa)$ from (3.47) but, as explained in Section 2.3, one can always rely on numerical methods to obtain arbitrarily close approximations. Based on these functions, it is then possible to characterize the distribution of component sizes associated to a randomly selected *node* through its generating function $H_0(x)$ given by

$$H_0(x) = x \left\{ p(0) + \sum_{\kappa=1}^{\infty} p(\kappa) \left[\hat{H}_1(x|\kappa - 1) \right]^{\kappa} \right\},$$

which is a direct counterpart of (2.32) for uncorrelated networks, now taking into account that degree correlations require conditioning the generating function $\hat{H}_1(x|\kappa - 1)$ on the excess degree $\kappa - 1$ of the randomly chosen node. Given $H_0(x)$, the induced average component size ϱ is given by

$$\varrho = H_0'(1),$$

which may be computed as follows:

$$H_0'(1) = p(0) + \sum_{\kappa=1}^{\infty} p(\kappa) \left[\hat{H}_1(1|\kappa - 1) \right]^{\kappa}$$

$$+ \sum_{\kappa=1}^{\infty} \kappa \, p(\kappa) \left[\hat{H}_1(1|\kappa - 1) \right]^{\kappa-1} \hat{H}_1'(1|\kappa - 1)$$

$$= 1 + \langle \kappa \rangle \sum_{\kappa=1}^{\infty} \zeta(\kappa) \hat{H}_1'(1|\kappa - 1).$$

Therefore, differentiating (3.47) and solving for $\left[\hat{H}_1'(1|\kappa) \right]_{\kappa=0,1,2,...}$ we readily arrive at the following matrix expression:

$$\rho = 1 + \langle \kappa \rangle \, \hat{\zeta}' \, M^{-1} \, \hat{\zeta}, \tag{3.48}$$

where $\hat{\zeta} = (\hat{\zeta}(\kappa))_{\kappa \geq 0}$ is the vector of excess degree frequencies for a neighboring node and M is the matrix whose elements are of the form

$$m_{\kappa,\kappa'} = \kappa \hat{\xi}(\kappa, \kappa') - \hat{\zeta}(\kappa')\delta_{\kappa,\kappa'} \qquad (\kappa = 0, 1, 2, \ldots),$$

where, as usual, $\delta_{\kappa,\kappa'}$ is the Kronecker delta (i.e. $\delta_{\kappa,\kappa'}$ is equal to 1 if $\kappa = \kappa'$ and 0 otherwise).

In view of (3.48), the point of divergence at which a giant component arises is given by the condition $\det M = 0$, which generalizes the conclusion $(z_2 - z_1 = 0)$ obtained in Section 2.3 for an uncorrelated random network. In turn, the inequality $\det M > 0$ is the counterpart for the requirement (2.23) established by Molloy and Reed (1995) [202] for a random uncorrelated network to "spread indefinitely" from a randomly selected node – that is, for the existence of a component with a significant fractional size.

When such a giant component exists, we can adapt customary arguments as well to compute its fractional size. Let $1 - \hat{w}_\kappa$ denote the probability that a randomly selected link with one of its endnodes displaying excess degree κ does *not* belong to the giant component. This is equivalent to saying that the other endnode of this link, whose degree κ' is distributed according to

$$\hat{p}(\kappa'|\kappa) = \frac{\hat{\xi}(\kappa, \kappa')}{\hat{\zeta}(\kappa)} \qquad (\kappa' = 0, 1, 2, \dots)$$

must not belong to the giant component either. But then, by consistency, none of the remaining κ' links of this other endnode must lead to the giant component, which leads to the following equations:

$$1 - \hat{w}_\kappa = \frac{1}{\hat{\zeta}(\kappa)} \sum_{\kappa'=1}^\infty \hat{\xi}(\kappa, \kappa')\,(1 - \hat{w}_{\kappa'})^{\kappa'} \qquad (\kappa = 0, 1, 2, \dots).$$

(3.49)

These consistency conditions are analogous to (2.34), but now must involve separate probabilities $\hat{w}_{\kappa'}$ for each of the possible degrees κ' of the neighboring nodes. Having obtained $(\hat{w}_\kappa)_{\kappa \geq 0}$ from (3.49), we can then determine the probability w that a randomly selected node belongs to the giant component, which of course is equal to the fractional size of this component. We simply need to note that the probability $1 - w$ that a randomly selected node does not belong to the giant component can be computed as the probability that none of its links connect to the giant component, i.e.

$$1 - w = p(0) + \sum_{\kappa=1}^\infty p(\kappa)\,(1 - \hat{w}_{\kappa-1})^\kappa,$$

where we use the fact that a node of degree κ has an excess degree $\kappa - 1$ and, therefore, the probability that any one of its links does not connect to the giant component is $(1 - \hat{w}_{\kappa-1})$.

Newman (2002*b*) [214] shows how to apply the previous techniques to the study of specific contexts. In particular, he focuses on a parametrized binomial family of degree distributions that can accommodate both the possibility that the degree correlations be assortative or disassortative (i.e. high/low degree nodes tend to be connected to other nodes of the same kind or the opposite). In this context, he explores how such correlations affect the giant-component inception *threshold* as well as its *size* (above the threshold), finding

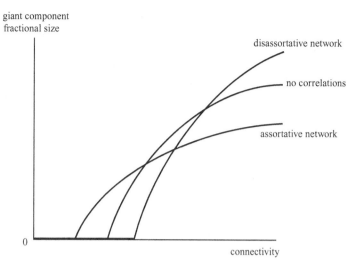

Figure 3.5. The fractional size of the giant component as a function of the connectivity, depending on the nature of the degree correlations. After Newman (2002*b*) [214]

both that the theory and the simulations deliver the following insightful conclusions.

If the network is assortative, then the giant-component threshold is lower than in the uncorrelated case but, once it sets in, its fractional size becomes eventually smaller. By contrast, when the network is disassortative, the giant-component threshold is higher than in the uncorrelated case but, eventually, the size of the giant component becomes larger. These conclusions are quite intuitive. For, if there is positive degree correlation, then the high-degree nodes tend to be "close together" and therefore the chances of triggering a large component are enhanced. However, once a large component starts to arise, the correlation itself that helped its inception must tend to limit its size in comparison with the scenario with no degree correlations. Of course, the intuition for the case with negative correlations is just the opposite: they make it harder for a large component to coalesce but, once enough of a critical mass is in place, it "spreads" faster. This state of affairs is depicted in Figure 3.5.

As explained in Section 2.3, a different mechanism whereby a network may end up displaying interesting local structure is through linkage correlations. These could induce, for example, some positive amount of clustering if they increase the probability that two nodes be linked when they share a common neighbor. Or, alternatively, linkage correlations could produce high cohesiveness if their effect is to introduce a negative bias against the establishment of links between nodes that are, in a certain sense, different.

Newman (2003*c*), (2003*d*) [217, 218] has shown that the generating-function methods introduced above to study degree correlations can be adapted to address these other kinds of internode correlations.[17] We shall not elaborate on this approach in any detail here. It is worth noting, however, that interesting parallelisms arise between the effects of clustering and degree correlations on the long-run behavior of epidemic processes. This transpires quite clearly, for example, in the study of SIR epidemics conducted by Newman (2003*d*) [218] for a certain family of random networks with parametrizable clustering. Basically, his conclusions are as depicted in Figure 3.5, but with the notion of increasing assortativeness replaced by increasing clustering and that of connectivity replaced by some suitable measure of "transmissibility" (which compounds both connectivity and the probabilities of infection and cure in a SIR context). He finds, specifically, that a rise in clustering has the following contradictory effects:

1. it lowers the transmissibility threshold for the inception of a large-scale epidemic (i.e. one involving a significant fraction of nodes);
2. it reduces the fractional size of such epidemic for high enough levels of transmissibility.

The above conclusions reflect essentially the same qualitative considerations displayed in Figure 3.5 for degree correlations, but now pertaining to increased clustering *in lieu* of growing assortativeness.

---

[17] Eguíluz and Klemm (2002) [94] also study the implications of clustering for SIS epidemics within a family of highly clustered and scale-free networks introduced in Klemm and Eguíluz (2002*a*) [177]. Their analysis suggests that, despite the scale-free distribution of connectivities in the underlying network, a positive threshold on the spreading rate is required for infection to take a sizable hold. It is not totally clear, however, whether this behavior should be attributed to high network clustering, to the particular form of disassortative (i.e. negative) correlations introduced by the network formation mechanism, or even to both.

CHAPTER 4

Neighborhood Effects in Diffusion and Play

In social contexts, the diffusion of information and/or behavior often exhibits features that do not match well those of the epidemic models discussed in Chapter 3. This concerns, specifically, the transmission mechanism contemplated by those models, which was assumed to be independent of the local (neighborhood) conditions faced by the agents concerned.

In the epidemic formulation of diffusion, the transmission of infection (or information) to a healthy (or uniformed) agent is tailored to her total exposure, i.e. the absolute number of infected neighbors. But in the spread of many social phenomena – mainly if there is a factor of persuasion or coordination involved – relative considerations tend to be important in understanding whether some new behavior or belief is adopted. Generically, we shall speak of these relative considerations operating on the diffusion process as *neighborhood effects*. They are the object of the present chapter, where we study their implications in a number of different setups.

4.1 NEIGHBORHOOD-DEPENDENT DIFFUSION IN RANDOM NETWORKS

In this starting section, we revisit the epidemic models considered in Chapter 3, now under neighborhood effects. First, in Subsection 4.1.1, the focus is on a SIR-like context where diffusion is irreversible and thus one may naturally conceive of diffusion as occurring through a *wave* of a certain reach. Next, in Subsection 4.1.2, we turn to a setup where diffusion spreads in a way akin to SIS-epidemics, with adoption/infection being only temporary. In this latter case, the concern is the extent of long-run *prevalence*.

To fix ideas, it may be useful to think of the diffusion process as pertaining, for example, to the adoption of a particular technology or the purchase of some commodity. In either of these two cases, the idea that neighborhood effects shape agents' decisions can be simply motivated as follows: when an agent is confronted with the possibility of fresh adoption/purchase, her decision depends on, say, the persuasion efforts exerted on her (for or against) by each of her neighbors in the social network. More formally, those neighborhood effects may be captured through a collection of functions

$$f_\kappa : \{0, 1, 2, \ldots, \kappa\} \to \mathbb{R} \qquad (\kappa = 0, 1, 2, \ldots), \qquad (4.1)$$

where each f_κ applies to all those agents with κ neighbors. The interpretation here is that, for any κ and $r \in \{0, 1, \ldots, \kappa\}$, $f_\kappa(r)$ specifies the "disposition" toward adoption for an agent who has r out of her κ neighbors adopting. Typically, this disposition will be identified with the probability (rate or mass, depending on context) that such an adoption occurs.

One possible specification in this respect is given by functions $\{f_\kappa\}_{\kappa=0}^{\infty}$ that have

$$f_\kappa(r) = \alpha r \qquad (\alpha > 0, \ \kappa = 0, 1, 2, \ldots; \ r = 0, 1, \ldots, \kappa).$$

This reflects a situation where no genuine neighborhood effects (in the sense suggested above) are present – the drive toward adoption only depends on the *total* number of neighboring adopters. In contrast, an alternative specification where such neighborhood effects do operate markedly is given by functions $\{f_\kappa\}_{\kappa=1}^{\infty}$ that satisfy $f_0(0) = 0$ and for each $\kappa = 1, 2, \ldots,$

$$f_\kappa(r) = \vartheta(r/\kappa) \qquad (r = 0, 1, \ldots, \kappa)$$

for some nondecreasing function $\vartheta : [0, 1] \to \mathbb{R}$. A further particularization of this case is obtained when ϑ is a step function. Thus, there is a threshold $\phi \geq 0$ such that

$$\vartheta(r/\kappa) = \begin{cases} 0 & \text{if } r/\kappa < \phi \\ \nu & \text{if } r/\kappa \geq \phi \end{cases}$$

for some $\nu > 0$. In this case, adoption/purchase occurs with positive probability if, and only if, the *fraction* of neighbors who have adopted/purchased is no lower than a given threshold ϕ.

4.1.1   Diffusion Waves under Permanent Adoption

The issue of how diffusion waves (i.e. unidirectional processes of propagation) advance in a large population has been studied by Watts (2002) [285] under the assumption that the underlying social network is a large random network with some given degree distribution $p \equiv \{p(\kappa)\}_{\kappa=0}^{\infty}$. As advanced, the transmission mechanism for adoption (or "infection," if we interpret this term widely) is assumed subject to neighborhood effects. Specifically, it is postulated that, in order for a node to adopt along a diffusion wave, a certain *fraction* of its neighbors must have adopted. This required fraction is labeled the node's *propensity*.

In principle, the propensity of a particular node could be idiosyncratic to it. For simplicity, however, let us suppose that all nodes have their propensity determined *ex-ante* in the *same* stochastic manner. That is, even though they may be heterogenous *ex-post*, each node has its actual propensity determined by the same random variable $\tilde{\phi}$ defined on $[0, 1]$, independently of the identity of the node or any other of its characteristics (e.g. its degree). Of course, the fact that nodes are *ex-ante* symmetric does *not* imply that all of them, independently of their degree, are equally likely to adopt. Indeed, if we denote by $q_\kappa(r)$ the probability that a node with r infected neighbors be infected itself, we have

$$q_\kappa(r) = \Pr\left[\tilde{\phi} \le \frac{r}{\kappa}\right], \tag{4.2}$$

which is obviously decreasing in κ.

Our main concern here is to understand the conditions under which a *global diffusion wave* may occur in large networks, with "a small seed triggering a giant cascade." Or, more precisely, the question is when a relatively small (infinitesimal) subset of original adopters may lead to a large wave that eventually involves a *significant* fraction (positive, generally short of one) of all nodes.

To address the problem formally, it is useful to start from a situation where $\tilde{\phi}$ and $\{p(\kappa)\}_{\kappa=0}^{\infty}$ are such that the diffusion wave only has a local reach, i.e. it spans only an infinitesimal fraction of the whole (infinite) set of nodes. In this case, the diffusion path followed by the process must, almost surely, involve no cycles.[1] Typically, therefore, the process of adoption along this path occurs through the influence of just *one* (adopting) neighbor. This implies that, for any particular node of degree κ that comes to be "hit" by the wave, the relevant requirement for its adoption (and, therefore, for its involvement in the further propagation of the process) is that its propensity be no larger than $\frac{1}{\kappa}$. The probability of this event is

$$q_\kappa \equiv \Pr\left[\tilde{\phi} \le \frac{1}{\kappa}\right], \tag{4.3}$$

which is simply obtained from the particularization of (4.2) to $r = 1$.

Now, the analysis is quite parallel to that undertaken in Section 3.2 pertaining to the problem of *resilient* SI diffusion, with the above q_κ playing the same role as the operating probabilities q_κ in that case – the same notation is used, to stress the parallelism. We may also define generating functions $F_0, F_1, \hat{F}_1$ and $H_0, H_1, \hat{H}_1$, with an interpretation that is also analogous to that of their former counterparts in the study of resilient diffusion. Thus, in particular, the average size of diffusion waves is given by $H_0'(1)$, where

$$H_0'(1) = F_0'(1) + \frac{F_0'(1)\hat{F}_1(1)}{1 - \hat{F}_1'(1)}, \tag{4.4}$$

so that the "giant-cascade threshold" at which a global diffusion wave arises is defined by the condition

$$1 - \hat{F}_1'(1) = 0, \tag{4.5}$$

---

[1] Recall that an analogous point was used in Section 2.3 when studying the rise of a giant component in a large random network.

which leads to the divergence of $H_0'(1)$. As in (3.2) we have that

$$\hat{F}_1(x) = \sum_{\kappa=1}^{\infty} \zeta(\kappa) \, q_\kappa \, x^{\kappa-1} = \frac{1}{\langle \kappa \rangle} \sum_{\kappa=0}^{\infty} \kappa \, p(\kappa) \, q_\kappa \, x^{\kappa-1},$$

and therefore

$$\hat{F}_1'(x) = \frac{1}{\langle \kappa \rangle} \sum_{\kappa=0}^{\infty} \kappa(\kappa - 1) p(\kappa) \, q_\kappa \, x^{\kappa-2},$$

which allows one to rewrite (4.5) as follows:

$$\sum_{\kappa=0}^{\infty} \kappa(\kappa - 1) p(\kappa) \, q_\kappa = \langle \kappa \rangle . \tag{4.6}$$

The previous condition implicitly defines the *critical points* at which diffusion waves display a qualitative transition between zero and positive fractional size. The latter occurs when $\sum_{\kappa=0}^{\infty} \kappa(\kappa - 1) p(\kappa) \, q_\kappa > \langle \kappa \rangle$ or, equivalently, $\hat{F}_1'(1) > 1$. In general, of course, the solution of (4.6) depends on the the details of the underlying random network. To fix ideas, let us consider two paradigmatic cases (recall Subsection 2.1.3):

1. The *Poisson (or Erdös-Renyi) random network* whose degree distribution

   $$p_z^{ER}(\kappa) = \frac{e^{-z} z^{\kappa}}{\kappa!} \qquad (\kappa = 0, 1, 2, \ldots) \tag{4.7}$$

   is parametrized by the average degree $z > 0$.

2. The *scale-free random network* whose degree distribution

   $$p_\gamma^{SF}(\kappa) = \frac{1}{\mathcal{R}(\gamma)} \, \kappa^{-\gamma} \qquad (\kappa = 1, 2, 3, \ldots) \tag{4.8}$$

   is parametrized by the decay parameter $\gamma > 1$. In fact, we shall assume that $\gamma > 2$, so that the distribution induces a well-defined average degree.

The other factor that impinges on the solution of (4.6) is the distribution of the random variable $\tilde{\phi}$ that governs node propensities. In this respect, it is convenient to simplify matters and suppose that the node propensity is deterministic (as well as common to all nodes). That is, let us posit that there is some given $\phi_0 > 0$ such that $\Pr[\tilde{\phi} = \phi_0] = 1$. Then, from (4.3), we simply have that

$$q_\kappa = \begin{cases} 1 & \text{if } \frac{1}{\kappa} \geq \phi_0 \\ 0 & \text{otherwise.} \end{cases}$$

Alternatively, we may express matters equivalently by saying that

$$q_\kappa = 1 \Leftrightarrow \kappa \leq \kappa_0, \tag{4.9}$$

where, using standard notation, we make

$$\kappa_0 \equiv \left\lfloor \frac{1}{\phi_0} \right\rfloor,$$

i.e. κ_0 is the highest integer no larger than $\frac{1}{\phi_0}$. It is, therefore, the maximum degree a node can have and still adopt in the presence of a *single* adopting neighbor.

Consider first the case of a Poisson (Erdös-Rényi) random network and, in view of (4.6), define the function $\Upsilon^{ER}(z)$ as follows:

$$\Upsilon^{ER}(z) = \left[\sum_{\kappa=0}^{\infty} \kappa(\kappa - 1) p_z^{ER}(\kappa) q_\kappa \right] - z$$

$$= \left[\sum_{\kappa=2}^{\infty} \frac{e^{-z} z^\kappa}{(\kappa - 2)!} q_\kappa \right] - z.$$

Notice that the critical average degree z_c^{ER} which marks the appearance of a giant cascade corresponds to a zero of Υ^{ER}, i.e. has $\Upsilon^{ER}(z_c^{ER}) = 0$. Also note that if we introduce the simplifying assumption on node propensity given by (4.9), we can redefine the function Υ^{ER} as follows:

$$\Upsilon^{ER}(z) = \left[\sum_{\kappa=2}^{\kappa_0} \frac{e^{-z} z^\kappa}{(\kappa - 2)!} \right] - z.$$

As we increase the key parameter κ_0, the function Υ^{ER} behaves as depicted in Figures 4.1–4.4.

Figures 4.1–4.4 provide a quite sharp understanding of the conditions under which either local or global diffusion arise. First, they show that in order for a giant cascade to occur, κ_0 must be large enough – in particular, one must have that $\kappa_0 \geq 4$, so that a node with no more than four neighbors is sure to adopt even if it has just a single adopting neighbor. This simply reflects the intuitive idea that for widespread diffusion to occur there must be a sufficiently high frequency of nodes that are certain to propagate adoption. Or, in other words, it cannot happen that such marked "susceptibility" to adoption is restricted to only very low-degree nodes.

Second, we also observe from Figures 4.2–4.4 that, when the former condition is met (i.e. $\kappa_0 \geq 4$), there are two different transitions associated to a corresponding pair of critical thresholds, $\check{z}_c(\kappa_0)$ and $\hat{z}_c(\kappa_0)$, with $\check{z}_c(\kappa_0) \leq \hat{z}_c(\kappa_0)$. The lower threshold $\check{z}_c(\kappa_0)$ defines the critical point at which, as the average connectivity grows toward it (i.e. $z \nearrow \check{z}_c(\kappa_0)$), a giant cascade arises. Naturally, we find that $\check{z}_c(\kappa_0) > 1$ since, as explained in Section 2.2, a giant component (which has to be the backbone of such a cascade) only exists if the average degree is at least 1. In fact, the existence of such a giant component is not quite enough, but a "mild premium" of connectivity is needed to account for the possibility that a wave is prematurely stopped at high-degree nodes. However, since these high-degree nodes are very infrequent if z is close to 1, it turns out that the entailed premium $\check{z}_c(\kappa_0) - 1$ is always quite small.

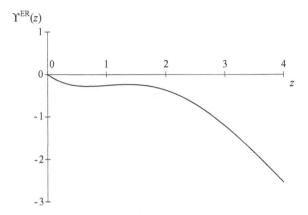

Figure 4.1. The function $\Upsilon^{ER}(z)$ for a Poisson random network with $\kappa_0 = 3$

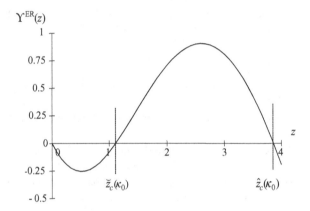

Figure 4.2. The function $\Upsilon^{ER}(z)$ for a Poisson random network with $\kappa_0 = 4$

But Figures 4.2–4.4 also show that the necessary condition $z \geq \check{z}_c(\kappa_0)$ is far from sufficient. Indeed, it is not so because global diffusion also requires that the network *not* be too highly connected. This is reflected by the existence of the second threshold $\hat{z}_c(\kappa_0)$ where a further transition occurs, now in the opposite direction. That is, if $z > \hat{z}_c(\kappa_0)$, the induced cascades become finite again. Their average size is given by the function in (4.4), that returns to well-defined in this range. The intuition here should be clear in view of previous discussion. If the network is densely connected, the frequency of high-degree nodes is so large that diffusion paths can hardly eschew them. When these nodes are encountered, diffusion typically stops there since it is unlikely that a high enough fraction of their (many) neighbors eventually adopts.

Thus, global diffusion requires that the average degree of the network lies in the intermediate range given by the interval $[\check{z}_c(\kappa_0), \hat{z}_c(\kappa_0)]$. This range, of course, depends on the adoption propensity of nodes, as captured by κ_0.

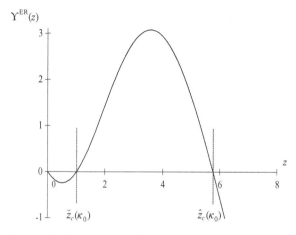

Figure 4.3. The function $\Upsilon^{ER}(z)$ for a Poisson random network with $\kappa_0 = 5$

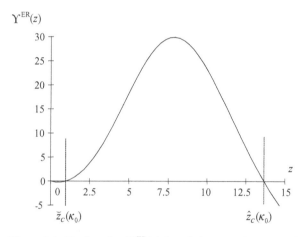

Figure 4.4. The function $\Upsilon^{ER}(z)$ for a Poisson random network with $\kappa_0 = 10$

Specifically, the more prone to adoption they are (i.e. the larger κ_0), the wider is that range. As it turns out, these and other similar predictions of the model are confirmed numerically by Watts (2002) [285], who conducts extensive simulations for Poisson random networks with a fixed common propensity.

Next, we further illustrate matters by undertaking a similar analysis for the case of scale-free networks. To do so, let us first define the function $\Psi^{SF}(\gamma)$ given by

$$\Psi^{SF}(\gamma) = \sum_{\kappa=1}^{\infty} \kappa(\kappa - 1) p_\gamma^{SF}(\kappa) \, q_\kappa - z, \tag{4.10}$$

where recall that $\gamma > 2$ is the decay parameter characterizing the corresponding scale-free degree distribution and, as usual, $z \equiv \langle \kappa \rangle$ denotes the average degree.

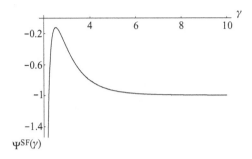

Figure 4.5. The function $\Psi^{SF}(\gamma)$ for a scale-free random network with $\kappa_0 = 8$

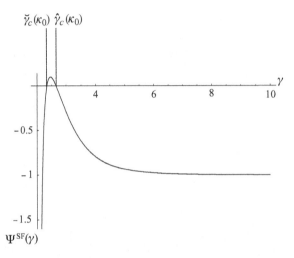

Figure 4.6. The function $\Psi^{SF}(\gamma)$ for a scale-free random network with $\kappa_0 = 9$

This function is the counterpart of the former $\Upsilon^{ER}(z)$ used in our analysis of Poisson networks, its zeros being the critical points satisfying (4.6). Now, in view of (4.8) and noting that the average degree is simply

$$z = \frac{\mathcal{R}(\gamma - 1)}{\mathcal{R}(\gamma)}, \tag{4.11}$$

we may rewrite (4.10) as follows:

$$\Psi^{SF}(\gamma) = \frac{1}{\mathcal{R}(\gamma)} \left[\sum_{\kappa=1}^{\infty} (\kappa - 1)\, \kappa^{-\gamma+1}\, q_\kappa - \mathcal{R}(\gamma - 1) \right],$$

which is an explicit function of γ alone. Then, under the maintained assumption that the adoption probabilities q_κ satisfy (4.9), we obtain

$$\Psi^{SF}(\gamma) = \frac{1}{\mathcal{R}(\gamma)} \left[\sum_{\kappa=1}^{\kappa_0} (\kappa - 1)\, \kappa^{-\gamma+1} - \mathcal{R}(\gamma - 1) \right].$$

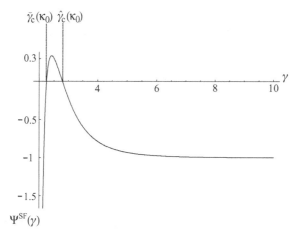

Figure 4.7. The function $\Psi^{SF}(\gamma)$ for a scale-free random network with $\kappa_0 = 10$

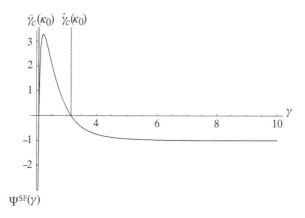

Figure 4.8. The function $\Psi^{SF}(\gamma)$ for a scale-free random network with $\kappa_0 = 20$

As before, we want to understand the behavior of Ψ^{SF} for different values of κ_0. This behavior is summarized in Figures 4.5–4.8.

We again find that, if κ_0 is large enough (specifically, $\kappa_0 \geq 9$), there are two transitions. These are associated to two corresponding thresholds $\check{\gamma}_c(\kappa_0)$ and $\hat{\gamma}_c(\kappa_0)$, for each value of κ_0. Notice that γ and z (the average degree given by (4.11)) move in opposite directions. Thus, as $\gamma \downarrow 2$ the average degree z grows unboundedly, while if $\gamma \to \infty$ then $z \downarrow 1$. The range $[\check{\gamma}_c(\kappa_0), \hat{\gamma}_c(\kappa_0)]$ where the dynamics induces giant cascades of diffusion also widens with κ_0, just as in the case of Poisson networks considered before. For example, one readily finds that as $\kappa_0 \to \infty$ the lower threshold $\check{\gamma}_c(\kappa_0) \downarrow 2$ and, therefore, the induced threshold $\mathcal{R}(\check{\gamma}_c(\kappa_0) - 1)/\mathcal{R}(\check{\gamma}_c(\kappa_0))$ that marks the maximum network connectivity consistent with global diffusion rises unboundedly.

Proceeding along the lines discussed in Section 3.2, it should be clear how one may also obtain for either of the scenarios considered (Poisson or scale-free networks) precise quantitative assessments concerning the *size* of diffusion cascades. To avoid repetitiveness, we dispense with a detailed account of these matters here. In fact, this exercise could be applied not only to the fractional size of a *giant* cascade when one exists, but also to the average size of *finite* cascades when global diffusion does not materialize (i.e. when the network parameters are not within the required range). Finally, note that it is also straightforward to extend the model to account for the possibility that nodes might be subject to some independent probability of "failure" (in which case they do not transmit/acquire the infection/information/behavior). To tackle this possibility, the approach would again be parallel to that undertaken in Section 3.2. Specifically, it would simply amount to reinterpreting the probabilities q_κ in (4.3) as embodying both considerations of propensity *per se* as well as the possibility of malfunctioning. The latter, in principle, could also depend on node degree, a possibility that is perfectly accomodated by the general framework.

4.1.2   Long-Run Prevalence under Temporary Adoption

Now we turn to a context where adoption still is subject to neighborhood effects but it is of a temporary nature. Thus, for example, if we think of the adoption decision as one involving the purchase of a certain good, a natural motivation is that the good in question is not indefinitely durable but, say, it breaks down or becomes obsolete at a certain rate. Then, under the assumption that this rate is exogenously determined, the process can be conceived as a SIS-like epidemics where, unlike what was posited in Section 3.4, the transmission mechanism may depend on relative neighborhood considerations.

A model of this sort has been recently studied by López-Pintado (2004) [192]. Time is modeled continuously, with the state of the system prevailing at any given time $t \geq 0$ consisting of a partition of the set of agents, N, into two classes: the *adopters* $A(t)$ and the *susceptible agents* $S(t)$. The former are those who adopted sometime in the past and are still "active" at t. The latter, on the other hand, are those who, even if they were adopters at some earlier time, enjoy no longer an active status and therefore are susceptible of adopting afresh if exposed to sufficiently strong local stimuli.

The architecture of social interaction that channels those local stimuli is represented by a random network with given degree distribution $p \equiv \{p(\kappa)\}_{\kappa=0}^{\infty}$. For any given agent/node that is in a susceptible state at some t, the rate at which it is taken to adopt depends on the current number r of adopting neighbors it has. Specifically, let us suppose that if the node in question has degree κ ($\kappa = 1, 2, \ldots$) its adoption rate is $f_\kappa(r)$, where each function $f_\kappa(\cdot)$ is as specified in (4.1). On the other hand, we make the assumption that an adopter (of any degree) reverts to a susceptible state at an exogenous uniform rate $\delta > 0$.

In line with the standard approach of continuous-time epidemic models, let us postulate that each $f_\kappa(\cdot)$ is a continuous and nondecreasing function satisfying

$f_\kappa(0) = 0$. That is, the adoption rate changes gradually with the number of adopting neighbors, cannot decrease as this number increases, and is zero if no such neighbors exist. It is also assumed that these functions are (weakly) concave so that, for each κ and r with $1 \le r \le \kappa - 1$, we have

$$f_\kappa(r) - f_\kappa(r-1) \ge f_\kappa(r+1) - f_\kappa(r). \tag{4.12}$$

This assumption is consistent, for example, with the epidemic framework studied by Pastor-Satorras and Vespignani (2001) [233] and discussed in Subsection 3.4.2 where, for all κ, $r = 0, 1, 2, \ldots (r \le \kappa)$,

$$f_\kappa(r) = r. \tag{4.13}$$

It rules out, however, contexts where the stimuli to adoption display "increasing returns" (as would be the case if the functions $f_\kappa(\cdot)$ were strictly convex). In this case, the model could generate multiple long-run behavior, in contrast with the long-run uniqueness shown below under (4.12) – see López-Pintado (2004) [192] for some examples.

As we did in Section 3.4 for the received SIS epidemics, we pursue here a mean-field analysis of the model. Under the "homogenous-mixing hypothesis" implicitly underlying this approach, a sufficient description of the system consists of the collection $\{\rho_\kappa(t)\}_{\kappa=0}^\infty$ specifying the frequency of nodes of each degree that are adopters at any given t. Then, in close analogy to (3.16), the law of motion of the system may be written as follows:

$$\dot{\rho}_\kappa(t) = -\delta\rho_\kappa(t) + \left[1 - \rho_\kappa(t)\right] \sum_{r=0}^{\kappa} \binom{\kappa}{r} [\theta(t)]^r \ [1 - \theta(t)]^{\kappa-r} \ f_\kappa(r)$$

$$(\kappa = 0, 1, 2, \ldots), \tag{4.14}$$

where we use the notational shorthand

$$\theta(t) \equiv \theta\left[\{\rho_{\kappa'}(t)\}_{\kappa'=0}^\infty\right]$$

to denote the probability that a randomly selected link points to an adopting node at t. For an easier comparison with (3.16), it is useful to divide through (4.14) by δ and, rescaling time, write

$$\dot{\rho}_\kappa(t) = -\rho_\kappa(t) + \lambda\left[1 - \rho_\kappa(t)\right] \sum_{r=0}^{\kappa} \binom{\kappa}{r} [\theta(t)]^r \ [1 - \theta(t)]^{\kappa-r} \ f_\kappa(r)$$

$$(\kappa = 0, 1, 2, \ldots), \tag{4.15}$$

where $\lambda \equiv 1/\delta$ may then be conceived as a benchmark adoption rate.

As usual, our first concern is to determine the stationary points of the dynamics $\{\rho_\kappa^*\}_{\kappa=0}^\infty$, obtained from (4.15) by setting $\dot{\rho}_\kappa(t) = 0$ for all κ. They are readily computed to be

$$\rho_\kappa^* = \frac{\lambda g_\kappa(\theta^*)}{1 + \lambda g_\kappa(\theta^*)} \qquad (\kappa = 0, 1, 2, \ldots), \tag{4.16}$$

where we use the following simplifying notation:

$$g_\kappa(\theta) \equiv \sum_{r=0}^{\kappa} \binom{\kappa}{r} \theta^r (1-\theta)^{\kappa-r} f_\kappa(r), \qquad (4.17)$$

and

$$\theta^* = \sum_{\kappa=1}^{\infty} \rho_\kappa^* \zeta(\kappa) \qquad (4.18)$$

is the induced stationary value for the probability that any link points to an adopting node. As explained in Subsection 3.4.2 (cf. (3.18)), the computation of θ^* in (4.18) relies on the degree distribution of neighboring nodes $[\zeta(\kappa)]_{\kappa=0}^{\infty}$, as given by (3.17). This simply reflects the fact that only such nodes can be reached by following a randomly selected link.

To solve for the stationary $\{\rho_\kappa^*\}_{\kappa=0}^{\infty}$, we start by combining (4.16) and (4.18) to obtain

$$\theta^* = \sum_{\kappa=1}^{\infty} \frac{\lambda g_\kappa(\theta^*)}{1 + \lambda g_\kappa(\theta^*)} \zeta(\kappa).$$

Under the maintained assumption of concavity of every $f_\kappa(\cdot)$, the function $\phi_\lambda(\theta)$, given by

$$\phi_\lambda(\theta) = \sum_{\kappa=1}^{\infty} \frac{\lambda g_\kappa(\theta)}{1 + \lambda g_\kappa(\theta)} \zeta(\kappa),$$

is concave. To see this, note that its first derivative is

$$\frac{d\phi_\lambda(\theta)}{d\theta} \equiv \phi_\lambda'(\theta) = \sum_{\kappa=1}^{\infty} \frac{\lambda g_\kappa'(\theta)}{(1 + \lambda g_\kappa(\theta))^2} \zeta(\kappa),$$

and derivating again we have

$$\phi_\lambda''(\theta) = \sum_{\kappa=1}^{\infty} \frac{\lambda g_\kappa''(\theta)(1 + \lambda g_\kappa(\theta)) - 2\left(\lambda g_\kappa'(\theta)\right)^2}{(1 + \lambda g_\kappa(\theta))^3} \zeta(\kappa).$$

Thus, in order to reach the desired conclusion, it is enough to show that, for each κ,

$$g_\kappa''(\theta) < 0. \qquad (4.19)$$

First, we compute

$$g'_\kappa(\theta) = \sum_{r=0}^{\kappa} \binom{\kappa}{r} f_\kappa(r) \left[r\theta^{r-1}(1-\theta)^{\kappa-r} - \theta^r(\kappa-r)(1-\theta)^{\kappa-r-1} \right]$$

$$= \sum_{r=0}^{\kappa-1} \left[\binom{\kappa}{r+1}(r+1)f_\kappa(r+1) - \binom{\kappa}{r}(\kappa-r)f_\kappa(r) \right] \theta^r (1-\theta)^{\kappa-r-1}$$

$$= \sum_{r=0}^{\kappa-1} \frac{\kappa!}{r!(\kappa-r-1)!} [f_\kappa(r+1) - f_\kappa(r)] \theta^r (1-\theta)^{\kappa-r-1}, \qquad (4.20)$$

where, in the last equality, we use the following identity:

$$\binom{\kappa}{r}(\kappa-r) \equiv \binom{\kappa}{r+1}(r+1).$$

Then, derivating again, we find

$$g''_\kappa(\theta) = \sum_{r=0}^{\kappa-1} \frac{\kappa!}{r!(\kappa-r-1)!} [f_\kappa(r+1) - f_\kappa(r)] \left[\begin{array}{c} r\theta^{r-1}(1-\theta)^{\kappa-r-1} \\ -(\kappa-r-1)\theta^r(1-\theta)^{\kappa-r-2} \end{array} \right]$$

$$= \sum_{r=0}^{\kappa-2} \left\{ \begin{array}{c} \frac{\kappa!(r+1)}{(r+1)!(\kappa-r-2)!} [f_\kappa(r+2) - f_\kappa(r+1)] \\ -\frac{\kappa!(\kappa-r-1)}{r!(\kappa-r-1)!} [f_\kappa(r+1) - f_\kappa(r)] \end{array} \right\} \theta^r (1-\theta)^{\kappa-r-2}$$

$$= -\sum_{r=0}^{\kappa-2} \left\{ \begin{array}{c} [f_\kappa(r+1) - f_\kappa(r)] \\ -[f_\kappa(r+2) - f_\kappa(r+1)] \end{array} \right\} \frac{\kappa!}{r!(\kappa-r-2)!} \theta^r (1-\theta)^{\kappa-r-2}.$$

Therefore, in view of (4.12), we indeed confirm that $g''_\kappa(\theta) < 0$ for all θ and κ, as desired.

Having thus proven that the function $\phi_\lambda(\theta)$ is concave, it follows from an argument already used in Section 3.4.2 that the necessary and sufficient condition for positive long-run adoption (i.e. for the persistence of a long-run share of adopting nodes) is simply

$$\phi'_\lambda(\theta)\big|_{\theta=0} = \sum_{\kappa=1}^{\infty} \frac{\lambda g'_\kappa(\theta)}{(1+\lambda g_\kappa(\theta))^2} \zeta(\kappa) \bigg|_{\theta=0} > 1. \qquad (4.21)$$

From (4.17) and (4.20), we respectively obtain $g_\kappa(0) = 0$ and

$$g'_\kappa(0) = \kappa \, f_\kappa(1).$$

Therefore, (4.21) can be rewritten as

$$\sum_{\kappa=1}^{\infty} \lambda\kappa f_\kappa(1) \zeta(\kappa) > 1$$

or

$$\lambda > \frac{\langle\kappa\rangle}{\sum_{\kappa=0}^{\infty} \kappa^2 f_\kappa(1) p(\kappa)} \equiv \lambda_c, \qquad (4.22)$$

where we use (3.17), with $p(\cdot)$ being the degree distribution of the underlying (generalized) random network and $\langle \kappa \rangle$ the induced average degree.

As a useful benchmark, we start the analysis by considering a scenario *without* neighborhood effects. Thus, let us first posit that there is some function $h(\cdot)$ such that $f_\kappa(r) = h(r)$ for every κ, i.e. the adoption rate is independent of neighborhood size. This leads to a critical threshold for the adoption rate given by

$$\lambda_c = \frac{\langle \kappa \rangle}{h(1) \sum_{\kappa=0}^{\infty} \kappa^2 \, p(\kappa)} = \frac{1}{h(1)} \frac{\langle \kappa \rangle}{\langle \kappa^2 \rangle}, \qquad (4.23)$$

where we naturally assume that $h(1) > 0$. If $h(r)$ is linear and normalized to satisfy (4.13), then $h(1) = 1$ and we recover the result due to Pastor-Satorras and Vespignani (2001) [233] discussed in Section 3.4.2. That is, long-run adoption prevails if, and only if, the adoption rate λ exceeds the ratio of first- and second-order moments of the degree distribution. As it will be recalled, this implies that in scale-free networks (where $\langle \kappa \rangle / \langle \kappa^2 \rangle = 0$) we have $\lambda_c = 0$ and, therefore, positive long-run adoption is assured as long as the adoption rate $\lambda > 0$. Indeed, (4.23) implies that this same conclusion extends to any context where adoption is free from neighborhood effects, in the sense indicated above.

In contrast, consider now the case where neighborhood effects *do* impinge on the adoption rate of agents. To fix ideas, a natural possibility is to posit that the adoption rate is equal to (or linear in) the fraction r/κ of adopting neighbors. Then, introducing this formulation into (4.22), the following striking implication results:

$$\lambda_c = \frac{\langle \kappa \rangle}{\sum_{\kappa=0}^{\infty} \kappa^2 \frac{1}{\kappa} \, p(\kappa)} = \frac{\langle \kappa \rangle}{\langle \kappa \rangle} = 1,$$

i.e. the critical threshold is equal to unity (in general, a constant), independently of what might be the underlying degree distribution of the network (scale-free, regular, Poisson, etc.). We find, therefore, that (linear) neighborhood effects render the issue of positive long-run adoption independent of network characteristics! This implies, in particular, that considerations that have proven crucial in the absence of neighborhood effects (e.g. the broadness of the degree distribution) appear to be totally irrelevant in the present case. In fact, this interesting theoretical insight finds good support in the numerical simulations conducted by López-Pintado (2004) [192] in a suitable discrete-time version of the model.

Heuristically, the intuition for such an "irrelevance result" hinges upon the struggle between two opposing forces. On one hand, when a degree distribution becomes broader, diffusion tends to be enhanced by the larger frequency of high-degree hubs, which act as prominent propagators. (This, in essence, is the intuition underlying the positive-prevalence result obtained for scale-free networks in the absence of neighborhood effects.) But, if neighborhood effects are present, high-degree nodes also find it harder to adopt (they require more adopting neighbors), which tends to offset their importance in the diffusion process. As it turns out, when the adoption rate is exactly linear in the fraction of adopting neighbors both forces precisely balance, yielding the aforementioned conclusion of network independence.

4.2 STRUCTURED NETWORKS: THE ROLE OF COHESIVENESS

So far in this chapter, our discussion of neighborhood effects in the phenomenon of diffusion has concentrated on scenarios where the pattern of social interaction is governed by a random network. This is certainly a good first step in the discussion of the problem but cannot be always judged satisfactory. For it abstracts from what, by the very nature of neighborhood effects, should play a key role in the analysis, namely, network structure.

Network structure often manifests itself in a variety of different correlations, e.g. degree correlations or clustering (linkage correlations), whose implications have been amply discussed in preceding chapters. Here, we turn to another structural feature of networks that should have an important bearing on diffusion: *cohesiveness* (recall Subsection 2.1.3). Specifically, we base our discussion on the elegant approach pursued by Morris (2000) [207], who casts the adoption decision of agents as one of optimal coordination with the choices made by their neighbors. Our emphasis here is on understanding the process as a *diffusion wave*, much like the problem was formulated in Subsection 4.1.1. The adoption decision of agents is, therefore, taken to be irreversible and the process unidirectional. In Section 4.3, we shall extend the analysis to the case where decisions are reversible (as well as noisy) and thus agents play a genuine coordination game in a flexible (and stochastic) setup.[2]

Let players be arranged along a given social network $\Gamma = (N, L)$, where we maintain the usual interpretation that its nodes are agents who interact locally with their immediate neighbors. Initially, all agents adopt the same choice (or action), which is labeled -1. Another choice then becomes possible, labeled $+1$. Let us suppose that the payoffs of an agent $i \in N$ when she interacts with another player $j \in \mathcal{N}^i$ is given (as a function of their respective choices) by the following table:

i \ j	$+1$	-1
$+1$	$1 + h$	$-1 + h$
-1	$-1 - h$	$1 - h$

$$(4.24)$$

---

[2] In fact, Morris (2000) [207] does contemplate the possibility that agents' choice be reversible. That is, his model allows agents to revert to their original choice if this becomes optimal later on. However, none of the essential insights gained from the model hinges upon this issue. Hence we prefer to postpone its consideration to Section 4.3, where choice reversibility, as well as the presence of noise, does indeed play a key role in the analysis.

where $h \in (-1, 1)$ is a key parameter of the model that, if different from zero, introduces a payoff bias in favor of one of the two actions.[3] An important assumption of the model is that each player i must display the *same* choice, -1 or $+1$, when interacting with *each* of her neighbors $j \in \mathcal{N}^i$. In this sense, therefore, one may view that choice as an (endogenously varying) attribute of the node/player in question, rather than of its links/interactions.

Given the incentives toward coordination entailed by the payoffs displayed in (4.24), it is clear that no player will ever want to switch actions (i.e. abandon action -1) unless someone else does so. In this light, the "diffusion question" is posed as follows. Suppose that a *small* part of the population (the "leaders") turn, for unmodeled reasons, to espousing action $+1$. When will this action spread to the rest of the population (or at least a significant part of it)?

The essential postulate here is that, after leaders' original moves, no agent will subsequently change to $+1$ unless she finds it profitable, given the choice profile exhibited by her neighbors. Formally, let $\mathbf{s}(t) = (s^1(t), s^2(t), \ldots, s^n(t)) \in \{-1, +1\}^n$ specify the action profile prevailing at some time t. Then, in view of (4.24), a switch to action $+1$ by any given agent i at the ensuing period $t + 1$ is to be judged profitable (i.e. a "myopic" best response) if

$$(1 + h) \left| \left\{ j \in \mathcal{N}^i : s^j(t) = +1 \right\} \right| + (-1 + h) \left| \left\{ j \in \mathcal{N}^i : s^j(t) = -1 \right\} \right|$$
$$> (-1 - h) \left| \left\{ j \in \mathcal{N}^i : s^j(t) = +1 \right\} \right| + (1 - h) \left| \left\{ j \in \mathcal{N}^i : s^j(t) = -1 \right\} \right|.$$

Thus, after some rearranging of terms, the relevant condition becomes

$$\frac{1}{z^i} \left| \left\{ j \in \mathcal{N}^i : s^j(t) = +1 \right\} \right| > \frac{1 - h}{2}, \tag{4.25}$$

which simply indicates that the *fraction* of individuals choosing $+1$ in i's neighborhood must exceed[4] the threshold $q \equiv \frac{1-h}{2}$. Diffusion, therefore, is modeled as an inherently frequency-dependent process where neighborhood effects are indeed paramount.

The threshold q is lower or higher than an "even split" of $1/2$ depending on whether action $+1$ enjoys, respectively, a positive bias ($h > 0$) or a negative one ($h < 0$). Naturally, the process of diffusion (in particular, the issue of whether it will span a wide range or not) is dependent on the value of q. But, on the other hand, it is clear that the reach of diffusion must also crucially hinge upon the architecture of the social network. Indeed, as advanced, a key feature of the network architecture that will turn out to have an important bearing on the problem is cohesiveness (cf. (2.11)). Recall that, roughly, a certain subset of nodes is said to be highly cohesive if all of them have "most" of their links

---

[3] Morris (2000) [207] parametrizes the payoff bias in a somewhat different way, i.e. through the coordination payoff earned by each of the two actions. The present formulation does not alter the nature of the results but is more in line with the framework subsequently used to discuss coordination setups in Section 4.3.

[4] For concreteness, a *strict* gain is required if the switch is to take place, but this has no important implications on the analysis.

connected to other nodes in that set. Heuristically, the main intuition to be gathered in this respect will be simple: in order for a diffusion wave to keep advancing steadily, its "front" cannot meet very cohesive groups of agents who have not yet adopted.

Before addressing matters formally, let us put forward a few simple examples that will illustrate some of the key ideas. First, consider the simplest possible context where the social network consists of a one-dimensional lattice with a unit neighborhood radius (i.e. $m = r = 1$ in the lattice networks of Subsection 2.1.2). Then, it should be clear that extensive diffusion can only take place if $q < 1/2$. For otherwise, if $q \geq 1/2$, only individuals that are "sandwiched" by two individuals belonging to the original seed of individuals adopting action $+1$ will ever switch to this action. In the end, this means that diffusion cannot go much beyond the original seed.

Now suppose that the lattice is bidimensional ($m = 2$). Let us continue to posit that the neighborhood radius $r = 1$, where we use the ordinary lattice distance $\varphi(\cdot)$ given by

$$\varphi(x, y) = |x_1 - y_1| + |x_2 - y_2|, \tag{4.26}$$

with x_i and y_i ($i = 1, 2$) standing for the lattice coordinates of the points x and y. Then, a straightforward adaptation of the former considerations indicate that the requirement for diffusion is that $q < 1/4$. Or, in general, for any arbitrary dimension m, the condition becomes $q < 1/(2m)$ so that overall diffusion becomes harder to attain as the richness of the underlying space (i.e. its dimension) grows.

In general, of course, the social network could build upon underlying structures (regular or not) that are *not* lattices. By way of illustration, let us consider two stylized examples considered by Morris (2000) [207]: group structures and hierarchical ones. They are respectively illustrated in Figures 4.9 and 4.10.

The first example has the population partitioned into different groups with the same number of individuals in each of them. Groups are indexed by $g = 1, 2, \ldots$, and they are arranged along a one-dimensional lattice in consecutive index order. In every group, the individuals belonging to it are indexed by $i = 1, 2, \ldots, m$. All individuals within a group are taken to be *completely* connected (i.e. they form a so-called clique). On the other hand, the only additional links of the social network are those that lie between agents who have the *same* individual index and belong to *adjacent* groups. Thus, in total, every agent (except, possibly those belonging to end groups if the network is finite) have $m + 1$ neighbors.

In the second example, individuals are arranged along a regular tree with a branching factor m. Two agents are then considered neighbors if they are directly connected in the underlying tree structure. All of them, therefore, have $m + 1$ links, with the exceptions of the root (who has only m links) and, if the tree is finite, the outermost "leaves" (who have just one link).

It will be formally shown below, as a direct implication of Morris' general results, that in the networks depicted in Figures 4.9 and 4.10 a common (necessary and sufficient) condition for overall diffusion is that $q < 1/(m + 1)$. Thus,

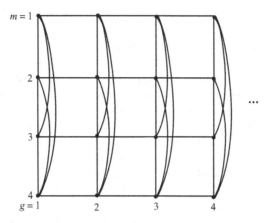

Figure 4.9. A network based on groups arranged along a one-dimensional lattice and $m = 4$ members per group, as considered by Morris (2000) [207]

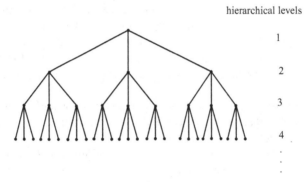

Figure 4.10. A network based on a hierarchical tree structure with a branching factor $m = 3$, as considered by Morris (2000) [207]

if m is large, widespread diffusion will only occur when q is rather low. This demanding requirement derives from a key feature that is displayed not only in both of those cases but, in fact, also arises in the lattice networks considered earlier. In all these different contexts, if a diffusion wave is to reach the whole population from a relatively small seed, payoffs must be such that agents are willing to adopt action $+1$ even when exposed to only *one* such adopting neighbor. To see why this happens, note that, in all those setups, any nonadopting agent lying precisely at the current frontier of a diffusion wave will have just *one* adopting neighbor lying at the "other side" of that frontier. Thus, only if that agent is indeed prepared to adopt under those circumstances can the wave succeed in moving forward.

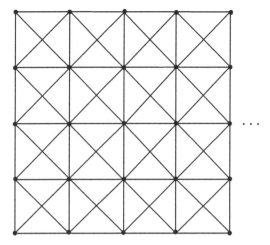

Figure 4.11. A regular network built upon a two-dimensional lattice, with the distance function given by (4.27) and the neighborhood radius $r = 1$, as considered by Morris (2000) [207]

Thus, somewhat disappointingly, in all these different examples we reencounter considerations that are strongly reminiscent of the "unstructured" (random-network) context studied in Subsection 4.1.1. There, due to the lack of network structure, we also found that a giant diffusion wave can only unfold if it can expand, *via* high-propensity agents, through the *weak* stimulus of just *one* adopting neighbor. Does this basic insight still hold beyond the construct of a random network? Is it applicable even when the pattern of interaction may exhibit significant local structure?

As it turns out, and in line with intuition, the answers to the former questions must, in general, be decidedly *negative*. To illustrate this point in the simplest possible fashion, let us revisit the case where the underlying structure is a lattice – say, a two dimensional one. Now, however, instead of defining the neighborhood of any given node in terms of the ordinary lattice distance (4.26), consider the alternative one given by

$$\tilde{\varphi}(x, y) = \max \{|x_1 - y_1|, \ |x_2 - y_2|\}. \tag{4.27}$$

Then, if we again consider a radius $r = 1$, the induced network is as illustrated in Figure 4.11 with every agent having exactly eight neighbors.

What is then required for overall diffusion in this case? We claim that, in contrast with the former lattice example, the condition $q < 3/8$ is now certainly sufficient. Thus, it is enough that adoption be profitable when three (or more) out of the eight neighbors have adopted. To see this, suppose, for example, that the process starts with a seed consisting of a completely connected "clique" of *nine* players. To be concrete, let this clique include the nodes with lattice coordinates $x = (x_1, x_2)$ as follows:

$$A(0) = \{x = (x_1, x_2) : x_1, x_2 = 0, 1, 2\}.$$

Then, if $q < 3/8$, the adopters after a first round of adjustment are given by the set

$$A(1) = A(0) \cup \{(3, 1), (1, 3), (-1, 1), (1, -1)\}.$$

And, proceeding iteratively, in the next rounds we have

$$A(2) = A(1) \cup \{(3, 0), (3, 2), (0, 3), (2, 3), (-1, 2), (-1, 0), (0, -1), (2, -1)\}$$
$$A(3) = A(2) \cup \{(1, -2), (1, 4), (3, -1), (3, 3), (4, 1), (-1, 3), (-1, -1), (-2, 1)\},$$

$$\vdots$$

which clearly has $A(t)$ grow without limit, eventually extending to the whole network.

The former discussion highlights the fact that, in general, the extent of overall diffusion must be expected to depend not only on payoffs but also on the precise architecture of the network. To address matters formally, we now introduce some new concepts and notation. Assume that the network is infinite, i.e. $n \to \infty$. Then, we say that *diffusion is possible* when there is some *finite* set of agents such that, if all of them initially choose action $+1$, the whole population will do so eventually. That is, in the limit, as the number of adjustment rounds $t \to \infty$, no individual of the population remains choosing the original action -1. As advanced, the analysis will rely on some measure of network cohesiveness. Formally, given any $r \in (0, 1)$, we declare a set of nodes M as $(1 - r)$-*cohesive* if its cohesiveness $\mathcal{H}(M)$, as defined by (2.10)–(2.11), is *at least equal* to $1 - r$.

Based on the former notions of diffusion and cohesiveness, a first immediate conclusion concerning the possibility of overall diffusion can be stated as follows:

Claim 1. *Given $q \in (0, 1)$, diffusion is* not *possible if, for every finite set of nodes M, the complement $\bar{M} = N \backslash M$ includes a nonempty subset V that is $(1 - q)$-cohesive, i.e. it enjoys a cohesiveness $\mathcal{B}(V) \geq 1 - q$.*[5]

To see the validity of this claim, consider any finite set M acting as the seed of the diffusion process and let V be the nonempty subset of the complement $\bar{M}$ that is $(1 - q)$-cohesive. We argue that no node in that subset can ever find it optimal to switch to action $+1$. The reason is that each of these nodes has at least a fraction $(1 - q)$ of its neighbors in the set V. Therefore, if all nodes in

---

[5] Notice that if the network is not fully connected (i.e. has more than one component), then any set M wholly lying in one component always has a subset of its complement $\bar{M}$ that is 1-cohesive. This obviously implies that diffusion would not be possible if we insist that the original seed has to be fully connected.

V are choosing action -1 at any t before diffusion reaches them, any one of them, say i, has

$$\frac{1}{z^i}\left|\{j \in \mathcal{N}^i : s^j(t) = -1\}\right| \geq 1 - q$$

or

$$q \geq 1 - \frac{1}{z^i}\left|\{j \in \mathcal{N}^i : s^j(t) = -1\}\right|$$

$$= \frac{1}{z^i}\left[z^i - \left|\{j \in \mathcal{N}^i : s^j(t) = -1\}\right|\right] = \frac{1}{z^i}\left|\{j \in \mathcal{N}^i : s^j(t) = +1\}\right|,$$

which is the negation of (4.25), since recall that $q \equiv \frac{1-h}{2}$. This implies that i must choose -1 at $t + 1$ as well as, of course, at any other future time.

Claim 1 can be equivalently reformulated as saying that, in order for diffusion to be possible, a *necessary* condition is that there is at least one cofinite set (i.e. a set whose complement is finite) such that none of its subsets is $(1 - q)$-cohesive. Next, we show that this necessary condition is also sufficient.

Claim 2. *Given $q \in (0, 1)$, suppose that there is a cofinite set such that none of its subsets is $(1 - q)$-cohesive. Then, diffusion is possible.*

The above statement follows from an argument polar to that underlying Claim 1. Suppose that a cofinite set U exists, none of whose subsets is $(1 - q)$-cohesive. Then, if all the agents in its (finite) complement $\bar{U}$ start by choosing action $+1$, there are some of the agents in U who have less than a fraction $(1 - q)$ of their neighbors in U. These will switch to action $+1$. The same logic can be iterated indefinitely to conclude that, as stated, the set of agents choosing action $+1$ must continuously increase until no player choosing action -1 is left in the population.[6]

Given the characterization afforded by Claims 1 and 2, it is clear that the possibility of diffusion depends on whether or not q exceeds some appropriate threshold, say ξ, that *solely* depends on the *architecture* of the network. Such a threshold ξ, therefore, fully characterizes the problem: diffusion is possible if, and only if, $q < \xi$. Often, it will be easy to compute this threshold precisely, as we did for the examples discussed above. But, even if this is difficult in some cases, one can always determine useful upper and lower bounds for ξ, as stated by the following further claims.

Claim 3. *Assume that every cofinite set of nodes contains a $(1 - p)$-cohesive subset. Then, $\xi \leq p$.*

---

[6] More precisely, note that we are implicitly taking the limits in t and n in this order. Thus, for any given n, we first observe that no player can remain choosing action -1 when $t \to \infty$. Therefore, as $n \to \infty$, the desired conclusion follows. This approach is slightly different from that pursued in Morris (2000) [207] where somewhat more delicate technical issues arise since the network is directly posited to be countably infinite.

Claim 4. *Suppose that Γ is fully connected and let $\bar{z}$ be such that $z^i \leq \bar{z}$ for all $i \in N$. Then, $\xi \geq 1/\bar{z}$.*

Claim 3 follows directly from the implications of cohesiveness on best-response adjustment. On the other hand, Claim 4 is a consequence of the fact that, in a *connected* network with maximum degree $\bar{z}$, no proper subgroup can display a cohesiveness higher than $(\bar{z} - 1)/\bar{z} = 1 - 1/\bar{z}$. To confirm the latter point, note that if a subgroup M had a higher cohesiveness, all of its nodes would have to be connected to nodes in M alone. This then would render M disconnected from $\bar{M} = N \backslash M$.

The upper and lower bounds resulting from Claims 3 and 4 may be used sometimes to determine *uniquely* the threshold ξ. This happens, for example, in the networks depicted in Figures 4.9 and 4.10. In the first case, $\bar{z} = m + 1$ so that, by virtue of Claim 4, $\xi \geq 1/(m + 1)$. But, on the other hand, observe that any cofinite set includes a subset V consisting of all those agents that are in groups $g \geq g_0$ for some large enough $g_0 \in \mathbb{N}$. Every individual in any such V has $\frac{m}{m+1}$ of her neighbors in V, so that this set is $\frac{m}{m+1}$-cohesive. Thus, by Claim 3, $\xi \leq 1 - \frac{m}{m+1} = 1/(m + 1)$. Combining both inequalities, we arrive at the conclusion that $\xi = 1/(m + 1)$, as indicated. An analogous reasoning applies also to the tree network illustrated in 4.10, where the role of g_0 in the former argument is now played by some particular level of the hierarchy.

In contrast with the approach pursued in Subsection 4.1.1, our concern here has been to study the conditions under which diffusion may spread from a small subset of the network to the *whole* of it – i.e. not merely a sizable fraction, possibly short of one. This might be justified if we deal with networks that, despite having possibly a complex architecture, exhibit some recurrent patterns. For in that case, partial and global diffusion is subject to essentially the same considerations. But there is nothing in the present framework that presumes those recurrences. Then, it could well be the case that diffusion waves are only able to attain a fractional size, which in turn might require that the seed lies in the right part of the network. It is easy to adapt Claims 1 and 2 to account for this possibility. If we rephrase matters by relaxing the former notion of (complete) diffusion to just unbounded (albeit possibly partial) diffusion, then the counterparts of those early claims would read as follows.

Claim 1′. *Given $q \in (0, 1)$, unbounded diffusion is never possible if, for every finite set of nodes M, the complement $\bar{M} = N \backslash M$ includes a $(1 - q)$-cohesive subset that is cofinite.*

Claim 2′. *Given $q \in (0, 1)$, suppose that there is a cofinite set such that the union of its maximal $(1 - q)$-cohesive subsets has an infinite complement (i.e. it is* not *cofinite). Then, unbounded diffusion is possible.*

The above two results highlight the fact that essentially the same qualitative considerations underlie diffusion when it is required to be complete as when the weaker goal is merely unbounded (but possibly partial) diffusion. In either case, that is, cohesiveness cannot be too high, at least for a significant part of the network.

To conclude, it is interesting to revisit the diffusion model of Watts (2002) [285] (cf. Subsection 4.1.1) in the light of the present theoretical framework. In particular, an important point to understand is how network structure (specifically, cohesion) affects the process of diffusion. This should help us draw a useful contrast between the present (possibly structured) scenario and the case where the social network is random (and thus unstructured).

Consider, for concreteness, the case of Poisson networks. Then, a good basis for the comparison is afforded by an alternative lattice network. More specifically, suppose that the latter network builds upon an underlying lattice of dimension $m = 2$. Finally, let us assume that payoffs in (4.24) are such that $q = 1/4$. In the terminology used in Subsection 4.1.1, this essentially corresponds to making $\phi_0 = 1/4$ (and therefore $\kappa_0 = 4$).

To carry out a comparison between both setups, it is natural to establish a correspondence between the average degree z of the Poisson network and the uniform (thus average) degree of the lattice network. But, as illustrated earlier, the latter does not only depend on the dimension of the lattice but also on the distance notion used on it and the neighborhood radius. Thus let us start with the ordinary lattice distance $\varphi(\cdot)$ given by (4.26) and suppose that the neighborhood radius $r = 1$. Then, we observe that in both contexts, the parameter configurations are precisely at the brink of global diffusion. For, on the one hand, in the lattice network we have that $q = 1/4 = 1/(2m) = \xi$. And, on the other hand, for the Poisson network we may read from Figure 4.2 that $z = 4\ (= 2m)$ is also (roughly)[7] at the critical point $\hat{z}_c$ where global diffusion ceases being possible.

Now let us consider what happens if, keeping the same framework of comparison, one increases, say doubles, the (average) degree. In the case where the network is random (Poisson), this leads deep into the overconnected region where a giant cascade is no longer possible (cf. Figure 4.2). Instead, for the lattice network, if the higher degree is attained by reconstructing the neighborhoods of nodes in term of the distance $\tilde{\varphi}(\cdot)$ specified in (4.27) – i.e. the social network is as depicted in Figure 4.11 – the implications are precisely the opposite. That is, the diffusion threshold rises from $\xi = 1/4$ to $\xi = 3/8$, which leads into a situation where unbounded (in fact, complete) diffusion materializes.

What is the basis for this sharply contrasting state of affairs? Of course, the answer must be tailored to the different extent of network structure prevailing in either case. When Poisson networks lie close to the upper threshold consistent with global diffusion, a rise in the frequency of high-degree nodes lowers the average susceptibility to adoption. In fact, this negative effects more than offsets

---

[7] More precisely, the critical point is $\hat{z}_c = 3.86$.

the positive one induced by increased connectivity. This essentially occurs because, in random networks, adoption among neighbors fails to be correlated. Instead, when lattice networks of a given dimension increase their degree, they also become more "dense". Such enhanced density also rises the fraction of adopting neighbors that enter the diffusion wave. In the end, this may favor (as in the particular case discussed) the eventual reach of the process.

4.3 STRATEGIC ADJUSTMENT IN LARGE COORDINATION SETUPS

Let us now consider a setup where players are still involved in a coordination game but, in contrast with the context studied in Section 4.2, their decisions are flexible (i.e. reversible) and noisy (e.g. subject to mistakes or/and experimentation). Many social contexts display these characteristics. Consider, for example, the phenomenon of technological adoption. In this context, it is natural to posit that an agent, if willing, should be able to reimplement her original choice of technology. This desire could arise, for example, if the agents with whom she interacts happen to revert to their original behavior. On the other hand, it is also plausible to postulate that decisions must be frequently made under incomplete – perhaps mistaken – information on payoffs. To return to the example of technological adoption, this might well occur if, say, the agent has no prior (or recent) experience with the alternative technology under consideration. In this sense, therefore, her choice may be conceived, at least occasionally, as experimental or "noisy".

When agents' decisions are both flexible and subject to noise, the induced adjustment dynamics need not be unidirectional or absorbing, as implicitly considered so far in this chapter. A new theoretical setup is needed to study the evolution of social behavior in this case. A stylized framework where these matters can be fruitfully addressed is afforded by the classical model of statistical physics known as the *Ising model* (or its generalization to any finite number of "spins," the so-called *Potts model*). The technical foundations of the Ising model and its interpretation in physics are outlined in Appendix B. Here, we focus on its economic motivation and provide a formal analysis of some simple contexts that will prove particularly useful. Indeed, because of its great tractability, some of the models of network formation considered in Chapter 6 will build upon this model to study the dynamics *on* the network that proceeds alongside the (co)evolution *of* the network itself.

Consider a large population N, whose pattern of bilateral interaction is given by a network $\Gamma = (N, L)$. For the moment, let us assume that there are only two possible actions, which are labeled $+1$ and -1. Each player i has to make the *same* choice in the interaction with *each* of her neighbors in $\mathcal{N}^i$. The payoffs accruing from each bilateral encounter are as given by the payoff table in (4.24), for every possible combination of own and partner's actions. Thus, payoffs are again parametrized by the value of h, which reflects the payoff bias (positive or negative) enjoyed by action $+1$ relative to action -1.

The population is to be thought of as very large, with a cardinality $n \to \infty$. Time is modeled continuously, $t \in [0, \infty)$. At any given t, the state of the system is given by the list $\mathbf{s}(t) = [s^i(t)]_{i \in N} \in \{-1, +1\}^n$ specifying the action chosen by each member of the population. For any given player $i \in N$, her payoff at t is given by

$$\pi^i(\mathbf{s}(t)) = (1 + h s^i(t)) \left| \{ j \in \mathcal{N}^i : s^j(t) = s^i(t) \} \right|$$
$$+ (-1 + h s^i(t)) \left| \{ j \in \mathcal{N}^i : s^j(t) = -s^i(t) \} \right|.$$

The adjustment dynamics is formulated as follows. Every agent i in the population receives an opportunity to revise her action at a constant rate, which may be normalized to unity. When any such opportunity arrives at some t, we postulate that she chooses either of the two possibilities, actions $\hat{s}^i = +1, -1$, with probabilities

$$\Pr(\hat{s}^i) \propto \exp \left\{ \beta \left[\pi^i(\hat{s}^i, \mathbf{s}^{-i}(t)) \right] \right\} \tag{4.28}$$

for some common parameter $\beta \geq 0$. As usual, the notation $\pi^i(\hat{s}^i, \mathbf{s}^{-i}(t))$ stands for the payoff obtained by player i when she chooses action $\hat{s}^i$ (possibly different from $s^i(t)$) and the choice of all agents $j \neq i$ is given by $\mathbf{s}^{-i}(t) \equiv (s^j(t))_{j \in N \setminus \{i\}}$. Of course, the above formulation merely implies that

$$\Pr(\hat{s}^i) = \frac{\exp \left\{ \beta \left[\pi^i(\hat{s}^i, \mathbf{s}^{-i}(t)) \right] \right\}}{\exp \left\{ \beta \left[\pi^i(+1, \mathbf{s}^{-i}(t)) \right] \right\} + \exp \left\{ \beta \left[\pi^i(-1, \mathbf{s}^{-i}(t)) \right] \right\}}.$$
$$\tag{4.29}$$

Conceptually, (4.29) may be understood as a noisy best response rule whereby a player myopically revises her choice toward the action that would provide her with the maximum instantaneous payoff. It is in the spirit of the well-known formulations of logistic quantal response equilibrium proposed by McKelvey and Palfrey (1995) [198], which has been provided with a natural bounded-rationality interpretation by Chen et al. (1997) [61]. In the modern evolutionary literature, it has also been amply used as a model for adjustment and learning by, for example, Blume (1993) [33], Durlauf (1997) [90], and Young (1998) [294].

The parameter β in (4.29) modulates the behavioral noise, i.e. the (probabilistic) extent to which an agent deviates from a genuine best response to the prevailing state of the system. The extreme case where $\beta \to \infty$ reflects a situation where the agent plays with full probability a best response to $\mathbf{s}^{-i}(t)$, i.e. any action $\hat{s}^i$ that yields the highest $\pi^i(s^i, \mathbf{s}^{-i}(t))$ for $s^i = \pm 1$. However, for any finite β, a suboptimal choice is also played with a positive probability. In the polar extreme, when $\beta = 0$, both actions are equiprobably chosen, irrespectively of their payoffs.

Formally, the model is equivalent to the Ising interacting particle system discussed in Appendix B with the following parameter identification $1/(kT) = \beta$; $J = 1$; $H = h$. We know, therefore, that the invariant probability distributions characterizing the long-run behavior of the process are the Gibbs measures ν satisfying (cf. (B.4)):

$$\nu(\mathbf{s}) = \frac{1}{Z} \exp\left[\beta\left(\sum_{(i,j)\in L} s^i s^j + h \sum_{i\in N} s^i\right)\right] \tag{4.30}$$

for every $\mathbf{s} \in \{-1, +1\}^N \equiv S$.

The key to solving the model is computing the normalizing factor

$$Z = \sum_{\mathbf{s}\in S}\left\{\exp\left[\beta\left(\sum_{(i,j)\in L} s^i s^j + h \sum_{i\in N} s^i\right)\right]\right\}. \tag{4.31}$$

This task is addressed next for two different frameworks.[8]

First, in Subsection 4.3.1, we consider a context where the network Γ is an infinite lattice network of dimension m. An explicit solution is provided for the simple case where $m = 1$, while for larger values of m we rely on the mean-field approximation discussed in Appendix C.1.

Second, in Subsection 4.3.2, the focus turns to networks with a tree structure (specifically, a so-called Bethe lattice), where again we provide an essentially exact solution of the model. This second case is interesting in itself, but also for its implications on random networks. Locally, these networks display a tree structure and thus can be reasonably well approximated (at least if the second-order moment of the degree distribution is bounded) by the solution obtained for strictly branching networks.

4.3.1   Lattice Networks

Let us start by assuming that Γ is a boundariless lattice network of dimension $m = 1$ and radius $r = 1$. Denote by Z_n the counterpart of (4.31) when the network consists of n nodes (formally, we shall later make $n \to \infty$). That is,

$$Z_n = \sum_{\mathbf{s}\in S}\exp\left\{\left[\beta\left(\sum_{i=1}^n s^i s^{i+1} + h\sum_{i=1}^n s^i\right)\right]\right\}, \tag{4.32}$$

where nodes are indexed consecutively along the lattice and, as usual, $i = n + 1$ is interpreted modulo n as $i = 1$. Clearly, each of the 2^n exponential terms in the above sum can be factorized to yield the following equivalent expression:

$$Z_n = \sum_{\mathbf{s}\in S}\left\{\prod_{i=1}^n \exp\left[\beta\left(s^i s^{i+1} + hs^i\right)\right]\right\}. \tag{4.33}$$

Alternatively, if we denote

$$V(s^i, s^j) \equiv \exp\left\{\beta\left[s^i s^j + \frac{1}{2}h(s^i + s^j)\right]\right\},$$

---

[8] Besides the self-contained discussion included in the appendix, the reader is referred to the excellent monograph by Baxter (1982) [26] for a detailed elaboration on the analytical methods used to study Ising models.

it is convenient to rewrite (4.33) as follows:

$$Z_n = \sum_{s \in S} \left\{ \prod_{i=1}^{n} V(s^i, s^{i+1}) \right\}. \tag{4.34}$$

Each of the four possible argument pairs of the function V can be arranged in the 2×2 matrix

$$\mathbf{V} = \begin{pmatrix} V(+1, +1) & V(+1, -1) \\ V(-1, +1) & V(-1, -1) \end{pmatrix} = \begin{pmatrix} \exp[\beta(1+h)] & \exp(-\beta) \\ \exp(-\beta) & \exp[\beta(1-h)] \end{pmatrix},$$

which then allows us to rewrite (4.34) in the following compact form:

$$Z_n = \operatorname{trace}[\mathbf{V}^n]. \tag{4.35}$$

Since $V(+1, -1) = V(-1, +1)$, the matrix $\mathbf{V}$ is symmetric. Therefore, elementary linear algebra allows us to write

$$\mathbf{V} = P \begin{pmatrix} \lambda_1 & 0 \\ 0 & \lambda_2 \end{pmatrix} P^{-1}, \tag{4.36}$$

where λ_1 and λ_2 are the eigenvalues of $\mathbf{V}$, which are real and simple by virtue of Perron's Theorem. Hence

$$\operatorname{trace}[\mathbf{V}^n] = (\lambda_1)^n + (\lambda_2)^n \tag{4.37}$$

given that, in view of (4.36), we have that $(\lambda_1)^n$ and $(\lambda_2)^n$ are the eigenvalues of $\mathbf{V}^n$.

As our interest is on the behavior of large systems, we focus on how average magnitudes grow for large n. Specifically, we want to compute

$$f(h, \beta) \equiv -\frac{1}{\beta} \lim_{n \to \infty} \left[\frac{1}{n} \ln Z_n \right], \tag{4.38}$$

which, as explained in Appendix B (cf. the analogue (B.5)), plays a key role in assessing the overall homogeneity in the population behavior. Just as the notion of magnetization is defined for spin (ferromagnetic) systems, we measure such homogeneity by

$$\mathcal{C}(\mathbf{s}) = \sum_{i=1}^{n} \frac{1}{n} s^i,$$

which we label the *index of social conformity*, or the "conformity index" for short.[9] It ranges from -1 to $+1$, corresponding to the two extreme situations

---

[9] Note that this measure of conformity is of a global kind in that it does *not* necessarily reflect how well coordinated, on average, are the neighboring individuals who *actually* interact. To illustrate the point, consider a state where the population is split into two equal and connected parts, each of these choosing a given but different action. (For example, assume n is even and let all individuals $i = 1, 2, \ldots, n/2$ choose action $+1$ while all the others choose -1.) This state yields an index of social conformity essentially zero although most of the interactions display perfect coordination. In effect, however, this kind of states are very unlikely and, therefore, local coordination and social conformity typically go hand in hand.

where social conformity is achieved at either of the two actions, -1 or $+1$, respectively. On the other hand, $C(s)$ displays a value close to zero when the population is split into two roughly equal-sized subsets that display a different action and, therefore, global heterogeneity is essentially at a maximum. In expected (or average) terms, the index of social conformity induced by the process in the long-run is obtained by integrating over the Gibbs distribution to obtain

$$C(h, \beta) \equiv \lim_{n \to \infty} \sum_{s \in S} \left\{ \nu(s) \left[\sum_{i=1}^{n} \frac{1}{n} s^i \right] \right\}.$$

Let λ_1 be the (single) largest eigenvalue of $\mathbf{V}$. Direct computation shows

$$\lambda_1 = \exp(\beta) \cosh(\beta h) + \sqrt{\exp(2\beta) \sinh^2(\beta h) + \exp(-2\beta)}.$$

Thus, from (4.35) and (4.37), we can rewrite (4.38) as follows:

$$f(h, \beta) = -\frac{1}{\beta} \ln \lambda_1 - \frac{1}{\beta} \lim_{n \to \infty} \frac{1}{n} \left[\ln \left(1 + \left(\frac{\lambda_2}{\lambda_1} \right)^n \right) \right] = -\frac{1}{\beta} \ln \lambda_1$$

$$= -\frac{1}{\beta} \ln \left[\exp(\beta) \cosh(\beta h) + \sqrt{\exp(2\beta) \sinh^2(\beta h) + \exp(-2\beta)} \right].$$

$$(4.39)$$

Then (cf. (B.6)), since

$$C(h, \beta) = -\frac{\partial}{\partial h} f(h, \beta),$$

we find

$$C(h, \beta) = \frac{\exp(\beta) \sinh(\beta h)}{\sqrt{\exp(2\beta) \sinh^2(\beta h) + \exp(-2\beta)}}, \qquad (4.40)$$

which provides a precise evaluation of what is the expected (or average) index of social conformity achieved in the long run for every possible values of h and β.

An important observation following from (4.40) is that, for any given (finite) β, the conformity index $C(h, \beta)$ depends *continuously* on h. This implies, in particular, that the situation where no global conformity materializes because of full payoff symmetry (i.e. the case where $C = 0$ owing to $h = 0$) is a robust state of affairs as h varies slightly. In general, of course, the *marginal* sensitivity of C to variations of h must hinge upon the magnitude of β. Thus, even in the presence of just a slight bias in favor of one of the actions (say, toward action $+1$ with $h > 0$), a large enough β will lead to some significant extent of conformity on this action (again, this dependence being continuous on β). The aforementioned considerations are illustrated in Figure 4.12, where we map the function $C(h, \beta)$ for a range of h centered around zero and $\beta \in [0, 1]$.

The situation is quite different for higher dimensions, i.e. when the lattice network has $m \geq 2$ (still the radius being $r = 1$). In particular, as explained in

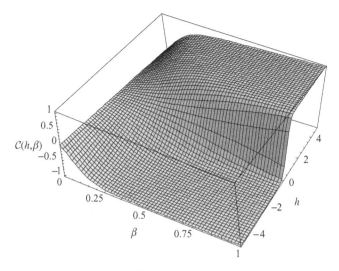

Figure 4.12. The expected index of social conformity, as given by (4.40), for a one-dimensional lattice network where $h \in [-5, 5]$ and $\beta \in [0, 1]$

Appendix B, the model then displays a first-order (discontinuous) transition as h changes sign. It is also clear that the methods used for the one-dimensional lattice cannot be extended beyond this case and a substantially more sophisticated approach is required to analyze the (Ising) model in a multidimensional context.[10] In fact, only for $m = 2$ and $h = 0$ is there a complete solution available, provided by Lars Onsager (1944) [226]. Often, therefore, the literature relies on mean-field techniques, which happen to provide quite a good approximation for the actual behavior of the system when $m \geq 4$. We refer the interested reader to Appendix C.1, where the essential features of this approach are explained in some detail.

According to the mean-field solution of the model, if β is large enough, the only stable equilibria of the system display some extent of social conformity, bounded away from zero, *even for infinitesimal h*. In fact, it turns out (cf. (C.1)) that the condition on β that is required for such a state of affairs is simply[11]

$$\beta > \frac{1}{m}.$$

This condition embodies the intuitive idea that, as the network becomes more highly connected, it becomes easier for the population to attain some measure of social conformity.

---

[10] In essence, the crucial difficulty arising in multidimensional contexts is that, unlike what occurs in one dimension, there are typically multiple paths connecting (and thus channeling influence) between nodes. This is again *not* a problem if the underlying network is a tree, which is what permits the analysis conducted in Subsection 4.3.2.

[11] Note that the counterpart of β in the traditional Ising model is given by $1/(kT)$.

As β grows above the former threshold, the extent of social conformity naturally rises as well, as measured by the consequent increase in the absolute value of $C(h, \beta)$. (Figure C.3 describes the situation.) One finds, in particular, that the *absolute* conformity index $|C(h, \beta)| \nearrow 1$ as $\beta \to \infty$, independently of the magnitude of h. This is akin to results obtained in the modern evolutionary literature. For example, in a model where players adjust their behavior as in (4.29), Young (1998) [294] shows that, when $\beta \to \infty$, the population eventually conforms to a single common action. The particular action thus singled out is independent of the underlying network, but sharply depends on a suitably formulated notion of "payoff bias" which generalizes the one considered here. Indeed, for a payoff scenario parametrized as in (4.24), it exactly coincides with the criterion associated to the sign of h – i.e. the action selected has the same sign as h. On the other hand, for the more general payoff structure considered by Young (1998) [294], it settles on the action that is comparatively "safer" (or risk-dominant, in the usual terminology).[12]

The previous discussion delineates an interesting interplay between payoffs (as captured by h) and the nature of agents' adjustment (as embodied by β) in shaping the long-run behavior of the social dynamics. The general conclusions obtained in this respect are hardly surprising:

- the stronger the payoff asymmetries, or/and
- the more sensitive agents' adjustment, or/and
- the higher the agents' interconnectivity in the social network

the more pronounced is the extent of social conformity eventually attained by the population in the long run.

The present coordination model also provides the first clear-cut manifestation in this monograph of a much more subtle phenomenon: sharp (first- or second-order) transitions. That is, abrupt discontinuities in the asymptotic dynamics of the system in response to slight changes of some of its key parameters. Such behavior, however, has been found only when the number of interacting dimensions (in this case, on the lattice) is high enough. This, in a sense, is a reflection of the idea that a complex dynamics can only arise when the pattern of connection among the interacting agents is dense enough. Indeed, this insight will be confirmed by much of our future analysis in a variety of different scenarios – again, for instance, in the next subsection. It will also play a preeminent role in our analysis and understanding of network formation processes in Chapter 6.

---

[12] Within a general 2×2 payoff table, risk dominance by one action is consistent with this action being the one that, in case of coordination, yields the lowest (equilibrium) payoff. This happens if such a lower payoff in case of coordination is more than offset by a payoff advantage in case of miscoordination. See Subsection 6.1.1 (specifically, the discussion concerning the coordination scenario given by the payoff table (6.3)) for an elaboration.

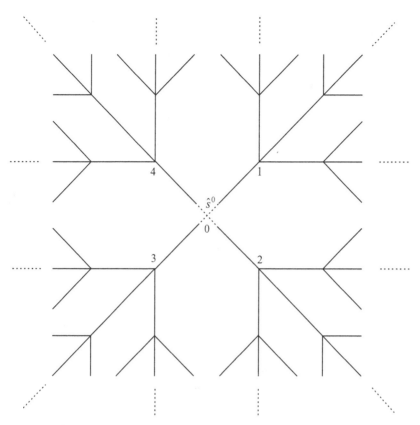

Figure 4.13. A Bethe lattice with a constant degree $u = 4$

4.3.2 Tree Networks

Let us now consider the case of networks that display a branching structure. More precisely, we shall focus on infinite *Cayley trees* where each node has the same number u of neighbors. Thus, the neighborhood $\mathcal{N}^i$ of each agent i consists of a single ancestor and $u - 1$ descendants. Such a construct is called a *Bethe lattice* (see Figure 4.13). Our interest in this lattice largely derives from the fact that, as we explain below in some detail, many random networks can be locally conceived as "random trees." This permits one to approach their analysis through an adaptation of the techniques used for Bethe lattices.

As before, we assume that every agent i interacts with all of her neighbors through a 2×2 bilateral game with payoff table given by (4.24). At every t, she has to choose the same action $s^i(t)$ in each of these encounters. This choice is revised at a constant independent rate in the exponential manner embodied by (4.29), with the common parameter $\beta \geq 0$ modulating deviations from myopic best response.

Again, the essential step in the analysis is the computation of

$$Z = \sum_{\mathbf{s} \in S} \left\{ \exp \left[\beta \left(\sum_{i \in N, \, j \in \mathcal{N}^i} s^i s^j + h \sum_{i \in N} s^i \right) \right] \right\}, \tag{4.41}$$

which in turn allows us to determine the Gibbs measures $v = [v(\mathbf{s})]_{\mathbf{s} \in S}$ that characterize the long-run behavior of the adjustment process (recall (4.30)). Given the essentially one-dimensional paths of the "diffusion" process in this context, one might feel inclined to follow an approach analogous to that pursued above for the one-dimensional lattice. Here, however, this is not a valid course since the two contexts differ in one crucial respect. While in the one-dimensional lattice the total "influence" (correlations) decays fast with distance, this is not true in the Bethe lattice. In the present case, the number of neighbors grows exponentially with distance. Therefore, even if any one of them indeed has its effect vanish as it becomes progressively more distant from the node in question, their *total* effect could well be of a significant magnitude.

Instead, the key idea underlying the procedure that will be used to solve the model crucially relies on the stationarity of the Bethe lattice. Intuitively, such a stationarity allows one to formulate *self-consistency* relationships among neighboring sites that should hold at *any* point in the network (cf. Baxter (1982) [26]). Clearly, the stationarity of a Bethe lattice crucially depends on its infinite depth. Our procedure, however, will stem from a finite tree, on which an increasing number of outer leaves are inductively added to arrive at a Bethe lattice in the limit.

We start, therefore, with a *finite* uniformly branching lattice (i.e. a Cayley tree) where the distance from the root (labeled node 0) to the outermost boundary nodes in the tree is some finite $r + 1 \in \mathbb{N}$. Let the node/agent 0 now be removed. This partitions the original network into u identical subtrees starting at nodes $1, 2, \ldots, u$. (See Figure 4.13 for an illustration of the procedure.) Denote by $\Gamma_{1r} = (N_{1r}, L_{1r}), \Gamma_{2r} = (N_{2r}, L_{2r}), \ldots, \Gamma_{ur} = (N_{ur}, L_{ur})$ the subtrees of depth r obtained after removing node 0. Then, the computation of (4.41) for the original Cayley tree, which is denoted by Z_{r+1}, can be decomposed in terms of the corresponding magnitudes for each of those subtrees $\{\Gamma_{kr}\}_{k=1}^{u}$ as follows.

For each state $\mathbf{s} \in S$, denote

$$Q_{0,r+1}(\mathbf{s}) \equiv \exp \left[\beta \left(\sum_{i \in N, \, j \in \mathcal{N}^i} s^i s^j + h \sum_{i \in N} s^i \right) \right]$$

so that

$$Z_{r+1} = \sum_{\mathbf{s} \in S} Q_{0,r+1}(\mathbf{s}). \tag{4.42}$$

Each of the terms $Q_{0,r+1}(\mathbf{s})$ may be factorized as follows:

$$Q_{0,r+1}(\mathbf{s}) = \prod_{i \in N} \exp\left[\beta\left(\sum_{j \in \mathcal{N}^i} s^i s^j + h s^i\right)\right]$$

$$= \exp(\beta h s^0) \prod_{k=1}^{u} Q_{kr}(s^0, \mathbf{s}^{N_{kr}}),$$
(4.43)

where $\mathbf{s}^{N_{kr}}$ stands for the actions displayed by the nodes N_{kr} in the subtree Γ_{kr} and

$$Q_{kr}(s^0, \mathbf{s}^{N_{kr}}) = \exp\left[\beta\left(s^0 s^k + \sum_{i \in N_{kr},\, j \in \mathcal{N}^i} s^i s^j + h \sum_{i \in N_{kr}} s^i\right)\right]$$

stands for the factor contribution to $Q_{0,r+1}(\mathbf{s})$ that is associated to the subtree Γ_{kr}. But now, proceeding analogously as before, if node k were eliminated from that subtree, the resulting sub-subtrees can be used to write the following recurrence relationship:

$$Q_{kr}(s^0, \mathbf{s}^{N_{kr}}) = \exp\left[\beta\left(s^0 s^k + h s^k\right)\right] \prod_{k'=1}^{u-1} Q_{kk',r-1}(s^k, \mathbf{s}^{N_{kk',r-1}}),$$
(4.44)

where $\mathbf{s}^{N_{kk',r-1}}$ stand for action profiles of nodes that lie in the subtree of depth $r-1$ whose root is the k'-th descendant of node k, and $Q_{kk',r-1}(\cdot)$ is the counterpart for that subtree of the former $Q_{kr}(\cdot)$.

This nested construction allows us to compute the expected conformity index (or "magnetization") attained at a Bethe lattice as follows. First, let

$$g_r(s^0) = \sum_{\mathbf{s}^{N_{kr}} \in \{-1,+1\}^{N_{kr}}} Q_{kr}(s^0, \mathbf{s}^{N_{kr}}) \qquad (s^0 = +1, -1),$$

which is proportional to the probability that agent 0 displays the particular choice s^0 in the Gibbs measure. This magnitude is obviously well defined, independently of k, since all subtrees associated to each of the descendants of node 0 are identical. Thus choosing, for example, $k = 1$ we can use (4.44) to write

$$g_r(s^0) = \sum_{s^1 \pm 1} \left\{\exp\left[\beta\left(s^0 s^1 + h s^1\right)\right] \prod_{k'=1}^{u-1} g_{r-1}(s^1)\right\}$$

$$= \sum_{s^1 \pm 1} \left\{\exp\left[\beta\left(s^0 s^1 + h s^1\right)\right] [g_{r-1}(s^1)]^{u-1}\right\},$$
(4.45)

where $g_{r-1}(\cdot)$ is simply the counterpart of $g_r(\cdot)$ for a subtree of depth $r-1$.

We are interested in determining $g_r(s^0)$ for $s^0 = \pm 1$ and large r. Once this is achieved, the expected conformity index can be obtained as

$$C_{r+1}(h, \beta) = \frac{1}{Z_{r+1}} \sum_{s^0 = \pm 1} \left\{ [s^0 \exp(\beta h s^0)] [g_r(s^0)]^u \right\},$$

where, from (4.42), we have

$$Z_{r+1} = \sum_{s^0 = \pm 1} \left\{ \exp(\beta h s^0) [g_r(s^0)]^u \right\}.$$

In fact, it will be sufficient to compute the ratio

$$x_r \equiv \frac{g_r(-1)}{g_r(+1)}.$$

between the two possible values of $g_r(s^0)$, $s^0 = \pm 1$. In view of (4.45), these two values satisfy the following recurrence relationships:

$$g_r(-1) = [g_{r-1}(-1)]^{u-1} \exp[\beta(1-h)] + [g_{r-1}(+1)]^{u-1} \exp[\beta(-1+h)]$$
$$g_r(+1) = [g_{r-1}(-1)]^{u-1} \exp[\beta(-1-h)] + [g_{r-1}(+1)]^{u-1} \exp[\beta(1+h)],$$

which in turn can be used to establish a corresponding recurrence between x_r and x_{r-1} $(= g_{r-1}(-1)/g_{r-1}(+1))$ through a function

$$x_r = \Phi(x_{r-1}),$$

where

$$\Phi(x) \equiv \frac{x^{u-1} \exp[\beta(1-h)] + \exp[\beta(-1+h)]}{x^{u-1} \exp[\beta(-1-h)] + \exp[\beta(1+h)]}. \tag{4.46}$$

As we make $r \to \infty$, the stationarity of the network implies that $x_r, x_{r-1} \to \hat{x}$, so that $\hat{x}$ must be a fixed point of Φ. Thus, we may compute $\hat{x}$ as a solution to the equation

$$\Phi(\hat{x}) = \hat{x} \tag{4.47}$$

then obtaining the induced conformity index as follows:

$$C(h, \beta) = \lim_{r \to \infty} C_r(h, \beta) = \frac{1}{Z} \sum_{s^0 = \pm 1} [\hat{x}^u s^0 \exp(\beta h s^0)],$$

where

$$Z = \lim_{r \to \infty} Z_r = \sum_{s^0 = \pm 1} [\hat{x}^u \exp(\beta h s^0)]$$

is the appropriate normalizing factor (4.41) for the (infinite) Bethe lattice.

The aim now is to investigate the set of solutions of the fixed-point equation (4.47). As the benchmark case, let us suppose that h is either zero or infinitesimal, i.e. there is no significant payoff bias in favor of any of the two actions. Then, $\hat{x} = 1$ is always a solution of (4.47). This simply reflects the fact

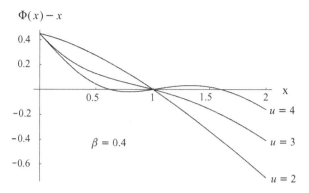

Figure 4.14. The fixed points of the function Φ given by (4.46) with $h = 0$, for an adjustment parameter $\beta = 0.4$ and Bethe lattices with a uniform degree given by three different values $u = 2, \ 3, \ 4$

that, under strict action symmetry, a social configuration where no action is singled out in any way may be sustained at equilibrium. In this equilibrium, the ratio $g_\infty(-1)/g_\infty(+1) = 1$, so that the probability that an arbitrary node/agent chooses either of the two possible actions ($+1$ or -1) is the same.

But the key question here is whether, for h in a neighborhood around zero, the solution $\hat{x} = 1$ can be regarded as stable. In full analogy with the analysis undertaken for the case where the network is an m-dimensional regular lattice (recall Subsection 4.3.1 and Appendix C.1), it all hinges upon whether or not the fixed-point equation (4.47) has multiple solutions. If it does, the aforementioned state associated to $\hat{x} = 1$ – that displays no social conformity – is unstable. And then, depending on the sign of the perturbation of h, the long-run state of the system displays an index of social conformity, positive or negative, that is bounded away from zero.

What determines whether or not the equilibrium is unique? Again, since the considerations involved are parallel to those explained for the m-dimensional lattice, we shall not revisit them in much detail here. In a nutshell, the gist of the analysis is that multiple solutions exist if the connectivity of the Bethe lattice (as given by u) is high enough or/and the sensitivity of players' adjustment (embodied by β) is strong. Or, somewhat more precisely, matters can be reformulated as follows. Given β, there is a threshold $\hat{u}$ on the degree (or branching factor) of the Bethe lattice such that if, and only if, $u > \hat{u}$ there is equilibrium multiplicity (and thus a first-order phase transition in h). Reciprocally, given the degree u, there is a threshold $\hat{\beta}$ such that equilibrium multiplicity arises if, and only if, $\beta > \hat{\beta}$. Each of these two statements is, respectively, illustrated in Figures 4.15 and 4.14 which explore the solutions of (4.47) for $h = 0$ within a specific parameter range for u and β.

As explained, much of our interest on Bethe lattices in the present context derives from the fact that, under suitable circumstances, they can be regarded as good approximations of large random networks. This happens, specifically,

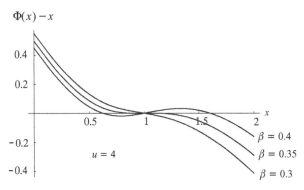

Figure 4.15. The fixed points of the function Φ given by (4.46) with $h = 0$, for a Bethe lattice with a uniform degree $u = 4$ and three different values of the adjustment parameter $\beta = 0.3,\ 0.35,\ 0.4$

when the second-order moment of the degree distribution of the random network is bounded.[13] In that case, the random network can be conceived as a "random tree," at least locally. Thus, while its connectivity (the "branching factor") is determined stochastically at every node by the corresponding degree distribution, the cycles (if they exist) are typically very long. This suggests that the approach used above to characterize the long-run behavior of the adjustment dynamics in a Bethe lattice can be adapted to the case of such random networks.

Indeed, this has been recently confirmed by Ehrhardt and Marsili (2004) [96], who have extended the previous techniques to provide an explicit solution of the Potts model in these random networks.[14] Their analysis builds on a recurrence relation akin to (4.45) – now a stochastic one – to obtain again the solution of the model as a fixed point. The form of this solution happens to be a natural adaptation of that obtained above for a Bethe lattice. It turns out, therefore, that equilibrium multiplicity (and the corresponding first-order phase transition) continues to hinge upon whether the underlying network displays (given β) a high enough connectivity.

A proper way of tackling coordination adjustment processes in random networks will prove particularly useful when we turn to studying processes of network coevolution in Chapter 6. In some of the models studied there, the network prevailing at any given point in time may be conceived as essentially

---

[13] As shown by Chung and Lu (2002) [62] and Cohen and Havlin (2003) [68], such a condition guarantees that the typical distance in the network does not grow with network size n more slowly than $\log n$. This is the crucial requirement that must be satisfied if the tree-like assumption is to represent a good approximation.

[14] Recall that the Potts model is a generalization of the Ising model that allows any arbitrary (finite) number of spins (or actions). An earlier study of the general Potts model in the context of random networks was carried out by Dorogovtsev *et al.* (2004) [85]. Their mean-field (approximate) approach, however, happens to be reasonably accurate only for random networks where all nodes display quite high connectivity.

random, i.e. characterized solely by the prevailing degree distribution. To have a good grasp, therefore, of how the profile of individuals' actions adapts to the currently prevailing network will be crucial to understand how, in turn, the network itself adjusts over time.

4.4 PERSISTENT INNOVATION

The models of diffusion considered so far are subject to a limitation that distorts a proper understanding of this phenomenon. Implicitly, it is supposed that "innovation" (i.e. the original stimulus triggering diffusion) is a once-for-all event that forever after defines the outcome of the process. It is presumed, therefore, that innovation is exogenous and independent of diffusion, the relationship between them being one-sided (from the former to the latter). But in the real world, of course, the situation is hardly like this. First, the situation prevailing at some point in time may be quite heterogenous and reflect, rather than the outcome of a single diffusion wave, the juxtaposition of different earlier processes of (partial) diffusion. Second, such heterogeneity in turn shapes crucially the process of innovation, thus affecting the future course of diffusion as well.

This richer view of matters requires modeling diffusion as *both* fueled by, as well as impinging on, a *persistent* process of innovation. Unfortunately, this is also bound to complicate matters substantially and may call for a somewhat different, possibly more eclectic, methodological approach. In what follows, we discuss a preliminary step along these lines undertaken by Arenas *et al.* (2000, 2002) [14, 15]. The model embodies two complementary driving forces: relatively infrequent updates (or "innovations"), followed by a rapid process of local diffusion (or "imitation"). By bringing them together, the objective is to shed light on how their rich interplay may shape in interesting ways the pace of change of the system.

The assumed social network is the simplest possible: agents are placed along a one-dimensional (boundariless) lattice, the neighbors of any given player $i \in N = \{1, 2, \ldots, n\}$ being those indexed $i - 1$ and $i + 1$ (modulo n) – cf. Subsection 2.1.2. The interaction between neighboring agents is conducted on the basis of their chosen actions, which are identified with nonnegative numbers $a^i \in \mathbb{R}_+$ for every agent $i = 1, 2, \ldots, n$. As usual, it is supposed that the same action must be chosen by each agent i in the interaction with both of her neighbors.

In line as well with former models, we posit that the benefits from interaction are enhanced by coordination. That is, the payoffs resulting from each bilateral interaction depend on the similarity of the actions displayed by the two agents involved. Specifically, they are given by a function $\psi : \mathbb{R}_+^2 \to \mathbb{R}$, where $\psi(a, a')$ represents the payoff of an agent choosing a when her partner chooses a'. For simplicity, suppose that it has the following form:

$$\psi(a, a') = a - \eta \left[1 - e^{-[a-a']_+} \right],$$

where $\eta > 0$ is a parameter of the model and $[x]_+ \equiv \max\{x, 0\}$. To fix ideas, one possible interpretation of this payoff formulation is as follows. Every action a has a payoff potential given by the magnitude of a itself. This potential, however, is only realized if the partner is "equally advanced;" otherwise, there is a penalty to be incurred (say, a loss due to incompatibility) that depends on the difference $a - a'$.

The law of motion of the process includes two separate components: innovation and diffusion. Each of these unfolds along a large number of "stages," all completed within every "period" – thus, in essence, we contemplate two different time scales. For simplicity, those two subprocesses are supposed to operate in sequence: first innovation, then diffusion. We now describe separately each of them, in reverse order.

Diffusion. It refers to the process by which, after an innovation, agents change their behavior over time through a chain of myopic best responses to what their neighbors do. Formally, let us index by $q = 1, 2, \ldots$ the stages of such adjustment. At each q, every individual i is given the opportunity to adapt her former action a^i_{q-1} to what her neighbors, $i - 1$ and $i + 1$, chose at stage $q - 1$.[15] Then, she is taken to play a best response, i.e.

$$a^i_q \in \arg\max_{a^i} \left[\psi(a^i, a^{i-1}_{q-1}) + \psi(a^i, a^{i+1}_{q-1}) \right] \tag{4.48}$$

under the following two constraints:

$$a^i_q \geq a^i_{q-1} \tag{4.49}$$

$$a^i_q \leq \max \left\{ a^{i-1}_{q-1}, a^i_{q-1}, a^{i+1}_{q-1} \right\}. \tag{4.50}$$

The first inequality, (4.49), simplifies matters by imposing a monotonicity on adjustment that rules out, for example, the complications that would result from the possibility of cyclical behavior. It is akin to the simplifying assumption made in our analysis of the diffusion model of Morris (2000) [207] in Section 4.2. Inequality (4.50), on the other hand, ensures that the decision problem of every agent has a bounded choice set and is therefore well defined. The motivation is that diffusion here purely reflects local imitation and, therefore, the scope of adjustment should be limited by the possibilities (say, technological know-how) available in an agent's neighborhood. In this sense, we introduce a difference between the present diffusion component of the dynamics and the other one that embodies innovation alone (see below).

Governed by (4.48)–(4.50), the diffusion process is taken to proceed from some initial action profile $\mathbf{a}_0 = \left[a^i_0 \right]_{i \in N}$ up the point at which no further changes take place. Clearly, this point arrives in finite time. In line

---

[15] This formulation differs slightly from that considered in Arenas *et al.* (2000, 2002) [14, 15], where revision opportunities are given in sequence to the different agents. The variation, however, has no significant implications on the analysis.

with our former terminology, the whole completion of any such process of imitation adjustment is called a *diffusion wave*.

Innovation. In between diffusion waves, an *innovation* occurs. This means that the action chosen by *one* randomly selected individual is subject to an upward shift. The magnitude of this shift is given by the realization of a random variable $\tilde{\sigma}$, taken to be uniform over the interval $[0, 1]$.

The overall dynamic process evolves along an indefinite sequence of periods $t = 0, 1, 2, \ldots$. At each $t > 0$, there is *one* innovation, followed by a *full* round of adjustments until a standstill is reached. Let $\mathbf{a}(t) = [a^i(t)]_{i \in N}$ be the action profile prevailing at the end of the adjustments (innovation plus the corresponding diffusion wave) conducted within period t. We are interested in two different features of the dynamics in the long run, i.e. as $t \to \infty$. A first one is the size of the diffusion waves, i.e. the number of agents

$$w(t) \equiv \left| \left\{ i \in N : a^i(t) \neq a^i(t-1) \right\} \right|$$

who change their behavior at any given t. In particular, we would like to understand the intertemporal heterogeneity exhibited by these diffusion waves, as reflected by their long-run distribution. A second object of interest is the aggregate change

$$Y(t) \equiv \sum_{i=1}^{n} \left[a^i(t) - a^i(t-1) \right]$$

induced by each of these waves, which is a measure of their effectiveness in furthering the advance of the system.

Naturally, the size of the diffusion waves and their entailed advances are influenced by the payoff parameter η. When η is low, one expects that diffusion should always involve waves spanning the full population and therefore $w(t) = n$ for all t. Indeed, it is easy to compute the specific upper bound below which this long-run state of affairs is guaranteed. Simply consider a situation where, starting from homogenous initial conditions in which all agents are choosing a common a, one agent (and only one) switches to some alternative $a + \Delta$ ($\Delta > 0$). Then, both of her neighbors (and subsequently the latter's neighbors, and so on) will find the adjustment to $a + \Delta$ profitable if

$$2(a + \Delta) - \eta(1 - e^{-\Delta}) > 2a$$

or

$$\eta < \frac{2\Delta}{1 - e^{-\Delta}}.$$

Suppose now, for simplicity, that the process starts with a uniform profile, say $\mathbf{a}(0) = (0, 0, \ldots, 0)$. Then, as long as

$$\eta \leq \lim_{\Delta \downarrow 0} \frac{2\Delta}{1 - e^{-\Delta}} = 2,$$

we can be sure that *any* innovation in the relevant support $[0, 1]$ is eventually adopted by all agents sometime along the induced diffusion wave. Therefore, a uniform profile is again restored once the wave is completed. The system advances in full coordination with a flat wavefront, no gradients ever persisting in the population profile after diffusion. Then, the expected rate of aggregate advance is $n/2$, in view of the assumed uniformity of the random variable $\tilde{\sigma}$ that governs the payoff increase of each innovation.

On the other hand, as η increases, the population action profile must start to display significant gradients along the process. Local heterogeneities, in other words, begin to arise among the actions adopted by neighbors, even after the completion of diffusion. In fact, if the situation is such that

$$\eta > \frac{2}{1 - 1/e} = 3.164$$

no innovation in $[0, 1]$ that might possibly materialize can generate *any* wave at all *if* the original profile is uniform. This happens because, in this case, neither of the two neighbors of the innovating agent finds it worthwhile to adopt the innovation. This impasse, of course, must be broken eventually since further innovations (by the same or other agents) will, almost surely, introduce steeper gradients in the action profile. Consequently, the incentives for adjustment become so strong that the pressure for adjustment overcomes any incompatibility costs.

The aforementioned considerations suggest that, as η increases to a value around 3 and beyond, progressively wider heterogeneity in wave sizes should be expected. This is indeed what is observed in the numerical simulations conducted by Arenas *et al.* (2002) [15], which are depicted in Figure 4.16. There we observe, on one hand, that when $\eta = 2$ the diffusion waves are of full system size – and thus homogenous – as explained above. But, for a value as low as $\eta = 3$, a significant dispersion in the long-run distribution of wave sizes starts to appear, while for a slightly higher value of $\eta = 3.5$ and beyond, the induced distribution already displays scale-free (i.e. "fully-fledged") heterogeneity. In this latter case, that is, the size distribution of diffusion waves is given by a clear-cut power law of the form

$$P(w) \propto w^{-\gamma} \tag{4.51}$$

for $w \neq 0$ and some $\gamma > 0$. In fact, a similar power-law (or scale-free) behavior is found for the distribution of total advances for that range of η, as presented in Figure 4.17. In both cases, the conclusions are qualitatively unaffected by changes in the population size n.

From the power-law distributions obtained for both the diffusion size w and total advance Y, it is natural to conjecture that there should also be a power relationship between w and Y (now increasing) when $\eta \geq 3.5$. This conjecture is confirmed by Figure 4.18, where one observes a relationship of the form

$$Y \propto w^{\alpha} \tag{4.52}$$

for some *given* $\alpha > 1$ that is independent of η (and also of n).

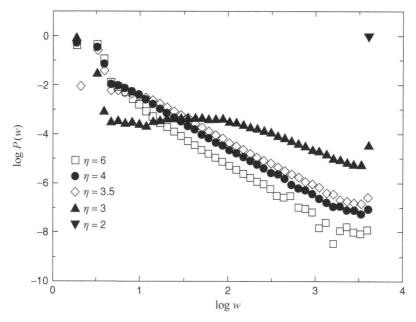

Figure 4.16. Long-run distribution for the size of the diffusion waves with a payoff parameter $\eta = 2$, 3, 3.5, 4, 6, and a population size $n = 4096$, as reported by Arenas *et al.* (2002) [15]. Both axes are in logarithmic scale – the horizontal axis measures the logarithm of the sizes of diffusion waves and the vertical axis the corresponding logarithm of their long-run frequency

The above numerical results indicate that if $\eta \geq 3.5$, the system generates distributions with no characteristic scales for either diffusion-wave sizes or the entailed advances. Now, however, let us no longer take η as an exogenous parameter but conceive it as a *control parameter* that can be set to attain some desired performance. For example, one may think of the model as representing a firm (say, its R&D department) that is to choose one among different possible lines of development of its range of products. Each such line is characterized by a corresponding value of η, reflecting a different degree of compatibility across "neighboring sublines" in the span of products covered by the firm. Then, it is natural to ask the question of what is the optimal value of η that attains optimal performance. To answer this question, of course, a precise definition of "performance" is required. One possibility might be to identify the level of performance with the rate of advance of the process along the upward "technological" ladder. In that case, it is obvious that the optimal choice involves a low η (specifically, $\eta \leq 2$) since, as explained above, this induces the largest diffusion waves and, therefore, the fastest pace of advance.

But it is conceivable that time *per se* might not be the primary issue, the objective being instead to *minimize* the number of adjustment instances required to reach a certain target level of total advance. This indeed would be the goal

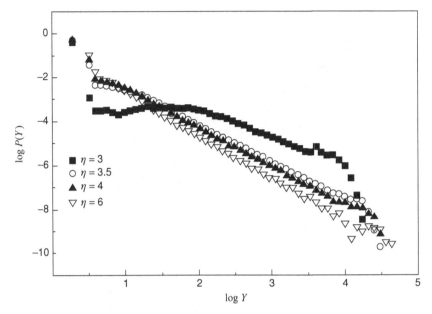

Figure 4.17. Long-run distribution for the total advances induced by the diffusion waves with a payoff parameter $\eta = 3$, 3.5, 4, 6, and a population size $n = 4096$, as reported by Arenas *et al.* (2002) [15]. Both axes are in logarithmic scale – the horizontal axis measures the logarithm of the advances and the vertical axis the corresponding logarithm of their long-run frequency

if, for example, adjustment is rather fast (or the discount of the future quite low) and every single adjustment that is implemented by an agent incurs a fixed adoption cost (independent of the size of adjustment).[16] Under these conditions, the relevant magnitude to be optimized is no longer the total advance $Y(t)$ attained at some t or the size $w(t)$ of its diffusion wave, but the ratio of the two, $Y(t)/w(t)$. In the limit, therefore, the objective would be to maximize

$$\rho \equiv \lim_{T \to \infty} \rho(T) = \lim_{T \to \infty} \frac{\sum_{t=1}^{T} Y(t)}{\sum_{t=1}^{T} w(t)}. \qquad (4.53)$$

The numerical results in this respect obtained by Arenas *et al.* (2002) [15] are summarized in Figure 4.19.

Figure 4.19 shows that the performance of the system increases monotonically over time (i.e. as the horizon T grows) and, moreover, converges to a

---

[16] In the context of our example, one could think of the opportunity cost of training for any new task along the technological ladder, when such training requires devoting a (fixed) amount of time that could have been otherwise used for production.

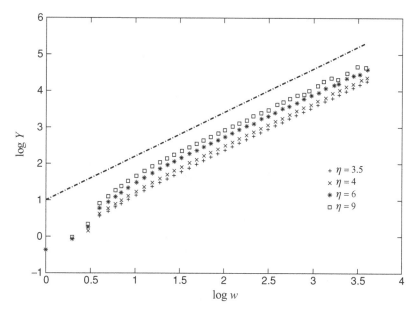

Figure 4.18. Power-law relationship (depicted in doubly logarithmic scale) between diffusion-wave size, w, and induced total advance, Y, as reported by Arenas *et al.* (2002) [15]

well-defined value for all η. It also indicates that optimal performance, as measured by ρ, is achieved at a value of η slightly above 3, i.e. just at the "brink" of the region where scale-free (often called "critical")[17] behavior starts to arise – recall Figures 4.16 and 4.17. This conclusion is unaffected by the size of the system, as shown by Figure 4.20. There we find that, even though the benefit from choosing η optimally increases (both marginally and in absolute terms) as the system size n grows, the specific choice of η that attains such optimality remains essentially unchanged.

To shed light on these conclusions, we pursue a route that integrates numerical and analytical methods in a "symbiotic" manner. The approach builds on some of the empirical regularities gathered from the numerical simulations and incorporates them as *assumptions* in a theoretical explanation of the observed features of optimal performance. We shall rely, in particular, on the following

[17] Bak *et al.* (1987, 1988) [18, 19] were the first to show that systems ("sandpiles") subject to a series of local perturbations or stimuli may generate critical behavior, i.e. a distribution of avalanche sizes that is scale-free. This has led to an immense body of theoretical literature on the phenomenon of so-called self-organized criticality (see e.g. the useful monograph by Jensen (1998) [164]). It has also been forcefully argued by some (e.g. by Bak (1996) [17]) that this phenomenon provides a new perspective to understand a wide variety of different processes in the physical, biological, or socioeconomic realms.

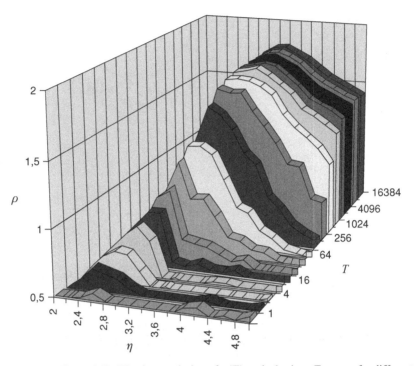

Figure 4.19. The time evolution of $\rho(T)$ as the horizon T grows, for different values of η and a population size $n = 512$, as reported by Arenas *et al.* (2002) [15]

two findings reported in Arenas *et al.* (2002) [15], which further refine the simulation results described above.

R1. There is a *scale-free region* $U = [\eta_0, \eta_1]$ for the parameter η such that if $\eta \in U$, the sizes of the diffusion waves w display a power-law distribution with a decay parameter γ that is increasing in η and satisfies $\gamma < 2$ for η close η_0.

R2. Within the scale-free region, the relationship between w and Y also displays (an increasing) power-law relationship with a constant exponent $\alpha > 1$, independent of η and population size n.

Based on R1 and R2, we now argue as follows. First note that, for any given time horizon T, we may obviously write

$$\rho(T) = \frac{\frac{1}{T} \sum_{t=1}^{T} Y(t)}{\frac{1}{T} \sum_{t=1}^{T} w(t)}$$

and, therefore, as $T \to \infty$,

$$\rho = \lim_{T \to \infty} \rho(T) = \frac{\bar{Y}}{\bar{w}},$$

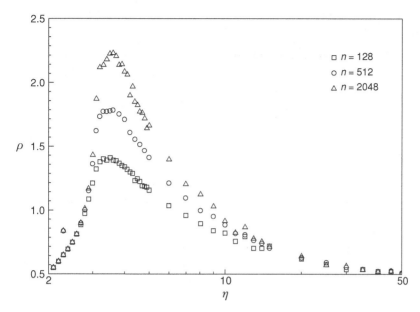

Figure 4.20. The long-run value of ρ, as given by (4.53) for different values of η and three system sizes, $n = 128, \ 512, \ 2048$, as reported by Arenas *et al.* (2002) [15]

where $\bar{Y}$ and $\bar{w}$ are the (well-defined) average magnitudes of total advance and diffusion-wave size derived from the long-run dynamics. Thus, in view of (4.51)–(4.52), for large n we can write (recall Footnote 9 of Chapter 2)

$$\rho \sim \frac{\int_1^n w^\alpha \ w^{-\gamma} \ \mathrm{d}w}{\int_1^n w \ w^{-\gamma} \ \mathrm{d}w}$$

or

$$\rho \sim \frac{2 - \gamma}{\alpha - \gamma + 1} \frac{n^{1+\alpha-\gamma} - 1}{n^{2-\gamma} - 1}.$$

When n is large, it can be readily seen that, depending on the parameter configuration under consideration, the above expression can be approximated as follows:

(A) $\rho \sim \frac{2-\gamma}{\alpha-\gamma+1} n^{\alpha-1}$ if $\gamma < 2$

(B) $\rho \sim \frac{\gamma-2}{\alpha-\gamma+1} n^{(\alpha-1)-(\gamma-2)}$ if $2 < \gamma < \alpha + 1$

(C) $\rho \sim \frac{\gamma-2}{\gamma-\alpha-1}$ if $\gamma > \alpha + 1$.

Then we claim that, for large systems, the optimal performance (i.e. the highest level for ρ) is attained at the value of η in the *scale-free region* where the induced power law has the lowest γ, i.e. at the *edge* of that region. This claim follows from an argument that can be divided into the following three steps.

- First, we discard that the optimal performance may be obtained under configuration (C) where $\gamma > \alpha + 1$. The reason is straightforward: in this parameter region, ρ is independent of n and therefore fails to exploit the (unbounded) scale effects associated to large system size that are indeed achievable in the other two regions.
- Second, we conclude that optimal performance can *neither* be achieved under configuration (B). To see this, note that since $\gamma > 2$ in that case, the aforementioned scale effects that prevail in region (B) are of a lower order than in region (A). Since, in view of R1, this latter parameter region is attainable for low enough η, optimality cannot be achieved in (B).
- Finally, we argue that, within (A), the highest value of ρ is attained for the lowest possible value of γ consistent with power-law behavior – i.e. for the lowest value of η within the scale-free region. This follows from the following two observations: (i) in view of R2, α is independent of η and n; (ii) the factor $\frac{2-\gamma}{\alpha-\gamma+1}$ is a decreasing function of γ (and thus of η).

Combining the above three considerations, the stated claim readily follows, i.e. the optimal ρ-performance is attained for a value of η "at the edge" of the scale-free region. As explained, this conclusion is in good accord with the numerical simulations depicted in Figures 4.19 and 4.20.

The analysis, in sum, reveals that when adjustment is costly (rather than urgent) the optimal pattern of diffusion occurs at the point where the population displays a delicate balance between heterogeneity and uniformity. On one hand, of course, the pull toward uniformity induced by diffusion is required if agents are to take advantage of the innovations arising elsewhere. But, on the other hand, too strong a homogenizing force is detrimental to performance since agents then adjust too often, thus bearing an unnecessarily high cost. As it turns out, the virtuous middle ground lies where "criticality" (i.e. a broad scale-free distribution in wave size) is close to turning into a state of affairs with a predominance of very large diffusion waves. Heuristically, this is reminiscent of the suggestive claim put forward by some authors (e.g. Kauffman (1993) [170]) to the effect that the long-run performance of large interacting systems is typically optimized "at the edge between order and chaos."

CHAPTER 5

Searching in Social Networks

The previous chapter has modeled diffusion and play as "reactive" phenomena, i.e. processes that unfold while agents *respond* to their current neighborhood conditions. In a polar fashion, another important (but "proactive") phenomenon that is often mediated through the social network is *search*. A paradigmatic instance of it arises when a certain agent/node faces a problem (or query) whose solution (answer) is to be found somewhere else in the social network. This is reminiscent of the famous experiment set up by Milgram (1967) [200] – recall Section 1.1 – where the task was to direct a letter to a "distant" individual through a chain of social acquaintances. In present times, the internet represents a search scenario where analogous issues appear. In this case, a typical problem consists of finding a desired piece of information by searching through the hyperlinks that connect the various webpages in the huge WWW network.

The effectiveness of search in these setups is inherently affected by network considerations. In general, of course, the way agents access disperse information must be crucially shaped by the architecture (topological characteristics) of the social network. Another consideration, equally important, is the knowledge that agents have on the social network itself. In line with our emphasis on complexity, the natural assumption to make in this respect is that such information is purely local. Sometimes, however, agents may be in the position to rely on some underlying "reference structure" (e.g. the arrangement of individuals along spatial or professional dimensions) to guide and thus improve their search. To understand the performance of search within these different scenarios is the leading objective of the first part of this chapter.

A second related issue that will attract our attention concerns the menace of congestion. This problem, specifically, tends to be important if the flow of information (or requests) that have to be *simultaneously* processed through the network is very high. For, in this case, some agents might end up burdened beyond their capacities, which in turn could impose long delays on the overall functioning of the network. The question of how the network must adapt in order to strike the best balance between search and congestion is intimately related to a central theme in organizational design. To shed some light on it is our aim in the last part of the chapter.

5.1 SEARCH IN RANDOM NETWORKS

Suppose that a "problem" (query or request) arrives at a randomly chosen node of a network but must be tackled by some other node, also randomly chosen. Then, the question being asked is simply how long will it take, on average, for the problem to find its solution if search has to be conducted through the network by a concatenation of local steps.

More precisely, let us suppose that the pattern of bilateral connections that can be used for search is modeled as a (large and almost surely connected) *random network*, in the manner described in Section 2.3. The actual network in place, therefore, may be conceived as a draw from the uniform stochastic ensemble characterized by some given degree distribution $\{p(\kappa)\}_{\kappa=0}^{\infty}$. Formally, our objective is to assess how the average delay $\lambda(n)$ in solving the problem "scales" with n, the size of the network, i.e. what is its growing order as $n \to \infty$.

Of course, the answer to this question must depend on the features of the algorithm/protocol at work. In particular, it should hinge upon the information that nodes are allowed to use in dealing with incoming problems. To start with the simplest case, let us consider the basic setup where any given node, in receiving a particular request, only knows whether it can address it or not. If the node can meet the request, it readily does so and search ends. Otherwise, it simply relays the request to one of its neighbors, randomly chosen, with an outright preference towards those neighbors that have not been asked before.[1]

In this setup, we argue that the average (or expected) delay, which will be denoted by $\lambda_0(n)$, is linear in n. To simplify the details of the argument, let us assume that the search process spends essentially no time at already visited nodes. That is, whenever at some point in the search process all neighboring nodes have already been visited before, the (randomly selected) node contacted in this case relays the request instantaneously. Then, it is easy to see that, at any given stage τ of the process, the probability q_τ that the request be met *precisely* at this stage (which naturally implies that it has not been done so before) is always equal to $1/n$. First, for $\tau = 1$, this probability is obviously $1/n$. Next, for $\tau = 2$, it is

$$q_2 = \left(1 - \frac{1}{n}\right) \frac{1}{n-1} = \frac{1}{n},$$

which simply reflects the fact that any of the $n - 1$ nodes that remained unchecked at the start of the second stage have the same probability of being the desired target. And, inductively, for any general $\tau = 3, 4, \ldots, n$, we have:

$$q_\tau = \left(1 - \frac{\tau - 1}{n}\right) \frac{1}{n - \tau + 1} = \frac{1}{n}.$$

---

[1] This implicitly assumes that the algorithm keeps a record of all formerly contacted nodes and carries this information along as search proceeds. An algorithm that does not enjoy this feature is studied in section 5.3.

Therefore, the expected delay is simply

$$\lambda_0(n) = \sum_{\tau=1}^{n} \tau q_\tau = \frac{n+1}{2},$$

which is indeed linear in system size, as claimed.

In a sense, the former case can be regarded as a worst-case scenario, since nodes are supposed to lack any information whatsoever, not only global but also local. In contrast, we may follow Adamic *et al.* (2001, 2003) [2, 1] and suppose that, in receiving a request, a node knows whether it can address such a request or one of its neighbors can do so. (Heuristically, one may suppose that every node is in perfect communication with each of its neighbors or, equivalently, that it stores the information they possess.) Further suppose that, if the node finds that the request cannot be met locally, it acts as before – i.e. it relays the request to one of its neighbors, randomly chosen, in the hope that one of this neighbor's neighbors may be able to tackle it.

In this second scenario, the logic used for the first setup can be readily adapted to conclude that the induced expected delay, now denoted $\lambda_1(n)$, satisfies:[2]

$$\lambda_1(n) \sim \frac{n}{\hat{z}} \tag{5.1}$$

where $\hat{z}$ is the average number of *additional* neighbors (i.e. the average *excess* degree) of a neighboring node. This conclusion simply follows from the fact that, at every unsuccessful stage along the search process, there is an average of $\hat{z}$ nodes (rather than one, as in the first scenario) that are discarded as possible solutions for the request.

Let $\hat{G}(x)$ stand for the generating function, given by (2.29), that characterizes the excess degree distribution of a neighboring node. We may then readily compute

$$\hat{z} = \hat{G}'(1) = \frac{\langle \kappa^2 \rangle - \langle \kappa \rangle}{\langle \kappa \rangle} = \frac{\langle \kappa^2 \rangle}{\langle \kappa \rangle} - 1. \tag{5.2}$$

In view of this expression, different cases need to be considered in evaluating (5.1). One possibility is that the degree distribution has finite first- and second-order moments and, consequently, both $\langle \kappa \rangle$ and $\langle \kappa^2 \rangle$ are uniformly bounded as $n \to \infty$. This requires that the degree distribution not be too widely distributed, as it happens for example if the degree distribution is Poisson (cf. (2.2)) or geometric (cf. (2.3)). Then, $\lambda_1(n)$ increases linearly with network size, just like in the worst-case scenario where nodes possess no information whatsoever. Note, in fact, that the same *qualitative* conclusion would apply if the local knowledge of nodes were to span, rather than just first neighbors, r-th order neighbors for some given (finite) $r \in \mathbb{N}$.

The alternative possibility is that the degree distribution has unbounded second-order moments, i.e. $\langle \kappa^2 \rangle \to \infty$ as $n \to \infty$. In this case, one needs to

---

[2] For the interpretation of the notation $\sim$, recall Footnote 9 of Chapter 2.

assess how the second-order moment grows with n in order to determine the corresponding behavior of $\lambda_1(n)$. To fix ideas, our ensuing discussion focuses on the case of scale-free networks where the degree distribution satisfies

$$p(\kappa) \propto \kappa^{-\gamma} \tag{5.3}$$

for some $\gamma \in (2, 3)$.

Naturally, as long as n remains finite, one cannot possibly posit that (5.3) applies for all $\kappa \geq 1$. Instead, the support of the distribution must be truncated at some finite threshold $\bar{\kappa}(n) < n$. In specific applications, the operational question arises of how to estimate a suitable value for such a threshold (sometimes referred to as the *maximum degree*). Here, we follow the heuristic suggestion put forward by Cohen *et al.* (2000) [66]. Essentially, they suggest that $\bar{\kappa}(n)$ should be computed as the *highest* value among all values $\tilde{\kappa}$ that satisfy the following condition:

> If the degree of all n different nodes in the network is independently selected according to the limit (untruncated) distribution satisfying (5.3) for all $\kappa \in \mathbb{N}$, the expected number of those that have a degree no lower than $\tilde{\kappa}$ is at least equal to 1.

Thus, what is postulated is that there is not even a single "full" node that is expected to display a degree $\kappa > \bar{\kappa}(n)$. Alternative suggestions in the same spirit have been proposed by other authors. For example, Aiello *et al.* (2000) [3] propose the more stringent threshold induced by the requirement that the expected number of nodes that have a degree *equal* to the threshold is (approximately) equal to unity.[3]

To compute $\bar{\kappa}(n)$ as suggested by Cohen *et al.* (2000) [66], first recall from (2.4) that, as $n \to \infty$, the limit degree distribution $\{p(\kappa)\}_{\kappa=1}^{\infty}$ is given by

$$p(\kappa) = \frac{1}{\mathcal{R}(\gamma)} \kappa^{-\gamma} \qquad (\kappa \in \mathbb{N}),$$

where $\mathcal{R}(\gamma)$ stands for the Riemann zeta function (cf. (2.5)). Alternatively, we can rely on the usual continuum approximation with density

$$p(\kappa) = (\gamma - 1) \kappa^{-\gamma} \qquad (\kappa \geq 1),$$

which is a suitable approximation for large n. Then, for any finite n, the maximum degree $\bar{\kappa}(n)$ may be simply estimated through the condition that the binomial distribution $B(\xi, n)$ with success probability

$$\xi = (\gamma - 1) \int_{\kappa=\bar{\kappa}(n)}^{\infty} \kappa^{-\gamma} \, d\kappa$$

---

[3] The intuitive basis for these different threshold choices should be clear. Depending on the realm of application, however, it should be emphasized that the event that some node does have a degree higher than the chosen threshold should be attributed positive probability even for large n. Thus, in this light, the suggested threshold is just to be regarded as a convenient approximation that essentially marks the particular point beyond which one simply assumes that the degree distribution starts to violate the power law and the probability decay is consequently much faster.

has an expected value of one. This amounts to requiring that

$$\xi n = 1,$$

or

$$[\bar{\kappa}(n)]^{-\gamma+1} = \frac{1}{n}, \tag{5.4}$$

so that, as n grows, the maximum degree satisfies:

$$\bar{\kappa}(n) \sim n^{\frac{1}{\gamma-1}}. \tag{5.5}$$

Given any large but finite n and the corresponding $\bar{\kappa}(n)$ computed as above, the (finite) second-order moment of the distribution may be approximated by

$$\langle \kappa^2 \rangle \simeq A(n) \int_{\kappa=1}^{\bar{\kappa}(n)} \kappa^2 \, \kappa^{-\gamma} \, d\kappa$$

for some suitable normalizing constant $A(n)$ given by

$$A(n) = \left[\int_{\kappa=1}^{\bar{\kappa}(n)} \kappa^{-\gamma} d\kappa \right]^{-1} = \frac{\gamma - 1}{1 - [\bar{\kappa}(n)]^{-\gamma+1}}.$$

Thus, in view of (5.2), we have that the average excess degree of a neighboring node – denoted by $\hat{z}(n)$ to reflect explicitly the dependence on the network size – satisfies:

$$\hat{z}(n) \simeq \left(\frac{\gamma - 2}{\gamma - 3} \right) \frac{1 - [\bar{\kappa}(n)]^{-\gamma+3}}{1 - [\bar{\kappa}(n)]^{-\gamma+2}} - 1.$$

Then, using (5.5), we find that, for large n,

$$\hat{z}(n) \sim \left(\frac{\gamma - 2}{\gamma - 3} \right) \frac{1 - n^{\frac{3-\gamma}{\gamma-1}}}{1 - n^{\frac{2-\gamma}{\gamma-1}}}. \tag{5.6}$$

Now, observe that, under our maintained assumption that $2 < \gamma < 3$,

$$\lim_{n \to \infty} n^{\frac{2-\gamma}{\gamma-1}} = 0$$

and, therefore, (5.6) may be rewritten as follows:

$$\hat{z}(n) \sim n^{\frac{3-\gamma}{\gamma-1}}$$

hence we conclude that the expected delay $\lambda_1(n)$ in the present case satisfies:

$$\lambda_1(n) \sim \frac{n}{\hat{z}(n)} \sim n^{1-\frac{3-\gamma}{\gamma-1}} = n^{\frac{2(\gamma-2)}{\gamma-1}}.$$

The former expression implies that, even qualitatively, quite different performance is attained by the random search algorithm at the two extremes of the contemplated range of γ. On one hand, as $\gamma \nearrow 3$, the expected delay grows almost linearly with n, just as in the scenario where nodes had no information on their neighbors. Instead, as γ falls, the expected delay grows with network size much more slowly, the rate becoming essentially logarithmic as $\gamma \searrow 2$.

These conclusions are consistent with the insights that were obtained for the case where the degree distribution displays bounded second-order moments. If internode degree variability is relatively low (e.g. γ is close to 3 in scale-free networks), random search cannot be very effective, even if nodes have direct information of the characteristics of their neighbors. The situation, however, is drastically different if the variance of the degree distribution becomes very large (e.g. γ draws close to 2 in scale-free networks). In that case, random search *cum* local information can benefit from the wide search scope enjoyed by high-degree nodes (some of which are then very large hubs) to accelerate the process very significantly.

As a slight variation on the previous search scenario, one may also consider the case where, at the time a request arrives to a node i, this node not only knows whether its immediate (first) neighbors $j \in \mathcal{N}^i$ can address the request but also has this same information (perhaps after readily asking its first neighbors) about all its *second-order* neighbors in $\mathcal{N}_2^i \equiv \{ j \in N : \exists k \in \mathcal{N}^i \text{ s.t. } j \in \mathcal{N}^k \} \setminus \mathcal{N}^i$. This simply amounts to having search cover new nodes at the rate at which, on average, *fresh* second neighbors arise. That is, search advances by checking whether the solution lies at any of the second neighbors of the node currently facing the request – of course, only those that have not been considered so far. (Note that the solution is sure *not* to lie with its first neighbors since, in that case, the process would have ended in the previous stage when the node in question was "asked".) Formally, that rate is given by the average number of new second neighbors of a typical neighboring node, which is simply equal to $[\hat{z}(n)]^2$ where $\hat{z}(n)$ is as specified above.[4]

Denote by $\lambda_2(n)$ the expected delay in the latter case for a network of size n. Then, by an immediate adaptation of the previous analysis, it follows (again for scale-free networks characterized by (5.3)) that

$$\lambda_2(n) \sim \frac{n}{[\hat{z}(n)]^2} \sim n^{1 - \frac{2(3-\gamma)}{\gamma-1}} = n^{\frac{3(\gamma-2)-1}{\gamma-1}}.$$

Therefore, as $\gamma \nearrow 3$ one continues to have that expected delay increases linearly with n while a logarithmic increase starts to emerge, not as γ approaches 2, but at the somewhat higher point where $\gamma \searrow 7/3$. This difference simply reflects the intuitive idea that, as the span of local information encompasses higher-order neighbors, search tends to proceed at a faster pace.

Adamic *et al.* (2001, 2003) [2, 1] also consider how search would be affected if the routing procedure may be responsive to the degree of neighboring nodes. Specifically, they posit that, rather than having currently "unsuccessful

---

[4] Here, we use the fact that clustering can be taken to vanish for large n. To see this, refer to (2.36) and note that, since $\gamma > 2$, the second-order moment of the degree distribution grows less than linearly in n when $\bar{\kappa}(n)$ is given by (5.5).

nodes" send the pending request to a randomly selected neighbor, the one who subsequently takes charge is the neighbor that has itself the most neighbors. Intuitively, this rule is motivated by the idea that, *a priori*, the more neighbors a node has, the more likely it is that one of them may meet the request. Under this modified procedure, it is natural to conjecture that search performance could be significantly enhanced, even when the degree distribution is not especially broad. For, under such procedure, search should be able to profit greatly from even a relatively small asymmetry across nodes' connectivities. Indeed, this conjecture has been elegantly confirmed by Adamic *et al.* (2001) [2] for the case of scale-free networks. We end our discussion by sketching informally the main gist of the argument.

In scale-free networks, even from the very early stages of search, the process rapidly finds (and thus thereafter becomes mostly based on) those nodes with the highest degree. That is, it exploits the informational advantages of the most connected nodes whose degree is close to $\bar{\kappa}(n)$, as defined by (5.4). Using (5.5), we may then estimate that the average delay, denoted by $\lambda_3(n)$, scales with network size as follows:

$$\lambda_3(n) \sim \frac{n}{n^{\frac{1}{\gamma-1}}} = n^{\frac{\gamma-2}{\gamma-1}}. \tag{5.7}$$

This rough assessment, which is (essentially)[5] in line with the rate computed by Adamic *et al.* (2001) [2], leads to the following interesting conclusions. First we have that, as $\gamma \searrow 2$, the average delay approximately scales logarithmically with network size, precisely the same conclusion that was obtained for search protocols that are insensitive to neighboring-node degree. In this sense, therefore, we find that having the search protocol display a degree bias is largely inconsequential when scale-free networks display a broad degree variance. If this happens, simpler procedures already display a good performance. Matters, however, are significantly affected in the opposite end of the relevant range for γ, i.e. as $\gamma \nearrow 3$. Then, (5.7) implies that

$$\lambda_3(n) \sim \sqrt{n}$$

which represents a substantial improvement over the linear scaling with network size obtained in the absence of degree preference for neighbor selection. Under such parameter conditions, therefore, a biased protocol allows search to take advantage of the asymmetries in node connectivities (that would otherwise be squandered) and consequently speed up, on average, the arrival at the target.

---

[5] Specifically, Adamic *et al.* (2001) [2] find that $\lambda_3(n) \sim n^{\frac{2(\gamma-2)}{\gamma}}$, which yields a higher-order delay than that following from (5.7) except for the border case where $\gamma = 2$. There are two main differences in their analysis. First, they assume that the "knowledge depth" of a node includes its second-neighbors, as contemplated in the search scenario associated to delay $\lambda_2(n)$ above. Second, they follow the formulation for maximum degree proposed by Aiello *et al.* (2000) [3] that was outlined in our earlier discussion. It is easy to see that this alternative formulation induces a threshold $\bar{\kappa}(n)$ that scales as $n^{1/\gamma}$, which in turn implies a slightly slower search rate than the one induced by (5.5).

5.2 SEARCH IN NETWORKS WITH AN UNDERLYING STRUCTURE

The analysis undertaken in Section 5.1 presumes an environment where the social network is dissociated from any underlying structure that might be known by agents and thus be helpful in search. But, in many real-world contexts, such a structure does exist and is fruitfully used in guiding search efforts and enquiries. An obvious substrate that shapes social interaction is physical space – even in the modern electronic age, agents tend to interact more often, or intensively, with those that live or work nearby. Similar considerations arise along professional, ethnic, religious, hobby, or preference dimensions. That is, any information of what are the attributes of the "target" in some of these respects can, and generally will, be used by agents in reaching it as fast and effectively as possible.

In this section, we address the problem in a number of different setups. First, we consider the simplest possible case where agents are orderly placed along a regular lattice. This generates obvious advantages in finding shortest paths but may instead force these paths to be inordinately long. As we know (recall Chapter 2), this problem is sharply mitigated if the regular lattice is perturbed by some random links, i.e. if we are in the presence of a so-called small world network. The mere existence of short average paths, however, may not be enough to guarantee that they can be found and thus effectively used by agents, if they enjoy only local network information. This brings us to the crucial problem of (operational) *searchability*. As we shall see, whether or not searchability obtains turns out to depend very delicately on how the random links are formed in relation with the underlying lattice – or, to put it differently, on the interplay between this structure and the long-range links that supplement it. Analogous but more robust considerations will be seen to arise if, as is plausible for many real-world problems, the underlying reference structure is hierarchic.

5.2.1 Lattice Networks

Let $\Gamma = (N, L)$ be a regular (and boundariless) lattice network of dimension m, as formulated in detail at the beginning of Section 2.4. For simplicity, let us suppose that the neighborhood of any given node i includes all those nodes j that are at unit distance (i.e. $r = 1$), the lattice distance $\varphi : N \times N \to \mathbb{R}$ being the ordinary one given by

$$\varphi(i, j) = \sum_{u=1}^{m} \left| x_u^i - x_u^j \right| \tag{5.8}$$

where $x^\ell = (x_1^\ell, x_2^\ell, \ldots, x_m^\ell)$ stands for the coordinates of any given node $\ell \in N$.

In this context, we consider a search problem identical to that put forward in Section 5.1. That is, problems/requests are taken to arise at different nodes but have to find their solution at other randomly selected nodes. Our objective again is to understand how *both* the network features and the routing procedure (or protocol) jointly impinge on the average delay required for solutions to be found.

Concerning the protocol, of course, its features should be a reflection of the *information* agents have about the network location where the different problems are solved. One extreme possibility, which is the counterpart of what was supposed for random networks, is to assume that the coordinates x^j of any target j are utterly unknown. Then, the situation is clearly akin to that studied in Section 5.1 for random networks with narrow degree distributions. Therefore, the average delay must scale *linearly* with network size $n = |N|$.

Another alternative, possibly more natural in the present case, is to assume that the coordinates of the solution are known at the time the problem arises. Then, if this information can be passed along, the protocol can take advantage of it and choose only shortest paths in the direction of the target. Obviously, every protocol that moves the problem to any of the neighbors whose lattice coordinates are closer (in one dimension) to the solution indeed attains shortest paths. The induced average delay $\lambda(n)$ then simply coincides with the average lattice distance $\bar{d}$, which for large n scales as (cf. Section 2.4)

$$\bar{d} \sim n^{1/m}. \tag{5.9}$$

Thus, if the lattice is one-dimensional, average delay grows linearly with n, just as in the case where no lattice information is used by the protocol. But if $m > 1$, the rate is slower and decreases with the dimension of the lattice. This simply reflects the fact that the higher is this dimension the closer together one can "pack" the different pairs of problem sources and solutions.

The latter considerations raise the question of whether, in some cases, the dimension of the lattice might be conceived as an *endogenous* feature of the situation.[6] Specifically, it may sometimes be reasonable to postulate that this dimension m depends on the population size n, as given by some function $m = f(n)$. Naturally, the properties displayed by the function $f(\cdot)$ must reflect the mechanism that is taken to endogenize the lattice dimension. To fix ideas, we now propose a stylized context that provides a simple-minded illustration.

Let the population be arranged within an infinitely dimensional lattice Ξ, where the range spanned along any given dimension is uniformly bounded by some $U \in \mathbb{N}$. Thus, formally, let us make $\Xi = \{0, 1, 2, \ldots, U\}^\infty$. By way of interpretation, each dimension may be conceived as a distinct characteristic that can be used to differentiate the agents of the population. The assumption, therefore, is that whereas there is just a finite number of different ways (at most U) in terms of which individuals can distinguish themselves for any *given* characteristic, there is an unbounded number of separate characteristics (geographic location, profession, preferences, etc.) that may be used to single out each of them. Intuitively, one may think of the number of dimensions actually spanned (or opened) by the population – i.e. the number of characteristics along

---

[6] The ideas discussed in the remainder of the present subsection originated in conversations with V. Bhaskar.

which one observes any differentiation – as the complexity of the environment in which agents live. In this sense, therefore, it seems reasonable to posit that the number of open dimensions increases with population size.

To be more specific, consider a given population composed of agents indexed by $i = 1, 2, \ldots n$, who enter into the world in that same order. Assume that, as agents enter, they spread along any of the open but yet unsaturated dimensions with the aim of occupying some coordinates in the lattice space of characteristics (a "niche") that is distinct from that of any other previous member of the population. Further suppose that, when this process can proceed no further (because all open dimensions are saturated), a new dimension is opened by the next individual that enters the population. Formally, we may suppose that dimensions $u = 1, 2, \ldots$ are opened in the same order as they are indexed and, while a certain dimension v has not yet been opened, individuals i who have already entered display the coordinate $x_v^i = 0$.

Let $\mu(n)$ stand for the number of open dimensions required to accommodate a population of cardinality n. Clearly,

$$U^{\mu(n)-1} \le n \le U^{\mu(n)}$$

or

$$\mu(n) - 1 \le \frac{\log n}{\log U} \le \mu(n)$$

and therefore

$$\mu(n) \sim \log n \tag{5.10}$$

which implies that, even though the "richness" of the environment indeed rises with population size, it does so very slowly.[7]

Finally, let us turn to what are the implications of this context for search. Still under the assumption that the search protocol may use information on the target coordinates, the combination of (5.9) and (5.10) imply that the average delay $\lambda(n)$ scales with population size as follows:

$$\lambda(n) \sim n^{\frac{1}{\log n}}.$$

This means that search delay grows very slowly with population size – indeed, growth is slower than logarithmic! Admittedly, the assumption that the effective lattice dimension grows logarithmically with population size might be far-fetched in many applications. The former considerations illustrate, however, that as long as it is plausible to posit that the richness of the environment rises with population size, only very moderate such increases can have a substantial bearing on search performance.

---

[7] Note that the uniform (and thus average) degree $z = 2\mu(n)$ also rises with n as $\mu(n)$ does. Therefore, in view of (5.10), the connectivity of every node increases logarithmically in population size. By way of comparison, it is interesting to observe that this is the same rate that marks the threshold for overall connectedness in the context of Poisson networks (cf. (2.15)).

5.2.2   Small Worlds

Here we maintain the assumption, admittedly very stylized, that agents are arranged along a regular lattice structure. However, in contrast with the previous subsection, the lattice dimension is kept fixed, independently of population size. We consider instead an enhancement of the model that is inspired in the small-world setup proposed by Watts and Strogatz (1998) [288]. That is, the basic lattice network is supplemented with some relatively low number of random (typically long-range) links. As explained in detail in Section 2.4, this formulation succeeds in generating the low average distances (as well as high clustering) that seem characteristic of so many real-world networks. But it also rules out, by construction, the wide internode diversity of connectivities that, as Section 5.1 suggests, might be required to attain a satisfactory search performance in the realm of *unstructured* networks. Since social networks typically display small variance and significant structure (recall Section 1.1), the present approach seems particularly well suited to the study of search in those cases. The hope is that, by an appropriate use of the underlying structure, one may still achieve effective search under those conditions.

However, as it has been repeatedly emphasized, the existence of short paths (which we know generally exist in small-world networks) and searchability are two conceptually distinct notions. Thus, even though it is apparent that the latter implies the former, what precisely might be required to attain the stronger desideratum of searchability in small-world networks is an intriguing issue. Kleinberg (2000*a,b*) [173, 174] has recently addressed it in the context of a simple and elegant model. In the remainder of this subsection, we present his model and discuss the interesting insights that result from it.

In essence, the aim of Kleinberg is to revisit the issue of search performance in a general setup that integrates the case of random networks (studied in Section 5.1) and lattice networks (considered in Subsection 5.2.1) as particular contexts. In such an enhanced setup, he asks the following questions: What are the topological properties required for searchability? Under what conditions does a fast-search algorithm exist for which delays grow slowly with population size?

Kleinberg's theoretical approach starts with agents placed in an m-dimensional lattice and connected to all those who lie within a given radius r in terms of the ordinary lattice distance φ defined by (5.8). Suppose, for concreteness, that $m = 2$. Then, the neighborhood of each agent i is given by

$$\mathcal{N}^i = \left\{ j \in N : \left| x_1^i - x_1^j \right| + \left| x_2^i - x_2^j \right| \leq r \right\},$$

where, as usual, (x_1^ℓ, x_2^ℓ) stand for the lattice coordinates of an arbitrary node ℓ.

Next, in the spirit of the small-world model of Watts and Strogatz (1998) [288], every agent is given q additional links that she can use to connect to individuals away from her neighborhood. Each of these q "global links" is selected randomly (and independently), with farther individuals being less likely choices. Specifically, it is posited that the linking probability decays according to a power law, so that the probability that any given node i is thus linked to some other $\ell \in N$ is proportional to

$$[\varphi(i, \ell)]^{-\gamma} = \left[\left|x_1^i - x_1^\ell\right| + \left|x_2^i - x_2^\ell\right|\right]^{-\gamma},$$

where $\gamma \geq 0$ is a parameter of the model modulating how close to i, on average, these new neighbors are located.

In Kleinberg's model, the parameter γ plays a key role in the analysis, since it determines the extent to which the creation of new connections is constrained by the underlying lattice. Heuristically, the effect of γ on the effectiveness of search is ambiguous:

(1) On one hand, a high γ implies that truly long-range global links are quite unlikely, which works against the distance-reducing potential of these additional links. In this sense, one may view a context with high γ as close to that of the original lattice, with the small-world potential of the global links being curtailed by their typically short range.

(2) On the other hand, a low γ renders the global links genuinely random, which leads to a configuration that approximates a small-world network in the original sense of Watts and Strogatz (1998) [288]. The internode distances, therefore, are generally short. This advantage, however, is obtained at the cost of losing much of the "geographical" underpinning of global links that could otherwise be fruitfully used by a decentralized search protocol.

Of course, concerning (2) above, the important question is what must be understood as a *decentralized* protocol in the present context. Following Kleinberg (2000*a,b*) [173, 174], let us say that a protocol (or algorithm) qualifies as decentralized when it *combines* the features (and presumes the information) that have been contemplated for random (unstructured) networks in Section 5.1 *and* for lattice networks in Subsection 5.2.1. Thus, when a particular problem *en route* is currently lying unsolved at some i, this node can use only the following information in choosing where to dispatch it:

- the overall lattice structure, including its own position (coordinates);
- the lattice coordinates $x^* = (x_1^*, x_2^*)$ of the target node where the problem is solved;
- the characteristics/coordinates of all of its neighbors, including those with whom node i is connected through global links;
- the list of nodes (as well as their neighbors) already visited along the search path.[8]

---

[8] It is supposed, therefore, that the algorithm may avoid getting mired in indefinite cycles. This assumption is unnecessary for the result stated below, since the algorithm constructed for the best-case scenario ($\gamma = 2$) does not rely on the history of the search path. Instead, what it underscores is that any negative results that might be obtained for other parameter configurations are not to be attributed to the existence of those kind of cycles.

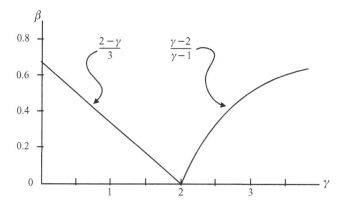

Figure 5.1. The dependence of the the exponent β given in (5.11) on the probability decay parameter γ, as illustrated in Kleinberg (2000a) [173]

Under these restrictions, Kleinberg shows two complementary results concerning the performance of decentralized protocols in a search environment as considered throughout.

Theorem A. *Let $\gamma = 2$. Then, there is a decentralized protocol whose induced average delay $\lambda(n)$ is bounded by a polynomial in $\log n$.*

Theorem B. *Let $\gamma \neq 2$. Then, if the network size n is large enough, there is some α (that may depend on q, r, and γ but not on n) such that the average delay of any decentralized protocol $\lambda(n)$ satisfies*

$$\lambda(n) \geq \alpha\, n^{\beta}$$

where

$$\beta = \begin{cases} \frac{2-\gamma}{3} & \text{if } \gamma < 2 \\ \frac{\gamma-2}{\gamma-1} & \text{if } \gamma > 2 \end{cases}. \tag{5.11}$$

The previous results are illustrated in Figure 5.1, which depicts the key effect on search performance induced by the parameter γ that modulates the distance of the global connections. It shows, in particular, that the optimal performance is attained at $\gamma = 2$, with a knife-edge situation occurring at that point. (For the general case, where the underlying lattice has dimension m, this happens where $\gamma = m$.) If γ is tuned at precisely the value of 2, search is relatively fast and the induced delay increases only as a polynomial function of the *logarithm* of network size. However, if γ is set any differently, matters are drastically worse, with delay increasing as some power of n. This implies that, as $n \rightarrow \infty$, search is infinitely faster when $\gamma = 2$ than for any other alternative value.

Kleinberg's proof of Theorem A is constructive. He puts forward a "gradient" algorithm that, at each stage of the search process, simple sends the problem to the neighboring node whose lattice distance to the (known) coordinates of the target node is lowest. When $\gamma = 2$, this routing procedure turns out to yield short average delays that increase polylogarithmically in population size. Interestingly, such a natural algorithm is the formal counterpart of the rule of thumb often used by individuals participating in small-world experiments. As reported, for example, in the "reverse small-world experiments" conducted by Killworth and Bernard (1978) [171] (see also the informal account by Milgram (1967) [200] of his early results), individuals typically proceed by "zooming" in on the characteristics ("coordinates") of the target.

While Theorem A indicates that making γ equal to the dimension of the lattice is sufficient to attain searchability, Theorem B establishes that this condition is also necessary. The mere notion that, in order to minimize delay, the decay rate γ must not be either too high or too low is intuitive enough. For, on the one hand, if γ is quite low, the long-range links that supplement the original network are little responsive to its lattice structure and, therefore, there is no clear sense in which the gradient algorithm can rely *consistently* on those links to approach the target. Admittedly, as long as the problem is far from its solution, it is true that random global links do work toward bringing it significantly closer. This benefit, however, tends to vanish fast. As the process advances, subsequent global links are ever less likely to bring the problem much closer to the target. This implies that the last stages of search (that will typically involve a substantial number if the network is large) must largely rely on moving in local steps along the underlying lattice. On the other hand, in the polar case when γ is quite high, the opposite considerations apply. Whereas the additional links will tend to be quite useful in the later stages of the search process, they are too local to be really helpful in the earlier ones.

Well beyond the simple qualitative understanding of the situation just outlined, the remarkable conclusion derived from Theorems A and B is that the "right balance" is precisely struck at the point where γ equals the dimension of the underlying lattice. Essentially, the reason for this sharp finding derives from the fact that, only in that case, the probability of having a global link of any given length is the same *at all scales*. To be more precise note that, in the two-dimensional case, the probability that any given global link spans some lattice distance in the range $[y, \alpha y]$ is of order $y^2 y^{-\gamma}$ for any large distance y and any factor $\alpha > 1$. Thus, indeed, this probability becomes independent of y only when $\gamma = 2$. Just in this case, therefore, do global links have the same (consistent) ability of moving towards the target, independently of the distance (scale) at which the search process is currently operating.

Kleinberg's model provides an effective setup to highlight the impact of network structure on searchability in the context of generalized small-world architectures. Its drawback, however, is that the theoretical framework proposed is quite rigid, hardly like what is typically observed in social environments. In real-world contexts, the reference structure guiding search is usually much richer (and also much less regular) than posited by Kleinberg's model. This has motivated Watts *et al.* (2002) [287] – and, independently, Kleinberg

(2001) [175] himself – to propose an approach that embodies a more intuitive and realistic description of the actual framework in which search is usually conducted in social environments. This approach, which presumes that the underlying reference structure is of a hierarchic nature, is discussed in the next subsection.

5.2.3   Hierarchic Structures

The main idea motivating the approach of Watts *et al.* (2002) [287] is that individuals organize their perception of the world in a hierarchical fashion. In the real world, they argue, people are often arranged – and thus can be "located" by other individuals – according to a nested (hierarchical) set of characteristics. These characteristics could be defined, for example, along geographic lines, with individuals being grouped by country, region, city, or neighborhood. Alternatively, the arrangement could reflect professional occupations, with workers being initially partitioned into, say, blue- and white-collar ones, then proceeding with further subdivisions in further classes (say sectors), and classes of classes (subsectors), etc., up to a certain level of job discrimination. Or, in contrast, the first divisions could be by sectors, subsectors, etc., only eventually having workers classified as blue- or white-collar. In general, *several* such criteria (e.g. geography *and* occupation) could be used separately by individuals in organizing their social space. But then, it is plausible that for any two individuals to feel (and also be assessed by others) as close, it would be enough that they are sufficiently similar according to *just one* of the relevant criteria.

To formalize matters, Watts *et al.* (2002) [287] resort to a formulation that is reminiscent of how evolutionary trees are used in biological contexts to categorize and explain the process of speciation. The different hierarchic criteria that organize the characteristic space are described through a corresponding collection of (branching) trees, $T_1, T_2, T_3, \ldots, T_H$, a separate one for each of the H categories under consideration. Moving downwards along any of these trees, every new branching represents a further refinement (i.e. a finer partition of individuals) according to more stringent criteria of the kind embodied by that tree. Thus, for example, if some T_h captures geographic proximity, a first branching might split the full territory under scrutiny in several countries, then a subsequent branching would identify regions, a third one correspond to cities, etc. And following a given path along the tree, an *end node* is reached that represents a maximal set of traits characterizing one of the elementary units used to classify individuals (e.g. the neighborhood in which they live). See Figure 5.2 for some simple illustrations.

Associated to each tree T_h, it is natural to define a *distance* function on its end nodes given by the number of steps back that are required to meet a common "ancestor." Thus, for any two of its end nodes, i and j, their distance $\psi^h(i, j)$ according to tree (or criterion) h is simply the number of branching (or refining) steps in which they happen to lie in different classes. Then, to aggregate the different measures of distance associated to each category, Watts *et al.* (2002)

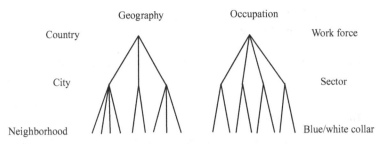

Figure 5.2. Two different trees organizing the social space according to two
alternative criteria: geographic proximity and occupation

[287] consider the *ultrametric distance* $u(\cdot, \cdot)$ obtained as the minimum across
all categories, i.e.

$$u(i, j) = \min_{h=1,\ldots,H} \psi^h(i, j) \tag{5.12}$$

for any pair of nodes, i and j.[9] Thus, as advanced, in order for two nodes to be
judged similar (or close) it is enough that they happen to be so in terms of just
one criterion.

Let us now particularize the above context by positing that each of the
different trees $T_h (h = 1, 2, \ldots, H)$ displays the same number of levels l and an
identical branching factor b (i.e. the same number of branches leave from each
intermediate node). Thus, for each tree, there is the same number of elementary
characteristics induced, $C_h = \{c_{hs}\}_{s=1}^{B}$, where we denote $B \equiv b^{l-1}$.

Each individual i displays a vector of social coordinates $x^i = (x_1^i, x_2^i, \ldots,$
$x_H^i) \in C_1 \times \cdots \times C_H$, one for each of the different criteria $h = 1, 2, \ldots, H$.
The assignment of the different coordinates x_h^i for each i is carried out independently across all those criteria. That is, the coordinate chosen for any *given*
individual i according to one criterion h is stochastically independent of the
coordinate selected according to any other criterion h'. This means, in particular, that the "dimensionality" of the population profile increases steeply as the
number H of criteria grows.

Such a hierarchic organization of individual characteristics allows one to
group agents correspondingly. Specifically, for any given criterion h, and for
each of the B different elementary characteristics in C_h that are possible for it,
the agents who display the same c_{hs} can be thought of as a group of individuals
enjoying the highest affinity according to that criterion. For simplicity, let us
suppose that there is the same number g of individuals in each of those B groups.
This implies, in turn, that the total number of individuals in the population (i.e.
the network size n) is simply given by $n = gB$.

Given that there are H different criteria, the population is partitioned into
the same number H of alternative ways. Furthermore, since the assignment of

---

[9] It is easy to see that $u(\cdot, \cdot)$ generally violates the triangle inequality and therefore fails to be a
proper metric.

characteristics is carried out independently for each criterion h, the partitions induced in each case must be typically different as well. These partitions, however, do not define the social network *per se* but only provide the *basis* on which it is constructed. The stochastic mechanism used to generate the social network from them is described next.

Consider each of the n different nodes/individuals in turn. For each of them, an average of z independent links are established in the following manner. First, there is a determination of the social distance d involved in the link to be formed. This is done by selecting d stochastically according to the probability

$$p(d) = c \, e^{-\alpha(d+1)},$$

where c is a normalization constant and α is a parameter measuring the degree of homophyly – the propensity to associate with people who are alike (i.e. are at a short social distance). Once d is thus chosen, the link in question is established with some node j in the set

$$U_d^i \equiv \{j \in N : u(i, j) = d\},$$

any of the possible candidates chosen with the same probability.

Having constructed the social network in the manner described, the search scenario confronted by individuals is formulated as the natural adaptation of that studied by Kleinberg (2000a,b) [173, 174] (cf. Subsection 5.2.2). That is, a problem is taken to arrive at a randomly selected node and it has to find its way to the solution, which lies at some other randomly selected node. The nature of the problem is perfectly known, in that the characteristics of the agent who may solve it are perfectly identified. Beyond this, however, any agent facing the task of routing an unsolved problem only has strictly local information, i.e. she merely knows the characteristics of those agents with whom she is directly connected. Agents lack, in particular, any precise population-wide information on the prevailing social network. With such limited information in hand, they are assumed to use a (decentralized) search protocol that is the natural counterpart of the Kleinberg's gradient rule considered in Subsection 5.2.2. It is implicit, therefore, that agents are aware of the hierarchical structure that defines the social space of characteristics and how it bears on the establishment of actual links.

The search/routing protocol used by the agents may specifically be described as follows. Consider a problem that arrives at some node i and can be solved by an agent j with coordinates $x^j = (x_1^j, x_2^j, \ldots, x_H^j)$. If $j \in \mathcal{N}^i$ (i.e. j is a neighbor of i in the social network that has materialized), then i sends the problem to j and it is immediately solved. Otherwise, agent i sends the problem to an agent $k \in \mathcal{N}^i$ for which the distance to j is minimal in the underlying social space, i.e. to anyone in the set

$$\{k \in \mathcal{N}^i : u(k, j) \le u(k', j) \ \forall k' \in \mathcal{N}^i\}.$$

The analysis by Watts *et al.* (2002) [287] is concerned with the average delay induced by such gradient search protocol, as it depends on the key parameters of the model, α and H – i.e. on the degree of homophyly and the richness of the social space of characteristics. They focus, in particular, on how this delay (the length of the search path) impinges on the probability of finding the target if, at each step, the request is passed along only with some probability.

Let $\pi \in (0, 1)$ be the fixed probability that, at each stage of the search process, an unfulfilled request is successfully relayed by the node in question to one of its neighbors. Under these circumstances, it is clear that the *ex-ante* probability that the target is eventually reached decreases geometrically with the length of the path it treads in quest of the solution. Thus, if one insists that the problem be eventually solved with some minimum probability q, this desideratum is equivalent to requiring that the corresponding path lengths λ should satisfy

$$\langle \pi^\lambda \rangle \geq q.$$

This in turn entails an upper bound on the expected path length that is sure to be met if

$$\langle \lambda \rangle \leq \frac{\log q}{\log \pi}.$$

As α and H change, the numerical conclusions obtained by Watts *et al.* (2002) [287] are summarized in Figure 5.3.

The first important observation is that when α is large (high homophyly), search works badly if the social space is very poor (i.e. $H = 1$). In that case, the fact that almost all links lie within homogenous groups allows for only too few "long-range" links that bridge wide gaps in social space between individuals with very different characteristics. As a consequence, when the population is large, most search paths happen to be too long and are aborted before they can find the target. The situation here is similar in spirit to that prevailed in Kleinberg's (2000a,b) [173, 174] model for $\gamma > 2$ (recall Subsection 5.2.2).

This problem, however, is interestingly mitigated if $H \geq 2$. For, in this case, the richer social space and the postulated independent assignment of individual characteristics in each of its dimensions provides an indirect way of closing the aforementioned wide gaps. Two very distant agents in the induced ultrametric are certainly very unlikely to have a direct link if homophyly is strong enough. However, because the triangular inequality does not generally hold in this case, there may well be an indirect but short path whose constituent links are formed with significant probability.

As a polar case, note that if α is small (low homophyly), very rich environments (high H) hinder effective search. Now, the considerations involved are analogous to those underlying Kleinberg's model for $\gamma < 2$, i.e. there is too little use of the underlying social structure, relative to the large complexity of the environment. Therefore, even though short paths surely exist, they cannot be found within a reasonable time horizon.

In general, as one might have expected, the best searching conditions are obtained for intermediate values of α. In such an intermediate range, some extent of homophyly renders the underlying social space of characteristics a

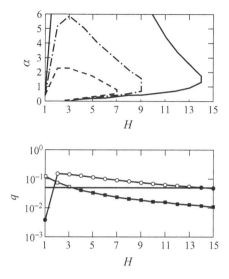

Figure 5.3. *The upper panel* shows the regions in H–α space where search is effective in the sense that at least 5% of the problems are solved (i.e. $q = 0.05$) when, at every node, only 75% of the unsolved problems are passed to a neighbor (i.e. $\pi = 0.75$). The situation is depicted for three network sizes, $n = 102\,400, 204\,800, 409\,600$, with the respective regions (solid, dot-dash, and dash) becoming progressively smaller. In all cases, the network is constructed with a branching factor $b = 2$ as well as a group size g and average degree z satisfying $g = z + 1 = 100$. *The lower panel* shows the change in the problem-solving probability (i.e. $\langle 0.75^\lambda \rangle$) for different values of H and two alternative values of α in the smaller network scenario ($n = 102\,400$). Squares correspond to the case $\alpha = 0$ and circles correspond to $\alpha = 2$. Finally, open symbols denote that the induced probability is above the threshold $q = 0.05$ while closed symbols indicates that it is below this threshold. After Watts *et al.* (2002) [287]

useful structure for search, but it is not so strong to become, in effect, counter-productive. In this sense, therefore, the insights are analogous to those derived from the model of Kleinberg (2000a,b) [173, 174]. These parallelisms notwithstanding, it is important to stress that marked contrasts also exist between the two approaches in at least two important respects. First, as we have already explained, the social structure that guides search in the present model is both more intuitive and robust[10] than Kleinberg's. Second, the parameter range where effective search is now possible does not represent a knife-edge state of affairs

---

[10] Even though the numerical simulations reported by Watts *et al.* (2002) [287] are undertaken under a number of simplifying regularity assumptions (e.g. common branching factor or the same number of levels per criterion), these simplifications hardly seem essential to their approach. In contrast, the lattice structure contemplated by Kleinberg (2000a,b) [173, 174] is inherently regular and any deviation from this regularity might well alter the analysis significantly.

but encompasses a wide region with plausible parameter values. Figure 5.3 underscores the fact, however, that if the environment becomes very complex (either because H rises or/and the population size n becomes larger), no value for the "design parameter" α exists which can tackle it successfully. Eventually, even the best-tuned search mechanism will be overwhelmed by the richness of the environment.

5.3 SEARCH AND CONGESTION

So far our analysis has implicitly supposed that each problem of search is essentially addressed in "isolation," i.e. independently of any other similar search activities undertaken in the same context at the same time. This can be a good approximation only under two rather extreme situations. One is that search requests arrive very slowly so that, typically, any one of them is already completed when another arises. A second alternative justification is that processing and "routing" search requests uses only scant resources (time, effort, etc.). Thus, in effect, the performance of agents/nodes is basically the same irrespectively of how many of those requests must be tackled simultaneously.

It is clear, however, that these extreme situations are more an exception than the rule in most real-world contexts. Think, for example, of an organization (say a firm) that confronts a steady flow of problems, many of which are difficult to identify, explain, or communicate. Then, one would expect that, when any particular agent faces a request that cannot be readily addressed, she will need significant time and effort to first grasp and then relay it to one of her "neighbors" in the organization network. This, of course, must prevent her from handling a large number of such problems simultaneously. In turn, it also raises the risk of congestion, i.e. the possibility that some problems remain unprocessed for some time and thus see its eventual solution delayed. Indeed, even if there is only *one* agent who faces acute congestion, the organization as a whole may well fear important delays (perhaps utter collapse) in its *overall* ability to perform satisfactorily.

In this section we address these issues from a number of different theoretical angles. First, we formalize explicitly the problem in an abstract framework where problems arise randomly in a given organization (network) at an exogenous rate. Then, our main concern is to study how the interplay between the process of problem generation and network architecture affects the performance of the organization, i.e. its ability to deliver the required flow of problem solving. Finally, we pose a design question: What is, given the exogenous demands imposed on the organization, the optimal design of its operating network?

In much of our analysis, the former issues are addressed in a minimalist setup where the organization/network does not have any underlying structure to build upon, nor faces any structural constraint in its (re)design. We end our discussion, however, with a reconsideration of the problem in a context that, in line with Subsection 5.2.3, postulates an underlying hierarchical structure.

Naturally, this structure (or "backbone") is taken to affect both the nature of the search problems as well as the scope of organizational design.

5.3.1 Network Architecture and Performance

Consider a given *connected* (and undirected) network $\Gamma = (N, L)$ that defines the information and communication flows involved in the operation of a certain organization. The set of nodes, N, defines the elementary units of the organization (its agents, task groups, departments, etc.). The links $ij \in L$ represent two-way communication channels between pairs of nodes, i and j, that are used to convey requests and pool information on their respective characteristics (e.g. their range of competencies and abilities). The mission of the organization is to "solve problems." These recurrently arise at every node but, typically, require the idiosyncratic competencies of some other node that can solve it. They have to be routed to that node, therefore, through a search protocol that defines the functioning routine of the organization and, naturally, has to respect its communication (network) structure.[11]

The search scenario confronted by the organization is, therefore, just as considered throughout this chapter. A key difference, however, is that search is no longer assumed to be a once-and-for-all phenomenon. Rather, problems arise repeatedly over time, at a pace that may well lead to the presence of several unsolved problems in the organization at any given point in time. This, in turn, may occasionally drive some nodes into the need to process/route several pending requests that are simultaneously calling for their attention.

Formally, the analysis follows the approach of Guimerà *et al.* (2002) [145] – see also Arenas *et al.* (2003) [13]. We suppose that, at each point in time (which is modeled continuously), problems make their first appearance in an organization at an exogenous rate ρ, independently at every node. Each problem originating at $i \in N$ has an "address" indicating the node k, randomly selected in $N\setminus\{i\}$, where it is to be solved. We posit, therefore, that the competence of every individual is restricted to a particular problem, which in turn can be solved

---

[11] There is a well-established body of economic literature that studies questions analogous to those considered here (i.e. the processing of simultaneous tasks by an organization), but mostly abstracts from the issue that mainly interests us here, i.e. congestion. This literature started with the work of Radner (1993) [243] and has been followed by a number of interesting papers, e.g. Bolton and Dewatripont (1994) [39] or van Zandt (1999a) [295] – see van Zandt (1999b) [296] for a good survey. In this literature, an organization is mostly viewed as an entity involved in the process of combining bits of information (or intermediate tasks) to conform the final output. The objective of any such organization is then to "time" (coordinate) the completion of all these bits in the best way, i.e. without any wasteful delay.

As mentioned, the bulk of this literature abstracts from considerations of congestion, although there are also some exceptions. Noted representatives are the papers by Garicano (2000) [122] and Beggs (2001) [27]. They contemplate, however, an *ex-ante* symmetry in the ability of agents in tackling different problems (even if they may differ in it *ex post*), which is quite different from the *exogenous* profile of specialization that implicitly characterizes the approach pursued here.

by that agent alone. In what follows, "problem k" refers to any problem that can be solved solely at node k.

Let us now define the protocol (rules) by which the problems travel through the organization until solved. Consider any given problem k lying at a node i ($i \neq k$) sometime along the process. Assuming that the protocol is time independent, its prescription at that juncture can be described through a probability vector $(p_{ij}^k)_{j=1,2,...,n}$, where each p_{ij}^k specifies the probability with which a problem k moves to node j when processed by i. Of course, since we assume that requests can only be passed to neighbors, we must have $\sum_{j \in \mathcal{N}^i} p_{ij}^k = 1$, i.e. the protocol has to respect the neighborhood structure $\{\mathcal{N}^i\}_{i \in N}$ induced by the network Γ.

Naturally, in line with our emphasis on *decentralized* procedures, our interest here is on protocols where, given the problem being faced a node, its routing can depend on only *local* features of the network. Among these features, the identity (thus competencies) of neighbors is certainly a key one, under the maintained assumption that such information is pooled locally. This implies that, for all i and k, we have

$$k \in \mathcal{N}^i \Rightarrow \left[p_{ik}^k = 1; \ p_{ij}^k = 0 \quad \forall j \neq k \right].$$

When the problem in question cannot be solved locally, the protocol must send the request to any of its neighbors according to some local-based criterion. One natural possibility might be to treat all neighbors symmetrically and have

$$p_{ij}^k = \frac{1}{|\mathcal{N}^i|}$$

for all $j \in \mathcal{N}^i$ when $k \notin \mathcal{N}^i$. Alternatively, the protocol could tailor its choice to the connectivity of neighbors (still a local network feature) and impose, for example, the following condition:

$$\left[j, \ell \in \mathcal{N}^i, \ k \notin \mathcal{N}^i, \ |\mathcal{N}^j| < |\mathcal{N}^\ell| \right] \Rightarrow p_{ij}^k = 0.$$

That is, in line with the rule considered at the end of Section 5.1, it could prescribe that only highest-degree neighbors receive the request.

In a compact fashion, the network-*cum*-protocol that guides the problems toward the solution can be formalized by a collection of communication matrices

$$\mathcal{P} \equiv \{ P^k \equiv (p_{ij}^k)_{i,j \in N} \}_{k \in N}. \tag{5.13}$$

By positing that

$$p_{kj}^k = 0 \quad \forall j, k \in N$$

each of the matrices P^k defines a pseudo-stochastic matrix that governs the finite-horizon stochastic process that comes at a halt when problem k reaches the homonymous node. These matrices are useful in computing the average delay involved in solving these problems, as presently explained.

First, for each $r \in \mathbb{N}$, let us compute:

$$q_{ij}^k(r) = \sum_{l_1, l_2, \dots, l_{r-1}} p_{il_1}^k p_{l_1 l_2}^k \cdots p_{l_{r-1} j}^k, \qquad (5.14)$$

which is the probability that a problem k, currently in i, will be at node j after r steps. Or, using matrix notation, we can simply define $Q^k(r)$ as the matrix whose ijth element is $q_{ij}^k(r)$ and satisfies

$$Q^k(r) = (P^k)^r = P^{k} \overset{(r \text{ times})}{\cdots} P^k. \qquad (5.15)$$

To be sure, it is important to stress that the above probabilities only capture the *expected position* of problem k after r steps in the *actual* operation of the search protocol – that is, there is no account of the delay (i.e. actual time) involved in such r steps effectively being completed. To address the latter, the *notional* formulation of the search protocol embodied by (5.15) needs to be complemented by the repercussions of congestion. For, in general, it is the processing burden supported by nodes (i.e. their backlog of pending requests) that determines the promptness with which each of their pending routing tasks is performed.

The issue of congestion presumes, of course, that each agent/node has only a limited processing capability. To model these processing limits, let us specifically assume that the nodes behave as *queues*. This means that they have unlimited storage capacity but instead process problems, in expected terms, at a constant rate – which is normalized to unity per time instant. By way of illustration, a simple scenario consistent with this formulation is one where each of the q_i pending problems faced by a node i at some point in time are all independently addressed at the same (uniform) rate $\frac{1}{q_i}$. In this case, the aggregate rate at which a single problem is processed is indeed $q_i \times \frac{1}{q_i} = 1$, as postulated.

In general, under our assumption of stationarity of the search process, the number of problems standing in the queue of a particular node i behaves like an infinite-state Markov process, with their arrival and departure times governed by corresponding Poisson processes. That Markov process, therefore, displays well-defined steady state probabilities and averages, as long as the fluctuations have finite variance. To compute those key magnitudes, we proceed as follows.

Denote by μ_{ij}^k the stationary *arrival* rate to node j of problems that appeared in the network at node i and have destination k. On the other hand, let ν_{ij}^k stand for the stationary *departure* rate from node j of problems which appeared in the network at node i with destination k. Then, since the problem arrival rate faced by a node is the sum of the arrival rates from the outside of the system (new problems) plus the arrival rates from other nodes, we can write[12]

$$
\mu_{ij}^k = \begin{cases} \frac{\rho}{n-1}\delta_{ij} + \sum_{l=1}^n v_{il}^k p_{lj}^k & \text{when } j \neq k \\ 0 & \text{when } j = k, \end{cases} \tag{5.16}
$$

where, as usual, δ_{ij} stands for a Kronecker delta as in (2.49). The term $\frac{\rho}{n-1}\delta_{ij}$ in the first line of the above expression reflects the fact that when a fresh problem arrives at node i (which occurs at the rate ρ), it is precisely of type k with the same probability as of any other type in $N\backslash\{i\}$. On the other hand, the second vanishing term simply derives from our assumption that any problem reaching its destination gets immediately solved and, therefore, does not get added to the queue.

When the system reaches a steady state, the average number of problems arriving at a node cannot exceed those that depart from it – otherwise, the stock of unsolved problems would explode, which is incompatible with stationarity. Thus, in the long run, one must have that $\mu_{ij}^k = v_{ij}^k$ for all i, j, k and therefore (5.16) may be rewritten as follows:

$$
\mu_{ij}^k = \begin{cases} \frac{\rho}{n-1}\delta_{ij} + \sum_{l=1}^n \mu_{il}^k p_{lj}^k & \text{when } j \neq k \\ 0 & \text{when } j = k. \end{cases} \tag{5.17}
$$

Let R^k be a diagonal matrix such that $r_{ij}^k = 1$ for $i = j \neq k$ and $r_{ij}^k = 0$ otherwise. Now, using the matrix notation $\mathcal{M}^k \equiv (\mu_{ij}^k)_{i,j \in N}$, we can write the equations in (5.17) in a more compact form as follows:

$$
\mathcal{M}^k = \frac{\rho}{n-1} R^k + \mathcal{M}^k P^k R^k,
$$

where the matrix R^k simply accounts for the fact that problems k that arrive at node k (either from outside the organization or some other node) are instantaneously solved and vanish. The above expression can be then used to solve for the matrix $\mathcal{M}^k$ and obtain

$$
\mathcal{M}^k = \frac{\rho}{n-1} R^k (I - P^k R^k)^{-1}. \tag{5.18}
$$

In order to interpret (5.18), it is useful to focus first on an instrumental (fictitious) scenario where time is discrete and there is never any delay when an intermediate node processes a request. Under these conditions, of course, the number of nodes visited by any given problem before it is solved is identical to the time it spends in the network. That is, the delay (number of periods)

---

[12] The queuing network considered here is closely related to what is known in the Operations Research literature as a multi-class Jackson network (see e.g. Chao, Miyazawa and Pinedo (1999) [60]). As in our case, these networks generate an ergodic Markov process whose invariant distribution is a *product measure*. It is precisely this property that permits analyzing the flow of problems faced by each node as a composition of independent Poisson processes. The useful implication of this fact is that the arrival rates coming from different sources add up to a combined arrival rate, as postulated in (5.16).

involved in finding the solution equals the number of intermediate routing steps *actually* completed by the search protocol.

Then further assume, still in a purely instrumental vein, that *one* problem of each type k is created at *each* node i in *every* period t with probability 1. In this case, it is clear that the $q_{ij}^k(r)$ defined in (5.14) can be reinterpreted as the probability that, at any given time $t(\geq r)$, there is a problem k which originated r periods ago in node i and is currently at node j. With this interpretation in mind, the expression

$$b_{ij}^k \equiv \begin{cases} \sum_{r=0}^{\infty} q_{ij}^k(r) & \text{when } j \neq k \\ 0 & \text{when } j = k \end{cases}$$

can be viewed as the limiting (or steady-state) *expected* number of problems k which arose in i sometime in the past and are currently (at some large t) passing through node j.[13]

Let B^k denote the matrix $(b_{ij}^k)_{i,j \in N}$ for any given k. This matrix is readily computed as follows:

$$B^k = \sum_{r=0}^{\infty} Q^k(r) R^k = \sum_{r=0}^{\infty} (P^k)^r R^k = (I - P^k)^{-1} R^k. \tag{5.19}$$

Now aggregating over all possible source-nodes i where problems may arise, and all target-nodes k where these problems are solved and disappear, one may define

$$\beta^j \equiv \sum_{i=1}^{n} \sum_{k=1}^{n} b_{ij}^k \tag{5.20}$$

for any given node j. In line with our previous discussion, one can interpret β^j as the expected number of problems (of any kind and with any origin) that are going through node j in the long run.

The notion defined in (5.20) can be viewed as a variation on the measure of *betweenness* discussed in Subsection 2.1.3. It is important, however, to contrast the present concept of betweenness embodied by β^i, which is of an *algorithmic* nature, with the *topological* concept b^i defined in (2.12). Naturally, the algorithmic β^i is *partially* a reflection of the topology of the network Γ (interagent communication must respect the network constraints). In general, however, the particular protocol $\mathcal{P}$ in use – as given by (5.13) – is also important to determine β^i. Indeed, it is straightforward to construct examples where the poor performance of an organization (i.e. its high congestion and long delays) is not at all the consequence of a bad communication structure (as given by the network) but of how this structure is inefficiently used by the communication protocol.

Let us now return to the original context in continuous time where problems arise at the rate ρ in every node and these have limited processing capability

---

[13] Note that $b_{ki}^k = 0$ for all $i \in N$ since, again, we assume that the problems that arrive (even from outside) at their destination become solved immediately and disappear.

(i.e. we abandon the instrumental discrete-time setup used to define (5.20)). Intuitively, it is clear that the betweenness profile $(\beta^i)_{i \in N}$ induced by the pair $(\Gamma, \mathcal{P})$ should play a central role in assessing the differential burden experienced by the different nodes. This intuitive idea can be made precise by noting that[14]

$$\left[I - P^k \right]^{-1} R^k = R^k \left[I - P^k R^k \right]^{-1},$$

so that, in view of (5.18) and (5.19), we may write

$$\mathcal{M}^k = \frac{\rho}{n-1} B^k.$$

Hence if we denote by $\varpi^j = \sum_{i=1}^n \sum_{k=1}^n \mu_{ij}^k$ the *total* arrival rate of problems to a node j (from every origin i and destination k) in a steady state, we find that

$$\varpi^j = \frac{\rho}{n-1} \beta^j \tag{5.21}$$

i.e. the stationary aggregate rate at which problems of any sort arrive at a node j is proportional to its *algorithmic* betweenness β^j.

Next, in order to assess the state of congestion of any given node i, the rate of problem arrival given by (5.21) must be compared with the rate of problem departure. Recall that the latter rate has been normalized to 1 for any nonidle node (i.e. a node that has at least one pending request). Therefore, at a steady state (where no node i can see the length of its queue grow without bound) we must have

$$\frac{\rho}{n-1} \beta^i \leq 1 \tag{5.22}$$

for every $i \in N$. In fact, this condition allows us to mark the point beyond which the network "collapses" because the number of pending problems starts to grow unboundedly. This happens whenever the exogenous arrival rate ρ is such that (5.22) becomes violated at *some* node (obviously, the node with highest betweenness). The above condition also indicates that the "critical" (i.e. maximum) ρ_c that the network can cope with, short of collapse, is

$$\rho_c = \frac{n-1}{\max_i \beta^i}. \tag{5.23}$$

Thus, quite naturally, we conclude that the highest processing burden the organization can bear is inversely proportional to the *highest algorithmic betweenness* incurred across all its agents/nodes.

---

[14] To verify this condition, simply rewrite it as

$$R^k \left[I - P^k R^k \right] = \left[I - P^k \right] R^k,$$

which is obviously satisfied since $R^k P^k = P^k$ because $p_{kj}^k = 0$ for all j.

Collapse, of course, is the ultimate manifestation of organizational failure. But aside from this extreme state of affairs, one may still wish to compare the relative performance of organizations that are all able to avert such an unbounded growth in the stock of unsolved problems. This could be done in terms of the (finite) size of such stock in the long run. This stock reflects, as its mirror image, the average delay incurred by problems before they are solved. The formal statement of such a relation between the stock of pending problems and their delay is known in Queue Theory (cf. Allen (1990) [7]) as Little's Law.[15]

Assume, therefore, that the organization at hand is capable of averting collapse. This implies, as explained, that $\frac{\rho}{n-1}\beta^i \leq 1$ for all $i \in N$ since every individual node must lie below its threshold of collapse. Being this the case, the following question naturally arises. If every node is, on average, able to handle all problems at the same rate as they come, why queues of any positive length might ever arise along the process? To understand the reason intuitively, note that the (unavoidable) fluctuations that are always present along the process induce inherently asymmetric effects on the length of queues. On one hand, when no problems stand in the queue of a certain node, the queue can obviously become no shorter. Instead, no matter how long a queue might be, there is always a positive probability that it increases even further. In heuristic terms, one could describe the basis of this asymmetry as follows: whereas upward fluctuations always increase congestion, downwards fluctuations cannot "anticipatorily save" on it. This, in the end, implies that queues of some positive length should be expected to persist even in the long run.

To understand now this issue formally, it is useful to rely on the master-equation approach that has been repeatedly used before to model jump processes – see e.g. Appendix C.2. In the present case, the (continuous-time) master equations must specify the rates at which queues see their length evolve over time. As will be recalled, the arrivals of problems to, and their departures from, each node i follow Poisson processes with rates equal to $\varpi^i = \rho\frac{\beta^i}{n-1}$ and unity, respectively. Therefore, if we denote by $p_t^i(m)$ the probability that node i displays a queue of size m at some t, the change in these probabilities over time is governed by the following differential equation:

$$\frac{\partial p_t^i(m)}{\partial t} = \left[\varpi^i p_t^i(m-1) + p_t^i(m+1)\right] - \left[\varpi^i p_t^i(m) + p_t^i(m)\right],$$

$$(m = 1, 2, \ldots), \qquad (5.24)$$

---

[15] More precisely, delay D is proportional to the stock U of pending problems in the long run. To see this, note that, under stationarity, the rate of problems solved, say S, must coincide with the rate of problems newly created, $Y = \rho n$. But, in turn, we have that $S = \sigma U$, where σ is the rate at which each of the pending problems is solved. Thus, from the equality $S = Y$, which may be rewritten as $\sigma U = \rho n$, we find that $\sigma = \frac{\rho n}{U}$. Therefore, since the expected delay of a typical unsolved problem is simply the reciprocal of the rate at which it is solved, we have $D = \frac{1}{\sigma} = \frac{1}{\rho n}U$, as claimed.

where the first bracket embodies the "inflow term" while the second one represents the "outflow term." Concerning inflow, note that a node i attains a queue of size m when one of the following two events take place:

(a) it formerly displayed a queue of size $m - 1$ and a new problem arrives (at the rate ω^i);
(b) its previous queue was of size $m + 1$ and a problem is processed (at the rate 1).

Items (a)–(b) explain the first bracket term of (5.24). As for its second term, just observe that a node i stops having a queue of length m either if a new problem arrives or a pending problem is solved. Naturally, equation (5.24) is only valid if $m \geq 1$. For $m = 0$, the counterpart equation is simpler and reads

$$\frac{\partial p_t^i(0)}{\partial t} = p_t^i(1) - \varpi^i \, p_t^i(0). \tag{5.25}$$

Now we note that, in the long-run, we must have

$$\frac{\partial p_t^i(m)}{\partial t} = 0 \qquad (m = 0, 1, 2, \dots),$$

so that the stationary distribution $\{p^i(m)\}_{m=0}^{\infty}$ can be obtained from (5.24)–(5.25) through the following equations:

$$\varpi^i \, p^i(m - 1) + p^i(m + 1) = (1 + \varpi^i) \, p^i(m) \qquad (m = 1, 2, \dots)$$
$$p^i(1) = \varpi^i \, p^i(0).$$

These equations can be readily solved to yield

$$p^i(m) = (1 - \varpi^i)(\varpi^i)^m \qquad (m = 0, 1, 2, \dots).$$

Hence the average size of the queue of node i in the long run is given by:[16]

$$\lambda^i = \sum_{m=0}^{\infty} m \, (1 - \varpi^i)(\varpi^i)^m = \frac{\varpi^i}{1 - \varpi^i}. \tag{5.26}$$

The average queue length of node i computed in (5.26) depends on both the exogenous rate ρ at which problems arrive to the organization as a whole as well as the centrality of this node in the organization, i.e. its algorithmic betweenness β^i. To see this, just note that these two factors indeed underlie the determination of ϖ^i in (5.21), so that an equivalent rewriting of the long-run queue size of node i is

$$\lambda^i = \frac{\frac{\rho}{n-1} \beta^i}{1 - \frac{\rho}{n-1} \beta^i}.$$

[16] Here, we use for queue size the same notation λ as was used for delay before (e.g. in Section 5.1). In view of the fact that, by Little's Law, one is proportional to the other, both can be seen as reflecting the same considerations.

Accounting now for the queue/delay situation prevailing in each of the nodes of the whole network, the following aggregate magnitude may be defined:

$$\lambda(\rho) = \sum_{i \in N} \frac{\frac{\rho}{n-1}\beta^i}{1 - \frac{\rho}{n-1}\beta^i}, \tag{5.27}$$

which may be called the *total stock of pending problems* prevailing in the long run (For convenience, we make explicit its dependence on the problem arrival rate ρ.) Such an aggregate measure of queue length is a natural standard of performance that can be used to assess the adequacy of the organization (as reflected by its communication network) to the demands imposed on it by the environment (as captured by ρ).

5.3.2   Optimal Network Design

Once we have a particular standard of organizational performance such as that embodied by $\lambda(\rho)$ in (5.27), the issue of *organizational design* naturally comes to mind. Specifically, we may wonder what is the best way of structuring the organization so that, given the resources available, its performance is optimized. This normative perspective, which was labeled "the designer's viewpoint" by Hurwicz (1960) [154]), has a long tradition in economics. It underlies, specifically, the large body of literature labeled Mechanism Theory. Here, we apply this approach to the framework discussed in Subsection 5.3.1, the objective being to find the "optimal network design" that best mitigates the problem of congestion and delay faced by an organization.

Let us start by redefining more flexibly the organization as a set of nodes/agents N and a given *number* of links, say m, which can be placed as desired as long as the overall network remains connected. This defines a family $\mathcal{G}$ of possible networks $\Gamma = (N, L)$, all of which have (say, exactly)[17] the postulated number of links. A natural condition for network connectivity requires that $m \geq n - 1$. On the other hand, to make the problem interesting we also assume that $m \ll \frac{1}{2}n(n-1)$, where the latter is the number of links in the completely connected network.

In general, of course, the optimal network design must depend on the environment faced by the organization, as captured by ρ. Intuitively, high values for ρ may be understood as a rapidly changing environment, where a lot of intraorganizational search and communication is required to address the new problems that arrive. In contrast, a low ρ would reflect a situation where the underlying conditions faced by the organization are rather stable. Therefore, much of the activity required from agents is "business as usual," and only quite occasionally they happen to require the assistance or know-how of other individuals in the organization.

---

[17] Thus, for simplicity, "free disposal" of links is ruled out, although the analysis would not be much affected by this possibility.

To address the problem formally, it is useful to formulate the design optimization problem in *betweenness space* as follows. First, note that the objective function $\lambda(\rho)$ in (5.27) that is to be minimized only depends on the network through the vector of node betweenness $\beta = (\beta^1, \beta^2, \ldots, \beta^n)$. To stress this fact, let us write $\lambda^\beta(\rho)$ as the delay induced by a network with n nodes and the betweenness profile β. In pursuing this approach, what remains to be described in order to have the design problem fully specified is the set of *feasible* betweenness profiles that are attainable for a network with n nodes and m links. In general, this is a difficult task to tackle, not only analytically but numerically as well. For the moment, we shall abstract from these difficulties by simply referring to the set of such admissible profiles as $\mathcal{B}$. Then, the design problem can be simply formulated as follows:

$$\min_{\beta \in \mathcal{B}} \lambda^\beta(\rho).$$

Consider first the case where ρ is very low. Then, congestion can hardly be an issue, since only a few pending problems will generally coexist in the organization. Therefore, the network should be structured to minimize path lengths as well as possible "routing mistakes" (which are possible since the protocol can only rely on local information). Clearly, this objective is best fulfilled by a star (or star-like) configuration where most nodes are solely connected to a central node (or core of nodes). To see this more precisely, note that, when $\rho \downarrow 0$, $\lambda^\beta(\rho)$ can be suitably approximated as follows:

$$\lambda^\beta(\rho) = \sum_{i \in N} \frac{\rho^{\frac{\beta^i}{n-1}}}{1 - \rho^{\frac{\beta^i}{n-1}}} \approx \frac{\rho}{n-1} \sum_{i \in N} \beta^i.$$

Then, the aforementioned conclusion readily follows from the following three observations:

1. The sum of algorithmic betweenness is never lower than the sum of topological betweenness, i.e. $\sum_{i \in N} \beta^i \geq \sum_{i \in N} b^i$, where the topological betweenness b^i is defined in (2.12).
2. As explained in Subsection 2.1.3, $\sum_{i \in N} b^i$ is essentially proportional to the average (topological) distance $\bar{d}$ in the network. Therefore, $\sum_{i \in N} b^i$ is minimized at a star network – or, if an exact star is not possible because $m > n - 1$, at a star-like network with a core-periphery dichotomy.
3. In a star(-like) network, algorithmic and topological betweenness essentially coincide.

Consider now the polar case where ρ is high, but not so high that the organization is sure to collapse (independently of how it designs its network). More precisely, let

$$\hat{\beta} \equiv \min_{\beta \in B} \max_{i \in N} \beta^i \tag{5.28}$$

denote the lowest maximum betweenness that can be attained over all feasible profiles $\beta \in \mathcal{B}$ and, correspondingly, denote by

$$\hat{\rho}_c \equiv \frac{n-1}{\hat{\beta}}. \tag{5.29}$$

Then, collapse can be averted by some feasible network design if, and only if, the problem arrival rate satisfies

$$\rho < \hat{\rho}_c.$$

Thus, assume that ρ satisfies the former inequality but is so high as to lie very close to $\hat{\rho}_c$. Then, in order to forestall collapse, the network architecture must be so precisely designed that, essentially, the lowest possible maximum betweenness is attained. This, in turn, requires that the network displays no large asymmetries across the betweenness of the different nodes. That is, the optimal network should be close to a homogenous network with only very little asymmetries across nodes – i.e. the induced betweenness profile must be basically uniform. If this is indeed the case, the corresponding (optimal) delay $\hat{\lambda}$ diverges as follows (cf. (5.28)-(5.29)):

$$\hat{\lambda} \sim \frac{1}{1 - \rho\frac{\hat{\beta}}{n-1}} = \frac{1}{1 - \frac{\rho}{\hat{\rho}_c}},$$

when $\rho \uparrow \hat{\rho}_c$.

What might be expected for genuinely intermediate values of ρ, not too close to the boundaries of the range $(0, \hat{\rho}_c)$? We now conjecture that a rather abrupt transition may arise, in view of the following features of the problem.

(a) Given ρ, the objective function $\lambda^\beta(\rho)$ to be minimized in betweenness space is an increasing and convex function of $\beta = (\beta^1, \beta^2, \ldots, \beta^n)$ – see (5.27). Furthermore, for each $K \geq 0$, its level sets

$$\{\beta : \lambda^\beta(\rho) = K\}$$

are symmetric with respect to the bisectrix of the positive orthant and concave to the origin, with their curvature "sharpening" as ρ rises. That is, they are essentially straight lines when $\rho \approx 0$ and are close to being kinked at the bisectrix when $\rho \approx \hat{\rho}_c$.

(b) Let $\beta^\circledast = (\beta^{\circledast 1}, \ldots, \beta^{\circledast n})$ denote the betweenness profile of a star(-like) network where the sum of algorithmic and topological betweenness is minimized. Then, the set $\mathcal{B}$ of feasible betweenness must lie in the following subspace:

$$H \equiv \left\{ \beta = (\beta^i)_{i \in N} \in \mathbb{R}^n : \sum_{i=1}^n \beta^i \geq \sum_{i=1}^n \beta^{\circledast i} \right\}.$$

This implies that the curvature of the lower boundary of $\mathcal{B}$, i.e.

$$\partial \mathcal{B} \equiv \left\{ \begin{array}{l} \beta = (\beta^i)_{i \in N} : \left[\tilde{\beta} \in \mathcal{B}, \tilde{\beta}^i < \beta^i \text{ for some } i \in N \right] \Rightarrow \\ \qquad \left[\tilde{\beta}^j \geq \beta^j \text{ for some } j \in N \right] \end{array} \right\}$$

cannot be uniformly convex to the origin. We may rely on this observation to advance that, provided the curvature of $\partial \mathcal{B}$ remains *qualitatively* the same throughout, it has to be concave.

Combine now the properties of the objective function described in (a) with the concavity of $\partial \mathcal{B}$ put forward in (b). Furthermore, let us make the simplifying assumption that the curvatures of the level curves $\{\beta : \lambda^\beta(\rho) = K\}$ and the frontier $\partial \mathcal{B}$ (both concave to the origin) are unambiguously comparable, i.e. either one is uniformly more concave than the other or *vice versa* (of course they would coincide in the borderline case). Then, the design problem may be understood along the lines illustrated in the simple two-dimensional diagram depicted in Figure 5.4.

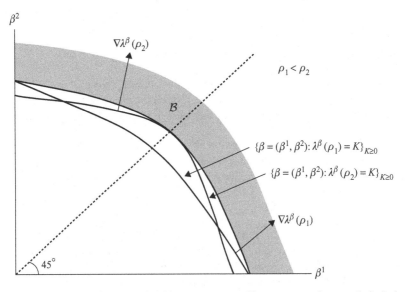

Figure 5.4. The optimal betweenness profile as ρ passes from a relatively low $\rho = \rho_1$ to a higher $\rho = \rho_2$. In the latter case, the optimal profile lies on the bisectrix of the positive orthant, where one of the level curves $\{\beta = (\beta^1, \beta^2) : \lambda^\beta(\rho_2) = K\}_{K \geq 0}$ is tangent to the lower frontier of $\mathcal{B}$. This corresponds to a point of minimum polarization. For the lower $\rho = \rho_1$, the level curves $\{\beta = (\beta^1, \beta^2) : \lambda^\beta(\rho_1) = K\}_{K \geq 0}$ display less curvature and the optimal profiles are corner solutions lying on each of the two axes. At these points, the polarization is at a maximum

We are interested in tracing the optimal configurations in betweenness space, as the problem burden imposed on the organization increases (i.e. as the arrival rate ρ grows). On one hand, point (a) above explains that this change is reflected in a progressively sharper "bending" of the level curves $\{\beta : \lambda^{\beta}(\rho) = K\}$. As this happens, Figure 5.4 illustrates that the optimal (tangency) points should tend to become less polarized and the betweenness asymmetries among nodes fall, at least weakly. In fact, point (b) suggests that a *discontinuous* transition might well be expected to take place at a certain threshold for ρ. In such an abrupt transition, as ρ exceeds that critical value, the optimal architecture switches from one where the betweenness profile is very polarized (corresponding to a star-like configuration) to another where it is uniform (the network then being essentially symmetric across all nodes).

To check the validity of these heuristic considerations, Guimerà *et al.* (2002) [145] resort to numerical simulations. For a variety of computationally amenable setups, they estimate how the optimal network architecture changes as the problem arrival rate varies from low values close to zero to a point near the maximum critical rate.[18] To provide a quantitative assessment of *network polarization*, the following measure is used:

$$\theta^{\beta} = \frac{\max_{i \in N} \beta_i - \langle \beta_i \rangle_{i \in N}}{\langle \beta_i \rangle_{i \in N}},$$

which attains its maximum value when the betweenness profile β corresponds to a star network and reaches a minimum of zero for a fully symmetric network. Denoting by $\theta^*(\rho)$ the polarization displayed by the optimal network when the arrival rate is ρ, their results are shown in Figure 5.5. They find, specifically, that when the arrival rate of new problems is low, extreme network polarization is optimal and remains so up to a certain critical value of the arrival rate. At that point, on the other hand, a sharp transition occurs whereby a symmetric network architecture becomes optimal for all higher values. These results support, at least within the small setups under consideration, the gist of the former discussion.

5.3.3 Networks with a Hierarchic Backbone

The twin issues of search and congestion have been addressed in the former two subsections in a context where there is no reference structure underlying the social network. The setup, therefore, was just like the one studied in Section 5.1, where agents had no information (other than purely local knowledge) that could be used to guide their search efforts. This, as will be recalled, contrasts with the alternative approach pursued in Section 5.2. There, we did postulate the

---

[18] Guimerá *et al.* (2002) [145] find the optimal network by simulated annealing, which is a procedure widely used to find a solution for complex optimization problems (cf. Stariolo and Tsallis (1995) [265]).

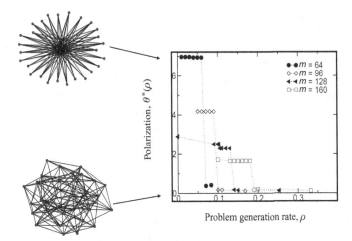

Figure 5.5. Polarization of the optimal structure as a function of ρ, for networks of size $n = 32$ and different number of links $m = 64, 96, 128, 160$. The star-like configuration (top) is optimal for low ρ, while an homogeneous configuration (bottom) is optimal for high ρ

existence of some such structure and found that it may allow agents to conduct search with an effectiveness that would not be attainable otherwise.

We now ask the question of how the existence of a suitable reference structure (an organizational backbone) may impinge on the problem of search and congestion. This issue has been recently addressed by Dodds, Watts and Sabel (2003) [84] – hereafter referred to as DWS. They conduct a numerical analysis of the problem in a complex scenario that is somewhat reminiscent of that studied by Watts *et al.* (2002) [287], discussed in Section 5.2.3. In what follows, we describe their approach and results.

The different components of the model proposed by DWS may be organized as follows.

(1) *Underlying structure*

There is a backbone of the organization that acts as a "coordinate system" within which both agents and problems can be located. This backbone is hierarchical and consists of L levels going from the highest level denoted by $\ell = 0$ (which includes the single *head* of the organization) to the lowest level $\ell = L - 1$. Each lower level stems from the immediately higher one, i.e. from the one with immediately *lower* index. Specifically, every individual of the higher level "manages" a number b of corresponding members at the lower level ($b > 1$). Overall, therefore, the total number of agents in the organization is

$$n = 1 + b + b^2 + \cdots + b^{L-1} = \frac{b^L - 1}{b - 1}.$$

(2) *Network formation*

Based on the underlying structure, the actual network of the organization is constructed by *adding* new links to it in a stochastic fashion.[19] A
natural interpretation of these links is that they are mostly of an informal character, supplementing the communication channels afforded
by the formal (hierarchical) chart of the organization.[20]

The selection of such "informal links" is jointly affected by two complementary considerations.

(a) On one hand, the separation between any two agents along the
backbone structure affects negatively their probability of being
connected by informal links. Roughly, two individuals are judged
to be close if neither of them needs to proceed to a much higher
level than her own to meet a common ancestor. The motivation
is that, in this case, those agents should find it relatively easy to
come together through few backbone-based intermediaries. The
importance of these considerations is governed by a parameter ζ,
as formally explained below.

(b) On the other hand, the probability that two agents be linked informally depends positively on the proximity of their closest common
ancestor to the head (or root) of the hierarchic backbone. One possible motivation here is that individuals in the managing echelons
of the organization enjoy more work flexibility. Thus, everything
else equal – in particular, concerning their relative distance considered in (a), individuals whose common ancestor is close to the
organizational apex are more likely to enjoy informal links. The
significance of this factor is controlled by a parameter λ, as indicated below.

To implement (a)–(b) formally, DWS define some suitable notions of
distance and depth, which are then used by the stochastic mechanism
of formation of new links. We describe each of these notions in turn.

Firstly, for each pair of agents i and j, denote by d_{ij} (or d_{ji}) the
difference between the hierarchical level of i (respectively, j) and that
of the closest ancestor of both i and j along the underlying backbone. In
general, of course, d_{ij} and d_{ji} are different unless i and j are placed at
exactly the same level of the organization. Based on these magnitudes,
the *organizational distance* $h(i, j)$ between i and j is defined by

$$h(i, j) = \sqrt{d_{ij}^2 + d_{ji}^2 - 2},$$ (5.30)

---

[19] Note, therefore, that in contrast with the model of Watts *et al.* (2002) [287] discussed in Subsection 5.2.3, the hierarchic structure *does* belong to the network.

[20] Recall our discussion in Subsection 1.2.8, where we stressed the importance of informal
links/relationships in the everyday operation of large and complex organizations.

which applies only to agents i and j who have $d_{ij} + d_{ji} \geq 2$ and, therefore, are *not* already linked by the backbone structure.[21]

Secondly, define the magnitude D_{ij} (which is equal to D_{ji}) as the *organizational depth* of i and j, which is measured by the backbone-distance from their closest common ancestor to the head of the organization. Clearly, D_{ij} simply coincides with the index of the organizational level at which such a common ancestor happens to be located.

Based on the above defined magnitudes, a total of m links are added to the backbone structure in the following manner. In sequence and without replacement, each possible link ij (not already part of the backbone structure) is selected stochastically with a probability $P(i, j)$ that satisfies the following expression:

$$P(i, j) \propto \left[\exp \left(-\frac{D_{ij}}{\lambda} \right) \right] \left[\exp \left(-\frac{h(i, j)}{\zeta} \right) \right], \qquad (5.31)$$

i.e. it is exponentially decreasing in both organizational distance and depth.

(3) *Problem generation*

Problems are generated from each node at some given rate per unit of time, which we continue to denote by ρ. Another parameter ξ controls how likely it is that the solution to the problem should lie far in the backbone from the originating node. Specifically, a problem that arises at some node i will find its solution at some node j with a conditional probability $q_i(j)$ that satisfies

$$q_i(j) \propto \exp \left(-\frac{h(i, j)}{\xi} \right).$$

Therefore, if ξ is small, the solution is likely to be found close to the originating node, while if it is large it can be found essentially anywhere with a comparable probability. Intuitively, the parameter ξ captures the typical complexity of the problems faced by the organization. When its problems are likely to be complex, their solutions may be found "anywhere," in locations that are generally far-away in the underlying backbone. This implies, in particular, that it is not possible to devise (or restructure) the organizational chart so as to match reasonably well a "typical" pattern of problem sources and solutions.

---

[21] Note that, accoding to (5.30), any two nodes that share the same immediate ancestor (manager) are taken to be at zero distance. This property will have important implications in the generation of certain networks – specifically, for the so-called local-team networks that are obtained for particular limit values of the parameters ζ and λ.

(4) *Information processing*

When a problem arises, its solution must be found by searching through the network, i.e. by passing it along until the target node is reached. In so doing, agents are assumed to follow a heuristic reasoning analogous to that used in Subsection 5.2.3. That is, they send the problem to the neighboring node (in either the formal or informal network) that is closest in the underlying backbone to the target node. This, in other words, implies that the problem will be sent to the neighbor that has the closest common ancestor with the node where the problem is solved. Of course, the problem will be passed directly to this node if it is one of the neighbors of the agent currently facing the problem.

Note that this search protocol relies on an implicit informational assumption analogous to that adopted throughout Section 5.2. It assumes that agents are aware of the backbone structure, can identify the position of every agent in it, and also know who can solve any given problem they might currently face. On the other hand, about all other details of the overall organizational network (which is formed as described above), they only have local information. They know, specifically, the backbone coordinates of their immediate neighbors (most importantly, of their informal contacts) but have no information whatsoever about how informal links connect other individuals in the organization. These information conditions are what DWS call "pseudoglobal knowledge."

It is important to understand the different role in search played by the backbone and the informal links. For example, if no informal links were present ($m = 0$), the path followed by any given problem would always be the same: it would work its way upward until the first common ancestor of the original and target node is met; thereafter, it would proceed downward along the unique path of the backbone hierarchy that reaches the solution. In contrast, when informal links are present, there are generally shortcuts that bypass common ancestors, using transversal links. These shortcuts directly connect nodes in the organization that are sometimes very far in the organizational chart – i.e. they only have common ancestors who lie very high up in the hierarchy. They afford, as we shall see, a two-fold advantage. First, of course, much shorter paths become available. Second, they tend to ease the congestion of upper nodes, which would otherwise be burdened by too many requests passing through them.

In the theoretical framework described, there are two kind of parameters: the environmental parameters and those that could be viewed (see below) as object of design.

Concerning the environmental parameters, the main ones are ρ and ξ. As discussed in Subsection 5.3.1, ρ captures the problem burden imposed on the organization and can be related to the rate at which the environment changes and thus organizational adaptation is required. The parameter ξ, on the other hand, embodies the typical complexity of the problems faced by the organization – cf. item (3) above. In a sense, both ρ and ξ reflect alternative dimensions impinging on the effective volume of internal search that the organization must undergo to tackle the problems that arrive to it. It thus seems sufficient to consider just one of them, as DWS do, focusing on ξ and keeping ρ fixed.

The parameters ζ and λ, on the other hand, may be regarded as objects of organizational design, much as in Subsection 5.3.2 alternative network architectures were assessed in terms of their induced search performance. Recall that those parameters govern the mechanism establishing the informal links that supplement the formal chart (backbone) and thus largely shape the overall topology of the organizational network. In a stylized fashion, ζ and λ may be interpreted as embodying the culture of the organization, which is itself the outcome (at least in part) of what rules and other internal arrangements are put in place when designing its functioning. Whatever is then the resulting organizational culture, it must surely impinge on the establishment of informal links. It should affect, for example, how easy it is to establish those links across different departments/divisions (captured by ζ) or how this depends on the position in the organizational hierarchy (embodied by λ).

But, of course, in addressing the issue of organizational design, one also needs a well-defined measure of organizational performance. DWS propose a two-fold criterion in this respect.

First, they suggest that one matter of concern should be the *maximum node centrality* of the network, akin to the value of $\hat{\beta}$ introduced by Guimerà *et al.* (2002) [145] and defined in (5.28). Again, therefore, we are interested in identifying the node that bears the highest processing burden, as it is *jointly* induced by the network, the algorithm, and the problem generation mechanism. The node with maximum centrality is the main bottleneck of the organization. Consequently, the magnitude of its processing burden represents a meaningful measure of how congested is the overall functioning of the organization.

Another dimension of performance highlighted by DWS is related to what we called *resilience* in Section 3.2. It asks the question of how robust is the overall connectedness of network to the removal (or failure) of a certain fraction of nodes. More precisely, such robustness is quantified as the fractional size of the largest remaining component when some n_r nodes are removed from the network.[22]

DWS conduct extensive numerical simulations in the theoretical framework described. Their most interesting results concern the case where the environmental parameter ξ lies in an intermediate range. Arguably, this is the context where the network architecture of the organization is most relevant. For, on one hand, only when ξ is not too low it generally happens that agents need

---

[22] Their results appear to be largely independent of the particular mechanism (biased or not) used in removing nodes.

to explore more than just locally around the problem source in order to find its solution. And, on the other hand, only if ξ is not inordinately high does the underlying backbone structure have any significant bearing on where the solution is to be expected. When ξ stays away from these two extremes, DWS find that the only kind of network design that fares well in both dimensions of interest (low centrality and high robustness) is what they call a *multiscale network*. It defines a class of networks obtained for intermediate values of the design variables ζ and λ. In those networks, the links added to the backbone span significant distances and do cover all hierarchic levels. However, they are more commonly found involving moderate distances and nodes in the upper part of the hierarchy.

The intuition for this conclusion can be explained by contrasting the performance of multiscale networks with that obtained for other configurations. The question, therefore, is why multiscale networks dominate any of the alternative possibilities. Following DWS, the alternative network configurations can be schematically categorized as follows.

- *Random networks,* obtained when $(\lambda, \zeta) \to (\infty, \infty)$. Then, the informal links are essentially independent of the underlying backbone.
- *Core-periphery networks*, prevailing when $(\lambda, \zeta) \to (0, 0)$. In this case, the uppermost nodes in levels $\ell = 0, 1$ form a highly connected core (a clique), while each of the agents in level 1 are the top managers of different unrelated branches (subtrees) that display virtually no informal links.
- *Random interdivisional networks*, occurring when $(\lambda, \zeta) \to (0, \infty)$. Here, informal links exist only between nodes that lie in different "divisions," i.e. have the single node that lies at the head of the hierarchic backbone as their unique common ancestor.
- *Local-team networks*, arising when $(\lambda, \zeta) \to (\infty, 0)$. Under these circumstances, informal links only connect individuals who have the same immediate ancestor (for which organizational distance is zero, as explained in Footnote 21). Thus, the organizational network consists of a hierarchy of closely knit groups (or "teams") in which each member is the ancestor of a corresponding group, also closely-knit, at the immediately lower level.

Now, as advanced, we argue that, when ξ lies within an intermediate range, multiscale networks dominate all former alternatives.

(a) *Multiscale networks are better than random networks.* The reason is that, while random networks are very robust, they do not contribute much to the ability of the original backbone in directing problems toward their targets. Under the maintained assumption that ξ is not too high, the location of the solution tends to be reasonably close to the node where the problem originates. Therefore, totally random links cannot be *consistently*[23] helpful all along the search path. These paths then come to rely too much on the upper nodes of the hierarchy, which imposes on them high centrality and the entailed congestion.

(b) *Multiscale networks are better than core-periphery networks.* The only informal links established in core–periphery networks involve the uppermost nodes in the two highest levels of the hierarchy, which form a completely connected clique. This feature is indeed effective in protecting the head of the organization from congestion but has the unfortunate consequence of being very fragile. If some of the (relatively few) nodes in level 1 become removed or faulty, the overall connectedness of the network suffers dramatically.

(c) *Multiscale networks are better than random interdivisional networks.* Here, the key issue is analogous to that which, as explained above, renders purely random links an ineffective complement of the backbone structure. In the present case, informal links are again too global and unrelated to the backbone to be really useful in search all along. They may well be useful in directing the problem to the right "division" in the early part of the search path. No further benefit, however, is to be gained from informal links later on. Overall, therefore, their role can only be of secondary importance in truly large organizations.

(d) *Multiscale networks are better than local-team networks.* This case is the polar opposite to the preceding one. If the organization network consists of a hierarchically arranged collection of local teams, informal links only exist within such teams. These links are then too local to really succeed in freeing search from the formal chart (i.e. the hierarchical backbone). Consequently, when problems arise that have the origin and target nodes at a significant distance, informal links are not of much use in opening short paths and alleviating the congestion of high-level nodes.

Thus as, the numerical simulations of DWS indeed confirm, *multiscale networks* (where both ζ and λ attain intermediate values) are best for robust search and network resilience when the process is guided by an underlying hierarchical structure. In a sense, their model complements the insights obtained in Subsection 5.2.3 with those derived from Subsection 5.3.2 and highlights the following interesting trade-off. On one hand, the underlying structure (be it hierarchical or a regular lattice) may improve performance by providing useful heuristics for search. But, on the other hand, when the search process is thus aided by a reference structure, there is the risk of exacerbating congestion if that structure funnels search too rigidly. Further insights on this important trade-off are likely to be gained from an analytical approach to the problem and the consideration of a wider diversity of underlying structures.

---

[23] In a sense, the considerations at work here are analogous to those highlighted in Subsection 5.2.2 for the model of Kleinberg (2000*a,b*) [173, 174].

CHAPTER 6

Search, Diffusion, and Play in Coevolving Networks

In this final chapter, we study the interplay of search, diffusion, and play in the formation and ongoing evolution of complex social networks. First, we illustrate how the issue of network formation is addressed by that part of the received economic literature that highlights its strategic dimension. As will be explained in Section 6.1, even though game-theoretic models are concerned with an undoubtedly important aspect of the phenomenon, they also display a significant drawback. Their standard methodology (i.e. the full-rationality paradigm) as well as many of their implicit assumptions (e.g. a largely stable environment) abstract from the inherent complexity that pervades the real world.

In contrast, the approach pursued in the bulk of this chapter adopts a polar standpoint. It stresses the complexity of social networks but, as a contrasting limitation, it largely eschews the strategic concerns that also play an important role in many cases. The analysis ranges from models where local search is the main driving force in network formation (Section 6.2) to those where the focus is on the interaction between network evolution and agents' embedded behavior (Section 6.3). Finally, a brief reconsideration of matters is conducted in Section 6.4, where it is also suggested that a genuine integration of strategic and complexity considerations should be one of the primary objectives of future network analysis.

6.1 GAME-THEORETIC MODELS OF NETWORK FORMATION

Here we shall not attempt to provide an extensive description of the large body of literature that studies network formation from a game-theoretic viewpoint.[1]

---

[1] For a very good overview of many of the recent developments in this area, the reader is referred to the volume of collected essays edited by Demange and Wooders (2005) [77]. It includes, in particular, surveys by Jackson (2005) [156] and Goyal (2005) [130] that provide an extended discussion of the issues and models that are illustrated here through our limited range of examples. On the other hand, the reader can also turn to the book edited by Dutta and Jackson (2003) [91], where some of the most influential articles in the early development of the network-formation literature are conveniently gathered.

Instead, the discussion will focus on some representative instances that illustrate well how strategic incentives impinge on problems of network formation. We shall concentrate, specifically, on the following setups:

- A *connections model* where agents must *bilaterally agree* on forming undirected links. These links yield not only immediate benefits from first neighbors but also additional ones from farther-away neighbors with a decay that depends on network distance.
- An *access model* in which agents have to *decide unilaterally* whom to connect to. These directed links give them access, without decay, to all the benefits that their partners either originally had or have acquired from linking to others.
- A model where agents play a *coordination game with their neighbors* and select both their partners (neighbors) as well as the strategies to adopt in the game. In correspondence to the network-formation assumptions underlying the connections and access models respectively, we shall consider two scenarios:
  A first one where links are *two-sided* (undirected) and must be agreed by the two agents involved.
  A second one where links are *one-sided* (directed) and are under the control of the connecting agent alone.

All of these contexts will first be studied from a static (equilibrium) viewpoint in Subsection 6.1.2 and then from a dynamic (long-run) perspective in Subsection 6.1.3. Some of them will also be revisited later on (e.g. in Subsections 6.2.1 and 6.3.1) when network formation is studied as the outcome of a "complex" dynamic process. A formal presentation of those four different setups of interaction is undertaken in the following Subsection.

6.1.1   Leading Scenarios

A Connections Model

The *Symmetric Connections Model* proposed by Jackson and Wolinsky (1996) [161] has become a popular benchmark in the modern network-formation literature. It contemplates a finite number of players $N = \{1, 2, \ldots, n\}$ that are connected through some undirected network $\Gamma = (N, L)$. For some given decay factor $\delta \in (0, 1)$ and some linking cost $c > 0$, the payoffs $\pi^i(\Gamma)$ earned by any particular player $i \in N$ are posited as follows:

$$\pi^i(\Gamma) = \sum_{j \neq i} \delta^{d(i,j)} - \frac{1}{2} c \kappa^i, \tag{6.1}$$

where, as usual, $d(i, j)$ stands for the geodesic distance between i and j in Γ (thus $d(i, j) = \infty$ if i and j lie in different components) and κ^i denotes the degree of node/agent i. These payoffs might be interpreted as capturing a process of bilateral communication channeled along the social network. Then, the key feature is that links are costly to both parties (i.e. they require equal investment of time or other resources) and the valuable information pooled across links deteriorates with distance.

An Access Model

We shall refer to the directed "connections model" without decay and linear payoffs studied in Bala and Goyal (2000) [21] as the *Linear Access Model*. It considers a set of players N who are connected through some network $\hat{\Gamma} = (N, \hat{L})$ that is *directed* – therefore, the existence of some link $(i, j) \in \hat{L}$ does not presume that the converse $(j, i) \in \hat{L}$ (cf. Subsection 2.1.1). Payoffs also reflect the direction of links. For any $i \in N$, let $\mathcal{A}^i(\hat{\Gamma})$ represent the set of agents who can be accessed by i in $\hat{\Gamma}$, formally defined as follows:

$$\mathcal{A}^i(\hat{\Gamma}) = \left\{ \begin{array}{l} \ell \in N : \exists\{j_1, j_2, \ldots, j_m\} \text{ s.t.} \\ (j_r, j_{r+1}) \in \hat{L} \text{ for all } r = 1, 2, \ldots, m - 1, \text{ with } j_1 = i \text{ and } j_m = \ell \end{array} \right\}.$$

Then, given some cost $c > 0$ involved in the formation of each link, the payoff of any particular player $i \in N$ is given by[2]

$$\pi^i(\hat{\Gamma}) = \left| \mathcal{A}^i(\hat{\Gamma}) \cup \{i\} \right| - c\hat{k}^i, \tag{6.2}$$

where $\left| \mathcal{A}^i(\hat{\Gamma}) \cup \{i\} \right|$ denotes the number of agents accessed by i – including herself – and $\hat{k}^i$ stands for her *outdegree* in $\hat{\Gamma}$, i.e. the number of links (i, j) that spring from i. One possible interpretation of these payoffs is again in terms of information flows. In contrast with the Symmetric Connections Model, however, it does not seem natural to conceive the entailed information acquisition as "communication," since it is one-directional and imposes a cost only on the party that "takes the initiative" (i.e. directs each link).

A Coordination Game Embedded in the Social Network

In this case, agents derive their payoffs from interacting with their neighbors according to a 2×2 coordination game analogous to that represented in (4.24). Now, however, let us allow for a general payoff table in which the payoffs earned by some agent i playing with some other j are given by

i \\ j	α	β
α	d	e
β	f	b

(6.3)

where the two possible actions are labeled α and β. Since the game is taken to be of coordination, we must have $d > f$ and $b > e$, i.e. the best response for a player who faces a single partner is to match the latter's choice. On the other

---

[2] Throughout this section, and for the sake of simplicity, we use the same notation to refer to the different payoff functions postulated by the different models. Bearing in mind which is the context under study, this should hopefully cause no confusion.

hand, to focus on the most interesting case, let us also assume that $d > b$ and $f + b > d + e$. In the parlance of game theory, it means that the Nash equilibrium (α, α) is *efficient* while the alternative Nash equilibrium (β, β) is *risk-dominant*. The first equilibrium is efficient because its induced payoffs (for both players) are higher than in the second. On the other hand, the equilibrium (β, β) is called risk-dominant because, under conditions of utter uncertainty (i.e. with a uniform subjective probability), the strategy β provides the highest expected payoff. Thus the coordination game poses a nontrivial problem of equilibrium selection where efficiency and risk-dominance embody conflicting criteria.

As indicated, given the pattern of interaction (formalized by some undirected network Γ), each player i is supposed to play the coordination game with each of her neighbors in $\mathcal{N}^i$. To make things interesting (i.e. to have the network be relevant in shaping agents' behavior), every player i is supposed to play the *same* action $a^i \in \{\alpha, \beta\}$ against everyone of her neighbors.[3] Concerning the nature of linking decisions, on the other hand, we consider two alternative scenarios: twosided and one-sided link creation. Each reflects alternative assumptions on whether game interaction requires bilateral consensus or not. Correspondingly, each of them also contemplates a different specification on how linking costs are shared.

1. *Two-sided link creation*

   This is the approach undertaken e.g. by Jackson and Watts (2002a) [159], who posit that links are undirected and thus "two-sided." The twosidedness of links has the following implications. First, as explained below (Subsection 6.1.2), it bears on the mechanism by which links are created: both players involved in any particular link should agree to it. An additional implication, naturally associated to the first, is that both players are assumed to contribute to the cost of creating the link (say equally). So let the *total* cost of each link be $c > 0$, and let $\psi(a^i, a^j)$ represent the payoffs to player i when she plays a^i and her partner j chooses a^j, as specified in (6.3). Then, the *overall* payoff $\pi^i(\mathbf{a}, \Gamma)$ obtained by player i when the prevailing network is $\Gamma = (N, L)$ and the action profile is $\mathbf{a} = (a^1, a^2, \ldots, a^n) \in \{\alpha, \beta\}^n$ has the following form:

$$\pi^i(\mathbf{a}, \Gamma) = \sum_{j \in \mathcal{N}^i} \psi(a^i, a^j) - \frac{1}{2}c\kappa^i, \tag{6.4}$$

   where, as usual, $\mathcal{N}^i = \{j \in N : (i, j) \in L\}$ stands for the neighborhood of i (induced by Γ) and $\kappa^i = |\mathcal{N}^i|$ is her degree.

---

[3] It is not always necessary to make this assumption in order for interesting network considerations to arise. But then the network must have implications that go beyond those strictly related to interaction. An example in this latter respect is discussed in Subsection 6.3.2, where we consider a context in which players are involved in *separate*, but *repeated*, interaction with all their neighbors according to a Prisoner's Dilemma. In this case, the network plays the key role of spreading strategically relevant information along the "parallel" repeated interaction that unfolds for every pair of neighboring players.

2. *One-sided link creation*

An alternative approach to network formation is pursued by Goyal and Vega-Redondo (2005) [135]. They posit that the underlying pattern of interaction is a *directed* network $\hat{\Gamma} = (N, \hat{L})$ and make the following two-fold assumption: (i) the cost c of each link (i, j) has to be incurred by the player i who directs it (whether or not the reciprocal link (j, i) is in place); (ii) any agent i interacts with everyone with whom she has a link, *whichever its direction*. Then, the payoff $\pi^i(\mathbf{a}, \hat{\Gamma})$ is given by

$$\pi^i(\mathbf{a}, \hat{\Gamma}) = \sum_{j \in \hat{\mathcal{N}}^i, i \in \hat{\mathcal{N}}^j} \psi(a^i, a^j) - c\hat{\kappa}^i, \qquad (6.5)$$

where $\hat{\mathcal{N}}^\ell$ represents the out-neighborhood of any node $\ell \in N$ in the directed network $\hat{\Gamma}$ (i.e. the set of neighbors to whom there is a direct link from ℓ) and $\hat{\kappa}^\ell$ stands for its outdegree. Naturally, such onesidedness of links has a counterpart in the network-formation mechanism, which is assumed unilateral. That is, each link is established under the exclusive control of the agent who directs it and then incurs its full cost (see below for the details).

6.1.2 A Static Equilibrium Approach

As explained, the different contexts just introduced presume different network-formation mechanisms at work and thus call for a different methodology to analyze them. In what follows, for didactical reasons, we start with the Linear Access Model (LAM), then proceed with the Symmetric Connections Model (SCM), to finish with the analysis of the coordination game under the two alternative formulations considered: one-sided and two-sided.

The Linear Access Model

In the LAM context, assuming that agents control their own links, they can evaluate the payoff implications of their linking decisions once they anticipate or predict the corresponding choices of others. This suggests modeling the network-formation process as a strategic-form game G where[4]

- each player $i \in N$ has a strategy space $S^i = \{M : M \subset N \setminus \{i\}\}$, with the interpretation that each $s^i \in S^i$ simply specifies the subset M of other players to whom i wishes to connect;

---

[4] The representation of a game in strategic form requires the specification of the set of strategies of all players and, for each of them, a payoff function that maps strategy vectors (or profiles) into payoffs. The reader unfamiliar with the very basic game theory that will be needed here can refer to the good introductory text by Watson (2002) [282] or, for more advanced and formal treatments, to Fudenberg and Tirole (1991) [116], Myerson (1991) [211], or Vega-Redondo (2003) [277]. In any of these references, one may find detailed explanations of the alternative ways in which a game can be represented and analyzed. The latter includes, in particular, the central notion of (strict) Nash equilibrium that is used below.

- for each strategy profile $\mathbf{s} = (s^1, s^2, \ldots, s^n)$, the induced payoff $\Pi^i(\mathbf{s})$ obtained by player i is given by

$$\Pi^i(\mathbf{s}) = \pi^i(\hat{\Gamma}(\mathbf{s})),$$

where $\pi^i(\cdot)$ is as specified by (6.2) and $\hat{\Gamma}(\mathbf{s})$ is the directed network $(N, \hat{L})$ where $(i, j) \in \hat{L} \Leftrightarrow j \in s_i$.

As standard in so many game-theoretic applications, we are interested in the Nash equilibria $\tilde{\mathbf{s}}$ of the game $G = [N, \{S^i\}_{i \in N}, \{\Pi^i\}_{i \in N}]$. In fact, Bala and Goyal (2000) [21] consider the more demanding notion of Strict Nash Equilibrium, where the choice $\tilde{s}^i$ of each player is required to be the unique optimal response to the strategies $\tilde{s}^j$ selected by the remaining players $j \neq i$.[5] More precisely, we have

Definition 5. *A strategy profile $\tilde{s}$ is a* Strict Nash equilibrium *of the game G if, for all $i \in N$ and every $s^i \in S^i$,*

$$\Pi^i(\tilde{\mathbf{s}}) > \Pi^i(s^i, \tilde{\mathbf{s}}^{-i}),$$

where $(s^i, \tilde{\mathbf{s}}^{-i})$ stands for the profile obtained from $\tilde{s}$ by replacing $\tilde{s}^i$ with s^i and keeping the remaining components unchanged at $\tilde{\mathbf{s}}^{-i} = (\tilde{s}^j)_{j \neq i}$.

It is not difficult to characterize the set of Strict Nash equilibria (SNE) of G, which naturally depend on the cost parameter c. A first observation is that the directed network $\hat{\Gamma}(\tilde{\mathbf{s}})$ induced by a SNE must have the property that, if it is not empty, each agent accesses everyone else. That is, one of the following exclusive statements must be true:

(i) $\mathcal{A}^i(\hat{\Gamma}(\tilde{\mathbf{s}})) = \varnothing$ for every $i \in N$;
(ii) $\mathcal{A}^i(\hat{\Gamma}(\tilde{\mathbf{s}})) = N \backslash \{i\}$ for every $i \in N$.

To see this, suppose (i) does not hold, so that at least one i has $\mathcal{A}^i(\hat{\Gamma}(\tilde{\mathbf{s}})) \neq \varnothing$. In fact, let i be one of the agents who accesses the largest number of other agents. Suppose, for the sake of contradiction, that she does *not* access everyone, i.e. there exists some j such that $j \notin \mathcal{A}^i(\hat{\Gamma}(\tilde{\mathbf{s}}))$. Then, we must also have that $i \notin \mathcal{A}^j(\hat{\Gamma}(\tilde{\mathbf{s}}))$, for otherwise $|\mathcal{A}^j(\hat{\Gamma}(\tilde{\mathbf{s}}))| > |\mathcal{A}^i(\hat{\Gamma}(\tilde{\mathbf{s}}))|$. But the possibility that $i \notin \mathcal{A}^j(\hat{\Gamma}(\tilde{\mathbf{s}}))$ is inconsistent with SNE, as we now explain. If j were to create the link (j, i) and delete any other links she might previously have, the set of agents thus accessed would be $\mathcal{A}^i(\hat{\Gamma}(\tilde{\mathbf{s}})) \cup \{i\}$. This would improve j's payoffs, either if she previously had some links or if she had no links. In the former case, she would increase the number of accessed agents at a linking cost that is no higher than before. In the latter case, she would turn from a zero payoff to a

---

[5] The motivation for such a stronger concept is that the ordinary notion of Nash equilibrium (which allows for players' best responses to be only weakly optimal) yields a huge multiplicity of equilibria in this case. Moreover, as we shall see in Subsection 6.1.3, strict Nash equilibria are the only outcomes toward which a natural adjustment dynamics converges globally.

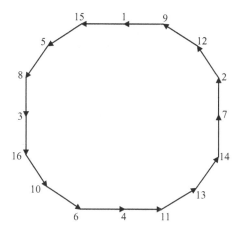

Figure 6.1. A directed wheel network in a population of 16 agents

positive one. (This follows from the fact that the induced payoff would be higher than that of i before, which could not have been negative at an equilibrium.) We may conclude, therefore, that $\mathcal{A}^i(\hat{\Gamma}(\tilde{s})) = N \backslash \{i\}$. But then it is clear that, at an equilibrium, every other k must have $\mathcal{A}^k(\hat{\Gamma}(\tilde{s})) = N \backslash \{k\}$ as well, since they can achieve this outcome by the single link (k, i).

Thus suppose that (ii) applies (i.e. (i) does not hold). Then, given that any player can access the rest of the population by connecting to a single agent, every player must support exactly *one* link. In fact, we now argue that the SNE network $\hat{\Gamma}(\tilde{s})$ must be a "wheel," with every agent receiving a link from only one other agent (cf. Figure 6.1). Now suppose otherwise, and let j and k be the two different players that support a link to some other i. In this case, it is clear that, say, player j would see her payoffs unaffected if, rather than supporting the link (j, i), she were to support instead the link (j, k). By so doing, the set of accessed agents would not change and neither would the cost be affected (i.e. it would continue to be that of a single link, c). But this is incompatible with the SNE notion, which requires that all players have *strict* incentives to stay with their equilibrium choices.

The former arguments establish the conclusion that every SNE network is either empty or a wheel. In fact, one can readily check that *both* architectures may be supported at a SNE if $c > 1$. In view of this characterization, it is finally of interest to compare the two possible equilibrium architectures with those that are efficient, in the sense of maximizing the aggregate payoff gains in the population. For concreteness, assume that $1 < c < n - 1$. Then, efficiency obviously requires that every agent accesses everyone else, provided this can be achieved through *just one* link per agent. But the latter proviso is indeed satisfied by a wheel network. This implies that the unique efficient architecture is the wheel and that, therefore, efficiency and (strict) equilibrium are compatible requirements in this case. Inefficiency, however, is also a possibility since we assume that $c > 1$. It will materialize if agents are somehow unable to "coordinate" their desire to become globally linked and no links are formed at all. Then, no agent is ready to form any link by herself, thus maintaining the empty network as an inefficient, but equilibrium, state of affairs.

The Symmetric Connections Model

Let us now consider the SCM, as introduced before. This context differs crucially from the LAM setup in that links are now undirected and their cost c is bilaterally shared by the two agents involved. Under these circumstances, it is natural to posit that the establishment of a *new* link between any two particular agents should occur if, and only if, both of them agree. And then, reciprocally, no *preexisting* link can be predicted to remain in place if any one of the two agents connected by it would benefit from its elimination. These are precisely the twin ideas embodied by the notion of *Pairwise Stability*, as originally formulated by Jackson and Wolinsky (1996) [161].[6]

To define matters formally, given any undirected network $\Gamma = (N, L)$, let $\pi^i(\Gamma)$ be as specified in (6.1). Furthermore, for any given $i, j \in N$, denote by $\Gamma \oplus ij$ the network $(N, L \cup \{ij\})$ and let $\Gamma \ominus ij$ stand for the network $(N, L \backslash \{ij\})$.[7]

Definition 6. *A particular network $\Gamma = (N, L)$ is said to be a* Pairwise-Stable network *(PSN) if the following two conditions are met:*

> (a) *There are no $i, j \in N$ such that both $\pi^i(\Gamma \oplus ij) \geq \pi^i(\Gamma)$ and $\pi^j(\Gamma \oplus ij) \geq \pi^j(\Gamma)$, one of these inequalities being strict.*
> (b) *For all $ij \in L$, neither $\pi^i(\Gamma \ominus ij) > \pi^i(\Gamma)$ nor $\pi^j(\Gamma \ominus ij) > \pi^j(\Gamma)$.*

---

[6] Alternatively, one could approach link formation in this case along the lines considered in the LAM context, but relying on a mechanism that reflects the two-sidedness of the situation. Specifically, following Myerson (1991) [211], one could still have the strategy spaces of each agent i defined as

$$S^i = \{M : M \subset N \backslash \{i\}\},$$

and the network $\Gamma(\mathbf{s}) = (N, L)$ induced by a strategy profile $\mathbf{s} = (s^1, s^2, \ldots, s^n)$ given by the condition

$$ij \in L \Leftrightarrow [j \in s_i \wedge i \in s_j].$$

A drawback of this formulation is that it exacerbates the coordination failures already witnessed in the LAM setup. By way of illustration, note that, independently of the parameters of the model (i.e. even for infinitesimal linking costs c), the strategy profile $(\varnothing, \varnothing, \ldots, \varnothing)$ is always a Nash equilibrium. Sometimes, it may be possible to mitigate this problem by considering (again, as in the LAM case) suitable refinements of Nash Equilibrium. This approach is pursued, for example, by Calvó-Armengol and Ilkiliç (2004) [51] (who consider the notion called Proper Equilibrium) or Goyal and Vega-Redondo (2004) [134] (who contemplate coalition-based refinements).

[7] Recall that when the link (i, j) is undirected (i.e. $(i, j) \in L \Leftrightarrow (j, i) \in L$) we have been using the shorthand notation ij throughout.

An important feature of the above notion of network stability is that link creation and link destruction are assessed separately. This has some analytical advantages but rules out what, in some cases, might be a relevant force leading to network instability. This concerns the possibility that two agents might gain by establishing a link between them if, simultaneously, they can eliminate a subset of their preexisting links with others.

Despite its relative weakness, the criterion of pairwise stability yields interesting network structure in the SCM context. Next, we list (and then prove) some of its implications for different ranges of the parameters, δ and c.

(i) If $c/2 < \delta - \delta^2$, the unique PSN is the *complete network* $\Gamma^c = (N, L^c)$, where $L^c = \{ij : i, j \in N\}$.

(ii) If $\delta - \delta^2 < c/2 < \delta$, a *star network* $\Gamma^s = (N, L^s)$ is pairwise-stable but, in general, other PSN exist. In a star network, there is some fixed i such that $L^s = \{ij : j \in N\}$.

(iii) If $c/2 > \delta$, any PSN $\Gamma = (N, L)$ is either *empty* or *connected*. In the latter case, every $i \in N$ has at least two links $ij, ik \in L, j \neq k$.

To establish the above points, we first argue that any PSN $\Gamma = (N, L)$ includes at most one (nonempty) component. Suppose, for the sake of contradiction, that two such components exist and let ij and $k\ell$ be two links lying in these different components. Then, it is enough to prove that i and ℓ would both gain from establishing the link $i\ell$.

On the one hand, note that, if Γ is a PSN, we must have

$$\pi^j(\Gamma) \geq \pi^j(\Gamma \ominus ij) \tag{6.6}$$

$$\pi^k(\Gamma) \geq \pi^k(\Gamma \ominus k\ell), \tag{6.7}$$

since otherwise the links ij and $k\ell$ could not be part of Γ. Now observe that it should also happen that

$$\pi^i(\Gamma \oplus i\ell) - \pi^i(\Gamma) > \pi^k(\Gamma) - \pi^k(\Gamma \ominus k\ell) \tag{6.8}$$

$$\pi^\ell(\Gamma \oplus i\ell) - \pi^\ell(\Gamma) > \pi^j(\Gamma) - \pi^j(\Gamma \ominus ij). \tag{6.9}$$

The basis for the first inequality is that when i links to ℓ, agent i obtains at least what k obtains in Γ from the link $k\ell$, in addition to δ^2 for the indirect connection with k that is channeled through ℓ. An analogous argument applies to the second inequality. Then, combining (6.6) and (6.9), we conclude that

$$\pi^\ell(\Gamma \oplus i\ell) > \pi^\ell(\Gamma),$$

while in view of (6.7) and (6.8) we have

$$\pi^i(\Gamma \oplus i\ell) > \pi^i(\Gamma).$$

The above two inequalities obviously contradict that Γ is a PSN.

We are now in a position to verify (i)–(iii). For (i), first note that $c/2 < \delta - \delta^2$ implies that any two players who share a common neighbor prefer to link directly rather than enjoy the indirect discounted benefits. Furthermore, note that since no PSN Γ can be empty (because $c/2 < \delta$), it must be connected (recall above). Combining both considerations, we conclude that Γ must be complete.

Concerning (ii), let $\Gamma^s = (N, L^s)$ be a star network centered on a particular i. Given that $\delta > c/2$, all links $ij \in L^s$ between i and any other peripheral j are sure to be worthwhile for both agents. On the other hand, since $c/2 > \delta - \delta^2$, no two peripheral players j, k will want to add the link jk to Γ^s since their entailed payoff gain (net of the linking cost) is negative. Thus Γ^s is indeed a PSN. To show that, in general, other pairwise-stable networks exist can be readily checked by constructing simple examples for $n > 3$.

Finally, to show (iii), it is enough to observe that if an agent i had only one link $ij \in L$ in a (nonempty) PSN $\Gamma = (N, L)$, then $\pi^j(\Gamma) - \pi^j(\Gamma \ominus ij) = \delta - c/2 < 0$. This implies that $\pi^j(\Gamma) < \pi^j(\Gamma \ominus ij)$, and therefore j should remove link ij.

Parallel to the discussion undertaken for the LAM context, it is of interest to contrast the implications of equilibrium (pairwise stability in this case) and efficiency (the maximization of the aggregate payoff), as it depends on the parameters of the model. Again, let us focus on the role of the linking costs c, for some given value of the decay rate δ. Clearly, for very low costs (i.e. $c/2 < \delta - \delta^2$), efficiency and pairwise stability both call for a complete network. Instead, when costs lie at the opposite extreme and $c/2 > \delta + (n - 2)\delta^2/2$, the opposite conclusion applies. That is, both efficiency and pairwise stability lead to an empty network.

The more interesting situation arises in the intermediate case where $\delta - \delta^2 < c/2 < \delta + (n - 2)\delta^2/2$. For this cost range, Jackson and Wolinsky (1996) [161] show that a network is efficient if, and only if, it displays a star architecture. Comparing this conclusion with (ii) and (iii) above, we see that there is at least the potential for a conflict between the two desiderata, pairwise stability and efficiency. Whereas in the range $c/2 \in (\delta - \delta^2, \delta)$ the two can be reconciled (since star networks are PSN, although not uniquely so in general), their clash is unavoidable if $c/2 \in (\delta, \delta + (n - 2)\delta^2/2)$.

For concreteness, let us focus on this latter case where the nature of the tension between efficiency and stability can be best explained. In a general sense, this conflict arises because agents (whose behavior is modeled through the pairwise stability notion) do *not* respond to the externalities that the SCM context naturally generates. More specifically, however, the problem involved may be of the two opposite types.

On one hand, we have the possibility of a coordination problem, akin to that already discussed in the LAM context. It may trap a large population, for example, in an empty network where the high payoff potential of a connected (say, star) network is utterly wasted. The reason is that, at an empty network, any two individuals who bilaterally consider the possibility of creating a link between them only compare their *private* benefits (δ) and their share of the linking cost ($c/2$). They ignore, therefore, the positive effect (externality) that such a link would have on third parties if a further link to either of them were also established.

But, polar to the aforementioned problem, (iii) also points to another possible source of inefficiency when the PSN is nonempty. It indicates that, if the "impasse" of an empty network is somehow averted, the opposite risk of overconnectedness is sure to materialize at a PSN. That is, it will be impossible to attain the efficient star architecture where not only connectedness but also short paths are obtained through just one link per each peripheral player. Instead, the strategic considerations underlying pairwise stability leads every agent to support, wastefully, at least two links. Again, the root of the problem is the noninternalization of externalities. But, in this case, the agent who blocks such an internalization is the center of the star. Surely, her contribution to efficiency would be crucial, as an intermediary in supporting short paths linking peripheral players. But she does not ripe any gain from that role and, consequently, is not ready to pay for a link more than what she strictly obtains from it, i.e. δ. Thus, when $\delta < c/2$ a star network cannot be pairwise stable and thus only inefficient architectures may be so.[8]

Network Formation and Social Coordination

We end our equilibrium analysis with the setup where agents not only choose how to link but also how to play a simple coordination game (recall the last part of Subsection 6.1.1). Two different network-formation scenarios are considered: two-sided and one-sided. In each of them, a different methodology of analysis must be applied, along the lines pursued for the SCM and LAM contexts, respectively.

1. Two-sided link creation. When links are two-sided and the corresponding cost is bilaterally shared, a suitable extension of the pairwise stability notion is in order. In the present case, a full description of the prevailing situation is what we shall call a *configuration*. It consists of a pair $\omega = (\mathbf{a}, \Gamma)$ that specifies both an action profile and a prevailing network. Associated to any such configuration, one can define a payoff $\pi^i(\mathbf{a}, \Gamma)$ for each agent $i \in N$, as given in (6.4). Then, inspired by the dynamic approach proposed in Jackson and Watts (2002*a*) [159] (see below), we put forward the following definition.

Definition 7. *A pair* $(\mathbf{a}, \Gamma)$ *is a* Pairwise-Stable configuration *(PSC) if*

(a) *There are no* $i, j \in N$ *such that both* $\pi^i(\mathbf{a}, \Gamma \oplus ij) \geq \pi^i(\mathbf{a}, \Gamma)$ *and* $\pi^j(\mathbf{a}, \Gamma \oplus ij) \geq \pi^j(\mathbf{a}, \Gamma)$, *one of these inequalities being strict.*

---

[8] To confirm that inefficient networks may indeed be pairwise stable, the reader may check that if $n = 6$ and $\delta < c/2 < (\delta + \delta^2 + \delta^3)(1 - \delta^2)$, any wheel network is a PSN.

(b) *For all $ij \in L$, neither $\pi^i(\mathbf{a}, \Gamma \ominus ij) > \pi^i(\mathbf{a}, \Gamma)$ nor $\pi^j(\mathbf{a}, \Gamma \ominus ij) > \pi^j(\mathbf{a}, \Gamma)$.*

(c) *For all $i \in N$, $\pi^i(\mathbf{a}, \Gamma) \geq \pi^i((a^i, \mathbf{a}^{-i}), \Gamma)$ for each $a^i \in \{\alpha, \beta\}$.*

Parts (a) and (b) of the previous definition are simply the counterparts of the corresponding ones in Definition 6, adapting the usual notation accordingly. Part (c), on the other hand, adds the requirement that the action chosen by any particular player be an optimal response to what others choose, given the network. In the same spirit as pairwise stability was formerly applied to networks alone, the present PSC notion maintains a separate evaluation of the different changes that modify a configuration, i.e. action revision, link creation, and link destruction.

When player interaction is given by a simple coordination game with payoff table as displayed in (6.3), the PSC's have a simple structure. Depending on the linking cost c, the following cases arise:

(i) If $c/2 < e$ ($= \min\{b, d, e, f\}$), then any PSC $\omega = (\mathbf{a}, \Gamma)$ has $\Gamma = \Gamma^c$ (where $\Gamma^c = (N, L^c)$ is the complete network with $L^c = \{ij : i, j \in N\}$) and a homogenous action profile that is either $\mathbf{a} = (\alpha, \alpha, \ldots, \alpha)$ or $\mathbf{a} = (\beta, \beta, \ldots, \beta)$.

(ii) If $e < c/2 < b$, then any PSC $\omega = (\mathbf{a}, \Gamma)$ has a network Γ that is partitioned into at most two completely connected components $\Gamma^\alpha = (N^\alpha, L^\alpha)$ and $\Gamma^\beta = (N^\beta, L^\beta) - N^\alpha$ or N^β empty – and a corresponding action profile $\mathbf{a} = (a^1, a^2, \ldots, a^n)$ that has $a^i = \alpha$ for all $i \in N^\alpha$ and $a^j = \beta$ for all $j \in N^\beta$.

(iii) If $b < c/2 < d$, then any PSC $\omega = (\mathbf{a}, \Gamma)$ has a network Γ that is partitioned into a completely connected component $\Gamma^\alpha = (N^\alpha, L^\alpha)$ and an empty subnetwork $\Gamma^\beta = (N^\beta, \varnothing)$ – possibly N^α or N^β empty – where $\mathbf{a} = (a^1, a^2, \ldots, a^n)$ has $a^i = \alpha$ for all $i \in N^\alpha$ and $a^i = \beta$ for all $i \in N^\beta$.

(iv) If $c/2 > d$, then any PSC $\omega = (\mathbf{a}, \Gamma)$ has $\Gamma = \Gamma^\varnothing \equiv (N, \varnothing)$.

All of the above conclusions are straightforward to check, so we shall only provide some brief clarifications for two of them. Concerning (i), note that if $c/2 < e$, all links are profitable for both parties and therefore every PSC must involve a complete network. This then implies that the action profile must be homogenous, since pairwise stability requires perfect coordination if the pattern of interaction is complete.[9] Finally, pertaining to (iii), it is worth stressing that

---

[9] To see this, consider a configuration with a complete network where m agents choose α and $n - m$ choose β. If $0 < m < n$, in order for such a configuration to satisfy Part (c) of Definition 7, the following two inequalities must hold:

$$d(m - 1) + e(n - m) \geq f(m - 1) + b(n - m)$$
$$dm + e(n - m - 1) \leq fm + b(n - m - 1),$$

where b, d, e, f are the payoffs specified in (6.3). These two inequalities, however, cannot hold simultaneously, given the assumption that the bilateral game is one of coordination.

a subnetwork with no links is one of the possibilities consistent with pairwise stability in this case only because the isolated players who choose β view this action choice as payoff-irrelevant given their lack of connections.

2. One-sided link creation. Now we suppose that links are one-sided, just as we had in the LAM context. Then, the agents' linking decisions can be modeled as part of an ordinary game. Adapting the former approach, its strategic-form representation G can be formulated as follows:

- for each player $i \in N$, her strategy space is $S^i = 2^{N \setminus \{i\}} \times \{\alpha, \beta\}$, where a typical $s^i = (M^i, a^i) \in S^i$ specifies the subset M^i of agents in $N \setminus \{i\}$ whom player i establishes a link with, together with the action a^i to be chosen in the coordination game;
- for each strategy profile $\mathbf{s} = [(M^1, a^1), (M^2, a^2), \ldots, (M^n, a^n)]$, the induced payoff $\Pi^i(\mathbf{s})$ for player i is defined by

$$\Pi^i(\mathbf{s}) = \pi^i(\mathbf{a}, \hat{\Gamma}(\mathbf{s})),$$

where $\pi^i(\cdot)$ is as specified in (6.5), $\mathbf{a} = (a^1, a^2, \ldots, a^n)$ is the action profile included in $\mathbf{s}$, and $\hat{\Gamma}(\mathbf{s}) = (N, \hat{L})$ is the directed network where $(i, j) \in \hat{L} \Leftrightarrow j \in M^i$.

We are again interested in the Strict Nash equilibria (SNE) of the above defined game G. Note that, in comparison with the PSC notion, the present equilibrium concept presumes a setup where agents have an enhanced adjustment flexibility in two key respects. First, they can control *jointly* any desired subset of their linking decisions. Second, they can *simultaneously* make linking adjustments and action revisions. Instead, what agents do *not* have, in comparison with the previous two-sided framework, is any control on their "passive" links. The basic assumption characterizing one-sided link creation is that such links cannot, or will not, be avoided. They would never be avoided, for example, if the game payoffs are all nonnegative and thus there is no reason (at least in a one-shot context) to object to "free" links.

Given any strategy profile $\mathbf{s} = [(M^1, a^1), (M^2, a^2), \ldots, (M^n, a^n)]$, let $L(\mathbf{s}) = \{ij : i \in M^j \vee j \in M^i\}$ and denote by $\Gamma(\mathbf{s}) = \{N, L(\mathbf{s})\}$ the *undirected* network reflecting the pattern of bilateral interaction induced by the directed network $\hat{\Gamma}(\mathbf{s})$, as defined above. Analogously, let $\mathbf{a}(\mathbf{s})$ stand for the corresponding action profile. Then, as the linking cost c varies, the set of SNE can be seen to change as follows (see Goyal and Vega-Redondo (2005)[135]):

(i′) If $c < \min\{b, f\}$, any SNE $\tilde{\mathbf{s}}$ induces a network $\Gamma(\tilde{\mathbf{s}}) = \Gamma^c$ (the complete network) and an action profile $\mathbf{a}(\tilde{\mathbf{s}})$ that is homogenous, i.e. either $\mathbf{a}(\tilde{\mathbf{s}}) = (\alpha, \alpha, \ldots, \alpha)$ or $\mathbf{a}(\tilde{\mathbf{s}}) = (\beta, \beta, \ldots, \beta)$.

(ii′) If $f < c < b$, any SNE $\tilde{\mathbf{s}}$ induces a network $\Gamma(\tilde{\mathbf{s}})$ that is partitioned into at most two completely connected components $\Gamma^\alpha = (N^\alpha, L^\alpha)$ and $\Gamma^\beta = (N^\beta, L^\beta)$ – possibly one of them empty – and a corresponding action profile $\mathbf{a}(\tilde{\mathbf{s}}) = (\tilde{a}^1, \tilde{a}^2, \ldots, \tilde{a}^n)$ that has $\tilde{a}^i = \alpha$ for all $i \in N^\alpha$ and $\tilde{a}^j = \beta$ for all $j \in N^\beta$.

(iii') If $b < c < d$, any SNE $\tilde{\mathbf{s}}$ induces a network $\Gamma(\tilde{\mathbf{s}})$ where either $\Gamma(\tilde{\mathbf{s}}) = \Gamma^c$ or $\Gamma(\tilde{\mathbf{s}}) = \Gamma^\varnothing$ (i.e. the network is complete or empty). In the first case, players display the homogenous action profile $\mathbf{a}(\tilde{\mathbf{s}}) = (\alpha, \alpha, \ldots, \alpha)$ while in the second case they display the homogenous action profile $\mathbf{a}(\tilde{\mathbf{s}}) = (\beta, \beta, \ldots, \beta)$.

(iv') If $c > d$, then any SNE $\tilde{\mathbf{s}}$ induces the network $\Gamma(\tilde{\mathbf{s}}) = \Gamma^\varnothing$.

The logic leading to (i')–(iv') is quite similar to that underlying (i)–(iv) for the previous two-sided context, so we shall not elaborate upon it here (see Goyal and Vega-Redondo (2005)[135] for details). The main difference resides in the fact that, because link-formation is now one-sided, the relevant parameter ranges must be adapted accordingly. Note, for example, that the case contemplated in (ii') is empty if, as it may well happen, $f > b$.

Equilibrium Network Formation: An Appraisal

The different models discussed in this section illustrate what tends to be a common feature in much of the strategic (equilibrium) analysis pursued by the game-theoretic literature on network formation – we refer again to Jackson (2005) [156] for a comprehensive survey. Based on the complementary tenets that agents are rational and enjoy "common knowledge" of the situation, the equilibrium predictions of the models tend to display specially simple network architectures: wheels, stars, complete, etc. These predictions, however, are markedly counterfactual. For, as explained in Chapter 1, social networks in the real world are typically very complex, at least when populations involved are large.

Admittedly, the simple theoretical predictions arising from the received game-theoretic literature afford a clear-cut (and thus certainly useful) account of the strategic forces at work in the formation of many social networks. This approach, however, is also bound to miss important features of the problem that stem from the vast complexity of many social networks. Network complexity, in particular, is expected to have a key bearing on the evolution of the network itself, thus impinging in an essential way on the process of network formation.

These methodological points have already been explained at some length before, so we shall not insist on them any further – recall, in particular, the discussion in Section 1.3. Partially motivated by these concerns, there is an important branch of the received literature that, relaxing the stringent assumptions that underlie equilibrium analysis, has undertaken an explicitly dynamic study of network formation. Agents are no longer assumed to be either unboundedly rational or fully aware of the details of their social environment. Rather, they are posited to adapt just gradually and in an uncoordinated fashion, as specific opportunities arrive to them. At any revision juncture, they are supposed to enjoy only limited understanding of the situation. This forces them to follow simple behavioral rules or react, say, in a myopic fashion to the current circumstances.[10]

In what follows, we review this dynamic approach for some of the benchmark models that have been studied in the present subsection through equilibrium analysis. In principle, one might hope that this could draw the analysis closer to the richness and complexity that we are after. In this respect, however, the results will turn out to be somewhat disappointing. An identification of what seems to be missing – in essence, we shall argue, a truly changing environment – will then naturally usher us into the models and approach that will occupy us in the rest of this chapter.

6.1.3   A Dynamic Long-Run Approach

In full parallelism to Subsection 6.1.2, we could have organized the present discussion by addressing in turn each of the four scenarios considered: the Linear Access Model, the Symmetric Connections Model, and the model of Network Formation and Social Coordination, both in its one- and two-sided versions. However, since the message to be gained is quite similar in each case, we focus instead on just two of them that illustrate well enough the range of considerations involved. Firstly, we shall discuss the Linear Access Model (LAM), where (a) link creation is *one-sided*; (b) there are no additional strategic dimensions; and (c) equilibrium is essentially unique. Secondly, we shall turn to the polar context where (i) link creation is *two-sided*, (ii) players interact according to a coordination *game*, and (iii) *equilibrium multiplicity* is an inherent feature and thus equilibrium selection becomes a central issue. Once these models are discussed and their main insights gathered, the present subsection will conclude with a critical appraisal of the dynamic approach to network formation, as exemplified by the aforementioned two scenarios.

The Linear Access Model, Revisited

In undertaking a dynamic analysis of the LAM context, we build on the traditional formulation of (bounded-rationality) learning in games – see Fudenberg and Levine (1998) [115] or Vega-Redondo (2003) [277]. It postulates that players simply best-respond, myopically, to the current behavior of others. This can be rationalized as a reasonable rule of thumb to be used when the underlying environment is too complex to be well comprehended and its evolution is gradual.

---

[10] There are also some recent interesting papers that have studied network formation when players are forward looking and react optimally to the anticipation of the subsequent (also optimal) behavior of others. See e.g. Watts (2002) [283] and Deroïan (2003) [80] in the context of the connections model (recall Subsection 6.1.1), or Page, Wooders and Kamat (2005) [231] and Dutta, Ghosal, and Ray (2005) [92] for a study of the problem in more general contexts.

Formally, let time be measured discretely and indexed by $t = 0, 1, 2, \ldots$. The state of the system is $\mathbf{s}_t$, the prevailing strategy profile. At every t, each player $i \in N$ is taken to enjoy a revision opportunity with some independent probability $p \in (0, 1)$, the same for everyone. If any given i receives such an opportunity, then she chooses a strategy s_t^i that maximizes her current payoffs, given the strategies formerly chosen by the remaining players. That is,

$$s_t^i \in \arg\max_{s^i \in S^i} \Pi^i\left(s^i, \mathbf{s}_{t-1}^{-i}\right), \tag{6.10}$$

where $\mathbf{s}_{t-1}^{-i}$ has the usual interpretation as the profile prevailing at $t-1$ that excludes the choice s_{t-1}^i adopted by i herself. In general, of course, there could be several choices at t consistent with (6.10). Then, every possible choice is assumed chosen with some (say equal) probability.

By construction, the SNE of the corresponding game – see Subsection 6.1.2 – *coincide* with the stationary points of the above best-response dynamics. That is, not only are these strategy profiles obviously stationary but, reciprocally, they are the only ones that qualify as such. Every $\mathbf{s} = (s^1, s^2, \ldots, s^n)$ that fails to be an SNE must have some i such that s^i is either *not* a best response or, at least, there is an alternative $\tilde{s}^i$ that is equally as good. Eventually, therefore, the dynamics must lead the system, almost surely (a.s.), away from it.

Bala and Goyal (2000) [21] show that the best-response dynamics formulated above eventually converges, a.s., to some SNE – i.e. to a wheel network or the empty network. To focus on the most interesting case, assume that $c \leq 1$ so that the empty network cannot be sustained at a SNE. Then, to establish the previous claim, it is enough to show that, starting from an arbitrary $\mathbf{s}_0$, there is an adjustment path $(\mathbf{s}_0, \mathbf{s}_1, \ldots, \mathbf{s}_T)$ that, in a finite number of steps, reaches a wheel network with positive probability. To start this chain, the fact that $c \leq 1$ allows us consider, without loss of generality, some initial $\mathbf{s}_0$ where every agent supports at least one link. Thereafter, the chain constructed includes the following two different adjustment phases.

First, consider a phase $(\mathbf{s}_0, \mathbf{s}_1, \ldots, \mathbf{s}_r)$ in which, for *every* $i \in N$, the set of accessed players $\mathcal{A}^i(\hat{\Gamma}(\mathbf{s}_t)) < n - 1$.[11] Then, at any given $t \leq r - 1$, let $i(t)$ be one of the players who is not in the set of accessed players $\mathcal{A}^{j(t)}(\hat{\Gamma}(\mathbf{s}_t))$ of some other $j(t)$. Suppose that $i(t)$ alone is given the opportunity to revise her strategy at $t + 1$. Since by supporting a single link to $j(t)$, player $i(t)$ can access $\mathcal{A}^{j(t)}(\hat{\Gamma}(\mathbf{s}_t)) \cup \{j(t)\}$, we can be sure that, after the revision, $i(t)$ accesses a number of other agents that is not lower than $\left|\mathcal{A}^{j(t)}(\hat{\Gamma}(\mathbf{s}_t))\right| + 1$, i.e. $\left|\mathcal{A}^{i(t)}(\hat{\Gamma}(\mathbf{s}_{t+1}))\right| \geq \left|\mathcal{A}^{j(t)}(\hat{\Gamma}(\mathbf{s}_t))\right| + 1$. Eventually, therefore, there is some finite r such that, for some $i \in N$, we have $\mathcal{A}^i(\hat{\Gamma}(\mathbf{s}_r)) = n - 1$.

Next, construct the phase $(\mathbf{s}_{r+1}, \mathbf{s}_{r+2}, \ldots, \mathbf{s}_T)$ as follows. For any $t \geq r$, let $i(t)$ continue to denote the player who singly revises her strategy at $t + 1$. For $t = r$, we choose $i(r)$ as one of the players who, given $\hat{\Gamma}(\mathbf{s}_r)$, is farthest away

---

[11] Of course, this phase could be empty (i.e. $r = 0$) if the initial $\mathbf{s}_0$ already includes some player i with $\mathcal{A}^i(\hat{\Gamma}(\mathbf{s}_t)) = n - 1$.

(in terms of the induced *directed* distance) from $i(r - 1)$, the last player who revised in the first phase. Suppose that $i(r)$ establishes a link with $i(r - 1)$ and deletes all others. Since $\mathcal{A}^{i(r-1)}(\hat{\Gamma}(\mathbf{s}_r)) = n - 1$ and $i(r - 1)$ did not previously rely on $i(r)$ to access any other player in $\hat{\Gamma}(\mathbf{s}_r)$, we have $\mathcal{A}^{i(r)}(\hat{\Gamma}(\mathbf{s}_{r+1})) = \mathcal{A}^{i(r-1)}(\hat{\Gamma}(\mathbf{s}_{r+1})) = n - 1$. Thus, in particular, this revision by $i(r)$ is consistent with (6.10). For subsequent t, we inductively choose $i(t)$ as one of the remaining players in the set $N \setminus \{i(r - 1), i(r), \ldots, i(t - 1)\}$ that is farthest away in $\hat{\Gamma}(\mathbf{s}_t)$ from the original $i(r - 1)$. We then assume that $i(t)$ establishes a link with $i(t - 1)$ and removes all other preexisting links. This is a best response and guarantees that

$$\mathcal{A}^{i(t)}(\hat{\Gamma}(\mathbf{s}_{t+1})) = \mathcal{A}^{i(t-1)}(\hat{\Gamma}(\mathbf{s}_{t+1})) = \cdots = \mathcal{A}^{i(r-1)}(\hat{\Gamma}(\mathbf{s}_{t+1})) = n - 1.$$

At $t = r + n - 1$, we have $\mathcal{A}^i(\hat{\Gamma}(\mathbf{s}_{t+1})) = n - 1$ for all i. Now, finally, let $i(r - 1)$ alone be provided with a revision opportunity. A best response for her is to establish a *single* link with $i(r + n - 1)$, which leads to a wheel network after a chain of adjustments of (finite) length $T = r + n$.

We conclude, in sum, that a dynamic analysis based on the adjustment process (6.10) reinforces the message obtained from our former static analysis. That is, even if players are only boundedly rational and have to learn how to reach equilibrium, a simple network architecture (i.e. the wheel, provided $c \leq 1$) is the sole outcome resulting from strategic behavior in the LAM context. In this context, however, it may be argued that the problem faced by the agents is particularly simple, since the induced game displays no equilibrium multiplicity that could muddle their adjustment process. In contrast, one might expect that the issue becomes substantially more involved when players interact through a coordination game and confront a nontrivial problem of equilibrium selection. As advanced, we now turn to analyzing this context within a network-formation mechanism that is assumed two-sided.

Network Formation and Social Coordination: Revisiting the Two-Sided Case

In Subsection 6.1.2, the equilibrium notion used in the static analysis of two-sided network-formation models was pairwise stability. Or, rather, a suitable elaboration of it when players' interaction is based on a (coordination) game. It is natural, therefore, to have the present dynamic analysis rely on the adjustment rule that implicitly underlies the concept of pairwise stability. This is the rule that, in the same spirit as the traditional best-response rule for ordinary games, embodies myopic adjustments on the part of agents. These adjustments, of course, should be conceived as either unilateral or bilateral, depending on the nature of the decision involved (i.e. action revision, link destruction, or link creation).

Proceeding now formally, time continues to be measured discretely and indexed by $t = 0, 1, 2, \ldots$. The state of the system $\omega_t = (\mathbf{a}_t, \Gamma_t)$ specifies the actions played by each player in the coordination game as well as the prevailing network. In line with the static PSC notion introduced in Definition 7, we postulate that, at every t, the following adjustment events (a)–(b) take place (in this order):

(a) A single pair of agents, i and j, is randomly selected (all pairs, say, selected with the same probability).
   - If the link ij is currently in place (i.e. $ij \in \Gamma_{t-1}$), then it is removed ($ij \notin \Gamma_t$) whenever at least one of the players strictly gains from this change – i.e. $\pi^i(\mathbf{a}_{t-1}, \Gamma_{t-1} \ominus ij) > \pi^i(\mathbf{a}_{t-1}, \Gamma_{t-1})$ or/and $\pi^j(\mathbf{a}_{t-1}, \Gamma_{t-1} \ominus ij) > \pi^j(\mathbf{a}_{t-1}, \Gamma_{t-1})$, where $\pi^\ell(\cdot)$ is as defined in (6.4).
   - If the link ij does not currently exist (i.e. $ij \notin \Gamma_{t-1}$) then it is created whenever $\pi^i(\mathbf{a}_{t-1}, \Gamma_{t-1} \oplus ij) \geq \pi^i(\mathbf{a}_{t-1}, \Gamma_{t-1})$ and $\pi^j(\mathbf{a}_{t-1}, \Gamma_{t-1} \oplus ij) \geq \pi^j(\mathbf{a}_{t-1}, \Gamma_{t-1})$ – i.e. neither player is harmed by it – with the gain being strict for at least one of them.
(b) A single player $i \in N$ is randomly selected (say uniformly). She is given the opportunity to revise her previous action and then selects $a_t^i \in \arg\max_{a^i \in \{\alpha, \beta\}} \pi^i(a^i, \mathbf{a}_{t-1}^{-i}, \Gamma_t)$, all of the admissible choices with some positive probability.

It should be clear that the stationary points of the above dynamics *coincide* with the pairwise-stable configurations, i.e. a state ω is stationary if, and only if, it defines a PSC. Indeed, it is also easy to check that the dynamics converges a.s. to some PSC from any arbitrarily chosen initial conditions. The interesting issue, therefore, is of a different sort – it concerns a problem of equilibrium selection. For, as explained in Subsection 6.1.2, when the linking cost is not too high in relation to payoffs (in particular, if $c/2 < b$) there is a significant multiplicity of pairwise-stable (or long-run) configurations. In fact, in the intermediate range where $e < c/2 < b$, such a multiplicity affects not only players' actions but also their network of interaction. In this case, *any* segmentation of the population into two components where a different action is homogeneously played turns out to be a PSC.

To address such a multiplicity problem, the modern game-theoretic (evolutionary) literature has explored the implications of adding some noise to the dynamics. In particular, Jackson and Watts (2002a) [159] enrich the above formulation with the inclusion of perturbations in both the link-revision stage (a) as well as in the action–revision stage (b).[12] More precisely, they replace

---

[12] Similar multiplicity problems also arise in the remaining two models studied in Subsection 6.1.2: the symmetric connections model, and the one-sided model of network formation and social coordination. The problem has also been tackled by adding noise to the "unperturbed dynamics." This leads to a clear-cut selection result in some cases, as explained by Jackson and Watts (2002b) [160] for the first scenario, and Goyal and Vega-Redondo (2005) [135] for the second one.

(a)–(b) by the following extended counterparts, also implemented in sequence at each t:

(a') Apply (a) and then reverse the outcome with some probability $\gamma > 0$.

(b') Apply (b) and then reverse the outcome with some probability $\varepsilon > 0$.

Since γ and ε are positive, the induced stochastic process is ergodic.[13] That is, independently of the initial configuration ω_0, the long-run behavior of the process is uniquely determined. In this sense, the multiplicity problem is resolved: the prediction of the model is identified with the unique invariant distribution $\mu_{\gamma,\varepsilon}$ to which the process converges over time.

Naturally, in consonance with the informal understanding of "noise," we want to think of both γ and ε as small, so that "most of the time" the adjustment is governed by rules (a) and (b) alone. Formally, this is captured by making both γ and ε converge to zero, in some prespecified ratio (positive and bounded). Then, the focus is on characterizing the limit invariant distribution $\mu_{\gamma,\varepsilon}$ as $\varepsilon = r\gamma \to 0$ for some $r > 0$. In what follows, I simply sketch the analysis and explain the main intuition, while I refer the interested reader to Jackson and Watts (2002a) [159] for the precise details.

Consider first the case where linking costs are low so that $c/2 < e$. Then, it is clear that, under the unperturbed dynamics (a)–(b), the process must converge a.s. to one of the two PSC's in which the network is complete and either everyone chooses α or everyone chooses β. Denote these states by ω^α and ω^β, respectively. By ergodicity, we also know that the process recurrently revisits ω^α and ω^β over time. Nay, if ε (and therefore γ) is low, it must lie at, or close to, either of them most of the time. The question then is which one of those two states will get the lion's share. Intuitively, it should be the state that is relatively more difficult to abandon through noise – or reciprocally, the one that is easiest to reach.

As it turns out, the resolution of this dilemma hinges upon considerations of risk dominance. The fact that the Nash equilibrium (β, β) has been posited to be risk dominant (recall Subsection 6.1.1) implies that the "basin of attraction" of ω^β for the unperturbed dynamics is the largest. When $\varepsilon \searrow 0$, this makes it "infinitely easier" to reach ω^β from ω^α than *vice versa*. In the end, this asymmetry implies that, for very low ε, the invariant distribution $\mu_{\gamma,\varepsilon}$ ends up attributing most of its weight to ω^β. One finds, therefore, that the *a priori* multiplicity problem is resolved in favor of action β – or, in the usual terminology, ω^β is the unique *stochastically stable state*.

Next, consider the only other case where an interesting multiplicity problem arises: $e < c/2 < b$.[14] Then, the large array of stationary states of the

---

[13] Simply note that, by resorting to noise alone, it is possible to perform a transition path across any two given states. Thus, the process displays a single recurrent class and is therefore ergodic.

[14] In the remaining cases, things are much less interesting. Thus, if $b < c/2 < d$, the more robust alternative to the empty network is a complete network with all agents playing α. Therefore, this is also the only stochastically stable configuration. On the other hand, if $c/2 > d$, every PSC involves an empty network and all are therefore essentially equivalent.

unperturbed dynamics that may "anchor" the overall dynamics is much wider – as indicated, it includes any partition of the population into two complete and action-homogenous components. What is the relative robustness to noise of each of them? As it happens, the two extreme such configurations, ω^α and ω^β, where all players are in the same (all-inclusive) component are *comparably* robust and also *more so* than any other. The intuition resides in the following observation.

If the process lies at either ω^α or ω^β, the only way in which the system can escape away is if, in the relatively short time lapse before the unperturbed dynamics settles down, *two or more* agents have their actions switch away (suboptimally) from the action adopted by everyone else. If they do so, there is some positive probability (corresponding to the unperturbed dynamics operating in a suitable order) that all others end up deleting their links to those deviants. The latter then become isolated, forming a sustainable (separate) component.

In contrast, we now argue that any other possible PSC can be destabilized by just *one* perturbation. As explained in Subsection 6.1.2, every alternative PSC in this case must have the overall network divided into two components, $(N^\alpha, \Gamma^\alpha)$ and (N^β, Γ^β). Then simply consider the possibility that, say, one of the agents $i \in N^\alpha$ switches to action β. Subsequently, it is possible (again, if the unperturbed dynamics operates in a suitable order) that i loses all her links with all other agents in N^α and forms links with those in N^β. This leads the process into a different PSC, thus showing that the original one can be "easily" destabilized by a single perturbation. Since such *relative* easiness is all what counts in the long run when ε and γ are very low, the following conclusion is consequently reached: If $e < c/2 < b$, only the states ω^α and ω^β – but *both* of them – are robust (i.e. stochastically stable) in the long run.

To summarize, it turns out that social learning leads to the same sharp predictions and simple network structures obtained from the static analysis. In fact, we find that those predictions are simplified still further if the basic adjustment dynamics is perturbed by some *small* noise. For example, even in those cases where multiple network and action configurations would be a priori possible, that perturbation always selects a *complete* network and a *homogenous* action profile. In this sense, therefore, we may assert that the dynamic approach does away with any modicum of complexity in the long run. That is, any genuinely local interaction structure or action diversity that would otherwise be consistent with equilibrium (i.e. pairwise stable) is essentially discarded in the long run by a small noise.

Network Formation: A Reappraisal from a Dynamic Viewpoint

The dynamic analysis of our leading network-formation scenarios underscores the same idea that was already gathered from the static approach.[15] It highlights,

---

[15] Analogous points could have been made concerning the other models introduced in Subsection 6.1.1 whose dynamic analysis has not been explicitly discussed.

in particular, that the game-theoretic approach typically pursued by the existing literature is unable to shed light on the network complexity observed in the real world. Certainly, a dynamic perspective that builds upon the assumption that players are boundedly rational and thus cannot "see through" the problem is a welcome first step in the right direction. As illustrated, however, it needs to be complemented with further moves toward a more realistic description of the situation if richer behavior is to ensue. Otherwise, the dynamics tend to act as a mere device for selection among different static equilibria, further simplifying the theoretical predictions.

Intuitively, there is an important feature missing from the received theoretical framework that is nevertheless prominent in the real world. It concerns the fact that, in most interesting situations, the underlying environment changes briskly over time. To account for this important feature, however, our models should not reflect a context that is essentially stationary, only "punctuated" (if at all) by occasional noise. For, in this case, nothing qualitatively different can eventually arise and the pressure toward simple equilibrium configurations is difficult to overcome. Instead, the models should contemplate an environment that is allowed to change continuously over time at a relatively fast pace – i.e. at a rate comparable to that at which agents' adjustment takes place. Under such conditions, agents must confront, face on, the implications of what evolutionary biologists label as the Red Queen Principle, after Lewis Carrol's (1872) [56] *Through the Looking Glass*: ". . . it takes all the running you can do to keep in the same place" (cf. Van Valen (1973) [274]). In the remaining part of this chapter, we discuss models that strive to incorporate some of this richness, either by considering environments that grow over time (Section 6.2) or that are subject to significant volatility (Section 6.3).

6.2 NETWORK-BASED SEARCH FOR PARTNERS IN A CHANGING ENVIRONMENT

In this section, we discuss network-formation models that embody alternative versions of both search and a changing environment. For concreteness, let us say that the creation of new links is carried out through *(network-based) search* when new partners are found by relying on *prevailing links*. This, of course, may have a variety of different materializations, as we illustrate below. It always means, however, that the current network has a crucial and *direct* bearing on the formation of new links.

Environmental change, on the other hand, will be considered in two different scenarios. First, in Subsection 6.2.1, we shall study models with a *growing* set of nodes (i.e. a context where new nodes keep forever entering). This introduces a marked asymmetry between "young" and "older" nodes, each entering in a quite different environment. Second, in Subsection 6.2.2, we focus on models where the set of nodes is fixed but the network is subject to *persistent* and *significant volatility*. This reflects an environment where the circumstances (e.g. competencies, information, etc.) that underlay the value of preexisting links may easily become "obsolete," thus requiring continuous adaptation by the agents.

Overall, we shall find that the combination of search and a nonstationary environment introduces new forces in network evolution, in turn generating some of the interesting complexity we missed in previous models. In particular, it induces the wide heterogeneity and intricate architecture displayed by many social networks in the real world.

6.2.1   A Growing Environment

As indicated, the alternative models to be discussed here all display network-based search in link creation and a growing environment. Even though they are quite different in their motivation and details, all of them are analyzed through a common methodology, i.e. a mean-field continuum approach, where the by-now familiar techniques of mean-field analysis are applied to the continuum idealization of a discrete framework.[16]

These models also induce many common regularities. Specifically, they all share a complex topology with a broad degree distribution, a relatively high clustering, and low average distances. Some of them can also be seen to display the positive degree correlations among neighboring nodes that are prevalent in many social networks (cf. Section 2.3). For the sake of focus, however, our formal analysis will concentrate on characterizing the induced degree distributions. These distributions will turn out to be scale-free in every case (at least for the high degree range), which suggests viewing this regularity as an implication of the twin features shared by all these models: growth and network-based search.

Meeting Partners in Action

Probably the simplest possible materialization of the notion of network-based search is the one postulated by Dorogovtsev *et al.* (2001) [89]. In a growing setup where new nodes enter over time, they posit that any new node just connects to both endnodes of randomly selected links (among all those currently in place). In a sense, we can view the process as reflecting a situation where agents can only be met when interacting with some other node. Thus, naturally, it follows that more active agents (i.e. those with more links) are more "visible" and thus will be *preferentially* chosen by entering nodes. Indeed, as we shall see, the

---

[16] The unified approach applied here to the analysis of the different models borrows heavily from Fosco (2004) [111]. Its mean-field continuum methods were first applied to the field of complex network analysis by Barabási and Albert (1999) [24]. It contrasts with the master-equation or rate-equation approaches pursued heretofore in this monograph (e.g. in the analysis of the Barabási–Albert model itself conducted in Section 2.5). Whereas the master-equation methodology provides an exact solution for large networks (i.e. asymptotically in n), the continuum approach delivers an accurate description only for nodes with a large degree (i.e. requires a further limit exercise on the degree κ to be genuinely applicable).

model turns out to be essentially indistinguishable from the original model with linear preferential attachment studied by Barabási and Albert (1999) [24].

Formally, let us start with a discrete version of the setup where, at each $t = 1, 2, \ldots$, there is a new node entering the network. Denote by $N(t)$ the nodes that have arrived up to (including) t. At the beginning of the process ($t = 0$) the set $N(0)$ includes m_0 nodes that, say, are completely connected among themselves. Thereafter, when a new node enters at any given t, it establishes an even number m of different links with an equal number of preexisting nodes $i \in N(t - 1)$. Specifically, suppose that it first randomly selects $m/2$ *links* (among those previously formed) and then connects to *both endnodes* of those links.[17] This means that, at large t, the probability ξ_t^i that any of the preexisting nodes $i \in N(t - 1)$ be selected by the newcomer is roughly equal to

$$\xi_t^i = m/2 \frac{\kappa_{t-1}^i}{\frac{1}{2} \sum_{j \in N(t-1)} \kappa_{t-1}^j},$$

where, in line with our notational conventions, κ_{t-1}^ℓ stands for the degree of any given node ℓ at $t - 1$. Thus, since

$$\sum_{j \in N(t-1)} \kappa_{t-1}^j = m_0(m_0 - 1) + 2m(t - 1),$$

the probability that i be selected can be approximated, for large t, as follows:

$$\xi_t^i \simeq \frac{\kappa_{t-1}^i}{2t}. \tag{6.11}$$

To analyze the long-run implications of the model, we now resort to a continuum idealization of it where the degree of any node i at some t is regarded as a nonnegative real (thus continuous) variable, denoted by $\kappa^i(t)$. Correspondingly, time is modeled continuously as well and, in view of (6.11), it is postulated that the rate at which a node i with degree $\kappa^i(t)$ increases this degree is governed by the following differential equation:

$$\frac{d\kappa^i(t)}{dt} = \frac{\kappa^i(t)}{2t}$$

with the initial condition $\kappa^i(t^i) = m$, where t^i denotes the point in time at which node i enters the network. The above differential equation is separable, so that it can be readily seen to yield the following solution:

$$\kappa^i(t) = m\sqrt{\frac{t}{t_i}} \qquad (t \geq t^i). \tag{6.12}$$

---

[17] Of course, this raises some caveats in the early stages of the process when, in view of the relatively small numbers, the procedure should be adapted in order to avert duplication (or multigraphs). We ignore this problem, however, since we are solely interested in asymptotic results for large networks, where it is irrelevant.

This expression provides a tangible manifestation of one of the key, albeit obvious, features of the model: on average, older nodes (i.e. those with lower t^i) display a larger connectivity. Based on (6.12), the probability that a particular node i display at some t a degree $\kappa^i(t)$ below a certain level κ can be written as

$$\Pr{}_t(\kappa^i(t) < \kappa) = \Pr{}_t\left(t^i > \frac{m^2 t}{\kappa^2}\right).$$

Since all nodes are *a priori* identical and enter at a constant rate, the probability distribution of entering times t^i for any $i \in N(t)$ is, for large t, approximately uniform over the interval $[0, t]$. Therefore, as $t \to \infty$, we have

$$\Pr{}_t\left(t^i > \frac{m^2 t}{\kappa^2}\right) \to 1 - \frac{m^2}{\kappa^2} \equiv P(\kappa),$$

where $P(\kappa)$ is the long-run cumulative degree distribution. The corresponding density is given by

$$p(\kappa) = \frac{dP(\kappa)}{d\kappa} = 2m^2 \kappa^{-3},$$

which, as advanced, coincides with the degree distribution resulting from the Barabási–Albert (BA) model with preferential attachment – cf. (2.56), derived for the case where only one link is formed by each entering node.

It is interesting to note, however, that despite the similarity between the degree distributions induced by the BA model and the present one, there are significant differences in other respects. These concern, for example, the respective levels of clustering. In the BA model, the clustering index satisfies $\mathcal{C} \sim n^{-3/4}$, so that it vanishes as the system size grows (recall Section 2.5). In contrast, in the present model, clustering remains bounded away from zero and, moreover, has an interesting degree dependence. To see this, consider for simplicity the case where $m = 2$ and let i be any given node with degree κ^i. Then, on one hand, the number of possible pairs among i's neighbors is $\kappa^i(\kappa^i - 1)/2$. On the other hand, the number of those pairs of nodes who are themselves neighbors is $\kappa^i - 1$. (By construction, each new neighbor obtained at $t > t^i$ contributes one such pair, whilst the first two neighbors obtained at the time t^i of entry only contribute one.) Combining both considerations, we have

$$C^i = \frac{2(\kappa^i - 1)}{\kappa^i(\kappa^i - 1)} = \frac{2}{\kappa^i}, \tag{6.13}$$

i.e. a node's clustering is inversely related to its degree. Interestingly enough, such inverse relationship is a feature displayed, quite sharply, by the empirical evidence reported for some social networks – see e.g. the results of Goyal *et al.* (2003) [132] on research collaboration networks among economists.

Search Through Nonaffiliating Referral

We now turn to another simple growing framework that has been proposed by Krapivsky and Redner (2001) [185], who label it *Growing Networks with Redirection* (GNR). Their model requires introducing a direction in links, as explained in Section 2.5 when discussing their more basic setup "without redirection." Intuitively, the network-formation process can be understood as the *disjunctive* composition of random search *or* referral in a growing network. As a new node i enters, first it randomly selects a node j (among those that formerly entered). Then, i either forms a link with j (so j becomes i's "ancestor") or, *alternatively*, asks j to refer i to j's own ancestor, say ℓ. In this latter case, i forms a link with ℓ (thus becoming a "descendant" of ℓ). Since referral and immediate linking are alternative (i.e. mutually excluding) possibilities, we describe the mechanism as one of *nonaffiliating referral*.

Formally, let us again start with a formulation in discrete time $t = 0, 1, 2, \ldots$. At every t, a new node j enters and chooses at random *one*[18] node i in the set $N(t-1)$ of those who have entered up to that point. (The initial $N(0)$ can be chosen as any finite nonempty set, arbitrarily connected.) Then, with probability $r \in (0, 1)$, node j establishes a link with i, while with the complementary probability $(1 - r)$ the link is directed to i's (unique) ancestor.

For large t, the probability $\check{\xi}_t^i$ that any of the preexisting nodes $i \in N(t-1)$ is selected by the newcomer is roughly given by

$$\check{\xi}_t^i = r \frac{1}{|N(t-1)|} + (1-r) \frac{\check{\kappa}_{t-1}^i}{\sum_{\ell \in N(t-1)} \check{\kappa}_{t-1}^\ell}, \tag{6.14}$$

where, adapting previous notation for outdegree (cf. (6.5)), $\check{\kappa}_t^\ell$ stands for the *indegree* – or number of descendants – of any given node ℓ at t.[19] For large t, (6.14) can be approximated as follows:

$$\check{\xi}_t^i \simeq r \frac{1}{t} + (1-r) \frac{\check{\kappa}_{t-1}^i}{t}.$$

Hence, in the continuum version of the model, we can write the following differential equation:

$$\frac{d\check{\kappa}^i(t)}{dt} = r \frac{1}{t} + (1-r) \frac{\check{\kappa}^i(t)}{t}, \tag{6.15}$$

---

[18] The GNR studied by Krapivsky and Redner (2001) [185] contemplates the creation of just one link per entering node. However, the analysis can be generalized to any number m of such links, as shown by Rozenfeld and ben-Avraham (2004) [250].

[19] As explained in Footnote 33 of Chapter 2, the distinction between indegree and total degree is irrelevant in the present context since the difference between them is uniformly equal to one for every node (see below for an elaboration). However, we choose to focus on the indegree here, because the distinction will be relevant in subsequent developments.

with the initial condition

$$\check{\kappa}^i(t^i) = 0, \qquad\qquad (6.16)$$

where, as before, t^i denotes the entry time of node i. The separability of the differential equation (6.15) readily yields the following solution:

$$\check{\kappa}^i(t) = \frac{At^{1-r} - r}{1 - r},$$

where A is an integration constant. Relying on the initial condition (6.16), we find $A = r(t^i)^{-(1-r)}$ so that

$$\check{\kappa}^i(t) = \frac{r}{1 - r}\left[\left(\frac{t}{t^i}\right)^{1-r} - 1\right].$$

To determine the long-run (in)degree distribution, we now proceed as above. First, we find that

$$\Pr_t(\check{\kappa}^i(t) < \kappa) = \Pr_t\left(t^i > \frac{t}{\left(\kappa\frac{1-r}{r} + 1\right)^{\frac{1}{1-r}}}\right),$$

so that, by the uniform distribution of entering times, we have that, as $t \to \infty$,

$$\Pr_t(\check{\kappa}^i(t) < \kappa) \to 1 - \left(\kappa\frac{1-r}{r} + 1\right)^{-\left(\frac{1}{1-r}\right)} \equiv \check{P}(\kappa),$$

which induces the density

$$\check{p}(\kappa) = \frac{d\check{P}(\kappa)}{d\kappa} = \frac{1}{r}\left(\kappa\frac{1-r}{r} + 1\right)^{-\left(\frac{2-r}{1-r}\right)}.$$

Clearly, since the total degree of a node $\kappa^i = \check{\kappa}^i + 1$, its corresponding distribution $\{p(\kappa)\}_{\kappa=1}^\infty = \{\check{p}(\kappa - 1)\}_{\kappa=1}^\infty$ is of an equivalent form (cf. Footnote 19).

Consider, by way of illustration, the particular case where $r = 1/2$ (i.e. there is an equal probability of linking to the first randomly selected node or to the one she refers). Then, we have

$$p(\kappa) \propto \kappa^{-3},$$

just as in the BA preferential-attachment model – or as in the model above labeled "Meeting Partners in Action" (MPA). However, as was explained for the latter case, it is worth stressing again that, even though the induced degree distributions are alike in all three models (BA, MPA, and the present one), this similarity does *not* translate to other topological properties such as clustering. Here, since the induced network is always a tree, we have that $C^i = 0$ uniformly for all i. This contrasts, for example, with the degree-dependent expression (6.13) obtained for the MPA context, where all nodes display positive clustering.

Search Through Affiliating Referral

In the spirit of the previous GNR model, Jackson and Rogers (2004) [158] have proposed a network-formation mechanism that accommodates a wider set of considerations. For certain "benchmark" configurations of the parameters, this mechanism will be seen to induce a degree distribution that coincides with that arising in the GNR context (at least if we focus on the mean-field continuum description of the network dynamics). For other parameter values, however, it spans a significantly richer set of possibilities that, as the authors themselves do, can be compared with empirical evidence in a number of different setups.

As usual, we start with a discrete-time formulation, a single node entering at every $t = 0, 1, 2, \ldots$. The new node j that enters at any given t is first taken to identify m_r nodes within the set $N(t-1)$ of those currently present. (Here, we may take $N(0)$ as any finite and, say, fully connected set of initial nodes.) After identifying those m_r nodes, node j independently establishes a directed link to each of them with probability p_r. Using previous terminology, the nodes for which those links are *actually* established may be called j's ancestors. On the other hand, *independently* of the linking decisions made in that first stage, node j also considers the possibility of forming additional links to some of the ancestors of the m_r nodes identified in the first stage of the procedure. Thus, regardless of what links have been actually established with those m_r nodes, it is supposed that node j identifies m_s additional "candidate nodes" among the ancestors of those nodes. Then, a link is established independently for each of those m_s candidates with probability p_s.

In the setup just described, we are again interested in determining the probability that any of the preexisting nodes i at t is selected as an ancestor of the entering node. For large t, this probability can be approximated by

$$\xi_t^i = m_r p_r \frac{1}{|N(t-1)|} + p_s m_s \frac{\check{\kappa}_{t-1}^i}{\sum_{j \in N(t-1)} \check{\kappa}_{t-1}^j}, \qquad (6.17)$$

where recall that $\check{\kappa}_{t-1}^\ell$ stands for the indegree (number of descendants) of any given node ℓ at $t-1$. Clearly, the total indegree $\sum_{j \in N(t-1)} \check{\kappa}_{t-1}^j$ (i.e. the aggregate number of descendants) is equal to the total outdegree (or aggregate number of ancestors). In expected terms, the latter is equal to $(p_r m_r + p_s m_s)|N(t-1)|$, which can be approximated by $t(p_r m_r + p_s m_s)$. Consequently, denoting the *expected outdegree* of a randomly selected node by $m \equiv p_r m_r + p_s m_s$, the probability in (6.17) can be approximated as follows:

$$\xi_t^i \simeq p_r \frac{m_r}{t} + p_s \frac{m_s}{mt} \check{\kappa}_{t-1}^i. \qquad (6.18)$$

Recasting now the network-formation process in a continuum framework, we can rely on (6.18) to write the differential equation:

$$\frac{d\check{\kappa}^i(t)}{dt} = p_r \frac{m_r}{t} + p_s \frac{m_s}{mt} \check{\kappa}^i(t), \qquad (6.19)$$

where we consider the initial condition $\check{\kappa}^i(t^i) = 0$, denoting by t^i the entry time of node i.[20]

Assuming $p_s m_s > 0$, denote $\chi \equiv \frac{p_r m_r}{p_s m_s}$. Then, proceeding as in the previous two models, it is immediate to find that the solution of the above (separable) differential equation is

$$\check{\kappa}^i(t) = \chi m \left[\left(\frac{t}{t^i} \right)^{\frac{p_s m_s}{m}} - 1 \right].$$

Therefore, for any given κ, we have

$$\Pr_t \left[\check{\kappa}^i(t) < \kappa \right] = \Pr_t \left[t^i > t \left(\frac{\kappa}{\chi m} + 1 \right)^{-\frac{m}{p_s m_s}} \right].$$

Since entering times may be assumed uniformly distributed, it follows that, as $t \to \infty$,

$$\Pr_t \left[\check{\kappa}^i(t) < \kappa \right] \to 1 - \left(\frac{\kappa}{\chi m} + 1 \right)^{-\frac{m}{p_s m_s}} \equiv \check{P}(\check{\kappa}),$$

which in turn implies that the density for the *indegree* distribution is given by

$$\check{p}(\kappa) = \frac{d\check{P}(\kappa)}{d\kappa} = \frac{m(\chi m)^{\frac{m}{p_s m_s}}}{p_s m_s} (\kappa + \chi m)^{-(\frac{m}{p_s m_s} + 1)}.$$

Thus, for large κ, the *total-degree* distribution $p(\kappa)$ is scale-free with

$$p(\kappa) \propto \kappa^{-(\frac{m}{p_s m_s} + 1)}.$$

Note that if $p_r = r$, $p_s = 1 - r$, and $m_r = m_s = 1$, expression (6.19) that governs the mean-field dynamics for node degrees in the present setup is formally identical to its counterpart (6.15) in the GNR model. Therefore, the two lead to an identical degree distribution in the long run.

Concerning other important features of the network, however, there is no such correspondence between the two models. This happens, for example, in the case of clustering. Even if the parameter values are as specified before, the induced network clustering does not match that of the GNR model. This, of course, is just as we found in our earlier comparison of the GNR, BA, and MPA models: despite their similarity in the degree distributions, they display substantially different levels of clustering. In the present case, this conclusion readily transpires from the mean-field analysis conducted by Jackson and Rogers (2004) [158], through which they obtain an explicit estimate of network clustering in the long run that is different from that obtained in those other models.

---

[20] Jackson and Rogers (2004) [158] consider $\check{\kappa}^i(t^i)$ – i.e. the initial number of descendants of an entering node – a flexible parameter of the model.

A mean-field approach is also used by Jackson and Rogers (2004) [158] to identify other interesting long-run features of the network.[21] In particular, they find some extent of assortativeness (i.e. positive degree correlation between connected nodes), a feature often encountered in social networks. As explained in Section 2.5 in some detail (see also the model by Vázquez (2003) [275] discussed below), such positive degree correlations are to be expected, in general, as a consequence of the temporal asymmetry among nodes (young and old) inherent in any growing-network environment.

Surfing the Network

Still remaining within a growing environment, we finally present a model that is largely inspired by the work of Vázquez (2003) [275]. The model conceives link creation as the result of new nodes "surfing" through the network along paths whose length is stochastically determined. Such a surfing process can be shown to deliver long-run networks that display many of the key attributes of complexity, e.g. a large degree heterogeneity, significant clustering, or internode degree correlations. In line with our former analysis, however, we shall concentrate our efforts on understanding the broad (scale-free) degree distributions induced by the model.

At every $t = 1, 2, \ldots$, we posit that there is a *single* node/agent that is searching for new connections. Thus, while its search lasts, it is the only node visiting other nodes (and possibly creating new links to them, as explained below). In carrying out these visits, the searching node "surfs" through the current network in a way that is reminiscent of how individuals tend to establish their (hyper)links in the World Wide Web. Specifically, upon entrance, it starts by visiting one of the existing nodes, randomly selected. Thereafter, the process is governed by the following mechanism.

Surfing mechanism: Let ℓ be the agent who is actively searching at any given t. Denote by $\hat{\Gamma}(t) = (N(t), \hat{L}(t))$ the directed network prevailing at the end of this period. Suppose that agent ℓ has visited some particular node $j \in N(t)\backslash\{\ell\}$ at t. Then, as the process moves into the subsequent period $t + 1$, one of the following two exclusive events takes place:

- With probability q_s, node ℓ continues its search. Then, it randomly chooses one of the directed links $(j, i) \in \hat{L}(t)$ to visit node i.
- With the complementary probability $1 - q_s$ node ℓ stops search. In that case, a new node $\ell' = \ell + 1$ enters and starts its search by visiting a randomly selected node in $N(t)$.

---

[21] Jackson and Rogers (2004) [158] consider as well a number of variants of their base framework presented here. Especially interesting is one where the probabilities p_r and p_s with which a newcomer actually links with the "candidate nodes" met by search depend on the latter's characteristics. In particular, they study the case where, in the spirit of BA's preferential attachment, the linking probabilities increase with the degree of those nodes.

In analogy with former notation, let $\check{\xi}^i_t$ stand for the probabilities that an "incumbent" node i is visited by the node searching at t. For a large random network, these probabilities must approximately satisfy

$$\check{\xi}^i_t = \frac{1 - q_s}{|N(t)| - 1} + q_s \sum_{(j,i)\in \hat{L}(t-1)} \check{\xi}^j_{t-1} \frac{1}{\hat{\kappa}^j_{t-1}},$$

where recall that $\hat{\kappa}^j_{t-1} = \left|\{i : (j, i) \in \hat{L}(t - 1)\}\right|$ is the outdegree of node j at t. The above expression simply reflects the idea that an incumbent node i can be visited either if it is selected as the first contact by a new node or, alternatively, one of its neighbors j was visited in the previous period by a node that continues searching.

In general, we may assume that the searching node only establishes links to a fraction of the nodes visited (e.g. only to those visited nodes that are deemed interesting). Let q_c denote the probability that a visit effectively leads to a link. Then, the probability that a node i receives a link by the searching node at t is simply $\check{\zeta}^i_t \equiv q_c \check{\xi}^i_t$.

Denote by $\overline{\check{\xi}}_t \equiv \left(\check{\xi}^i_t\right)_{i \in N(t)}$ the *average* visiting probability faced at t by incumbent nodes $i \in N(t)$ and let $\overline{\hat{\kappa}}_t \equiv \left(\hat{\kappa}^i_t\right)_{i \in N(t)}$ stand for the *average outdegree* prevailing across those nodes. In a mean-field analysis of the model, the linking probability $\check{\zeta}^i_t$ faced by any given node node i can be approximated as follows:

$$\check{\zeta}^i_t = q_c \left[\frac{1 - q_s}{N(t)} + q_s \frac{\overline{\check{\xi}}_t}{\overline{\hat{\kappa}}_t} \check{\kappa}^i_t \right], \tag{6.20}$$

where $\check{\kappa}^i_t$ is the indegree of node i at t.

Let us now rely on the continuum approximation of the model, where (6.20) is transformed into the following differential equation:

$$\frac{d\check{\kappa}^i(t)}{dt} = q_c \left[\frac{1 - q_s}{N(t)} + q_s \frac{\overline{\check{\xi}}(t)}{\overline{\hat{\kappa}}(t)} \check{\kappa}^i(t) \right].$$

Using the fact that the incumbent population grows at the same rate $(1 - q_s)$ at which surfing nodes abandon search (i.e. $N(t) = (1 - q_s)t$), the above expression can be rewritten as

$$\frac{d\check{\kappa}^i(t)}{dt} = q_c \left[\frac{1}{t} + q_s \frac{\overline{\check{\xi}}(t)}{\overline{\hat{\kappa}}(t)} \check{\kappa}^i(t) \right]. \tag{6.21}$$

Next note that, by the accounting identity that must be verified by the total out- and in-degree of the whole network, the average outdegree and the average indegree must coincide, i.e.

$$\overline{\hat{\kappa}}(t) = \overline{\check{\kappa}}(t),$$

where, in analogy with the outdegree notation, $\overline{\check{k}}(t)$ denotes the average inde-gree. On the other hand, since $\overline{\check{k}}(t)$ is the expected visiting probability faced by any incumbent node, it follows that

$$\overline{\check{k}}(t) = \frac{q_c \overline{\check{\xi}}(t) N(t) t}{N(t)} = q_c \overline{\check{\xi}}(t) t,$$

and therefore

$$\frac{\overline{\check{\xi}}(t)}{\overline{\check{k}}(t)} = \frac{\overline{\check{\xi}}(t)}{\overline{\check{k}}(t)} = \frac{1}{q_c t},$$

which, introduced in (6.21), leads to the following differential equation:

$$\frac{d\check{k}^i(t)}{dt} = q_c \frac{1}{t} + q_s \frac{\check{k}^i(t)}{t}, \tag{6.22}$$

to be solved with the initial condition $\check{k}^i(t^i) = 0$, where t^i again denotes the entry time of node i.

It is straightforward to see that the solution of (6.22) is given by

$$\check{k}^i(t) = \frac{q_c}{q_s} \left[\left(\frac{t}{t^i} \right)^{q_s} - 1 \right].$$

Therefore, as $t \to \infty$, the long-run cumulative distribution for network inde-gree, $\check{P}(\cdot)$, is given by

$$\check{P}(\kappa) = 1 - \left(1 + \frac{q_s}{q_c} \kappa \right)^{-\frac{1}{q_s}},$$

where $\kappa = 0, 1, 2, \ldots$, now stands for the different possible *indegrees* and the corresponding density is

$$\check{p}(\kappa) = \frac{d\check{P}(\kappa)}{d\kappa} = \frac{1}{q_c} (1 + \frac{q_s}{q_c} \kappa)^{-(\frac{1}{q_s}+1)}.$$

By varying the probability q_s in the interval $(0, 1]$, one obtains a whole family of scale-free degree distributions spanning the full range $[2, \infty)$ for the decay parameter. The induced network, on the other hand, should also display a significant topological structure in other respects – e.g. it is clear that sub-stantial levels of clustering are bound to arise from local search in the presence of a high q_s. In fact, for a closely related model, Vázquez (2003) [275] shows that the induced long-run network does exhibit sizable clustering, as well as an inverse relationship between local clustering and node degree, and a significant extent of internode degree correlations.

Heterogeneity and Structure in Growing Networks

The four alternative models of network formation discussed in the present subsection illustrate how different forms of *network-based search* may operate in a growing environment. The interesting point to note is that all of them generate the large internode heterogeneity and nontrivial structure that have been highlighted as essential features of complex networks.

Our analysis has mostly focused on characterizing the long-run degree distributions arising in each case. In this respect, the aforementioned heterogeneity across nodes is well evinced in the scale-free property displayed by those distributions (i.e. they all satisfy a power law, at least for large degrees). But, as succinctly outlined, those network formation models are also found to generate a significant structure in a number of other interesting dimensions. Concerning clustering, for example, even the simplest setup considered (what we have labeled "meeting partners in action") exhibits a significant amount of overall clustering as an obvious consequence of network-based search. This context also yields a negative relationship between a node's own clustering index and its degree, a feature sharply in line with some empirical evidence. An additional manifestation of network structure concerns internode correlations. These arise, in particular, when search is conducted through referral (affiliating or not) and is a reflection of the temporal asymmetry intrinsic to a growing environment.

In the next subsection, we dispense with the assumption of a growing environment and consider instead a setup where the (large) set of nodes remains fixed throughout the whole process. The change in the environment, therefore, must be channeled in a different way: it is imposed by a sizable measure of what we call *volatility*. As we shall see, such volatility, in interplay with a process of network-based search, delivers novel dynamic features and fresh theoretical insights.

6.2.2   A Volatile Environment

In a sense, the network-growing models studied in Subsection 6.2.1 fail to capture a fully fledged changing environment. For, in the long-run limit (which is the focus of the analysis), the overall conditions faced by each of the incoming agents stay essentially constant. Change, in other words, is to be regarded in those models as a transient phenomenon, not a persistent one. In contrast, it may be argued that if environmental change is indeed conceived as an essential feature of the situation, it should remain important over time, even asymptotically.

Here, we discuss a model proposed by Marsili *et al.* (2004) [196] that does enjoy this feature. Specifically, it contemplates a fixed population that is involved in a network-formation process subject to recurrent and disruptive volatility. In essence, therefore, network evolution can be seen as a struggle between *volatility* and *search*. Next, we present each of these two components of the dynamics in turn.

For convenience, let us model time continuously, with $t \in [0, \infty)$. At every t, the state of the system is identified with the prevailing network $\Gamma(t) = (N, L(t))$, which simply specifies the set of undirected links $L(t)$ that are in place at that time between the agents in the (fixed but large) population N.

We postulate that each of these links disappears at a constant rate λ. This is the phenomenon that we call *volatility*. A possible motivation for it derives from the idea that, due to unmodeled exogenous circumstances (e.g. changes in the environment), each link may be rendered useless, obsolete, or otherwise disappears. Alternatively, one might conceive such a process of link decay – which affects each node in proportion to its degree – as a reflection of the difficulties to maintain a large number of links operational. Whatever its interpretation, however, the important assumption here is that there is some disrupting noise that operates at a *significant* rate throughout the process. This contrasts, for example, with the role played by noise in the evolutionary approaches discussed in Subsection 6.1.3, where it is assumed to remain infinitesimally small all along.

As a balance against the pressure of volatility toward the elimination of existing links, agents continuously attempt to create new links. As before, the core of this process is modeled as the outcome of *network-based search*. More specifically, we posit that, at a given rate ξ, each agent $i \in N$ receives the opportunity to search through the network for the creation of a new link. This means that she explores locally the linking possibilities available through the following two-step mechanism. First, she selects at random one of her neighbors $j \in \mathcal{N}^i(t) \equiv \{k : ik \in L(t)\}$. Then, *via* that chosen neighbor j, agent i contacts one of the agents $\ell \in \mathcal{N}^j(t) \backslash \{i\}$, randomly selected from this set. If ℓ and i are not already neighbors at t (i.e. they are genuinely *second*-neighbors), then the link $i\ell$ is created and added to $L(t)$. Otherwise (i.e. they are in fact *first*-neighbors), the existing link simply remains in place.

In addition to such network-based search, it is also technically convenient to assume that there is a supplementary mechanism of *global search* that operates only infrequently. That is, at a (relatively low) rate η, each individual receives the opportunity to form a link with some randomly selected agent in the *whole* of $N \backslash \{i\}$. And again, if this link is not already present, it is then created and added to $\Gamma(t)$. This global search mechanism is mainly geared toward breaking the impasse that would otherwise arise if, say, the system starts (or ever reverts to) a very sparse and strongly fragmented network. That state of affairs would become fully irreversible in the absence of even a modicum of global search.

Overall, therefore, the process includes three components, that we have labeled as *volatility*, *network-based search*, and *global search*. As indicated, the first two represent the core of the process (i.e. the main driving forces), while the last one is taken to operate at a very slow pace (i.e. only very occasionally). Thus, without loss of generality, we normalize $\lambda = 1$ (recall that time is modeled continuously) and then focus the analysis on the role of ξ for some given (low) value of η.

To study the model, we again rely on mean-field analysis, but now on one which does *not* resort to a continuum approximation. The essential features of the approach (in particular, the requirement of self-consistency imposed on the solution) are reviewed in some detail in Section C.2 of the appendix. It builds upon the hypothesis that the network prevailing at any given t can be suitably described as a (pseudo-)random[22] network with some degree distribution p_t. Under this assumption, the first required step is to specify the *jump rates* at which a typical node i changes (i.e. increases or decreases by one link) its current degree κ^i.

In the mean-field formulation, the jump rates applying to a typical node i may be taken to depend only on its current degree κ^i. First, concerning the *decay rate* $\varpi_t^-(\kappa^i)$ at which one of the neighbors is lost, we can simply write

$$\varpi_t^-(\kappa^i) = \kappa^i \tag{6.23}$$

since each link vanishes at a constant rate $\lambda = 1$. The determination of the *link-creation rate* $\varpi_t^+(\kappa^i)$, on the other hand, is substantially more involved. It can be written in the following general form:

$$\varpi_t^+(\kappa^i) = \alpha_t + \beta_t \mathbb{I}_+(\kappa^i) + \gamma_t \kappa^i, \tag{6.24}$$

where $\mathbb{I}_+(\cdot)$ is the positive indicator function,[23] and α_t, β_t, and γ_t capture the contributions to link creation that are due to the following considerations:

- α_t specifies the contribution that is due to global search. Obviously, this term is independent of i's degree.
- β_t captures the contribution that is based on local (network-based) search that *originates in node i*. This term is positive only if this node has any neighbors (i.e. if $\kappa^i > 0$). But provided this happens, the expected effect is again independent of i's degree.
- γ_t captures the contribution resulting from local search performed by the neighbors of i. Since this search is independently performed by the different neighbors of i, the aggregate effect on this node must be proportional to its current degree κ^i.

The specific values of α_t, β_t, and γ_t depend on the state of the system (captured by the current p_t), as well as on the nature and details of the different processes of search involved. First, we have

$$\alpha_t = \eta + (n-1)\eta \frac{1}{n-1} = 2\eta, \tag{6.25}$$

where n is the population size. Implicit in this expression is the idea that n is so large that there is just a negligible probability that a randomly met agent be already a neighbor. With this proviso in mind, (6.25) simply reflects the fact that a link is created through global search if either the agent in question receives

---

[22] Throughout, we maintain the assumption that the prevailing network is random (i.e. displays a degree distribution p_t *and* lacks internode degree correlations) while still allowing for positive uncorrelated clustering. The network, therefore, is *not* a random network in the sense considered in Chapter 2, which motivates the label *pseudo-random network*. In this idealized construct, the degree distribution and the clustering index are the two independent features describing the network.

[23] That is, $\mathbb{I}_+(x) = \begin{cases} 1 & \text{if } x > 0 \\ 0 & \text{if } x \leq 0. \end{cases}$

an opportunity for global search or one of the $n - 1$ remaining agents do and end up meeting that agent.

Next, we argue that

$$\beta_t = \xi \times \Pr_t\left[\kappa^j \geq 2 \mid j \in \mathcal{N}^i(t)\right] \times (1 - \mathcal{C}_t), \tag{6.26}$$

where $\Pr_t\{\cdot \mid \cdot\}$ represents (conditional) probabilities computed in terms of the current p_t, and $\mathcal{C}_t$ denotes the clustering index prevailing at t – cf. (2.8). To understand (6.26), note that a new link is created by a node i that has some neighbors (i.e. $\kappa^i > 0$) when, simultaneously, the following events happen: (a) it receives a local-search opportunity (at the rate β_t); (b) its chosen neighbor j has at least one other neighbor (i.e. j's degree is at least 2); and (c) a randomly chosen neighbor of j is not a neighbor of i – which happens with probability $(1 - \mathcal{C}_t)$. To be sure, note that, in the latter respect, again we rely on the mean-field postulate that all nodes can be treated symmetrically, now pertaining to clustering.

Finally, we claim that γ_t can be approximated as follows:

$$\gamma_t = \xi \times \left\langle \frac{1}{\kappa^\ell} \,\middle|\, \ell \in \mathcal{N}_2^i(t) \right\rangle_t \times (1 - \mathcal{C}_t), \tag{6.27}$$

where $\left\langle \frac{1}{\kappa^\ell} \mid \ell \in \mathcal{N}_2^i(t) \right\rangle_t$ stands for the (conditional) expected value of $1/\kappa^\ell$ computed in terms of p_t across all $\ell \in \mathcal{N}_2^i(t)$. To see this, consider any single node j that is a neighbor of i (there are κ^i of them, which explains that γ_t is multiplied by κ^i in (6.24)). This neighbor of i contributes (roughly)[24] a total of $\kappa^j - 1$ second neighbors of i. Let ℓ be one such typical second-neighbor and let κ^ℓ be its degree. The probability that, when ℓ receives a local-search opportunity (at the rate ξ), it routes its search through j is $1/\kappa^\ell$. On the other hand, the probability that j directs ℓ to i is $1/(\kappa^j - 1)$. Thus, in all, the probability that ℓ reaches i in this manner is $(1/\kappa^\ell) \times (1/(\kappa^j - 1))$. Since, on the other hand, one must account for a total of $\kappa^j - 1$ second-neighbors accessible through j, the combined rate at which any of those nodes receives a search opportunity and reaches i is $\xi(1/\kappa^\ell) \times (1/(\kappa^j - 1)) \times (\kappa^j - 1) = \xi \times 1/\kappa^\ell$. This explains the first two terms of (6.27). Finally, its last term $(1 - \mathcal{C}_t)$ simply reflects, as before, the probability that ℓ and i in the above considerations (that are both neighbors of j) are not themselves neighbors. See Figure 6.2 for an illustration.

Now, we want to trace the dynamics of the degree distribution p_t. To this end, we focus on the induced evolution of the generating function

$$G_{0,t}(x) = \sum_{\kappa=0}^{\infty} p_t(\kappa)\, x^\kappa$$

---

[24] Here, for the sake of simplicity, the effect of clustering on the number of second-neighbors of i accessible though j is ignored. We also ignore the possibility that i might be the only neighbor of j.

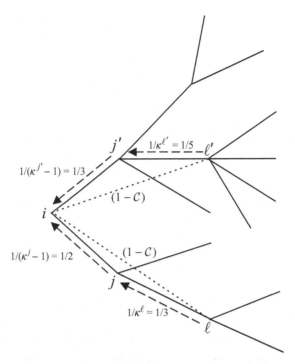

Figure 6.2. Nodes ℓ and ℓ' receive independent opportunities of local search and may establish a link with i. The dashed arrows indicate the search route that would lead them to i, with the corresponding probabilities attached. The links $i\ell$ and $i\ell'$ would then form (short-dashed segments) with ex-ante probability equal to $1 - C$

that characterizes the prevailing p_t over time. Using (6.23)–(6.24), we can write

$$
\begin{aligned}
\frac{\partial G_{0,t}(x)}{\partial t} &= \sum_{\kappa=0}^{\infty} \frac{\partial p_t(\kappa)}{\partial t} x^\kappa \\
&= \sum_{\kappa=0}^{\infty} x^\kappa \left\{ \begin{array}{c} p_t(\kappa-1)\varpi_t^+(\kappa-1) + p_t(\kappa+1)\varpi_t^-(\kappa+1) \\ -p_t(\kappa)\varpi_t^+(\kappa) - p_t(\kappa)\varpi_t^-(\kappa) \end{array} \right\} \\
&= \sum_{\kappa=0}^{\infty} x^\kappa \left\{ \begin{array}{c} \left[\alpha_t + \beta_t \mathbb{I}_+(\kappa-1) + \gamma_t(\kappa-1)\right] p_t(\kappa-1) \\ +(\kappa+1)\, p_t(\kappa+1) \\ -\left[(\alpha_t + \beta_t \mathbb{I}_+(\kappa) + \gamma_t\kappa) + \kappa\right] p_t(\kappa) \end{array} \right\} \\
&= (1-x)\left\{ (1-\gamma_t x)\frac{\partial G_{0,t}(x)}{\partial x} - (\alpha_t + \beta_t)G_{0,t}(x) + \beta_t G_{0,t}(0) \right\}.
\end{aligned}
$$

$$(6.28)$$

As usual, we are interested in the long-run stationary distribution p, as it depends on some corresponding $\alpha, \beta,$ and γ (the stationary values of $\alpha_t, \beta_t,$ and γ_t). In order to stress such dependence, we may denote this distribution by $p(\alpha, \beta, \gamma) \equiv \{p(\kappa; \alpha, \beta, \gamma)\}_{\kappa=0}^{\infty}$ and by $G_0(x; \alpha, \beta, \gamma)$ its corresponding generating function. Then, the postulated stationarity implies

$$\frac{\partial G_0(x; \alpha, \beta, \gamma)}{\partial t} = 0, \tag{6.29}$$

which, in view of (6.28), can be expressed equivalently in terms of the following differential equation:

$$(1 - \gamma x)\frac{\partial G_{0,t}(x; \alpha, \beta, \gamma)}{\partial x} - (\alpha + \beta)G_{0,t}(x; \alpha, \beta, \gamma)$$
$$+ \beta G_{0,t}(0; \alpha, \beta, \gamma) = 0.$$

The above differential equation in x can be readily checked to yield the following solution:

$$G_0(x; \alpha, \beta, \gamma) = \frac{\beta + \alpha(1 - \gamma x)^{-\frac{\alpha+\beta}{\gamma}}}{\beta + \alpha(1 - \gamma)^{-\frac{\alpha+\beta}{\gamma}}}, \tag{6.30}$$

which determines the generating function characterizing the long-run degree distribution $p(\alpha, \beta, \gamma)$, as a function of α, β, and γ.

But, reciprocally, the values of α, β, and γ that prevail in the long run depend on the limit degree distribution. In fact, this is merely trivial for the case of α since (6.25) directly furnishes it as a function of the parameter η alone. In the cases of β and γ, however, such dependence does genuinely arise. Specifically, note that expression (6.26) for β includes the term $\Pr\left[\kappa^j \geq 2 \mid j \in \mathcal{N}^i(t)\right]$ and expression (6.27) for γ contains $\left\langle \frac{1}{\kappa^\ell} \right\rangle$, where both must be computed in terms of $p(\alpha, \beta, \gamma)$. This indicates that the determination of the long-run state of the system indeed requires addressing a nontrivial *self-consistency problem*.

To tackle this problem, first note:[25]

$$\Pr\left[\kappa^j \geq 2 \mid j \in \mathcal{N}^i(t)\right] = 1 - G_1'(0) = 1 - \frac{G_0'(0)}{G_0'(1)}, \tag{6.31}$$

where we use the fact that node j is known to be a neighbor of i and, therefore, we need to use for it the degree distribution corresponding to a neighboring node. That is, its distribution is characterized by the generating function $G_1(x) = \frac{x \, G_0'(x)}{G_0'(1)}$ (recall Appendix A). On the other hand, it can be shown that[26]

$$\left\langle \frac{1}{\kappa^\ell} \,\middle|\, \ell \in \mathcal{N}_2^i(t) \right\rangle = \frac{1 - G_0(0)}{G_0'(1)}. \tag{6.32}$$

---

[25] To lighten notation, we again revert to dispensing with the dependence of $G_0(x)$ and $G_1(x)$ on α, β, and γ. Once the nature of the self-consistent problem has been clarified, this should generate no confusion.

[26] Note that

$$\sum_{\kappa=1}^{\infty} [(1/\kappa)\zeta(\kappa)] = \sum_{\kappa=1}^{\infty}\left[\left(\int_0^1 x^{\kappa-1}dx\right)\zeta(\kappa)\right] = \int_0^1 \frac{1}{x}\left[\sum_{\kappa=1}^{\infty} x^\kappa \zeta(\kappa)\right]dx$$

$$= \int_0^1 \frac{1}{x}\frac{xG_0'(x)}{G_0'(1)}dx = \frac{1}{G_0'(1)}\int_0^1 G_0'(x)dx$$

$$= \frac{G_0(1) - G_0(0)}{G_0'(1)} = \frac{1 - G_0(0)}{G_0'(1)}.$$

Thus, introducing (6.31) and (6.32) into (6.26) and (6.27), respectively, the conditions that reflect a self-consistent determination of α, β and γ are as follows:

$$\alpha = 2\eta \tag{6.33}$$

$$\beta = \xi(1 - C)\left(1 - \frac{G_0'(0)}{G_0'(1)}\right) \tag{6.34}$$

$$\gamma = \xi(1 - C)\left(\frac{1 - G_0(0)}{G_0'(1)}\right), \tag{6.35}$$

where $G_0(x) \equiv G_0(x; \alpha, \beta, \gamma)$ is as defined in (6.30), and C is the clustering index displayed by the network in the long run.

In principle, C could be treated as an additional parameter of the model, possibly calibrated through numerical simulations. It turns out, however, that the *endogenous* (co-)evolution of clustering, in interplay with the distribution of network connectivity, represents a fundamental feature of the overall dynamics. This point is underscored by the simulation results obtained by Marsili *et al.* (2004) [196], which are illustrated in Figure 6.3.

Figure 6.3 shows that, in an intermediate range of the key parameter ξ (with η kept fixed, at a suitably small value), the model allows for two different long-run states. In one of them, the network enjoys a high average connectivity and a relatively low clustering; in the other long-run state, the network is very sparse and the clustering is high. Both of these possibilities are dynamically stable, each arising from different initial conditions. In fact, one can conceive these conditions as the outcome of "history." Thus, for example, if ξ has changed gradually from originally low (high) values and the process has adjusted fast to it, the equilibrium along the lower (higher) branch is to be expected. This also induces the phenomenon called *hysteresis*. Once a transition has occurred – say to the high-connectivity equilibrium, after ξ has gone above the corresponding threshold – any return of ξ to previous lower levels does *not* revert the system to the original low-connectivity equilibrium. Such a rich behavior, however, is incompatible with (6.33)–(6.35), whose solution is easily seen to be unique, for any *fixed* C, throughout the whole parameter range. This suggests that, if one is to shed light on the true behavior of the model, it is important to let clustering change *endogenously* and integrate it into the overall solution of the model.

To achieve this integration, and in consonance with the rest of analysis, it is natural to rely on mean-field theory to model the clustering dynamics. Then, one can impose on it a corresponding stationarity condition, counterpart of that embodied by (6.29) for the degree distribution. Specifically, let

$$Q^i(t) \equiv \left|\left\{j\ell \in L(t) : j, \ell \in \mathcal{N}^i(t)\right\}\right|$$

stand for the number of links that exist at t between the neighbors of a typical node $i \in N$. In a mean-field description of the situation, where the clustering

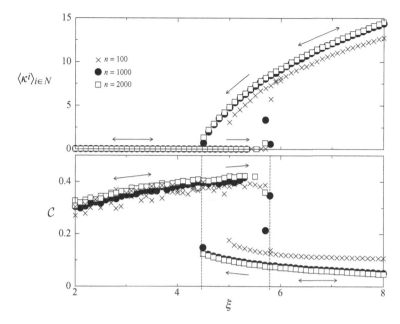

Figure 6.3. Average degree (upper panel) and clustering index (lower panel) obtained through numerical simulations in a suitably discretized version of the model proposed by Marsili *et al.* (2004) [196]. The rate of global search is fixed at $\eta = 0.001$ and three network sizes are considered, $n = 100, 1000, 2000$, with significant finite-population effects only arising for $n < 2000$. The arrows signify possible changes in the long-run state of the system as ξ changes gradually in the indicated directions and the system adjusts accordingly. The intermediate outcomes observed at the points of phase transition reflect the fact that, at those junctures, the empirical distribution derived from the simulations has two "peaks" of comparable magnitudes. Both remain significant only if the population is relatively small and the effect tends to vanish when $n = 2000$

continues to be assumed uniform throughout the network, we may posit

$$Q^i(t) = C_t \frac{\kappa^i(\kappa^i - 1)}{2}.$$

Thus, the decay rate ϑ_t^- at which the transition $Q^i \to Q^i - 1$ takes place is given (as a function of κ^i) by

$$\vartheta_t^-(\kappa^i) = C_t \frac{\kappa^i(\kappa^i - 1)}{2},$$

again a simple consequence of the fact that each of the existing links vanishes at a rate $\lambda = 1$. Reciprocally, by considerations analogous to those underlying

(6.26)–(6.27), the rate ϑ_t^+ at which $Q^i \to Q^i + 1$ can be approximated as follows:

$$
\vartheta_t^+(\kappa^i) = \xi\, \mathbb{I}_+(\kappa^i)\, \Pr_t\left[\kappa^j \geq 2 \mid j \in \mathcal{N}^i(t)\right] (1 - C_t)
$$
$$
+ \xi\, \kappa^i\, \mathbb{I}_+(\kappa^i - 1)\left\langle \frac{1}{\kappa^j} \,\middle|\, j \in \mathcal{N}^i(t) \right\rangle_t (1 - C_t).
$$

The first term is just as before – it reflects local (network-based) search originating in node i. The second term, on the other hand, captures the increase in clustering that occurs when a search opportunity (at the rate ξ) is received by some neighbor $j \in \mathcal{N}^i(t)$. In this case, a new link between the neighbors of i is established if the following events simultaneously happen: (a) agent j routes her search through i; (b) agent i happens to have at least another neighbor ℓ different from j (in that case, the rate is proportional to κ^i); and (c) agents j and ℓ are not neighbors (which happens with probability $(1 - C_t)$).

In the limit, when clustering remains stationary at some given level $\mathcal{C}$, we must have

$$
\left\langle \vartheta^-(\kappa^i) \right\rangle = \left\langle \vartheta^+(\kappa^i) \right\rangle,
$$

where the expectation is taken with respect to the long-run degree distribution p, restricted to nodes with at least one link. By usual methods, the above condition can be transformed into the following equation:

$$
\frac{\mathcal{C}}{2} G_0''(1) = \xi(1 - \mathcal{C})(2 - G_0(0))\left(1 - \frac{G_0'(0)}{G_0'(1)}\right). \tag{6.36}
$$

In combination with (6.33)–(6.35), this equation can be used to obtain the stationary solutions of the mean-field model in α, β, γ and, now, also in $\mathcal{C}$.

The aforementioned solutions are depicted in Figure 6.4, as reflected by the induced average degree and average clustering. We find the same qualitative pattern found in the numerical simulations summarized in Figure 6.3. For some suitably fixed η, three different regions obtain as the rate of local search varies. First, when local search is sluggish (i.e. the rate $\xi < \xi_1$), volatility dominates the process and the induced long-run state – as captured by the unique equilibrium $(p, \mathcal{C})$ in the mean-field theory – displays a very sparse network with a low connectivity and high clustering. In the intermediate range where $\xi \in [\xi_1, \xi_2]$ the mean-field solution gives rise to three long-run equilibria, the ones exhibiting extreme connectivity and polar clustering being stable while the other one is unstable. Finally, when search is relatively brisk and $\xi > \xi_2$, the model again leads to a unique long-run state, but now with a high connectivity and low clustering.

To summarize, the behavior of the model as its key parameter ξ varies (and η is fixed at a low value) is characterized – both in the simulations and the mean-field solution – by the following salient features:

(a) Sharp (discontinuous) transitions, in response to slight changes of ξ.
(b) Coexistence of polar equilibrium configurations, within a sizable range of ξ.

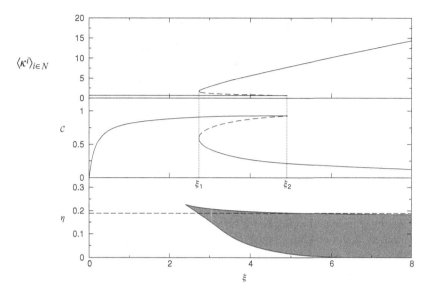

Figure 6.4. Solutions of the mean-field model embodied by equations (6.33)–(6.36). The upper and middle panels show how the average degree and clustering index depend on ξ, for a fixed value of $\eta = 0.19$. The solid lines trace the stable equilibria while the dashed line corresponds to the unstable equilibria. The lowermost panel, on the other hand, shows the regions in the $\xi - \eta$ space that lead to a single solution (white region) or two stable solutions (grey region). The dashed horizontal line in this space reflects the range of parameters considered in the upper two panels

(c) Hysteresis, as ξ changes gradually, whereby equilibrium selection is shaped by recent "history."

As explained in Section 1.3, these are features that may be regarded as a mark of the complexity induced by the social-network dynamics. They cast the process of network formation in sharp contrast with the strategic approach to the problem discussed in Section 6.1. Here, the network is in continuous flux, while agents' relentless search efforts struggle against the disintegrating forces induced by volatility. In the long-run, what results is a well-defined structure that remains inherently complex throughout and may react in sharp and subtle ways to the underlying circumstances (parameters). As a countervailing consideration, however, it should be stressed that payoffs and incentives play essentially no role in the present approach. This is an obviously important shortcoming, since social processes are largely steered by agents who, even if not unboundedly rational, often take their decisions in a purposeful manner. The consequent need of introducing nontrivial incentive considerations into complex-network analysis will be the main point stressed in our closing discussion of Section 6.4.

6.3 NETWORK EVOLUTION AND PLAY

The previous section has focused on setups where agents' sole dimension of choice is "networking," just as it was the case, for example, in the first two models studied in Section 6.1 (i.e. the Linear Action and the Symmetric Connections Models). Now, we are interested in how play and networks interact, along the lines of the last two strategic setups considered in that early section. Specifically, we reconsider the problem of (complex) network formation in a context where agents' choice concerns not only their links but also the strategy to be adopted in the game played with their neighbors.

In principle, there are many different ways in which network formation and game play can interact along the resulting coevolutionary process. Here, for concreteness, we begin by considering a coordination scenario that is analogous to the one considered in Section 6.1, i.e. agents are involved in a coordination game with their neighbors. Thus, on one hand, when adjusting their behavior in the game, they tend to adapt their choice to what most of their neighbors do. But, on the other hand, the way players behave in the coordination game naturally affects network-formation decisions as well. It determines, specifically, whether linking opportunities are judged profitable (because agents are well coordinated) and thus they indeed materialize. In this setup, one expects that the long-run pattern of play that eventually arises should have a key bearing on and, reciprocally, be affected by, the characteristics of the corresponding long-run network (e.g. on its connectivity). To shed light on this interplay is the main purpose of Subsection 6.3.1. There we study a model along the aforementioned lines where volatility continues to exert an important influence on the process.

Next, in Subsection 6.3.2, we discuss, but much more succinctly, other alternative instances where network formation still coevolves in interesting ways with agents' play. We consider, specifically, three different scenarios, corresponding to three alternative strategic situations. In the first two of them, interacting (i.e. neighboring) players face a conflict between cooperation and opportunistic incentives, as modeled by the classical Prisoner's Dilemma. In one case, agents play a one-shot version of this game and react through simple imitation rules to their neighbors' behavior. In the other one, agents interact repeatedly (i.e. according to a repeated version of the game) and must rely on the network to access any strategically relevant information – in particular, information on how their partners behaved in the past with third parties. In both instances, we shall find that the evolution of the network is able to sustain cooperation in cases where a fixed network architecture would fail. Finally, the third scenario considered involves a process of technological diffusion that is mediated by the prevailing network. Again, the fact that the network is allowed to change over time alongside the technology (in particular, by promoting links among agents that are not too dissimilar technologically) is found to have a key impact on the overall dynamics of the process.

6.3.1 Playing a Coordination Game

Consider a fixed (and large) population of agents N who are involved in a coevolutionary process of network formation and bilateral coordination. This is the setup studied by Ehrhardt *et al.* (2005) [97], where the state of the system must specify not only how nodes/agents connect to each other (i.e. the prevailing network) but also their choice of strategy in the underlying game. Thus let again have time be modeled continuously, with $t \in [0, \infty)$. On one hand, the state $\omega(t)$ at any such t must describe the current network $\Gamma(t)$ – or, equivalently, the set of existing (undirected) links $L(t)$ between the agents in N. On the other hand, the state has to include as well the *single*[27] action (or strategy) $a^i(t)$ chosen by every agent $i \in N$ in the game played with each of her neighbors $j \in N^i(t) = \{j \in N : ij \in L(t)\}$.

We shall postulate that the game is symmetric and of pure coordination, involving q different strategies. More precisely, let $S = \{s_1, s_2, \ldots, s_q\}$ be its (common) strategy space. Then, the payoff earned by any particular player i when she chooses a^i and her neighbor j selects a^j is given by $\psi(a^i, a^j)$, where

$$\psi(a^i, a^j) = \begin{cases} 1 & \text{if } a^i = a^j \\ 0 & \text{otherwise.} \end{cases}$$

This formulation partly generalizes the coordination context considered in Section 6.1 by contemplating an arbitrary number of strategies, but is partly more restrictive as well since it rules out any asymmetry across actions.[28]

In sum, a sufficient description of the situation prevailing at any given t is given by the state $\omega(t) = (\mathbf{a}(t), \Gamma(t))$ that includes the action profile $\mathbf{a}(t) = (a^1(t), a^2(t), \ldots, a^n(t)) \in S^n$ and the current network $\Gamma(t)$. The system dynamics, therefore, has to operate on these two dimensions, actions and links. Each of the two corresponding components of the process is now presented in turn: first the network dynamics, then the action dynamics.

Network dynamics: As before, the network changes through *search* and *volatility*.

- **Search:** Here, we simplify matters and consider only global (i.e. network-independent) search, formulated as follows. At every t, every agent $i \in N$ receives the opportunity of forming a link at a rate η. When such an opportunity arrives to i, she meets a randomly selected $j \in N \setminus \{i\}$ and considers the possibility of establishing the link ij (provided, of course, that it is not already in place). The link is

---

[27] Recall Subsection 6.1.1 and the considerations explained in Footnote 3.

[28] Specifically, the coordination scenario considered in Section 6.1 coincides with the present one if $q = 2$ and the payoff table (6.3) is particularized to $d = b = 1$ and $e = f = 0$. Also note that we now abstract from any explicit account of linking costs since they are peripheral to our main concerns here. Implicitly, however, the formulation for link creation postulated below implicitly presumes a linking cost c such that $0 < c < 1$.

formed with probability 1 if the two agents concerned are suitably coordinated, i.e. if $a_i(t) = a_j(t)$. Otherwise, the link is formed only with
some "small" probability ε (possibly zero). The implicit motivation
here is that only when players are well-coordinated the contemplated
link yields positive payoffs and thus players are strongly inclined to
establish it.

- **Volatility:**   Just as in the model studied in Subsection 6.2.2, existing
links are taken to vanish at a constant rate, which is normalized to
unity.[29]

Action dynamics: Agents adjust their game strategies, on the other hand, as in
the Ising model discussed in Chapter 4 and Appendix B – or, more precisely,
according to its generalization to any arbitrary number of "spins" that is generally called the Potts model. It is assumed that, at every t, each agent $i \in N$ is
given the opportunity to revise her strategy at a rate $\nu > 0$. If this event happens,
she chooses each $s_r \in S$ $(r = 1, 2, \ldots, q)$ with a probability

$$\Pr(s_r) \propto \exp \beta \left| \left\{ j \in \mathcal{N}^i(t) : a^j(t) = s_r \right\} \right|,$$

where, as usual, $\mathcal{N}^i(t)$ stands for the set of neighbors of i in $\Gamma(t)$, and $\beta > 0$
is the parameter that controls "behavioral noise" (cf. Section 4.3). Assume
that $\nu \gg \max[1, \eta]$ so that action adjustment is much faster than network
change. Then, as a suitable approximation, we may suppose that at any point
in time at which the network dynamics comes into operation the action profile is at an equilibrium (long-run) state of the action dynamics. In such a
situation, the key variable of interest is the probability that two randomly selected nodes display coordinated behavior (i.e. choose the same action). This
probability can be conditioned on whether these nodes belong or not to the
same network components. On one hand, if they lie in *different components*,
their coordination can only happen "by chance," i.e. with probability $1/q$.
Alternatively, if we consider two nodes that belong to the *same component*,
the only such contingency enjoying a significant probability is that the two
nodes in question belong to the *giant component* of the network (i.e. the
unique component of a significant size when the population is large). In that
case, the probability that these nodes be coordinated on the same action will
be denoted by $\varphi(\beta)$ – see below for a procedure to estimate this probability.
Qualitatively, one always has that $\varphi(\beta) > 1/q$ if $\beta > 0$, and $\varphi(\beta)$ converges to
1 as $\beta \to \infty$.

Building upon the previous considerations, we can now approach the analysis
of the network dynamics through mean-field methods analogous to those used

---

[29] In line with our above formulation for search and link creation, it might be reasonable to posit
that the rate of link destruction depends on whether or not the two agents involved in the
link under revision are coordinated on the same choice. This would not alter the gist of the
analysis and is therefore eschewed in order to highlight the essential (minimal) elements of
the model.

in Subsection 6.2.2. This requires specifying the jump rates at which the links of a typical node i are created and destroyed. We address each of these two possibilities in turn.

First, concerning link decay, the rate at which a node i with degree κ^i loses one of its links is given by

$$\varpi_t^-(\kappa^i) = \kappa^i. \tag{6.37}$$

This simply reflects the fact node i loses *each* of its κ^i links at a constant unitary rate.

On the other hand, in order to determine the link creation rate $\varpi_t^+(\kappa^i)$, the above discussion indicates that we need to estimate the probability that two randomly selected nodes both belong to the giant component of the prevailing network. To this end, let us make the simplifying assumption that the network prevailing at any t is well approximated as random with degree distribution p_t. Then, following Section 2.3, denote by w_t the fraction of *nodes* in the giant component and by $\hat{w}_t$ the fraction of existing *links* that connect such nodes. Applying (2.34)–(2.35), these magnitudes may be computed from the following equations:

$$1 - \hat{w}_t = \frac{1}{\sum_{\kappa'=1}^{\infty} \kappa' p_t(\kappa')} \sum_{\kappa=1}^{\infty} \kappa p_t(\kappa)(1 - \hat{w}_t)^{\kappa-1} \tag{6.38}$$

$$w_t = 1 - \sum_{\kappa=0}^{\infty} p_t(\kappa)(1 - \hat{w}_t)^{\kappa}. \tag{6.39}$$

Having thus determined w_t and $\hat{w}_t$, we now argue that the rate of link creation of a node i with degree κ^i has the following form:

$$\varpi_t^+(\kappa_i) = 2\eta \left\{ \begin{array}{l} [w_t \, (1-(1-\hat{w}_t)^{\kappa_i})] \, [\varphi(\beta) + (1-\varphi(\beta))\varepsilon] \\ + [1 - w_t(1-(1-\hat{w}_t)^{\kappa_i})] \, [1/q + (1-1/q)\varepsilon] \end{array} \right\}, \tag{6.40}$$

where recall that $\varphi(\beta)$ stands for the probability that two nodes in the giant component be coordinated on the same action. The above expression reflects the set of different contingencies under which a typical node i of degree κ_i ends up adding one more link to some randomly selected node j. They may be explained as follows:[30]

- First, the link ij is created with probability $[\varphi(\beta) + (1 - \varphi(\beta))\varepsilon]$ if both i and j belong to the giant component. As indicated, this is the only relevant event that needs to be considered for the case when the two nodes are in the same component. The *a priori* probability for that event is $[w_t \, (1 - (1 - \hat{w}_t)^{\kappa_i})]$, which is the product of the

---

[30] Note that, for a large network with bounded average degree, the probability that the link ij is already in place is essentially zero.

probability w_t that the (randomly selected) node j belongs to the giant component *and* the probability $(1 - (1 - \hat{w}_t)^{\kappa_i})$ that node i belongs to the giant component (the latter is equivalent to saying that none of its κ_i links point to the giant component). This explains the first term within brackets in the above expression.

- Second, the link ij is created even if i and j do not both belong to the giant component with probability $[1/q + (1 - 1/q)\varepsilon]$. This contributes the term $[1 - w_t(1 - (1 - \hat{w}_t)^{\kappa_i})][1/q + (1 - 1/q)\varepsilon]$.
- Finally, note that all of the former considerations arise either if node i is given the revision opportunity and selects any other j or, alternatively, any one of the $(n - 1)$ other nodes j is given this opportunity and selects the particular node i in question (a selection that happens with probability $1/(n - 1)$). This is the reason for the factor 2 multiplying the rate η on the right-hand side of (6.40).

Proceeding now as in Subsection 6.2.2, we want to study the dynamics of the generating function $G_{0,t}(x)$ that characterizes the degree distribution prevailing at each t, as given by

$$\frac{\partial G_{0,t}(x)}{\partial t} = \sum_{\kappa=0}^{\infty} \frac{\partial p_t(\kappa)}{\partial t} x^\kappa$$

$$= \sum_{\kappa=0}^{\infty} x^\kappa \left\{ \begin{array}{c} p_t(\kappa-1)\varpi_t^+(\kappa-1) + p_t(\kappa+1)\varpi_t^-(\kappa+1) \\ - p_t(\kappa)\varpi_t^+(\kappa) - p_t(\kappa)\varpi_t^-(\kappa) \end{array} \right\}.$$

To simplify matters, let us start by assuming that $\beta \to \infty$ so that we may make $\varphi(\beta) = 1$, i.e. any two nodes in the giant component are sure to be coordinated in one of the q actions. Then, relying on (6.37) and (6.40), it is straightforward to see that the law of motion of $G_{0,t}(x)$ can be rewritten as follows:

$$\frac{\partial G_{0,t}(x)}{\partial t} = (1-x)\frac{\partial G_{0,t}(x)}{\partial x} - 2\eta(1-x)\left[\tilde{\varepsilon} + (1-\tilde{\varepsilon})w_t\right] G_{0,t}(x)$$
$$+ 2\eta(1-x)(1-\tilde{\varepsilon}) w_t G_{0,t}((1-\hat{w}_t)x), \qquad (6.41)$$

where we use the short-hand notation $\tilde{\varepsilon} \equiv 1/q + (1 - 1/q)\varepsilon$.

Our aim is to characterize the long-run states of the system where the degree distribution p remains unchanged. In view of (6.41), this requires that the corresponding generating function $G_0(x)$ satisfies

$$(1 - x)\frac{\partial G_0(x)}{\partial x} - 2\eta(1 - x)\{[\tilde{\varepsilon} + (1 - \tilde{\varepsilon})w] G_0(x)$$
$$+ (1 - \tilde{\varepsilon}) w G_0((1 - \hat{w})x)\} = 0$$

or

$$\frac{\partial G_0(x)}{\partial x} = 2\eta \{[\tilde{\varepsilon} + (1 - \tilde{\varepsilon})w] G_0(x) - (1 - \tilde{\varepsilon}) w G_0((1 - \hat{w})x)\}.$$
$$(6.42)$$

Here, w and $\hat{w}$ are the stationary probabilities associated to p that correspond to selecting at random a node or link, respectively, in the giant component. Naturally, as a counterpart of (6.38)–(6.39), these probabilities must satisfy

$$1 - \hat{w} = \frac{1}{\sum_{\kappa'=1}^{\infty} \kappa' p(\kappa')} \sum_{\kappa=1}^{\infty} \kappa \, p(\kappa)(1 - \hat{w})^{\kappa-1} \tag{6.43}$$

$$w = 1 - \sum_{\kappa=0}^{\infty} p(\kappa)(1 - \hat{w})^{\kappa}. \tag{6.44}$$

Given any particular values for w and $\hat{w}$, one may integrate (6.42) numerically to any desired degree of accuracy. Then, in combination with (6.43)–(6.44), again we have a system that needs to be solved simultaneously in a self-consistent fashion for any given value of $\tilde{\varepsilon}$ and η. Our objective is to trace how these two parameters impinge on the solution – in particular, on the overall connectivity of the network, as captured by its average degree. The results, both theoretical and numerical, are depicted in Figure 6.5.

The mean-field theory and the numerical simulations are in reasonably good agreement. Both show the same qualitative behavior as $1/\eta$ (which can be conceived as the effective volatility rate) varies in the range $(0, \infty)$. When η is very low, the network connectivity is correspondingly low and the average connectivity is roughly equal to

$$\langle \kappa^i \rangle_{i \in N} = \frac{2\tilde{\varepsilon}}{1/\eta}. \tag{6.45}$$

This is a consequence of the fact that, under these conditions, the network is fragmented into a large collection of very small components and, therefore, new links are created at the rate $2\eta\tilde{\varepsilon}$. When this creation rate is balanced against the unitary rate at which existing links disappear, one obtains (as a ratio between the two) the average connectivity specified in (6.45).

Then, if starting from such low values, η increases gradually (and the system is given the opportunity to adjust to a stationary state), the average connectivity continues to grow continuously along the lower branch of (stable) equilibria in Figure 6.5. This behavior changes drastically at a certain point (i.e. when $\eta = \eta_1$ in the mean-field solution and at a somewhat lower value in the numerical simulations). If η continues growing beyond that point the adjustment of system leads to a large (discontinuous) increase in network connectivity, bringing about a sharp qualitative change in the state. The situation keeps adjusting gradually in the same direction if η increases even further. But if it then were to "change course" and begin falling, the network dynamics would display hysteresis, i.e. it would remain at a relatively connected state down to some η_2 that is significantly lower that the value η_1 at which the upward transition took place.

Finally, it is of some interest to relax the condition $\beta \to \infty$ and consider instead a scenario where strategy adjustment is subject to some noise (i.e. β is finite). Heuristically, one might expect that a lower β, by rendering

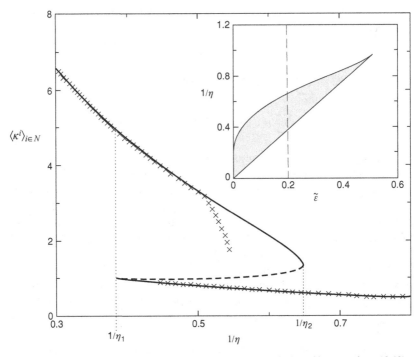

Figure 6.5. Mean-field solution of the model, as induced by equations (6.42)–(6.44). The diagram shows the dependence of the average degree on the inverse of the link-creation rate η for a fixed value of $\tilde{\varepsilon} = 1/q + (1 - 1/q)\varepsilon = 0.2$. The solid lines trace the stable equilibria whereas the dashed ones correspond to unstable ones. The points marked by $\times$ are obtained by simulations for networks with a total number of nodes $n = 20000$. The inset shows the regions in the parameter space that lead to a single solution (white region) or two stable solutions (grey region). The dashed vertical line in this space reflects the parameter conditions (i.e. value of $\tilde{\varepsilon}$) considered in the main diagram

network-based coordination more difficult, should play a role analogous to a lower rate of link creation (or, equivalently, a higher volatility). Indeed this can be shown to be true, not only numerically but also analytically.

For an analytical approach to the problem, Ehrhardt *et al.* (2005) [97] rely on the mean-field solution to the Potts model on random networks that was developed by Ehrhardt and Marsili (2004) [96] – recall Subsection 4.3.2. Doing so, one can estimate the coordination probability $\varphi(\beta)$ contemplated in (6.40) and, proceeding as above, obtain a self-consistent mean-field solution for the model in this general case. This analysis is found to support the indicated role of β, analogous to that of η. That is, as β grows, discontinuous transitions arise, with a region where the model displays equilibrium multiplicity (with a high- and low-connectivity phase) as well as hysteresis. When the system is in a phase with high conectivity, the giant component of the network also displays a high

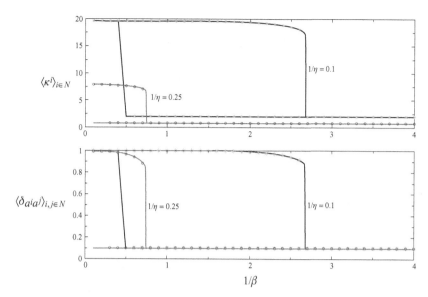

Figure 6.6. Effect of the noise parameter β on the long-run behavior of the system in a context with $q = 10$, $\varepsilon = 0$, and two different values of $\eta = 4$, 10. The diagram shows both the theoretical prediction (solid lines) and the simulations for a population size $n = 1000$. The upper pannel depicts the average degree $\langle \kappa^i \rangle_{i \in N}$, while the lower one presents the effect on the coordination probability $\langle \delta_{a^i a^j} \rangle_{i,j \in N}$ that two randomly selected nodes i and j have $\delta_{a^i a^j} = 1$ (i.e. display the same action)

fractional size. Therefore, the probability $\langle \delta_{a^i a^j} \rangle_{i,j \in N}$ that *any* two randomly selected nodes i and j be coordinated on the same action (i.e. $\delta_{a^i a^j} = 1$) is also expected to be high. These theoretical predictions, compared with numerical simulations, are depicted in Figure 6.6.

The dynamic behavior encountered in the present model is quite akin to that observed in Subsection 6.2.2 for a process of network formation that, nevertheless, relies on markedly different forces and takes place in quite different circumstances – in particular, it is based on *local* search and displays *no* strategic dimension. Such resemblance in dynamic performance suggests that certain key regularities may be expected to arise in a wide array of otherwise dissimilar social environments. More specifically, the main insight that transpires from both setups can be succinctly described as follows. Whenever a central characteristic underlying network formation (e.g. low network clustering in one model, high coordination of behavior in the other) is reinforced as part of the process of network buildup, the resulting complex dynamics tends to display the three features that have been highlighted here: sharp transitions, equilibrium coexistence, and hysteresis. Further illustration of this idea will be found in Section 6.3.2, within a still quite different setup that models diffusion and growth.

6.3.2   Other Strategic Setups

Finally, as advanced, we briefly discuss three other scenarios where network formation and play also unfold along a complex coevolutionary process.

A One-Shot Prisoner's Dilemma

The Prisoner's Dilemma provides a classical paradigm to study the conflict between efficiency and individual (opportunistic) incentives. In particular, it has been amply studied in a context where agents interact locally and shape their behavior by simple local rules. Well-known examples of the latter are the models studied by Nowak and May (1992) [225], Nowak *et al.* (1994) [224], and Eshel *et al.* (1998) [104], where agents play the Prisoner's Dilemma with their neighbors in some given network structure, regular or not. Only seldom, however, has this structure been allowed to change as part of the process.[31] Here, we outline one such approach, which has been proposed and studied by Zimmermann *et al.* (2004) [297] (see also Eguíluz *et al.* (2005) [95]).

The model includes a given population of agents, N, who live in an intertemporal setup modeled in discrete time. In every period $t = 0, 1, 2, \ldots$, individuals are arranged as specified by the prevailing (undirected) network Γ_t, and each of them can be defined as either a *cooperator* or a *defector*. An agent $i \in N$ is said to be a cooperator at t if she chooses $a_t^i = C$ (cooperation), while she is labeled a defector if she chooses $a_t^i = D$ (defection). It is worth emphasizing that agent i is assumed to play the same action with *all* of her neighbors $j \in \mathcal{N}_t^i$. This stands in contrast with the alternative model that will be studied subsequently.

The payoffs that are obtained by i from the bilateral interaction with any given j are as described by the following payoff table:

i \ j	C	D
C	ζ^{ij}	$\zeta^{ij} - u$
D	$\zeta^{ij} + v$	0

(6.46)

where ζ^{ij} $(= \zeta^{ji})$ is the (symmetric) positive payoff resulting from *joint cooperation* and the payoff from *joint defection* is normalized to 0. On the other hand, $u \geq \zeta^{ij}$ represents the *cost* from unilateral cooperation, whereas $v > 0$ stands for the extra *benefit* of unilateral defection.

---

[31] In a similar spirit, however, there is a vast body of group-selection literature postulating that the population is segmented in groups, the persistence or relative size of these groups being shaped by the pressure of selection or/and migration. This literature has its roots in the seminal work of Wynne-Edwards (1962) [293], which has been formalized, among others, by Eshel (1972) [103], Boyd and Richerson (1990) [42], or Vega-Redondo (1996) [276] using the tools of modern evolutionary theory. The key contrast between such group-selection theories and the present approach is that those theories implicitly presume that the network consists of disjoint and completely connected cliques – i.e. separate groups.

The state of the system $\omega_t = (\mathbf{a}_t, \Gamma_t)$ evolves over time by the composition of *strategy revision* and *network update*. For expositional simplicity, these two components of the dynamics may be viewed as operating sequentially at every t.

> **Strategy revision** *Every* agent $i \in N$ revises her former strategy a_{t-1}^i by mimicking the behavior of the individual who, at $t - 1$, obtained the highest *total* payoff in her neighborhood, including herself. If the two strategies, C and D, provided the same payoff, either of them is chosen with the same probability.
>
> **Network update** Let i be any given agent whose strategy revision has led her to imitating a defecting neighbor $j \in \mathcal{N}_t^i$. Then, with some probability $p \in [0, 1]$, agent i "rewires" her link $ij \in \Gamma_{t-1}$ to some other $\ell \in N$, randomly selected. On the other hand, a player who has imitated a cooperator does not rewire any of her links.

Thus, in sum, it is posited that every agent *simultaneously* revises her strategy at every t and, if this revision involves imitating a defector, the link connecting to the latter is rewired with some probability p. A possible rationale for this formulation is that, when an agent sees that one of her neighbors is not only doing better than herself but is also a defector, she feels some inclination to discontinue the relationship and look for a more rewarding partner.

The probability p parametrizes the so-called *plasticity* of the network. If it is equal to zero, the network remains fixed throughout and, correspondingly, one expects that only low levels of cooperation may be sustained in the long-run. Instead, when $p > 0$, it may be conjectured that, because network adjustment penalizes defectors, the process may succeed in limiting their numbers significantly. Indeed, this is what has been shown by Zimmermann *et al.* (2004) [297] through extensive numerical simulations. They find, in fact, that even a *very small* rewiring probability can have dramatic effects in the long-run behavior of the system.

Specifically, the numerical simulations are conducted for the case where $\zeta^{ij} = 1$ for all $i, j \in N$, and thus every pair of agents is taken to play the *same* Prisoner's Dilemma game. Concerning the other payoff parameters, on the other hand, the cost of defection is fixed to $u = 1$, while the value of v is allowed to vary in order to modulate the gains from unilateral defection.

The process starts with a random network, constructed to exhibit some given average connectivity. This connectivity remains fixed throughout since network update (see above) does not change the total number of links nor, of course, the average degree. Initially, the process is also seeded with some given fraction of cooperators, randomly placed on the network. Under these conditions, the system turns out to settle, eventually, in one of two long-run states. (There is again, therefore, equilibrium multiplicity, the long-run outcome depending on both the specific initial conditions materialized as well as the ensuing randomness.) In one of those long-run states, the whole population gravitates toward defection. Instead, in the alternative one, some positive fraction of

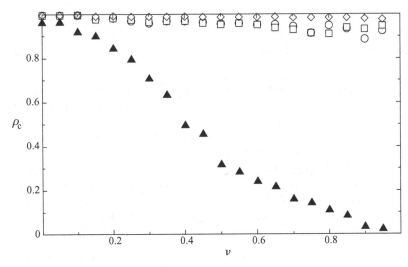

Figure 6.7. Fraction ρ_c of cooperators in the cooperative long-run state of the model proposed by Eguíluz *et al.* (2004) [95], as a function of p and v. Full triangles represent the case $p = 0$, while circles, squares, and diamonds represent, respectively, the cases $p = 0.01$, 0.1, 1. The numerical results pertain to a population consisting of $10\,000$ nodes arranged in a network with average degree $\langle \kappa^i \rangle = 8$. The initial fraction of cooperators is set at 0.6

cooperators, ρ_c, remains stable in the long run. The dependence of ρ_c on the two free parameters of the model, p and v, is depicted in Figure 6.7.

The simulation results show that even a very moderate extent of network plasticity (i.e. a low value of p) has drastic effects on the ability of the population to sustain cooperation in the long run. If $p = 0$ (and thus the network remains "frozen" throughout), the long-run fraction of cooperators decreases sharply as the extra benefit v from unilateral defection rises. In contrast, just a low $p = 0.01$ forcefully checks this effect: the entailed network plasticity allows for an almost complete state of cooperation to persist over time, even for quite high values of v.

Finally, it is of some interest to note that, as explained in detail by Zimmermann *et al.* (2004) [297], such cooperative outcome is sustained through a particular network architecture that affords the required robustness. As the process unfolds, that is, cooperators end up arranging themselves in a hierarchic (tree-like) manner. This implies that each of them has a highly connected (and thus successful) cooperator in her neighborhood. It also implies, therefore, that no defector connecting "from the outside" can have her isolate defection payoff stand out as worth imitating.

Repeated Prisoner's Dilemma

Suppose now that, within every period $t = 0, 1, 2, \ldots$, players directly connected in the prevailing social network Γ_t are involved in a *Repeated Prisoner's*

Dilemma. Thus, unlike in the former scenario, the game played within each period has itself an intertemporal dimension that should impinge on agents' behavior. Further lines of contrast with the previous one-shot scenario can be summarized as follows:

1. For each pair of connected players i and j ($ij \in \Gamma_t$), the Prisoner's Dilemma (PD) is *idiosyncratic* to the relationship and may also *change over time*. Specifically, the payoff table for the PD stage game is taken to be of the form given by (6.46), where the cooperation payoff attainable at any given t is denoted by ζ_t^{ij}, generally different across player pairs.

2. The Repeated Prisoner's Dilemma (RPD) played by any pair of connected players is *choice-independent* of any other in the following sense: the actions chosen along their bilateral repeated game are not constrained in any way by the choices those agents make (or have made) in the RPD's they currently play with other individuals of the population.

3. Depending on the social norm in place (see below), the different RPD's played by the same individual at some t may be *strategically related*. [This occurs when, for some player i, the choice she makes at stage q in the RPD she plays with some $j \in \mathcal{N}_t^i$ affects, at a later stage $q' > q$, the behavior of a different neighbor $\ell \in \mathcal{N}_t^i$ in the corresponding RPD played by i and ℓ.]

A model with the features listed above has been studied by Vega-Redondo (2005) [278] – see also Vega-Redondo *et al.* (2005) [279]. At every t, the population is involved in a collection of "parallel" RPD's played by every pair of agents i and j with $ij \in \Gamma_t$. Naturally, the overall pattern of behavior displayed at t must depend on the (equilibrium) social norm of behavior that prevails in the society. Let us consider two possibilities in this respect.

Bilateral Convention (BC). Under this norm, each different RPD is not only choice independent but also strategically independent. Then, it readily follows from standard considerations in the theory of repeated games that joint cooperation between any given i and j, $ij \in \Gamma_t$, may be supported as a (bilateral Subgame-Perfect)[32] equilibrium if, and only if, their current cooperation payoff ζ_t^{ij} is high enough, given the discount rate δ at which players discount future stage payoffs. More precisely, the requirement is that

$$\zeta_t^{ij} \geq \frac{1 - \delta}{\delta}. \tag{6.47}$$

---

[32] See Footnote 4 for various game theory references where the concept of Subgame-Perfect Equilibrium (the suitable one for multistage games) is explained in detail.

Multilateral Convention (MC). Under this alternative social norm, a player i is supposed to punish a neighbor j not only after j has defected on i but also when i learns that j has defected on some of j's other neighbors. The key assumption in this respect is that information on any defection that has occurred in third-party interactions "travels" along the network by neighbor-to-neighbor communication, only one link at every stage. This implies that, in order for such information to flow promptly between the different neighbors of a particular individual i, the prevailing network Γ_t must display a high "generalized clustering" in the vicinity of that node. Specifically, the relevant concern here is the distance between the neighbors of i, where the paths that go through i itself must naturally be excluded in computing that distance. It can be shown that, under MC, the criterion for any two given neighbors i and j to cooperate at some t is

$$\zeta_t^{ij} \geq \frac{1-\delta}{\delta} - \sum_{\ell \in \mathcal{N}_t^i} \left[\zeta_t^{i\ell} + \frac{1-\delta}{\delta} \right] \delta^{d_t^i(j,\ell)}, \qquad (6.48)$$

where $d_t^i(j, \ell)$ represents the aforementioned distance between j and ℓ, both neighbors of i. In comparison with (6.47), the gist of (6.48) can be simply explained as follows. Under MC, the incentives for cooperation between i and j are significantly higher than for BC (i.e. the corresponding requirement weaker) *if* there are many valuable neighbors of i who are not far from j, and *vice versa*. For, in this case, player i is deterred from defecting with j (and *vice versa*) by the threat of early ruining the high-cooperation potential that is otherwise attainable with their other valuable neighbors.

Let us now describe the induced network dynamics. Given the network Γ_{t-1} that prevailed at $t-1$, the network Γ_t that forms at t is derived from the sequential operation of three adjustment mechanisms. Reminiscent of those considered in Subsection 6.2.2, they can be outlined as follows.

Payoff update. For every link $ij \in \Gamma_{t-1}$, the "cooperation value" of the link ζ_{t-1}^{ij} is updated with some probability λ. In that event, a new payoff is redrawn afresh according to some given distribution. Heuristically, we may continue speaking of this phenomenon as "volatility," in the sense that its tendency will be to deteriorate the value of existing links and thus lead to their removal (see below). In line with this interpretation, λ is called the *volatility rate*.

Search. Every agent $i \in N$ is given the option of local and global search with respective probabilities ξ and $(1 - \xi)\eta$ for some $\xi, \eta \in (0, 1)$. *Local* search is conducted along the current component of i in Γ_{t-1} by meeting all those individuals who lie within a certain prespecified radius r. *Global* search, instead, involves meeting one randomly selected node in the population at large. In either case, for each of the individuals j thus met by i, a value ζ^{ij} is independently drawn for the cooperation payoff that *would* materialize if the link ij were indeed established. Every player can support at most a certain number of links. In view of this constraint, each player chooses the maximal set of links that display the highest cooperation value.

Decay. Given the payoffs and social network resulting from the operation of the first two adjustment steps, the prevailing social norm (BC or MC) then determines which links can be used to sustain cooperation. Those that cannot do so are simply removed to yield the network Γ_t that defines the pattern of (repeated) interaction that applies in period t.

The main focus of the analysis is to understand how the effective rate of volatility λ/ξ impinges on the ability of the population to sustain a dense network of cooperative behavior. Relatedly, another important concern is to discern the *endogenous* features of the network architecture that underlie the "struggle" of the society to maintain high levels of cooperation. Naturally, the answer to these questions must crucially depend on the prevailing social norm, BC or MC. These issues have been studied by Vega-Redondo (2005) [278], both through mean-field techniques and numerical simulations. For brevity, we focus only on the latter, which are summarized in Figures 6.8–6.9 for each of the two social norms under consideration.

Figure 6.8 shows that, under the social norm BC (i.e. when every pairwise interaction has to be supported bilaterally), increasing volatility has a significant and *progressively more* acute effect on the density of the social network. Indeed, at a certain point, the level of connectivity/cooperation experiences an abrupt discontinuous fall that is reminiscent of the sharp downward transition witnessed in the model discussed in Subsection 6.2.2. There is, however, an important difference to be stressed between the two cases, which concerns the evolution of clustering. In the present case, clustering – in the generalized sense measured by the inverse of average neighbors' distance – does *not* rise but instead falls as volatility grows.[33] The simple reason for it is that the radius r of local search is chosen large (in fact, it is set at $r = n - 1$). This is done in order to highlight the contrast between the implications of the two social norms (BC and MC), minimizing the limitations imposed by search. Under these conditions, clustering has no major impact on search and, therefore, its sharp fall at the transition is simply a reflection of the corresponding abrupt change in network connectivity.

The situation is markedly different under the social norm MC, as shown in Figure 6.9. In this case, the decrease in network connectivity is only gradual as volatility rises. This contrasting state of affairs is essentially rooted in the twin behavior displayed by generalized clustering, which is depicted in the lower panel. As the environment becomes more volatile (and thus cooperation tends to be less persistent), the social network adapts endogenously to minimize the damage. Thus, even if no player consciously harbors that aim, the social network increases its cohesiveness by lowering the distances between neighbors. This in turn has the important effect of deterring opportunistic behavior through the

---

[33] Note that the effective volatility rate can be thought of as the inverse of the (effective) search rate so that an increase in the volatility rate λ in the present model is analogous to a decrease of the search rate in the model discussed in Subsection 6.2.2.

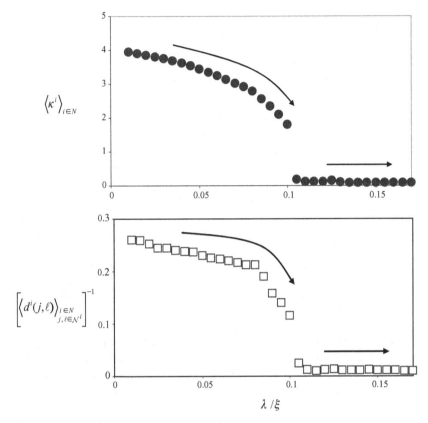

Figure 6.8. Average degree (upper panel) and the inverse of average neighbors' distance (lower panel) derived from numerical simulations in the model of Vega-Redondo (2005) [278] under the social norm BC. The diagrams depict the long-run state obtained as the effective volatility rate λ/ξ is increased gradually from very low levels, for a fixed value of $\eta/\xi = 0.01$. Other parameter values are set as follows: $\delta = 0.75$, $\xi = 0.1$, and $u = v = 4$ in the payoff table (6.46), with the fresh values of ζ^{ij} drawn uniformly from the interval [0.4, 1.4]. Finally, the radius of local search is set to $r = n - 1$, so that the "local" search of an agent reaches all individuals in her component

threat of fast, and thus effective, punishment. In the end, overall cooperation can be maintained at levels that would be otherwise unattainable if either (a) the alternative norm BC were in place, or (b) the network topology remained fixed in the face of a growing volatility.

Diffusion and Growth

Finally, we turn to a context where, unlike what has been considered so far, the range of behavior of nodes (agents) is not fixed but changes over time as induced

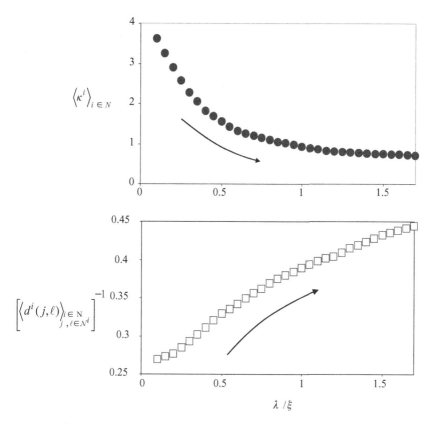

Figure 6.9. Average degree (upper panel) and the inverse of average neighbors' distance (lower panel) derived from numerical simulations in the model of Vega-Redondo (2005) [278] under the social norm MC. The rest of conditions are identical to those of Figure 6.8

by two complementary forces. On one hand, there is a process of *growth* that proceeds independently for each node. On the other hand, there is a process of *diffusion* across nodes that is mediated by the social network. A natural interpretation here is that the behavior of nodes reflects, say, technological choices, whose evolution is jointly governed by individual-based innovation and network-based imitation.

As usual, the social network is also assumed to change over time through the corresponding processes of link creation and destruction. While the latter is modeled exogenously (i.e. as the outcome of persistent volatility), link creation is postulated to be endogenous, depending crucially on the behavior displayed by the nodes in question. Specifically, it is assumed that only if their behavior is sufficiently similar, a link between them is created with significant a probability. Intuitively, the motivation is akin to that explained in Subsection 6.3.1 for a coordination scenario.

A model with the aforementioned features has been recently studied by Marsili *et al.* (2005) [195]. It can be briefly described as follows. At every $t = 0, 1, 2, \ldots$, the population displays a certain action profile $\mathbf{a}_t \in \mathbb{R}^n$, the particular a_t^i displayed by any given agent i hereafter referred to, for conciseness, as her "technological level." The state of the system also includes the social network Γ_t that specifies the undirected links $ij \in L_t$ prevailing at t. Corresponding to each of the two elements of a state, the law of motion of the system must include two components, technology adjustment and network adjustment, as described next.

Technological adjustment. At every t, each individual independently receives the opportunity to change her technological level with probability $v > 0$. In this event, the adjustment involves two consecutive steps. First, the agent first matches – say, by imitation – the highest technological level in her immediate neighborhood (including herself). Second, she experiences some idiosyncratic and independent technological shock χ_t^i, normally distributed with zero mean and finite variance. Overall, the new technological level becomes

$$a_t^i = \max \left\{ a_{t-1}^j : j \in \mathcal{N}_{t-1}^j \cup \{i\} \right\} + \chi_t^i.$$

Network adjustment. The network changes due to the creation of new links and the decay of preexisting ones. Each of these two mechanisms is now described in turn.

Link creation. At every t, each individual independently receives the opportunity to form a new link with probability $\eta > 0$. When this event occurs, she meets one randomly selected $j \in N \backslash \{i\}$ and, provided $ij \notin \Gamma_{t-1}$, considers establishing the link ij. She is taken to form it with *full probability* if the two agents are sufficiently similar – specifically, if $\left| a_t^i - a_t^j \right| \leq \bar{d}$, where $\bar{d}$ is a parameter of the model. Instead, if the former inequality does not apply, the link ij is formed only with a "small" probability ε.

Link decay. At every t, each existing link $ij \in \Gamma_{t-1}$ vanishes with probability $\lambda > 0$.

The model yields a dynamic performance analogous to that already encountered in a variety of quite different setups. In particular, if actions/technological choices adjust fast (i.e. $v \gg \eta, \lambda$), the network-formation process displays abrupt transitions, hysteresis, and equilibrium multiplicity as the effective intensity of link creation η / λ varies over its full range. In the present context, however, this performance has, as its mirror image, an interesting counterpart along the new dimension of technological change. That is, when the network transition occurs, the model also induces sharp changes (as well as hysteresis and equilibrium multiplicity) on the average rate at which technology grows

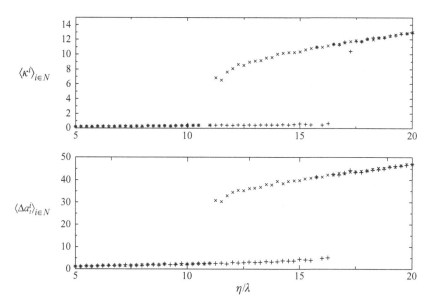

Figure 6.10. Average degree (upper panel) and average "technological" growth rate (lower panel), derived from numerical simulations in the model studied by Marsili *et al.* (2005) [195]. The crosses ($\times$) represent the long-run states derived from initial conditions with high connectivity while pluses ($+$) represent long-run states resulting from initial conditions with low connectivity. When the two symbols overlap (or are close by), the simulations point to equilibrium uniqueness; instead, they suggest equilibrium multiplicity when they stand apart. Thus, for high (low) values of η/λ, we find that a unique long-run state arises with a high (respectively, low) average connectivity. Instead, within an intermediate coexistence region, both situations may arise, depending on initial conditions. The simulations were conducted for $\bar{d} = 2$ and $\varepsilon/\lambda = 0.001$

over time. These results, obtained from numerical simulations,[34] are summarized in Figure 6.10.

The behavior depicted in Figure 6.10 is similar to that found in Subsection 6.2.2 (cf. Figure 6.3). In that case, however, the essential mechanism leading to sharp transitions was a change in network clustering, a feature playing no significant role in the present context. Here, any large shift in equilibrium long-run outcomes derives from the interplay between the evolution of the network and the associated change in agents' behavior. It occurs when, say,

---

[34] For simplicity, the model has been described to operate in discrete time. In effect, however, the discrete periods are to be conceived as very short so that, in the simulations, at most one adjustment event is allowed to take place in each of them. In this sense, the discrete-time formulation must be regarded as approximating a continuous-time process.

an increase (possibly small) in the rate of link creation leads to a network that starts being dense enough to represent a significant homogenizing device. Then, a forceful feedback into link creation itself is triggered, which strengthens the aforementioned trend toward homogenization and sparks a snowball effect. The mechanism at work is similar to that underlying the coordination setup studied in Subsection 6.3.1. The main difference is that, in the present case, the behavioral dimension of the process is no longer bounded within a fixed limited range. Thus when the network makes a sharp transition into a new configuration, the pace of technological advance also shifts into a new regime, as evinced by the lower panel of Figure 6.10.

6.4 INCENTIVES AND COMPLEXITY IN SOCIAL NETWORKS

In this final chapter, we have addressed the central issue of network (co-)evolution from two different perspectives. First, Section 6.1 has illustrated the approach pursued by the game-theoretic literature, whose emphasis is on understanding how agents' incentives and strategic interaction shape the architecture of the social network. As explained, this literature largely abstracts from considerations pertaining to the potential complexity of the situation. It either tackles the problem through a (static) equilibrium methodology or studies instead the long-run behavior of a suitably formulated process of social learning. In the first case, a common presumption is that agents can somehow "see through" the intricacies of the situation and attain a network configuration that is consistent with their incentives – i.e. a configuration that is immune to profitable deviations by small groups of agents. In contrast, the dynamic approach typically focuses on scenarios where the individual-based learning process is convergent, in which case strategic stability (or equilibrium) is again ensured in the long run.

The second part of this chapter (Sections 6.2 and 6.3) has, on the other hand, studied network evolution with an accent on the implications of large-scale complexity. This approach, which can be labeled "phenomenological," has aimed at grasping how simple and natural rules of adjustment may generate some of the long-run regularities found in empirical evidence. In this endeavor, however, the role played by agents' incentives in modeling the situation has been only marginal. Yet, unquestionably, benefits, costs, and the entailed agents' incentives are often key to the networking decisions and the associated behavior observed in social environments. At a basic level, of course, an assessment of own payoffs provides the guide and motivation for agents' choices. But, at a higher level, it is also some estimation of others' payoffs that agents use, with varying degrees of sophistication, to anticipate their partners' behavior. In general, ignoring those payoff-related considerations risks missing some of the essential (strategic) factors that shape the dynamics of many social networks.

A proper account of *both* complexity and incentives should, therefore, underpin a satisfactory theory of social networks.[35] If the environment is genuinely complex, however, it seems untenable to assume (as is standard in game-theoretic applications) that the pattern of interaction is perfectly known by everyone. Instead, a natural alternative is to posit that individuals enjoy only local information, i.e. their accurate knowledge is restricted to a small neighborhood. Thus, while agents may have some true aggregate information (say, on the overall *distribution* of "local conditions"), they are uncertain as to how this is patched together to conform the whole network. By casting the setup as an incomplete-information game, Galeotti and Vega-Redondo (2005) [120] undertake a preliminary step in addressing this problem. They study, in particular, a context where the underlying network is random (characterized by a given degree distribution) and players' payoffs display multiplicative complementarities. (See also the independent work by Sundararajan (2005)[266], who focuses on supermodular games and allows for incomplete information.) This approach is extended to other payoff scenarios (including payoff substitutabilities) and varying information radii by Galeotti *et al.* (2005) [119]. One of the primary aims of these papers is to understand how equilibrium behavior adapts when changes occur in either the topological properties of the network or the extent of information possessed by the agents.

Naturally, complexity and incentives should also be brought to bear on the study of *network formation processes*. In developing a research program in this vein, it is quite conceivable that some of the issues and methods that will emerge are similar to those already involved in our discussion of growing/evolving complex networks. For example, the idea that link creation and destruction should result from a combination of search and players' incentives has already been put forward, albeit in too simplified a form, in some of our models. In general, the interaction between incentives and network structure (say, clustering) is also bound to play a key role in many applications. This suggests, in particular, that the identification of complexity with uncorrelated randomness that characterizes much of the complex-network literature is too crude a route to be widely applicable. The need to overcome this simplistic view of complexity has already been raised at different points of this monograph. We have also highlighted, however, the significant difficulties, conceptual and methodological, which will have to be confronted in doing so. Genuine advance on this front should be one of the main lines of development of the field in the years to come.

---

[35] For another defense of this standpoint, see the recent survey by Jackson (2006) [157], who also provides a rich manifold of economic applications that illustrate the relevance of network theory to economic analysis. Further elaboration upon this question can be found in the Afterword, where we close the monograph with some general perspective on the field of complex social networks and a brief discussion of future avenues of research.

Afterword

The primary purpose of this monograph has been twofold. Firstly, the objective has been to provide a systematic account of some of the basic models and techniques developed by the modern theory of complex networks. In addition, a second motivation has been to illustrate the broad range of socioeconomic phenomena to which this theory can be naturally applied. In the latter pursuit, our approach is polar to that commonly espoused by classical game theory and economic analysis. It stresses the implications of complexity on the interaction structure, while downplaying the role of incentives in shaping agents' behavior. But, as repeatedly argued, neither of those one-sided perspectives can be judged satisfactory. In general, both complexity and incentive considerations should *jointly* play a key role in any proper understanding (and thus modeling) of most social phenomena.

To further elaborate on this point, it is useful to recapitulate what are some of the main benefits to be expected from explicitly accounting for *complexity* in the analysis of socioeconomic environments.

- First, of course, the theoretical approach undoubtedly becomes more realistic since, indeed, we find that so many interesting social problems in the real world are embedded in a complex and ever-changing social network (cf. Chapter 1). It is fitting, therefore, that those problems should also be modeled in ways that respect such underlying complexity.
- Second, new theoretical features arise (e.g. scale-free behavior or sharp dynamic transitions) that are intimately associated to complexity. This in turn helps shed light on diverse empirical evidence (say, the evolution of social pathologies, scientific collaboration, or interfirm partnerships) where those features play a quite prominent role.
- Third, the large scale inherent to complex phenomena naturally leads to a statistical description of the situation, where the focus lies on aggregate regularities rather than individual detail. This, in turn, permits a methodological approach (e.g. asymptotic analysis, mean-field

theory, etc.) that is able to deliver sharp results that would otherwise be unattainable from more "microscopic" modeling.

But, now reciprocally, we may also ask: what is to be gained from a suitable account of *incentives* in the study of social problems? Again, a threefold response – in essence parallel to that above – seems in order. By so doing, it may well be argued, the analysis becomes more realistic, new theoretical features arise, and a well-developed methodology (game theory in this case) can be fruitfully applied. All this has already been spelled and illustrated before, so we need not elaborate on it here. We finish, therefore, with a brief discussion of some of the issues and insights that may be expected to mark the fertile integration of incentives and complexity that is advocated here.

As the very organization of the monograph reflects, *diffusion*, *search*, and *play* are regarded here as three of the essential building blocks involved in most social-network phenomena. In fact, the central idea that implicitly motivates our endeavor is that complex behavior in social contexts often results from the *simultaneous* interplay of those processes. It is fair to say, however, that the way in which such three "components" have been separately modeled in Chapters 3–5 does not easily lead to their rich integration into a unified scenario. A key goal of future research, therefore, should be to develop a theoretical framework where suitable formulations of all of them are effectively made to *coevolve*.

Of course, in such an enriched context, agents' payoffs and their corresponding incentives must play an essential modeling role. For example, they should be involved in any suggested explanation of, say, when agents enter a diffusion wave, how they play with their neighbors, or the resources they devote to searching for valuable information. In the real world, of course, given the complexity of the environment, agents can only count on *relatively simple* decision rules to guide such behavior. One might hope, however, that when such bounded-rationality considerations are suitably modeled in a learning setup, the interactive evolutionary processes thus induced can shed some light on the intricate and subtle performance observed in network-based social dynamics.

Yet, traditionally, dynamic analysis in economics (even when evolutionary in nature) has revolved around the notions of equilibria – or stationary states – and their corresponding stability, local or global. We have argued at some length that the complexity witnessed in social environments cannot be possibly understood by focusing alone on the equilibria – static or dynamic – that arise in a *fixed* setup. The reason is that an essential underpinning of that complexity is the continuous volatility impinging on the environment in an essentially unpredictable fashion. This, in effect, forces the system to lie persistently far from equilibrium, in ceaseless flux. The entailed adaptation of the system should then be conceived, and thus modeled, as a disequilibrium phenomenon.

Unswerving adaptation, to be sure, does not preclude the formation of some stable structures (e.g. a recognizable network architecture) or the materialization of other long-run regularities (e.g. some specific amount of network clustering or a well-defined degree distribution). In this sense, the situation is reminiscent of what has been found in other realms of science such as nonlinear thermo-dynamics.[1] The so-called Rayleigh–Bénard convection is a good case in point. In 1900, the French physicist Henri Bénard discovered that when a thin layer of fluid is subject (by *constantly* heating it from below) to a suitable thermal gradient – neither too large not too small – a convection motion arises by which the molecules are set in motion defining a complex hexagonal pattern. This, in modern times, has become a paradigmatic example of how a continuous exter-nal perturbation (the heat flow in this case) may give rise to an *ordered* system in persistent *disequilibrium*.

The analogy with a social network subject to the continuous pressure of volatility may be useful. As the social network faces a continuous disrupting force that affects, say, the stability of its links, its architecture will tend to reconfigurate itself. In so doing, it may achieve certain stable properties that survive despite – nay, because of – such a sustained pressure (provided the latter is of "manageable proportions"). But that stability of overall key features of the network cannot be expected to entail a corresponding stability of the network itself. In general, the network will keep continuously changing, just as the molecules continue to move along the "convection rolls" in Bénard's thermodynamic experiment. Indeed, it is their relentless change that generates the resulting structure in the first place.

An evolving social network represents a *flexible structure* of interaction and this is precisely what renders a "network organization" (i.e. a network econ-omy, a network industry, a network firm) such an effective arrangement in the presence of fast environmental change – cf. Subsection 1.2.8. In fact, the ability to reconcile structure and change appears to be one of the essential attributes that distinguishes a *successful* network organization in a volatile environment. What is the best way of achieving this state of affairs, and what are the risks and benefits involved, are important questions for which we hardly have good answers as yet. They stand out, therefore, as central questions to be addressed by future research. Indeed, to understand how network structure and adaptabil-ity may be harmonized in a changing setup is an important issue of concern in many different areas of application – not only in economics but in biochem-istry, ecology, or sociology as well. It thus represents a good final illustration of the theme that has run throughout the whole monograph: the field of com-plex networks, by its genuinely interdisciplinary nature, lends itself naturally to research efforts that cut across traditional scientific boundaries. It is my hope that this monograph may help in this undertaking.

---

[1] See the classical book by Prigogine and Stengers (1984) [241] a lucid and engaging piece elabo-rating upon the relationship between nonequilibrium behavior ("chaos") and structure ("order"). Recall as well the work of Kauffman (1993) [170] mentioned at the end of Chapter 4.

Generating Functions

Let $\{p(\kappa)\}_{\kappa=0}^{\infty}$ be the distribution of a discrete random variable which, for our present purposes, we shall generally conceive as the node degree distribution of some random network. Its generating function G_0 is defined by

$$G_0(x) = \sum_{\kappa=0}^{\infty} p(\kappa)\, x^{\kappa}.$$

The key feature that marks the usefulness of a generating function is that it *fully* characterizes the distribution (and therefore, its moments of all orders). To see this observe that, for each $\kappa = 0, 1, 2, \ldots,$

$$p(\kappa) = \frac{1}{\kappa!} \left. \frac{d^{\kappa} G_0}{dx^{\kappa}}(x) \right|_{x=0}$$

so that the whole distribution can be recovered from G_0 through successive differentiation.

The former derivations require evaluating the different derivatives of G_0 at $x = 0$. If we switch instead to evaluating them at $x = 1$, the generating function may be used to determine the moments of the distribution of any order. First, by considering the generation function itself (i.e. the "derivative of 0-th order"), we simply obtain

$$G_0(1) = \sum_{\kappa=0}^{\infty} p(\kappa) = 1,$$

which follows from the mere fact that $\{p(\kappa)\}_{\kappa=0}^{\infty}$ embodies a well-defined probability distribution. Then, by derivating G_0 once and evaluating the resulting function at $x = 1$ we obtain the mean (first-order moment):

$$\left. \frac{dG_0}{dx}(x) \right|_{x=1} \equiv G_0'(1) = \sum_{\kappa=0}^{\infty} \kappa\, p(\kappa) = \langle \kappa \rangle.$$

In general, for any r-th order moment, we simply need to iterate r times the operator $\left(x \frac{d}{dx}\right)$ that consists of a differentiation with respect to x, followed by a multiplication by x. When the resulting function is evaluated at $x = 1$, we obtain

$$\left[\left(x\frac{d}{dx}\right)^r G_0\right](x)\bigg|_{x=1} = \langle\kappa^r\rangle.$$

For example, if the degree distribution is Poisson (cf. (2.2)), the generating function is of the form

$$G_0(x) = \sum_{\kappa=0}^{\infty}\frac{1}{\kappa!}e^{-z}z^{\kappa}\,x^{\kappa} = e^{-z}\sum_{\kappa=0}^{\infty}\frac{1}{\kappa!}(zx)^{\kappa} = e^{z(x-1)},$$

and it is easily confirmed that the first three moments are

$$\left[\left(x\frac{d}{dx}\right)G_0\right](x)\bigg|_{x=1} = z$$

$$\left[\left(x\frac{d}{dx}\right)^2 G_0\right](x)\bigg|_{x=1} = z(1+z)$$

$$\left[\left(x\frac{d}{dx}\right)^3 G_0\right](x)\bigg|_{x=1} = z(1+3z+z^2).$$

Starting with some given generating function G_0 as a point of reference, it is often convenient to work from it to determine the generating functions of distributions associated to the original one. For example, under the interpretation of G_0 as the generating function for the degree distribution of a random network, it is immediate to obtain its relationship with the counterpart G_1 characterizing the degree distribution $\{\zeta(\kappa)\}_{\kappa=0}^{\infty}$ of a *neighboring* node. In view of (2.20), we may write

$$G_1(x) = \sum_{\kappa=0}^{\infty}\zeta(\kappa)\,x^{\kappa} = \sum_{\kappa=0}^{\infty}\frac{p(\kappa)\,\kappa}{\sum_{\kappa'=0}^{\infty}p(\kappa')\,\kappa'}x^{\kappa}$$

$$= \frac{1}{\langle\kappa\rangle}\sum_{\kappa=0}^{\infty}p(\kappa)\,\kappa x^{\kappa} = \frac{1}{\langle\kappa\rangle}x\sum_{\kappa=0}^{\infty}p(\kappa)\,\kappa x^{\kappa-1}$$

$$= \frac{x\,G_0'(x)}{G_0'(1)}. \tag{A.1}$$

As a further example, we may also be interested in the distribution induced on the excess degree, i.e. the number of links of a neighboring node other than the one through which it is accessed. Its distribution $\{\hat{\zeta}(\kappa)\}_{\kappa=0}^{\infty}$ is given by

$$\hat{\zeta}(\kappa) = \zeta(\kappa+1) \qquad (\kappa = 0, 1, \dots),$$

and therefore its generating function $\hat{G}_1$ is

$$
\begin{aligned}
\hat{G}_1(x) &= \sum_{\kappa=0}^{\infty} \hat{\zeta}(\kappa)\, x^\kappa = \sum_{\kappa=0}^{\infty} \frac{p(\kappa+1)(\kappa+1)}{\sum_{\kappa'=0}^{\infty} p(\kappa')\, \kappa'} x^\kappa \\
&= \frac{1}{G_0'(1)} \sum_{\kappa=1}^{\infty} p(\kappa)\, \kappa\, x^{\kappa-1} \\
&= \frac{1}{G_0'(1)} \sum_{\kappa=0}^{\infty} p(\kappa)\, \kappa\, x^{\kappa-1} = \frac{G_0'(x)}{G_0'(1)}.
\end{aligned}
\tag{A.2}
$$

Thus we find that $\hat{G}_1$ differs from G_1 only in the leading factor x, which is now absent since the link used for accessing the neighboring node is not counted.

Two useful properties of generating functions are worth highlighting, since they are repeatedly used throughout the text. They both refer to how to compute the generating function of a random variable that is obtained from a certain collection of other m independent random variables, $\tilde{Y}_1, \tilde{Y}_2, \ldots, \tilde{Y}_m$.

- Firstly, consider the case of a random variable $\tilde{W}$ that results from a *probability mixture* of the $\tilde{Y}_i$. This means that its probability distribution $\{p_W(\kappa)\}_{\kappa=0}^{\infty}$ is given by

$$
p_W(\kappa) = \sum_{i=1}^{m} \alpha_i\, p_{Y_i}(\kappa),
$$

  where $\{p_{Y_i}(\kappa)\}_{\kappa=0}^{\infty}$ is the probability distribution of $\tilde{Y}_i$, $\alpha_i \geq 0$ for all $i = 1, 2, \ldots, n$, and $\sum_{i=1}^{m} \alpha_i = 1$. Then, if we denote by G_W and G_{Y_i} their respective generating functions, it is straightforward to see that

$$
G_W(x) = \sum_{i=1}^{m} \alpha_i\, G_{Y_i}(x).
\tag{A.3}
$$

- Secondly, let $\tilde{U}$ be the random variable that results from the sum of the other m random variables, i.e.

$$
\tilde{U} = \tilde{Y}_1 + \tilde{Y}_2 + \cdots + \tilde{Y}_m
$$

  so that the realizations of $\tilde{U}$ consist of the addition of one independent realization of each of the m different $\tilde{Y}_i$'s. Then, it can be readily checked that the generating function of $\tilde{U}$, G_U, satisfies

$$
G_U(x) = G_{Y_1}(x) \times G_{Y_2}(x) \times \cdots \times G_{Y_m}(x).
\tag{A.4}
$$

To fix ideas and illustrate matters, let us continue to focus on a random network context where the generating function G_0 characterizes the underlying degree distribution. Suppose that we are interested in finding the probability distribution of the *total* number of neighbors of m randomly selected nodes. The number of neighbors corresponding to each of these nodes is equally distributed, as characterized by the generating function G_0. Therefore, by (A.4), the distribution of interest is generated by $[G_0]^m$, i.e. the function G_0 raised to the power m. To see this, write

$$[G_0]^m(x) = \left[\sum_{\kappa=0}^{\infty} p(\kappa) x^{\kappa}\right]^m = \sum_{\kappa=0}^{\infty} \upsilon(\kappa) x^{\kappa},$$

where, for the moment, each $\upsilon(\kappa)$ merely refers to the coefficient of x^{κ} in the power expansion of $[G_0]^m$. Clearly, for any $\kappa = 0, 1, 2, \ldots$ we have

$$\upsilon(\kappa) = \sum_{\substack{\kappa_1, \kappa_2, \ldots, \kappa_m \\ \kappa_1 + \kappa_2 + \cdots + \kappa_m = \kappa}} p(\kappa_1) p(\kappa_2) \cdots p(\kappa_m),$$

which, as it should, is the probability that m nodes are randomly selected and their total degree is κ. This shows that $[G_0]^m$ indeed is the desired generating function.

Now imagine that we are interested in finding the distribution of the total number of *third* neighbors that can be accessed through *one* of the neighbors (randomly selected) of a particular node i. Assume that node i has m direct neighbors (i.e. $z^i = m$) and it is known that, out of these, one of them (say j) has two other neighbors, while the remaining $m - 1$ have three additional neighbors. Let $\hat{G}_1$ be the generating function characterizing the excess degree of a neighboring node, which is derived from G_0 as given by (A.2). First, we can apply (A.4) and state that the number of third neighbors that can be accesses through j is distributed as characterized by $(\hat{G}_1)^2$, whereas those that can be accessed through the remaining $m - 1$ players is as characterized by $(\hat{G}_1)^3$. Then, applying (A.3), it follows that the overall distribution of interest is simply characterized by a generating function $\tilde{G}$ defined by

$$\tilde{G}(x) = \frac{1}{m}[\hat{G}_1]^2(x) + \frac{m-1}{m}[\hat{G}_1]^3(x).$$

The Ising Model

The model of ferromagnetic interaction proposed by Ernst Ising in his dissertation (cf. Ising (1925) [155]) has become a canonical framework to study particle interaction in statistical physics. It involves a (large) set of particles, $N = \{1, 2, \ldots, n\}$, positioned along a regular lattice of a certain dimension m. Each of these particles can be conceived as a microscopic magnet that is in one of two possible states (or spins), $+1$ or -1. Ferromagnetic interaction occurs between *immediately* neighboring particles, with a tendency to display the same state. Overall, the *energy* displayed by any given configuration of the system $\mathbf{s} = (s^1, s^2, \ldots, s^n) \in \{-1, +1\}^N \equiv S$ is defined to be

$$E(\mathbf{s}) = -J \sum_{\{ij:\, j \in \mathcal{N}^i\}} s^i s^j \tag{B.1}$$

for some $J > 0$ where, as usual, $\mathcal{N}^i$ stands for the neighborhood of i in the underlying m-dimensional lattice.[1]

Physical systems naturally gravitate toward minimizing energy, an outcome that is achieved in the present case when *all* spins are aligned at either $+1$ or -1. But this principle of energy minimization has to be balanced against the competing principle of entropy maximization by which "disorder" is generated in any physical system. Josiah Willard Gibbs (1902, 1981) [124] showed that the precise way in which these competing principles must be balanced is embodied by the probability measures ν (now called Gibbs measures or Gibbs states) that assign to any particular state of the system $\mathbf{s}$ a probability $\nu(\mathbf{s})$ that is *proportional* to the following magnitude

$$e^{-E(\mathbf{s})/kT} = \exp\left[\frac{J}{kT} \sum_{i,j} s^i s^j\right], \tag{B.2}$$

---

[1] Here we define the (immediate) neighborhood of i as the set of points j that lie *one* step apart in the lattice. That is, if $x^i = (x_1^i, x_2^i, \ldots, x_m^i)$ and $x^j = (x_1^j, x_2^j, \ldots, x_m^j)$ denote their respective coordinates, then

$$\mathcal{N}^i = \{j \in N : \sum_{u=1}^m |x_u^i - x_u^j| = 1\}.$$

where k is a constant known as the "Boltzman constant," T is the (absolute) temperature of the system, and the indices i and j are interpreted as taken *only for neighboring nodes*. The key, therefore, to solve the model is to compute the normalization factor (or partition function)

$$Z = \sum_{s \in S} \exp \left[\frac{J}{kT} \sum_{i,j} s^i s^j \right],$$ (B.3)

so that we can then obtain

$$v(\mathbf{s}) = \frac{1}{Z} \exp \left[\frac{J}{kT} \sum_{i,j} s^i s^j \right]$$ (B.4)

for every $\mathbf{s} \in S$.

Often, it is assumed that, besides the interaction among neighboring particles, there is also an external magnetic field of magnitude H (positive or negative) that interacts separately with each individual particle. This amounts to replacing (B.1) by

$$E(\mathbf{s}) = -J \sum_{i,j} s^i s^j - H \sum_i s^i$$

as the appropriate energy of the system, then adapting (B.2) and (B.3) accordingly.

A key magnitude to be measured in the present context is called the *magnetization*. It is identified with the expected average value of the spins, as given by

$$M(H, T) = \frac{1}{n} \sum_{s \in S} (s^1 + s^2 + \cdots + s^n) v(\mathbf{s})$$

$$= \frac{1}{n} \left\{ \frac{1}{Z} \sum_{s \in S} (s^1 + s^2 + \cdots + s^n) \exp \left[\left(J \sum_{i,j} s^i s^j + H \sum_i s^i \right) / kT \right] \right\}.$$

The magnetization of the system measures the expected degree of "alignment" of the system on a given spin. In our adaptation of the Ising model to social contexts, it is interpreted as a reflection of the expected extent of social conformity.

We are typically interested in computing $M(H, T)$ for large systems, i.e. under the so-called "thermodynamic limit" obtained by making $n \to \infty$. To this end, it is useful to define the *free energy* of the system as

$$f(H, T) = - \lim_{n \to \infty} \frac{1}{n} kT \ln Z,$$ (B.5)

where Z (a function of H and T, as well as n) is given by (B.3). Then, it readily follows that

$$M(H, T) = -\frac{\partial}{\partial H} f(H, T).$$ (B.6)

The Ising model can also be studied as a stochastic dynamic system. Then, the corresponding *interacting particle system* (cf. Liggett (1985) [189]) is conceived as a Markov process in continuous time where the state space is $S = \{-1, +1\}^{\mathbb{Z}^m}$ – that is, the underlying network is directly assumed to be an infinite lattice of dimension m. In this context, it is postulated that, at each point in time $t \geq 0$, every node i updates its current spin $s_i(t)$ at a constant rate. If such an updating opportunity arrives, the "switch" to spin $s^i \in \{-1, +1\}$ is conducted with a probability proportional to

$$\exp\left\{\frac{1}{kT} s^i \left[J \sum_{j \in \mathcal{N}^i} s^j(t) + H \right] \right\}. \tag{B.7}$$

The relationship between this dynamics and our first approach to the Ising model derives from the fact that every Gibbs measure ν satisfying (B.4) is an invariant probability measure of the process. As we explain next, the key reason for it is that ν is *reversible* (i.e. it satisfies a suitable "balance condition"), which in turn implies time invariance.

To convey the crux of the argument in the simplest fashion, it is convenient to reformulate the process in a finite and discrete-time setup. Thus, let us postulate that there are only a finite number of nodes n (say, arranged in a boundariless lattice of dimension m) and time proceeds discretely ($t = 0, 1, 2, \ldots$). In this context, further assume that, at every t, the process chooses a single node i at random, its spin then being switched with the probability given by (B.7). With the complementary probability, therefore, the spin of i remains unchanged and $s^i(t + 1) = s^i(t)$.

Let $\Pi \equiv \left[\pi(\mathbf{s}, \mathbf{s}')\right]_{\mathbf{s}, \mathbf{s}' \in S}$ be the transition matrix of the Markov chain arising in such a discrete setup, where $\pi(\mathbf{s}, \mathbf{s}')$ stands for the conditional probability that the process transits from $\mathbf{s}$ to $\mathbf{s}'$. The first point to note is that the probability measure ν given by (B.4) is the unique one that satisfies the following balance condition:

$$\nu(\mathbf{s})\, \pi(\mathbf{s}, \mathbf{s}') = \nu(\mathbf{s}')\, \pi(\mathbf{s}', \mathbf{s}) \tag{B.8}$$

for all $\mathbf{s}, \mathbf{s}' \in S$. This condition, of course, holds trivially if $\mathbf{s}$ and $\mathbf{s}'$ differ in more that one component since, in that case, $\pi(\mathbf{s}, \mathbf{s}') = 0$. If instead $\mathbf{s}$ and $\mathbf{s}'$ only differ in one component, say that corresponding to node i (i.e. $s^j = s^{j\prime}$ for all $j \neq i$), we have

$$\pi(\mathbf{s}, \mathbf{s}') = \frac{1}{n} \frac{\exp\left[\frac{1}{kT} s^{i\prime} \left(J \sum_{j \in \mathcal{N}^i} s^j + H \right)\right]}{\sum_{\hat{s}^i = \pm 1} \exp\left[\frac{1}{kT} \hat{s}^i \left(J \sum_{j \in \mathcal{N}^i} s^j + H \right)\right]}$$

and therefore, as claimed,[2]

$$
\begin{aligned}
&v(\mathbf{s})\,\pi(\mathbf{s},\mathbf{s}') \\
&= \frac{\exp\left[\frac{1}{kT}\left(J\sum_{j,\ell}s^{j}s^{\ell}+H\sum_{j}s^{j}\right)\right]}{\sum_{\tilde{\mathbf{s}}\in S}\exp\left[\frac{1}{kT}\left(J\sum_{j,\ell}\tilde{s}^{j}\tilde{s}^{\ell}+H\sum_{j}\tilde{s}^{j}\right)\right]} \\
&\quad\times\frac{1}{n}\frac{\exp\left[\frac{1}{kT}s^{i'}\left(J\sum_{j\in\mathcal{N}^{i}}s^{j}+H\right)\right]}{\sum_{\hat{s}^{i}=\pm1}\exp\left[\frac{1}{kT}\hat{s}^{i}\left(J\sum_{j\in\mathcal{N}^{i}}s^{j}+H\right)\right]} \\
&= \frac{\exp\left[\frac{1}{kT}s^{i}\left(J\sum_{j\in\mathcal{N}^{i}}s^{j}+H\right)\right]\exp\left[\frac{1}{kT}\left(J\sum_{j\neq i\neq\ell}s^{j}s^{\ell}+H\sum_{j\neq i}s^{j}\right)\right]}{\sum_{\tilde{\mathbf{s}}\in S}\exp\left[\frac{1}{kT}\left(J\sum_{j,\ell}\tilde{s}^{j}\tilde{s}^{\ell}+H\sum_{j}\tilde{s}^{j}\right)\right]} \\
&\quad\times\frac{1}{n}\frac{\exp\left[\frac{1}{kT}s^{i'}\left(J\sum_{j\in\mathcal{N}^{i}}s^{j}+H\right)\right]}{\sum_{\hat{s}^{i}=\pm1}\exp\left[\frac{1}{kT}\hat{s}^{i}\left(J\sum_{j\in\mathcal{N}^{i}}s^{j}+H\right)\right]} \\
&= \frac{\exp\left[\frac{1}{kT}s^{i'}\left(J\sum_{j\in\mathcal{N}^{i}}s^{j}+H\right)\right]\exp\left[\frac{1}{kT}\left(J\sum_{j\neq i\neq\ell}s^{j}s^{\ell}+H\sum_{j\neq i}s^{j}\right)\right]}{\sum_{\tilde{\mathbf{s}}\in S}\exp\left[\frac{1}{kT}\left(J\sum_{j,\ell}\tilde{s}^{j}\tilde{s}^{\ell}+H\sum_{j}\tilde{s}^{j}\right)\right]} \\
&\quad\times\frac{1}{n}\frac{\exp\left[\frac{1}{kT}s^{i}\left(J\sum_{j\in\mathcal{N}^{i}}s^{j}+H\right)\right]}{\sum_{\hat{s}^{i}=\pm1}\exp\left[\frac{1}{kT}\hat{s}^{i}\left(J\sum_{j\in\mathcal{N}^{i}}s^{j}+H\right)\right]} \\
&= v(\mathbf{s}')\,\pi(\mathbf{s}',\mathbf{s}).
\end{aligned}
$$

Finally, we note that the reversibility of v indeed implies that it must be an invariant probability measure since

$$
\sum_{\mathbf{s}'\in S}v(\mathbf{s}')\,\pi(\mathbf{s}',\mathbf{s})=v(\mathbf{s})\sum_{\mathbf{s}'\in S}\pi(\mathbf{s},\mathbf{s}')=v(\mathbf{s}) \tag{B.9}
$$

for all $\mathbf{s}\in S$ and, therefore, in matrix form, we can compactly write

$$
v\,\Pi=v,
$$

as required by time invariance.

When the system is finite, the process is obviously ergodic and, consequently, the unique Gibbs measure satisfying (B.9) characterizes the long-run behavior of the process. Nevertheless, when $n\to\infty$, such ergodicity is no longer guaranteed, i.e. several Gibbs measures may exist. As it turns out, the issue of ergodicity crucially depends on the dimension m of the underlying lattice structure (see below). Independently of the lattice dimension, however, Gibbs measures are always reversible, i.e. satisfy the counterpart of the detailed

---

[2] Recall that all index pairs in the sums are to be interpreted as referring to neighboring nodes.

balance condition (B.8).[3] In every case, therefore, they remain invariant distributions of the process when $n \to \infty$.

An exact solution of the Ising model in the thermodynamic limit was provided by Ising (1925) [155] himself for the case $m = 1$. It is discussed in some detail in Section 4.3, where we show that the process is ergodic (i.e. has a unique invariant measure) for any $T > 0$. When $m = 2$, the problem is substantially more difficult and was only completely tackled much later by Lars Onsager (1944) [226] for $h = 0$. There is no exact solution yet known for the Ising model in still higher dimensions. It is known, however, that if $m \geq 2$ the model displays sharp transitions in both h (at zero) and in T (at a suitably defined critical value). Whereas the former transition is of "first-order" (i.e. embodies a discontinuous change in the magnetization of the system as h changes), the second one is of "second-order" (i.e. reflects a gradient discontinuity as T varies).

When the number of dimensions is large (specifically, it is enough that $m \geq 4$), the Ising model has its particles so densely connected that a mean-field ("global") approach to it delivers a good approximation. This is explained in Appendix C.1, where we provide a mean-field solution of the Ising model and show the nature of the aforementioned (first- and second-order) transitions. Finally, we note that another context in which the Ising model has been exactly solved is the Bethe lattice – an infinite Cayley tree in which every node has the same degree. This context is discussed in Subsection 4.3.2, as a way to approximate the case of random networks.

---

[3] See e.g. Theorems 2.14 and 2.15 in Chapter IV of Liggett (1985) [189].

Mean-Field Theory

Mean-field theory has been one of the main approaches traditionally used in the study of phase transitions of physical systems. It dates back to the early 20th century, when it was first applied by Pierre Weiss and others to the analysis of the phenomenon of ferromagnetism. (See, for example, the classical monograph by H. E. Stanley (1971) [264] for a historical account of these developments and an introduction to the field of phase transitions.)

Mean-field theory is usually applied to the analysis of complex systems where the interaction among a large number of individual "particles" proceeds along many dimensions. Under these conditions, the intuitive idea underlying the approach can be simply explained as follows. If the nature of interaction is rich (i.e. highly dimensional), it should be possible to capture the overall behavior of the system through a stylized model of the situation in which the host of effects impinging on each individual entity is replaced by a suitable mean field. In such a mean-field approach, the average description of the system is tailored to a suitable aggregate (or average) of the large number of individual effects exerted by the population at large. The self-referential nature of the exercise is thus apparent: the average state of the system is both an explanatory variable and the variable itself to be explained. This suggests that, in many cases, mean field theory must seek a self-consistent solution. This is why it is also often labeled *self-consistent field theory*.

In what follows, we outline two applications of mean-field theory to contexts that are of central importance in this monograph: (i) the Ising model of local interaction in a large and (possibly complex) network; (ii) continuous-time network evolution governed by endogenous jump processes.

C.1 THE MEAN-FIELD ISING MODEL

Consider an extension of the Ising model described in Appendix B in which, unlike for the two contexts studied in Section 4.3, the underlying network is possibly complex.[1] Suppose that, for every site i, we replace its ferromagnetic

---

[1] See Le Bellac (1988) [187] for a good and detailed discussion of the mean-field analysis of the Ising model.

interaction with each of its neighbors with an average effect. That is, the energy displayed at site i,

$$E^i = -J \sum_{j \in \mathcal{N}^i} s^i s^j - s^i H$$

is replaced by

$$\hat{E}^i = -J \sum_{j \in \mathcal{N}^i} s^i \langle s^\ell \rangle_{\ell \in N} - s^i H = -\left[J \sum_{j \in \mathcal{N}^i} \langle s^\ell \rangle_{\ell \in N} + H \right] s^i$$

$$= -\left[J z^i \langle s^\ell \rangle_{\ell \in N} + H \right] s^i,$$

where $\langle s^\ell \rangle_{\ell \in N}$ is the average spin of the system and, as usual, z^i is the degree of node i. Now, assuming that the expected number of neighbors of each particle is some given $q > 0$,[2] we may further approximate the above expression and write, for each site i,

$$\hat{E}^i(s^i) = -(qJM + H)s^i,$$

where we substitute the expected magnetization M for the average spin. As explained in Appendix B, solving the model requires the computation of the (approximate) partition function

$$\hat{Z} = \sum_{s \in S} \exp\left[-\frac{1}{kT} \sum_i \hat{E}^i(s^i) \right]$$

$$= \sum_{s^1 = \pm 1} \sum_{s^2 = \pm 1} \cdots \sum_{s^n = \pm 1} \exp\left[\frac{1}{kT} \sum_i (qJM + H)s^i \right]$$

$$= \left\{ \sum_{s^1 = \pm 1} \exp\left[\frac{1}{kT}(qJM + H)s^1 \right] \right\}$$

$$\times \left\{ \sum_{s_2 = \pm 1} \exp\left[\frac{1}{kT}(qJM + H)s^2 \right] \right\} \times \cdots$$

$$\times \left\{ \sum_{s_n = \pm 1} \exp\left[\frac{1}{kT}(qJM + H)s^n \right] \right\}$$

$$= 2^n \left\{ \frac{1}{2} \left[\exp\left[\frac{1}{kT}(qJM + H) \right] + \exp\left[-\frac{1}{kT}(qJM + H) \right] \right] \right\}^n$$

$$= 2^n \cosh^n \left[\frac{1}{kT}(qJM + H) \right].$$

---

[2] This assumption is of course not appropriate when the network displays a broad distribution. For a mean-field solution of the Ising model in a (broadly distributed) scale-free network, see Bianconi (2002) [29]. There she finds qualitatively very different behavior from that shown here – in particular, the magnetized phase turns out to be the only possibility for all finite temperatures in the thermodynamic limit.

Thus, as $n \to \infty$, the free energy (recall (B.5)) is given by

$$f(H, T) = -kT \lim_{n \to \infty} \left\{ \frac{1}{n} \ln 2^n + \frac{1}{n} \ln \left[\cosh^n \left(\frac{1}{kT}(qJM + H) \right) \right] \right\}$$

$$= -kT \left\{ \ln 2 + \ln \left[\cosh^n \left(\frac{1}{kT}(qJM + H) \right) \right] \right\},$$

and the magnetization $M \equiv M(H, T)$ can be readily computed from the following equation (cf. (B.6)):

$$M = -\frac{\partial}{\partial H} f(H, T) = \frac{\sinh \left(\frac{1}{kT}(qJM + H) \right)}{\cosh \left(\frac{1}{kT}(qJM + H) \right)}$$

$$= \tanh \left(\frac{1}{kT}(qJM + H) \right).$$

The former equation imposes a *self-consistent condition* on M, which is convenient to rewrite as follows:

$$\frac{1}{kT}(qJM + H) = \tanh^{-1}(M).$$

The solution in M of the previous equation is illustrated in Figure C.1 for the case where there is no external magnetic field ($H = 0$). The key observation to be made here is that the number of solutions of the equation depend on whether $\frac{qJ}{kT}$ is larger than $\frac{d}{dx} \tanh^{-1}(0) = 1$. That is, it depends on whether

$$T < T_c \equiv \frac{qJ}{k}. \tag{C.1}$$

If the condition in (C.1) is met, there are two equilibria displaying nonzero magnetization levels, in addition to the equilibrium with zero magnetization (which always exists for all T). The latter equilibrium, however, can be shown to be unstable. Thus, if $H > 0$ (no matter how small) the system will settle on the equilibrium with positive magnetization M_0, while it will do so on the one with $-M_0$ if $H < 0$. There is, in other words, a sharp discontinuous transition as H is changed slightly away from zero – see Figure C.2 for an illustration. In statistical physics, it is called a *first-order phase transition*.

If the system is large but finite (and thus ergodic), the alternative polar equilibrium whose nonvanishing magnetization is opposite to that of the external field must be regarded as a *metastable* configuration. That is, even though its *relative* persistence is much less marked than that of the stable configuration, the system may remain close to it for a very long stretch of time under some initial conditions. More specifically, that time is expected to rise exponentially, in expected terms, as the network size grows. This phenomenon, which goes under the name of ergodicity breakdown, is common in large stochastic systems. Indeed, it plays an important role in the analysis of network formation processes conducted in Chapter 6.

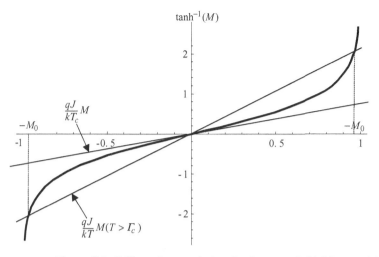

Figure C.1. Self-consistent solution for the mean-field Ising model for an external magnetic field $H = 0$ and different temperatures, $T = T_c$ and $T < T_c$

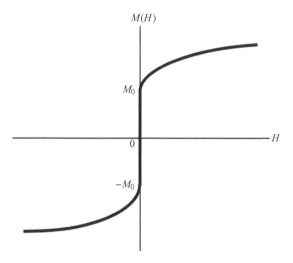

Figure C.2. First-order phase transition in the Ising model as a function of the external magnetic field for a temperature $T < T_c$

Alternatively, one may fix the external magnetic field at $H = 0$ – or more precisely, at an infinitesimal, say positive, value – and then trace the change of magnetization as temperature changes. Then, of course, for $T \geq T_c$, the induced magnetization $M(T) \equiv 0$. However, at $T = T_c$ there is a discontinuous change in the slope of the function $M(\cdot)$, with (positive) magnetization growing as T falls below T_c, this growth proceeding at a decreasing pace (in view of the curvature displayed by $\tanh^{-1}(M)$). Such a discontinuous behavior of the slope

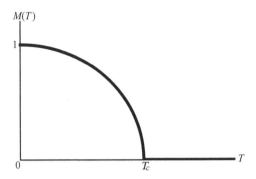

Figure C.3. Second-order phase transition in the Ising model as a function of the (absolute) temperature of the system, for an external magnetic field $H = 0$

of the function $M(\cdot)$ is called a *second-order phase transition*, and is illustrated in Figure C.3.

C.2 MEAN-FIELD ANALYSIS OF EVOLVING NETWORKS

Some of the models of network evolution considered in Chapter 6 are studied through mean-field (self-consistent) analysis. Here, this dynamic approach is outlined in an abstract setup, so as to highlight the essential common features. The general understanding of matters thus obtained should prove useful when turning to the study of specific applications.

Consider an evolving "infinite" network that, at every point in (continuous) time $t \in \mathbb{R}_+$, may be suitably described as a *random* network with some corresponding degree distribution $p_t \equiv \{p_t(\kappa)\}_{\kappa=0}^{\infty}$. The stochastic rules that govern its law of motion specify the rates at which links are created and deleted. Since time is modeled continuously, at most *one* change may occur at every instant, almost surely. That is, the probability that several such events might coincide at any given t is zero and thus may be safely ignored. This, in essence, leads to conceiving the dynamics as a collection of "parallel" *jump processes* (cf. Gardiner (1985, Ch. 7) [121]), each of them dictating the rates at which the respective node i has its degree κ^i rise or fall by one link.

Let $w^{i+}(t)$ and $w^{i-}(t)$ denote the rates at which either of those two possibilities (link creation and destruction) occur for any particular node i at some t, i.e.

$$w^{i+}(t) = \text{rate}\left[\kappa^i(t) \to \kappa^i(t) + 1\right]$$
$$w^{i-}(t) = \text{rate}\left[\kappa^i(t) \to \kappa^i(t) - 1\right].$$

The mean-field approach involves treating all nodes of the same degree in a symmetric fashion. Thus, concerning their transition rates, we simply postulate that

$$w^{i+}(t) = \varpi_t^+ \left(\kappa^i(t)\right) \tag{C.2}$$

$$w^{i-}(t) = \varpi_t^- \left(\kappa^i(t)\right) \tag{C.3}$$

for some node-independent $\varpi_t^+ (\cdot)$ and $\varpi_t^- (\cdot)$. Such internode symmetry allows us, in turn, to specify a set of master equations for the state of the system (i.e. the degree distribution p_t) as follows:

$$\frac{\partial p_t(\kappa)}{\partial t} = p_t(\kappa - 1)\varpi_t^+ (\kappa - 1) + p_t(\kappa + 1)\varpi_t^- (\kappa + 1) \tag{C.4}$$

$$- p_t(\kappa)\varpi_t^+ (\kappa) - p_t(\kappa)\varpi_t^- (\kappa)$$

for every degree $\kappa = 0, 1, 2, \ldots$. The different terms on the right-hand side of (C.4) represent the flows impinging on the number (frequency) of nodes displaying each of the possible degrees.[3] The first two terms correspond to net inflows. They embody the fact that a node may *freshly* come to display a certain degree κ in two different ways: either it formerly had degree $\kappa + 1$ and loses a link, or its previous degree was $\kappa - 1$ and gains a new link. Similarly, the latter two terms represent outflows and simply reflect that any node previously displaying degree κ will stop doing so if either it gains or loses one link.

Generally, we find it useful to characterize the degree distribution p_t prevailing at any t by its generating function

$$G_{0,t}(x) = \sum_{\kappa=0}^{\infty} p_t(\kappa) x^\kappa.$$

Then, building upon the master equations (C.4), the dynamics of this generating function can be formulated as follows:

$$\frac{\partial G_{0,t}(x)}{\partial t} = \sum_{\kappa=0}^{\infty} \frac{\partial p_t(\kappa)}{\partial t} x^\kappa$$

$$= \sum_{\kappa=0}^{\infty} x^\kappa \left\{ \begin{array}{c} p_t(\kappa - 1)\varpi_t^+ (\kappa - 1) + p_t(\kappa + 1)\varpi_t^- (\kappa + 1) \\ - p_t(\kappa)\varpi_t^+ (\kappa) - p_t(\kappa)\varpi_t^- (\kappa) \end{array} \right\}. \tag{C.5}$$

A common objective is to characterize the stationary states of the network, as captured by some corresponding degree distributions. Of course, in order for any such distribution $\hat{p}$ to define a stationarity state of the process, its generating function must be stationary as well. In view of (C.5), this requires that

$$\sum_{\kappa=0}^{\infty} x^\kappa \left\{ \begin{array}{c} \hat{p}(\kappa - 1)\hat{\varpi}^+ (\kappa - 1) + \hat{p}(\kappa + 1)\hat{\varpi}^- (\kappa + 1) \\ - \hat{p}(\kappa)\hat{\varpi}^+ (\kappa) - \hat{p}(\kappa)\hat{\varpi}^- (\kappa) \end{array} \right\} = 0 \tag{C.6}$$

---

[3] Note that, of course, we must have $\varpi^- (0) = 0$ at all t.

for all x, given some suitably considered transition rates $\{\hat{\varpi}^+(\kappa), \hat{\varpi}^-(\kappa)\}_{\kappa=0}^{\infty}$ that are consistent with $\hat{p}$. In essence, therefore, finding a stationary state of the process involves obtaining a *self-consistent solution* of the model where

  (a) the degree distribution $\hat{p}$ gives rise to the contemplated transition rates $\{\hat{\varpi}^+(\kappa), \hat{\varpi}^-(\kappa)\}_{\kappa=0}^{\infty}$;
  (b) the transition rates $\{\hat{\varpi}^+(\kappa), \hat{\varpi}^-(\kappa)\}_{\kappa=0}^{\infty}$ induce the long-run degree distribution $\hat{p}$.

The specific details of the model shape how the prevailing network topology bears on the current rates of link creation and destruction. Those modeling details, therefore, determine directly condition (a). On the other hand, condition (b) is simply a result of the stationarity requirement (C.6), which can be used to find the particular long-run distribution induced by any given in- and out-flow rates.

Bibliography

[1] Adamic, L. A., R. M. Lukose, and B. A. Huberman (2003) "Local search in unstructured networks," in S. Bornholdt and H. G. Schuster (eds.), *Handbook of Graphs and Networks: From the Genome to the Internet*, Berlin: Wiley VCH.

[2] Adamic, L. A., R. M. Lukose, A. R. Puniyani, and B. A. Huberman (2001) "Search in power-law networks," *Physical Review* E **64**, 046135.

[3] Aiello, W., F. Chung, and L. Lu (2000) "A random graph model for massive graphs," in *Proceedings of the 32nd Annual ACM Symposium on Theory of Computing*, 171–180, New York: Association of Computing Machinery.

[4] Albert, R. and A.-L. Barabási (2002) "Statistical mechanics of complex networks," *Review of Modern Physics* **74**, 47–97.

[5] Albert, R., H. Jeong, and A.-L. Barabási (1999) "Diameter of the world-wide web," *Nature* **401**, 130–131.

[6] Albert, R., H. Jeong, and A.-L. Barabási (2000) "Error and attack tolerance of networks," *Nature* **406**, 378–382.

[7] Allen, O. (1990) *Probability, Statistics and Queueing Theory with Computer Science Applications,* New York: Academic Press.

[8] van Alstyne, M. (1997) "The state of network organization: a survey in three frameworks," *Journal of Organizational Computing and Electronic Commerce* **7**, 83–151.

[9] Amaral, L. A. N., A. Díaz-Guilera, A. A. Moreira, A. L. Goldberger, and L. A. Lipsitz (2004) "Emergence of complex dynamics in a simple model of signaling networks," *Proceedings of the National Academy of Sciences USA* **101**, 15551–15555.

[10] Amaral, L. A. N., A. Scala, M. Barthélémy, and H. E. Stanley (2000) "Classes of small-world networks," *Proceedings of the National Academy of Sciences USA* **97**, 11149–11152.

[11] Anderson, R. M. and R. M. May (1991) *Infectious Diseases of Humans*, Oxford: Oxford University Press.

[12] Angrist, J. and K. Lang (2002) "How important are classroom peer effects? Evidence from Boston's Metco program," *National Bureau of Economic Research*, Working Paper 9263.

[13] Arenas, A., A. Cabrales, A. Díaz-Guilera, R. Guimerà, and F. Vega-Redondo (2003) "Search and Congestion in Complex Networks," in R. Pastor-Satorras,

M. Rubí, and A. Díaz-Guilera (eds.) *XVIII Sitges Conference on Statistical Mechanics*, Berlin: Springer Verlag.

[14] Arenas, A., A. Díaz-Guilera, C. J. Pérez, and F. Vega-Redondo (2000) "Self-organized evolution in a socio-economic environment," *Physical Review E* **61**, 3466–3469.

[15] Arenas, A., A. Díaz-Guilera, C. J. Pérez, and F. Vega-Redondo (2002) "Self-organized criticality in evolutionary systems with local interaction," *Journal of Economic Dynamics & Control* **26**, 2115–2142.

[16] Bailey, N. T. J. (1975) *The Mathematical Theory of Infectious Diseases and Its Applications*, New York: Hafner Press.

[17] Bak, P. (1996) *How Nature Works*, New York: Copernicus.

[18] Bak, P., C. Tang, and K. Wiesenfeld (1987) "Self-organized criticality: An explanation of the $1/f$ noise," *Physical Review Letters* **59**, 381–384.

[19] Bak, P., C. Tang, and K. Wiesenfeld (1988) "Self-organized criticality," *Physical Review A* **38**, 364–374.

[20] Bala, V. and S. Goyal (1998) "Learning from neighbours," *Review of Economic Studies* **65**, 595–621.

[21] Bala, V. and S. Goyal (2000) "A non-cooperative model of network formation," *Econometrica* **68**, 1181–1230.

[22] Balconi, M., S. Breschi, and F. Lissoni (2002) "Networks of inventors and the location of university research: an exploration of Italian data," *Centre for Research on Innovation and Internationalisation Processes (CESPRI)*, Working Paper no. 127.

[23] Banerjee, A. (1992) "A simple model of herd behavior," *Quarterly Journal of Economics* **107**, 797–817.

[24] Barabási, A.-L. and R. Albert (1999) "Emergence of scaling in random networks," *Science* **286**, 509–512.

[25] Barnes J. A. (1954) "Class and committees in a Norwegian island parish," *Human Relations* **7**, 39–58.

[26] Baxter, R. J. (1982) *Exactly Solved Models in Statistical Mechanics*, London: Academic Press.

[27] Beggs, A. W. (2001) "Queues and hierarchies," *Review of Economic Studies* **68**, 297–322.

[28] Bender, E. A. and E. R. Canfield (1978) "The asymptotic number of labelled graphs with given degree sequences," *Journal of Combinatorial Theory* A **24**, 296–307.

[29] Bianconi, G. (2002) "Mean field solution of the Ising model on a Barabási-Albert network," *Preprint* cond-mat/0204455.

[30] Bikhchandani, S., D. Hirshleifer, and I. Welch (1992) "A theory of fads, fashion, custom, and cultural change as informational cascade," *Journal of Political Economy* **100**, 992–1026.

[31] Bikhchandani, S., D. Hirshleifer, and I. Welch (1998) "Learning from the behavior of others: conformity, fads, and informational cascades," *The Journal of Economic Perspectives* **12**, 151–170.

[32] Bloch, F., G. Genicot and D. Ray (2004) "Informal insurance in social networks," mimeo, GREQAM (Université de la Méditerranée), Georgetown University, and New York University.

[33] Blume, L. (1993) "The statistical mechanics of strategic interaction," *Games and Economic Behavior* **5**, 387–424.

[34] Boguñá, M. and R. Pastor-Satorras (2002) "Epidemic spreading in correlated complex networks," *Physical Review* E **66**, 047104.

[35] Boguñá, M., R. Pastor-Satorras, and A. Vespignani (2003) "Absence of epidemic threshold in scale-free networks with degree correlations," *Physical Review Letters* **90**, 028701.

[36] Bollobás, B. (1980) "A probabilistic proof of an asymptotic formula for the number of labelled regular graphs," *European Journal of Combinatorics* **1**, 311–316.

[37] Bollobás, B. [1985] (2001) *Random Graphs* (2nd edn), Cambridge: Cambridge University Press.

[38] Bollobás, B. and O. M. Riordan (2003) "Mathematical results on scale-free random graphs," in S. Bornholdt and H. G. Schuster (eds.), *Handbook of Graphs and Networks: From the Genome to the Internet*, Berlin: Wiley VCH.

[39] Bolton, P. and M. Dewatripont (1994) "The Firm as a Communication Network," *Quarterly Journal of Economics* **109**, 809–839.

[40] Boorman, S. A. (1975) "A combinatorial optimization model for transmission of job information through contact networks," *Bell Journal of Economics* **6**, 216–249.

[41] Bott E. (1957) *Family and Social Network*, London: Tavistock.

[42] Boyd, R. and P. Richerson (1990) "Group selection among alternative evolutionary stable strategies," *Journal of Theoretical Biology* **145**, 331–342.

[43] Broder, A., R. Kumar, F. Maghoul, P. Raghavan, S. Rajagopalan, R. Stata, A. Tomkins, and J. Wiener (2000) "Graph structure in the web," *Computer Networks* **33**, 309–320.

[44] Buchanan, M. (2002) *Nexus: Small Worlds and the Ground-breaking Science of Networks*, New York: Norton.

[45] Burt, R. S. (1992) *Structural Holes: The Social Structure of Competition*, Cambridge: Harvard University Press.

[46] Burt, R. S., R. M. Hogarth, and C. Michaud (2000) "The social capital of French and American managers," *Organization Science* **11**, 123–147.

[47] Buskens, V. (1998) "The social structure of trust," *Social Networks* **20**, 265–289.

[48] Caldarelli, G., A. Capocci, P. de los Rios, and M. A. Muñoz (2002) "Scale-free networks from varying vertex intrinsic fitness," *Physical Review Letters* **89**, 258702.

[49] Callaway, D. S., M. E. J. Newman, S. H. Strogatz, and D. J. Watts (2000) "Network robustness and fragility: Percolation on random graphs," *Physical Review Letters* **85**, 5468–5471.

[50] Calvó-Armengol, A. (2004) "Job contact networks," *Journal of Economic Theory* **115**, 191–206.

[51] Calvó-Armengol, A. and R. Ilkiliç (2004) "Pairwise stability and Nash equilibria in network formation," mimeo, Universitat Autònoma de Barcelona.

[52] Calvó-Armengol, A. and M. O. Jackson (2004) "The effects of social networks on employment and inequality," *American Economic Review* **94**, 426–454.

[53] Calvó-Armengol, A. and Y. Zenou (2004) "Social networks and crime decisions: the role of social structure in facilitating delinquent behavior," *International Economic Review* **45**, 939–958.

[54] Carlson, J. M. and J. Doyle (2002) "Complexity and robustness," *Proceedings of the National Academy of Sciences USA* **99**, 2538–2545.

[55] Carré, B. (1979) *Graphs and Networks*, Oxford: Clarendon Press.

[56] Carrol, L. (1872) *Through the Looking Glass and What Alice Found There*. London: Macmillan.

[57] Cartwright, D. and F. Harary (1956) "Structural balance: a generalization of Heider's theory," *Psychological Review* **63**, 277–292.

[58] Castells, M. (1996) *The Information Age: Economy, Society, and Culture, Volume I: The Rise of the Network Society*, Massachusetts: Blackwell Publishers.

[59] Castilla, E. J., H. Hwang, E. Granovetter, and M. Granovetter (2000) "Social Networks in Silicon Valley," in C.-M. Lee, W. F. Miller, M. G. Hancock, and H. S. Rowen (eds.), *The Silicon Valley Edge*, Stanford: Stanford University Press.

[60] Chao, X., M. Miyazawa and M. L. Pinedo (1999) *Queueing Networks: Customers, Signals and Product Form Solutions*, Chichester: Wiley.

[61] Chen, H.-C., J. W. Friedman, and J.-F. Thisse (1997) "Boundedly rational Nash Equilibrium: a probabilistic choice approach," *Games and Economic Behavior* **18**, 32–54.

[62] Chung, F. and L. Lu (2002) "The average distances in random graphs with given expected degrees," *Proceedings of the National Academy of Sciences USA* **99**, 15879–15882.

[63] Chwe, M. S.-Y. (2000) "Communication and coordination in social networks," *Review of Economic Studies* **67**, 1–16.

[64] Clark, J. and D. A. Holton (1991) *A First Look at Graph Theory*, Singapore: World Scientific.

[65] Clifford, P. and A. Sudbury (1973) "A model for spatial conflict," *Biometrika* **60**, 581–588.

[66] Cohen, R., K. Erez, D. Ben-Avraham, and S. Havlin (2000) "Resilience of the internet to random breakdowns," *Physical Review Letters* **85**, 4626–4628.

[67] Cohen, R., K. Erez, D. Ben-Avraham, and S. Havlin (2001) "Breakdown of the Internet under intentional attack," *Physical Review Letters* **86**, 3682–3685.

[68] Cohen, R. and S. Havlin (2003) "Scale-free networks are ultrasmall," *Physical Review Letters* **90**, 058701.

[69] Cohen, R., S. Havlin, and D. Ben-Avraham (2003) "Efficient immunization strategies for computer networks and populations," *Physical Review Letters* **91**, 247901.

[70] Coleman, J. S. (1988) "Social capital in the creation of human capital," *American Journal of Sociology* **94**, S95–S120.

[71] Coleman, J. S. (1990) *Foundations of Social Theory*, Cambridge: Harvard University Press.

[72] Coleman, J. S., E. Katz, and H. Menzel (1966) *Medical Innovation: A Diffusion Study*, New York: Bobbs Merril.

[73] Conley, T. G. and C. R. Udry (2001) "Social learning through networks: the adoption of new agricultural technologies in Ghana," *American Journal of Agricultural Economics* **83**, 668–673.

[74] Crane, J. (1991) "The epidemic theory of ghettos and neighborhood effects on dropping out and teenage childbearing," *American Journal of Sociology* **96**, 1226–1259.

[75] D'Aspremont, C. and A. Jacquemin (1988) "Cooperative and noncooperative R&D in duopoly with spillovers," *American Economic Review* **78**, 1133–1137.

[76] Delapierre M. and L. Mytelka (1998) "Blurring boundaries: new interfirm relationships and the emergence of networked, knowledge-based oligopolies," in

M. G. Colombo (ed.), *The Changing Boundaries of the Firm*, London: Routledge Press.

[77] Demange, G. and M. H. Wooders (eds.) (2005) *Group Formation in Economics: Networks, Clubs, and Coalitions*, Cambridge: Cambridge University Press.

[78] DeMarzo, P., D. Vayanos, and J. Zwiebel (2003) "Persuasion bias, social influence, and unidimensional opinions," *Quarterly Journal of Economics* **118**, 909–968.

[79] Dercon, S. and J. de Weerdt (2002) "Risk-sharing networks and insurance against illness," mimeo, June, University of Oxford (UK) and Katholieke Universiteit Leuven (Belgium).

[80] Deroïan, F. (2003) "Farsighted strategies in the formation of a communication network," *Economics Letters* **80**, 343–349.

[81] Dezsö, Z. and A.-L. Barabási (2002) "Halting viruses in scale-free networks," *Physical Review* E **65**, 055103.

[82] Diani, M. and D. McAdam (2003) *Social Movements and Networks: Relational Approaches to Collective Action*, Oxford: Oxford University Press.

[83] Dodds, P. S., R. Muhamad, and D. J. Watts (2003) "An experimental study of search in global social networks," *Science* **301**, 827–829.

[84] Dodds, P. S., D. J. Watts, and C. F. Sabel (2003) "Information exchange and the robustness of organizational networks," *Proceedings of the National Academy of Sciences* **100**, 12516–12521.

[85] Dorogovtsev, S. N., A. V. Goltsev, and J. F. F. Mendes (2004) "Potts model on complex networks," *European Physical Journal* B **38**, 177.

[86] Dorogovtsev, S. N. and J. F. F. Mendes (2001) "Scaling properties of scale-free evolving networks: Continuous approach," *Physical Review* E **63**, 056125.

[87] Dorogovtsev, S. N. and J. F. F. Mendes (2002) "Evolution of Networks," *Advances in Physics* **51**, 1079–1187.

[88] Dorogovtsev, S. N., J. F. F. Mendes, and A. N. Samukhin (2000) "Structure of growing networks with preferential linking," *Physical Review Letters* **85**, 4633–36.

[89] Dorogovtsev, S. N., J. F. F. Mendes, and A. N. Samukhin (2001) "Size-dependent degree distribution of a scale-free growing network," *Physical Review* E **63**, 062101.

[90] Durlauf, S. (1997) "Statistical mechanics approaches to socioeconomic behavior," in W. B. Arthur, S. N. Durlauf, and D. A. Lane (eds.), *The Economy as an Evolving Complex System II*, Reading, MA; Addison-Wesley, 81–104.

[91] Dutta, B. and M. O. Jackson (eds.) (2003) *Networks and Groups: Models of Strategic Formation*, Berlin: Springer-Verlag.

[92] Dutta, B., S. Ghosal, and D. Ray (2005) "Farsighted network formation," *Journal of Economic Theory* **122**, 143–164.

[93] Ebel, H., Mielsch, L.-I., and S. Bornholdt (2002) "Scale-free topology of e-mail networks," *Physical Review* E **66**, 035103.

[94] Eguíluz, V. M. and K. Klemm (2002) "Epidemic threshold in structured scale-free networks," *Physical Review Letters* **89**, 108701.

[95] Eguíluz, V. M., M. Zimmermann, C. J. Cela-Conde, and M. San Miguel (2005) "Cooperation and the emergence of role differentiation in the dynamics of social networks," *American Journal of Sociology* **110**, 977–1008.

[96] Ehrhardt, G. C. M. A. and M. Marsili (2004) "Potts model on random trees," *Preprint* cond-mat/0411226.

[97] Ehrhardt, G., M. Marsili, and F. Vega-Redondo (2005) "Emergence and resilience of social networks: a general theoretical framework," *Preprint* arXiv:physics/0504124.

[98] Ellison, G. (1993) "Learning, local interaction, and coordination," *Econometrica* **61**, 1047–1071.

[99] Ellison, G. and D. Fudenberg (1993) "Rules of thumb for social learning," *Journal of Political Economy* **101**, 612–643.

[100] Ellison, G. and D. Fudenberg (1995) "Word of mouth communication and social learning," *Quarterly Journal of Economics* **110**, 93–125.

[101] Erdös, P. and A. Rényi (1959) "On random graphs I," *Publicationes Mathematicae Debrecen* **6**, 290–297.

[102] Erdös, P. and A. Rényi (1960) "On the evolution of random graphs," *Publications of the Mathematical Institute of the Hungarian Academy of Sciences* **5**, 17–61.

[103] Eshel, I. (1972) "On the neighbor effect and the evolution of altruistic traits," *Theoretical Population Biology* **3**, 258–277.

[104] Eshel, I., L. Samuelson, and A. Shaked (1998) "Altruists, egoists, and hooligans in a local interaction model," *American Economic Review* **88**, 157–179.

[105] Fafchamps, M. (2002) "Spontaneous market emergence," *Topics in Theoretical Economics* **2**, Article 2, Berkeley Electronic Press at http://www.bepress.com.

[106] Fafchamps, M. and S. Lund (2003) "Risk-sharing networks in rural Philippines," *Journal of Development Economics* **71**, 261–287.

[107] Faloutsos, M., P. Faloutsos, and C. Faloutsos (1999) "On power-law relationships of the internet topology," *Computer Communications Review* **29**, 251–262.

[108] Fararo, T. J. and J. Skvoretz (1987) "Unification of research programs: integrating two structural theories," *American Journal of Sociology* **92**, 1183–1209.

[109] Fararo, T. J. and M. Sunshine (1964) *A Study of a Biased Friendship Net*, Syracuse: Syracuse University Press.

[110] Fell, D. A. and A. Wagner (2000) "The small world of metabolism," *Nature Biotechnology* **18**, 1121–1122.

[111] Fosco, C. (2004) "Local preferential attachment," mimeo, Universidad de Alicante.

[112] Foster, A. D. and M. R. Rosenzweig (1995) "Learning by doing and learning from others: human capital and technical change in agriculture," *Journal of Political Economy* **103**, 1176–1209.

[113] Frank, O. and D. Strauss (1986) "Markov graphs," *Journal of the American Statistical Association* **81**, 832–842.

[114] Freeman, L. C. (1984) "The impact of computer based communication on the social structure of an emerging scientific specialty," *Social Networks* **6**, 201–221.

[115] Fudenberg, D. and D. K. Levine (1998) *The Theory of Learning in Games*, Cambridge: MIT Press.

[116] Fudenberg, D. and J. Tirole (1991) *Game Theory*, Cambridge: MIT Press.

[117] Galaskiewicz, J. (1985) *Social Organization of an Urban Grants Economy: A Study of Business Philantropy and Nonprofit Organizations*, Orlando: Academic Press.

[118] Gale, D. and S. Kariv (2003) "Bayesian learning in social networks," *Games and Economic Behavior* **45**, 329–346.

[119] Galeotti, A., S. Goyal, M. Jackson, F. Vega-Redondo, and L. Yariv (2005) "Network games," in preparation.

[120] Galeotti, A. and F. Vega-Redondo (2005) "Strategic analysis in complex networks with local externalities," *California Institute of Technology*, Working Paper no. 1224.

[121] Gardiner, C. W. (1985) *Handbook of Stochastic methods for Physics, Chemistry, and the Natural Sciences* (2nd edn), Berlin: Springer-Verlag.

[122] Garicano, L. (2000) "Hierarchies and the Organization of Knowledge in Production," *Journal of Political Economy* **108**, 874–904.

[123] Geroski, P. A. (2000) "Models of technology diffusion," *Research Policy* **29**, 603–625.

[124] Gibbs, J. W. [1902] (1981) *Elementary Principles of Statistical Mechanics*, Woodbridge, CT: Ox Bow Press.

[125] Gilbert, E. N. (1959) "Random graphs," *Annals of Mathematical Statistics* **30**, 1141–1144.

[126] Girvan, M. and Newman, M. E. J. (2002) "Community structure in social and biological networks," *Proceedings of the National Academy of Sciences USA* **99**, 7821–7826.

[127] Glaeser, E. L., H. D. Kallal, J. A. Scheinkman, and A. Shleifer (1992) "Growth in Cities," *Journal of Political Economy* **100**, 1126–1152.

[128] Glaeser, E. L., B. Sacerdote, and J. A. Scheinkman (1996) "Crime and social interactions," *Quarterly Journal of Economics* **111**, 507–548.

[129] Govindan R. and A. Reddy (1997) "An analysis of internet inter-domain topology and route stability," *Proceedings of IEEE Infocom'97*, Kobe, Japan.

[130] Goyal, S. (2005) "Learning in networks," in G. Demange and M. H. Wooders (eds.), *Group Formation in Economics: Networks, Clubs, and Coalitions*, Cambridge: Cambridge University Press.

[131] Goyal, S. and S. Joshi (2003) "Networks of collaboration in oligopoly," *Games and Economic Behavior* **43**, 57–85.

[132] Goyal, S., M. van der Leij, and J. L. Moraga-González (2003) "Economics: an emerging small world?," Working Paper, University of Essex and Erasmus University.

[133] Goyal, S. and J. L. Moraga-González (2001) "R&D Networks," *RAND Journal of Economics* **32**, 686–707.

[134] Goyal, S. and F. Vega-Redondo (2004) "Structural holes in social networks," mimeo, University of Essex and Universidad de Alicante.

[135] Goyal, S. and F. Vega-Redondo (2005) "Network formation and social coordination," *Games and Economic Behavior* **50**, 178–207.

[136] Granovetter, M. (1973) "The strength of weak ties," *American Journal of Sociology* **78**, 1360–1380.

[137] Granovetter, M. [1974] (1995) *Getting a Job: a Study on Contacts and Careers* (2nd edn), Chicago: Chicago University Press.

[138] Granovetter, M. (1978) "Threshold models of collective behavior," *American Journal of Sociology* **83**, 1420–1443.

[139] Granovetter, M. (1985) "Economic action and social structure: the problem of embeddedness," *American Journal of Sociology* **91**, 481–510.

[140] Grassberger, P. (1983) "On the critical behavior of the general epidemic process and dynamic percolation," *Mathematical Bioscience* **63**, 157–172.

[141] Greif, A. (1993) "Contract enforceability and economic institutions in early trade: the Maghribi traders' coalition," *American Economic Review* **83**, 525–548.

[142] Griliches, Z. (1957) "Hybrid corn: an exploration in the economics of technical change," *Econometrica* **25**, 501–522.

[143] Grossman, J. (2002) "The evolution of the mathematical research collaboration graph," *Congressus Numerantium* **158**, 201–212.

[144] Guimerà, R., L. Danon, A. Díaz-Guilera, F. Giralt, and A. Arenas (2003*a*) "Self-similar community structure in a network of human interactions," *Physical Review E* **68**, 065103.

[145] Guimerà, R., A. Díaz-Guilera, F. Vega-Redondo, A. Cabrales, and A. Arenas (2002) "Optimal network topologies for local search with congestion," *Physical Review Letters* **89**, 248701.

[146] Guimerà, R., S. Mossa, A. Turtschi, and L. A. N. Amaral (2003*b*) "Structure and efficiency of the world-wide airport network," *Preprint* cond-mat/0312535.

[147] Gulati, R., N. Nohria, and A. Zaheer (2000) "Guest editors' introduction to the special issue: Strategic Networks," *Strategic Management Journal* **21**, 199–201.

[148] Hagedoorn, J. (2002) "Inter-firm R&D partnerships: an overview of major trends and patterns since 1960," *Research Policy* **31**, 477–492.

[149] Hagedoorn J., A. Link, and N. S. Vonortas (2000) "Research partnerships," *Research Policy* **29**, 567–586.

[150] Harding, D. J. (2003) "Counterfactual models of neighborhood effects: the effect of neighborhood poverty on dropping out and teenage pregnancy," *American Journal of Sociology* **109**, 676–719.

[151] Heider, F. (1946) "Attitudes and cognitive organization," *Journal of Psychology* **21**, 107–112.

[152] Heider, F. (1958) *The Psychology of Interpersonal Relations*, New York: Wiley.

[153] Holley, R. and T. M. Liggett (1975) "Ergodic theorems for weakly interacting infinite systems and the voter model," *The Annals of Probability* **3**, 643–663.

[154] Hurwicz, L. (1960) "Optimality and informational efficiency in resource allocation processes," in K. J. Arrow, S. Karlin and P. Suppes (eds.), *Mathematical Models in the Social Sciences*, Cambridge: Cambridge University Press.

[155] Ising, E. (1925) "Beitrag zur Theorie des Ferromagnetismus," *Zeitschrift für Physik* **31**, 253–258.

[156] Jackson, M. (2005) "A survey of network formation models: stability and efficiency," in G. Demange and M. H. Wooders (eds.), *Group Formation in Economics: Networks, Clubs, and Coalitions*, Cambridge: Cambridge University Press.

[157] Jackson, M. O. (2006) "The economics of social networks," to appear in R. Blundell, W. Newey, and T. Persson (eds.), *Proceedings of the 9th World Congress of the Econometric Society*, Cambridge: Cambridge University Press.

[158] Jackson, M. and B. Rogers (2004) "Search in the formation of large networks: how random are socially generated networks?," *California Institute of Technology, Division of the Humanities and Social Sciences*, Working Paper no. 1216.

[159] Jackson, M. O. and A. Watts (2002*a*) "On the formation of interaction networks in social coordination games," *Games and Economic Behavior* **41**, 265–291.

[160] Jackson, M. O. and A. Watts (2002*b*) "The evolution of social and economic networks," *Journal of Economic Theory* **106**, 265–295.

[161] Jackson, M. O. and A. Wolinsky (1996) "A Strategic model of social and economic networks," *Journal of Economic Theory* **71**, 44–74.

[162] Jacobs, J. (1984) *Cities and the Wealth of Nations: Principles of Economic Life*, New York: Random House.

[163] Jaffe, A. and M. Trajtenberg (1996) "Flows of knowledge from universities and federal laboratories: Modeling the flow of patent citations over time and across institutional and geographic boundaries," *Proceedings of the National Academy of Sciences USA*, **93**, 12671–12677.

[164] Jensen, H. J. (1988) *Self-organized criticality*, Cambridge: Cambridge University Press.

[165] Jeong, H., S. Mason, A.-L. Barabási, and Z. N. Oltvai (2001) "Lethality and centrality in protein networks," *Nature* **411**, 41–42.

[166] Jeong, H., B. Tombor, R. Albert, Z. N. Oltvai, and A.-L. Barabási (2000) "The large-scale organization of metabolic networks," *Nature* **407**, 651–654.

[167] Jin, E. M., M. Girvan, and M. E. J. Newman (2001) "Structure of growing social networks," *Physical Review* E **64**, 046132.

[168] Kamien, M. I., Muller E. and I. Zang (1992) "Research joint ventures and R&D cartels," *American Economic Review* **82**, 1293–1306.

[169] Katz, M. (1986) "An analysis of cooperative research and development," *RAND Journal of Economics* **17**, 527–543.

[170] Kauffman, S. A. (1993) *The Origins of Order: Self-Organization and Selection in Evolution*, Oxford: Oxford University Press.

[171] Killworth, P. and H. R. Bernard (1978) "The reversal small-world experiment," *Social Networks* **1**, 159–192.

[172] Kirman, A., D. K. Herreiner, and G. Weisbuch (2000) "Market organization and trading relationships," *Economic Journal* **110**, 411–436.

[173] Kleinberg, J. (2000*a*) "Navigation in a small world," *Nature* **406**, 845.

[174] Kleinberg, J. (2000*b*) "The small-world phenomenon: An algorithmic perspective," *Proceedings of the 32nd ACM Symposium on Theory of Computing*. Also appears as *Cornell Computer Science Technical Report* 99-1776 (October 1999).

[175] Kleinberg, J. (2001) "Small-world phenomena and the dynamics of information," *Advances in Neural Information Processing Systems* **14**, 431–438.

[176] Kleinberg, J., S. R. Kumar, P. Raghavan, S. Rajagopalan, and A. Tomkins (1999) "The Web as a graph: measurements, models and methods," in *Proceedings of the International Conference on Combinatorics and Computing*, no. 1627 in *Lecture Notes in Computer Science*, 1–18, Berlin: Springer-Verlag.

[177] Klemm, K. and V. M. Eguíluz (2002*a*) "Highly clustered scale-free networks," *Physical Review* E **65**, 036123.

[178] Klemm, K. and V. M. Eguíluz (2002*b*) "Growing scale-free networks with small-world behavior," *Physical Review* E **65**, 057102.

[179] Koch C. and G. Laurent (1999) "Complexity and the nervous system," *Science* **284**, 96–98.

[180] Kollock, P. (1999) "The production of trust in online markets," in Lawler, E. J., M. Macy, S. Thyne, and H. A. Walker (eds.), *Advances in Group Processes* **16**, Greenwich, CT: JAI Press.

[181] Krackhardt, D. (1987) "Cognitive social structures," *Social Networks* **9**, 109–134.

[182] Krackhardt, D., and J. R. Hanson (1993) "Informal networks: the company behind the chart," *Harvard Business Review* **71**, 104–111.

[183] Kranton, R. and D. Minehart (2000) "Networks versus vertical integration," *Rand Journal of Economics* **31**, 570–601.

[184] Kranton, R. and D. Minehart (2001) "A theory of buyer-seller networks," *American Economic Review* **91**, 485–508.

[185] Krapivsky, P. L. and S. Redner (2001) "Organization of growing random networks," *Physical Review* E **63**, 066123.

[186] Krapivsky, P. L. and S. Redner (2003) "Rate equations approach for growing networks," R. Pastor-Satorras, M. Rubi, and A. Díaz-Guilera (eds.), *XVIII Sitges Conference on Statistical Mechanics*, Berlin: Springer Verlag.

[187] Le Bellac, M. (1988) *Des Phénomènes Critiques aux Champs de Jauge*, Paris: InterEditions/Editions du CNRS.

[188] Lee, N. H. (1969) *The Search for an Abortionist*, Chicago: University of Chicago Press.

[189] Liggett, T. M. (1985) *Interacting Particle Systems*, New York: Springer-Verlag.

[190] Ligon, E., J. Thomas, and T. Worrall (2002) "Informal insurance arrangements with limited commitment: theory and evidence from village economies," *Review of Economic Studies* **69**, 115–139.

[191] Lippert, S. and G. Spagnolo (2002) "Network of relations," mimeo, University of Mannheim.

[192] López-Pintado, D. (2004) "Diffusion in complex social networks," working paper IVIE WP-AD 2004-33, Universidad de Alicante.

[193] Lubbers, M. J. (2003) "Group composition and network structure in school classes: a multilevel application of the p^* model," *Social Networks* **25**, 309–332.

[194] Magoni, D. and J. J. Pansiot (2001) "Analysis of the autonomous system network topology," *ACM Computer Communication Review* **31**, 26–37.

[195] Marsili, M., F. Vega-Redondo, and G. Ehrhardt (2005) "Diffusion and growth in an evolving network," forthcoming in the *International Journal of Game Theory*.

[196] Marsili, M., F. Vega-Redondo, and F. Slanina (2004) "The rise and fall of a networked society: a formal model," *Proceedings of the National Academy of Sciences USA* **101**, 1439–1442.

[197] Maslov, S. and K. Sneppen (2002) "Specificity and stability in topology of protein networks," *Science* **296**, 910–913.

[198] McKelvey, R. D. and T. R. Palfrey (1995) "Quantal response equilibria for normal form games," *Games and Economic Behavior* **10**, 6–38.

[199] McMillan, J. and C. Woodruff (1999) "Interfirm relationships and informal credit in Vietnam," *Quarterly Journal of Economics* **114**, 1285–1320.

[200] Milgram, S. (1967) "The small-world problem," *Psychology Today* **2**, 60–67.

[201] Mitchell J. C. (1969) "The concept and use of social networks," in J. C. Mitchell (ed.) *Social Networks in Urban Situations: Analyses of Personal Relationships in Central African Towns,* Manchester: Manchester University Press, 1–50.

[202] Molloy M. and B. Reed (1995) "A critical point for random graphs with a given degree sequence," *Random Structures and Algorithms* **6**, 161–179.

[203] Molloy, M. and B. Reed (1998) "The size of the giant component of a random graph with a given degree sequence," *Combinatorics, Probability and Computing* **7**, 295–305.

[204] Montgomery, J. (1991) "Social networks and labor market outcomes: toward an economic analysis," *American Economic Review* **81**, 1408–1418.

[205] Montoya, J. M. and R. V. Solé (2002) "Small world patterns in food webs," *Journal of Theoretical Biology* **214**, 405–412.

[206] Moreno, J. L. (1934) "Who shall survive? A new approach to the problem of human interrelations," Washington, DC: Nervous and Mental Disease Publishing Co. (Reprinted in 1953 by Beacon House, Beacon, NY.)

[207] Morris, S. (2000) "Contagion," *Review of Economic Studies* **67**, 57–78.

[208] Munshi, K. (2003) "Networks in the modern economy: Mexican migrants in the US labor market," *Quarterly Journal of Economics* **118**, 549–597.

[209] Munshi, K. (2004) "Social learning in a heterogeneous population: technology diffusion in the Indian green revolution," *Journal of Development Economics* **73**, 185–213.

[210] Murgai, R., P. Winters, E. Sadoulet, and A. de Janvry (2002) "Localized and incomplete mutual insurance," *Journal of Development Economics* **67**, 245–274.

[211] Myerson, R. (1991) *Game Theory: Analysis of Conflict*, Cambridge: Harvard University Press.

[212] Newman, M. E. J. (2001) "The structure of scientific collaboration networks," *Proceedings of the National Academy of Sciences USA* **98**, 404–409.

[213] Newman, M. E. J. (2002*a*) "Spread of epidemic disease on networks," *Physical Review E* **66**, 016128.

[214] Newman, M. E. J. (2002*b*) "Assortative mixing in networks," *Physical Review Letters* **89**, 208701.

[215] Newman, M. E. J. (2003*a*) "Random graphs as models of networks," in S. Bornholdt and H. G. Schuster (eds.), *Handbook of Graphs and Networks: From the Genome to the Internet*, Berlin: Wiley VCH.

[216] Newman, M. E. J. (2003*b*) "The structure and function of complex networks," *SIAM Review* **45**, 167–256.

[217] Newman, M. E. J. (2003*c*) "Mixing patterns in networks," *Physical Review E* **67**, 026126.

[218] Newman, M. E. J. (2003*d*) "Properties of highly clustered networks," *Physical Review E* **68**, 026121.

[219] Newman, M. E. J., S. Forrest and J. Balthrop (2002) "Email networks and the spread of computer viruses," *Physical Review E* **66**, 035101.

[220] Newman, M. E. J., C. Moore, and D. J. Watts (1999) "Mean-field solution of the small-world network model," preprint cond-matt/9909165 v2.

[221] Newman, M. E. J., C. Moore, and D. J. Watts (2000) "Mean-field solution of the small-world network model," *Physical Review Letters* **84**, 3201–3204.

[222] Newman, M. E. J. and J. Park (2003) "Why social networks are different from other types of networks," *Physical Review E* **68**, 036122.

[223] Newman, M. E. J., S. H. Strogatz, and D. J. Watts (2001) "Random graphs with arbitrary degree distributions," *Physical Review E* **64**, 026118.

[224] Nowak, M. A., S. Bonhoeffer, and R. M. May (1994) "Spatial games and the maintenance of cooperation," *Proceedings of the National Academy of Science USA* **91**, 4877–4881.

[225] Nowak, M. A. and R. M. May (1992) "Evolutionary games and spatial chaos," *Nature* **359**, 826–829.

[226] Onsager, L. (1944) "Crystal Statistics. I. A two-dimensional model with an order-disorder transition," *Physical Review* **65**, 117–149.

[227] Opp, K. D. and C. Gern (1993) "Dissident groups, personal networks, and spontaneous cooperation: the East German revolution of 1989," *American Sociological Review* **58**, 659–680.

[228] Orsenigo L., F. Pammolli, and M. Riccaboni (2001) "Technological change and network dynamics: lessons from the pharmaceutical industry," *Research Policy* **30**, 485–508.

[229] Otte, E. and R. Rousseau (2002) "Social network analysis: a powerful strategy, also for the information sciences," *Journal of Information Science* **28**, 441–453.

[230] Padgett, J. F. and C. Ansell (1993) "Robust action and the rise of the Medici: 1400–1434," *American Journal of Sociology* **98**, 1259–1319.

[231] Page, F. H., M. H. Wooders, and S. Kamat (2005) "Networks and farsighted stability," *Journal of Economic Theory* **120**, 257–269.

[232] Pastor-Satorras, R., A. Vázquez, and A. Vespignani (2001) "Dynamical and correlation properties of the Internet," *Physical Review Letters* **87**, 258701.

[233] Pastor-Satorras, R. and A. Vespignani (2001) "Epidemic spreading in scale-free networks," *Physical Review Letters* **86**, 3200–3203.

[234] Pastor-Satorras, R. and A. Vespignani (2002) "Immunization of complex networks," *Physical Review* E **65**, 036104.

[235] Pastor-Satorras, R. and A. Vespignani (2003) "Epidemics and immunization in scale-free networks," in S. Bornholdt and H. G. Schuster (eds.), *Handbook of Graphs and Networks*, Berlin: Wiley-VCH.

[236] Pastor-Satorras R. and A. Vespignani (2004) *Evolution and Structure of the Internet: A Statistical Physics Approach*, Cambridge: Cambridge University Press.

[237] Podolny, J. M. and K. L. Page (1998) "Network forms of organization," *Annual Review of Sociology* **24**, 57–76.

[238] Powell, W. W., D. R. White, K. W. Koput, and J. Owen-Smith (2005) "Network dynamics and field evolution: the growth of inter-organizational collaboration in the life sciences," *American Journal of Sociology* **110**, 1132–1205.

[239] Price, D. J. de S. (1965) "Networks of scientific papers," *Science* **149**, 510–515.

[240] Price, D. J. de S. (1976) "A general theory of bibliometric and other cumulative advantage processes," *Journal of American Society for Information Science* **27**, 292–306.

[241] Prigogine, I. and I. Stengers (1984) *Order Out of Chaos*, New York: Bantam Books.

[242] Radaev, V. (2001) "The development of small entrepreneurship in Russia," *World Institute for Development Economics Research*, Discussion Paper No. 2001/135.

[243] Radner, R. (1993) "The organization of decentralized information processing," *Econometrica* **61**, 1109–1146.

[244] Rapoport, A. (1957) "A contribution to the theory of random and biased nets," *Bulletin of Mathematical Biophysics* **19**, 257–271.

[245] Rapoport, A. and W. J. Horvath (1961) "A study of a large sociogram," *Behavioral Science* **6**, 279–291.

[246] Rauch, J. E. (2001) "Business and social networks in international trade," *Journal of Economic Literature* **39**, 1177–1203.

[247] Redner, S. (1998) "How popular is your paper? An empirical study of the citation distribution," *European Physical Journal* B **4**, 131–134.

[248] Rees, A. (1966) "Information networks in labor markets," *American Economic Review* **56**, 559–566.

[249] Rogers, E. M. [1962] (1995) *Diffusion of Innovations* (4th edn), New York: Free Press.

[250] Rozenfeld, H. D. and D. ben-Avraham (2004) "Designer nets from local strategies," *Physical Review* E **70**, 056107.

[251] Ryan, B. and N. C. Gross (1943) "The diffusion of hybrid seed corn in two Iowa communities," *Rural Sociology* **8**, 15–24.

[252] Sacerdote, B. (2001) "Peer effects with random assignment: results for Dartmouth roommates," *Quarterly Journal of Economics* **116**, 681–704.

[253] Saxenian, A. (1994) *Regional Advantage: Culture and Competition in Silicon Valley and Route 128*, Cambridge, Massachusetts: Harvard University Press.

[254] Scala, A., L. A. N. Amaral and M. Barthélémy (2001) "Small-world networks and the conformation space of a lattice polymer chain," *Europhysics Letters* **55**, 594–600.

[255] Scott, J. (2000) *Social Network Analysis: A handbook*, Newbury Park, CA: Sage Publications. (1st edn 1991.)

[256] Siganos, S., M. Faloutsos, P. Faloutsos, and C. Faloutsos (2003) "Power-laws and the AS-level internet topology," *IEEE/ACM Transactions on Networking* **11**, 514–524.

[257] Simon, H. A. (1955) "On a class of skew distribution functions," *Biometrika* **42**, 425–440.

[258] Snijders, T. A. B. and C. Baerveldt (2003) "A multilevel network study of the effects of delinquent behavior on friendship evolution," *Journal of Mathematical Sociology* **27**, 123–151.

[259] Snow, D. A., L. A. Zurcher, and S. Ekland-Olson (1980) "Social networks and social movements: a microstructural approach to differential recruitment," *American Sociological Review* **45**, 787–801.

[260] de Sola Pool, I. and M. Kochen (1978) "Contacts and influence," *Social Networks* **1**, 5–51.

[261] Solé, R. V. and J. M. Montoya (2001) "Complexity and fragility in ecological networks," *Proceedings of the Royal Society* B **268**, 2039–2045.

[262] Solomonoff, R. and A. Rapoport (1951) "Connectivity of random nets," *Bulletin of Mathematical Biophysics* **13**, 107–117.

[263] Sporns, O. (2002) "Network analysis, complexity, and brain function," *Complexity* **8**, 56–60.

[264] Stanley, H. E. (1971) *Introduction to Phase Transitions and Critical Phenomena*, Oxford: Oxford University Press.

[265] Stariolo, D. A. and C. Tsallis (1995) "Optimization by simulated annealing: recent progress," in D. Stauffer (ed.) *Annual Review of Computational Physics* II, Singapore: World Scientific.

[266] Sundararajan, A. (2005) "Local network effects and network structure," *Working Paper CeDER-05-02*, Center for Digital Economy Research, Leonard N. Stern School of Business, New York University.

[267] Sutherland, E. H. [1924] (1947) *Principles of Criminology* (4th edn), Chicago: J. B. Lippincott.

[268] Topa, G. (2001) "Social interaction, local spillovers, and unemployment," *Review of Economic Studies* **68**, 261–295.

[269] Townsend, R. M. (1994) "Risk and insurance in village India," *Econometrica* **62**, 539–591.

[270] Travers J. and S. Milgram (1969) "An experimental study of the small world problem," *Sociometry* **32**, 425–443.

[271] Tyler, J. R., D. M. Wilkinson, and B. A. Huberman (2003) "Email as spectroscopy: automated discovery of community structure within organizations," in *Proceedings of the International Conference on Communities and Technologies*, Netherlands: Kluwer Academic Publishers.

[272] Uzzi, B. (1996) "The sources and consequences of embeddedness for the economic performance of organizations: the network effect," *American Sociological Review* **61**, 674–698.

[273] Valente, T. W. (1996) "Social network thresholds in the diffusion of innovations," *Social Networks* **18**, 69–89.

[274] Van Valen, L. (1973) "A new evolutionary law," *Evolutionary Theory* **1**, 1–30.

[275] Vázquez, A. (2003) "Growing network with local rules: preferential attachment, clustering hierarchy, and degree correlations," *Physical Review* E **67**, 056104.

[276] Vega-Redondo, F. (1996) "Long-run cooperation in the one-shot prisoner's dilemma: A hierarchic evolutionary approach," *BioSystems* **37**, 39–47.

[277] Vega-Redondo, F. (2003) *Economics and the Theory of Games*, Cambridge: Cambridge University Press.

[278] Vega-Redondo, F. (2005) "Building up social capital in a changing world," forthcoming in *Journal of Economic Dynamics and Control*.

[279] Vega-Redondo, F., M. Marsili, and F. Slanina (2005) "Clustering, cooperation, and search in social networks," *Journal of the European Economic Association* **3**, 628–638.

[280] Wasserman, S. and K. Faust (1994) *Social Network Analysis: Methods and Applications*, Cambridge: Cambridge University Press.

[281] Wasserman, S. and P. E. Pattison (1996) "Logit models and logistic regressions for social networks: I. An introduction to Markov graphs and p^*," *Psychometrika* **61**, 401–425.

[282] Watson, J. (2002) *Strategy: An Introduction to Game Theory*, New York: W.W. Norton & Company.

[283] Watts, A. (2002) "Non-myopic formation of circle networks," *Economics Letters* **74**, 277–281.

[284] Watts, D. J. (1999) *Small Worlds*, Princeton: Princeton University Press.

[285] Watts, D. J. (2002) "A simple model of global cascades on random networks," *Proceedings of the National Academy of Sciences USA* **99**, 5766–5771.

[286] Watts, D. J. (2003) *Six Degrees: The Science of a Connected Age*, New York: Norton.

[287] Watts, D. J., P. S. Dodds, and M. E. J. Newman (2002) "Identity and search in social networks," *Science* **296**, 1302–1305.

[288] Watts D. J. and S. H. Strogatz (1998) "Collective dynamics of 'small-world' networks," *Nature* **393**, 440–442.

[289] White, H., S. Boorman, and R. Breiger (1976) "Social structure from multiple networks. I.: Blockmodels of roles and positions," *American Journal of Sociology* **81**, 730–780.

[290] White, J. G., E. Southgate, J. N. Thompson, and S. Brenner (1986) "The structure of the nervous system of the nematode C. Elegans," *Philosophical Transactions Royal Society London* B **314**, 1–340.

[291] Williams, R. J. and N. D. Martinez (2000) "Simple rules yield complex food webs," *Nature* **404**, 180–183.

[292] Wormald, N. C. (1981) "The asymptotic connectivity of labelled regular graphs," *Journal of Combinatorial Theory* B **31**, 156–167.

[293] Wynne-Edwards, V. C. (1962) *Animal Dispersion in Relation to Social Behavior*, Edinburgh: Oliver & Boyd.

[294] Young, P. (1998) *Individual Strategy and Social Structure*, Princeton: Princeton University Press.

[295] van Zandt T. (1999*a*) "Real-time decentralized information processing as a model of organizations with boundedly rational agents," *Review of Economic Studies* **66**, 633–658.

[296] van Zandt, T. (1999*b*) "Decentralized information processing and the theory of organizations," in Murat Sertel M. (ed.), *Contemporary Economic Issues, Volume 4: Economic Behaviour and Design*, London: MacMillan.

[297] Zimmermann, M., V. M. Eguíluz, and M. San Miguel (2004) "Coevolution of dynamical states and interactions in dynamic networks," *Physical Review* E **69**, 065102(R).

Index